ANTHONY SKEWS

Evolutionary Politics

Socialism for Social Species

First edition

ISBN: 978-0-646-82606-6

Cover art by Adam Renvoize

This book was professionally typeset on Reedsy.
Find out more at reedsy.com

"Sociobiology actually leads you to leftism."

Kim Stanley Robinson,
28 February 2019

Contents

II Application

Acknowledgement

First of all, my thanks to the members of the Cultural Evolution Society whose research and depth of scientific expertise provided much of the inspiration for this book. My particular appreciation is due to David Sloan Wilson, Samuel Bowles, Herbert Gintis, Robert Boyd and Peter Richerson – each of whom have written masterpieces whose quality and insight this work can only approach.

I'd also like to thank the students and staff of the Graduate Institute of International and Development Studies in Geneva, who put up with me as I did the research that forms the foundation of this text. In particular, I'd like to acknowledge my thesis supervisor Dr Ravinder Bhavnani, as well as my teachers Cedric Dupont, Karsten Donnay, David Sylvan, Keith Kraus, Neus Torbisco-Casals, Brian McQuinn and Achim Wennmann. All of you may recognise fragments of your ideas scattered across this book, for which I am grateful.

Finally, my sincerest regards to the friends and sparring partners who have provided a sounding board for my ideas over the last several years. In Solidarity.

Reclaiming Darwin

Why should political scientists, activists and leaders study nature?

Politics is the process by which societies make collective decisions: the mechanisms – sometimes cooperative, sometimes competitive – through which their internal and external strategies are chosen. Academic sociology and anthropology have come to understand politics as an interaction between beliefs, actions, values and narratives[1]. While the natural environment constrains the actions a society can take, it is ideas, stories and values that motivate individuals to follow norms, take risks or organise collectively. One simply cannot describe a social agent based solely on its physical and thermodynamic properties, as one might a natural agent such as a proton, DNA molecule, bacterium, or black hole.

But this dichotomy between the social and natural is an illusion. No bright line divides social species from nature: to the degree that humans display unmatched behavioural complexity, the difference is one of scale and uniqueness, not kind[2]. New research in cultural evolution, mathematical biology, and evolutionary game theory is revealing the underlying structures of social behaviour[3]. Sociologists are not wrong to focus on the symbols, beliefs and ideas that motivate individual action; they simply lack a cohesive account of why *certain* symbols, beliefs and ideas come to exist and not others. The Russian-American geneticist Theodosius Dobzhansky wrote in 1973 that "nothing in biology makes sense except in the light of evolution"[4];

---

[1] Durkheim, "The Rules of Sociological Method" (1895).

[2] Proudhon, "What is Property?" (1831), Chapter V.

[3] Mesoudi et al. (2006) at pgs. 329-347; Mesoudi (2017); Gintis (2009).

[4] Dobzhansky (1973) at pgs. 125-129.

and nothing in society or culture makes sense except in light of cultural evolution[5].

That is not to say that political philosophy is rendered obsolete by the natural sciences. This book explicitly rejects the normative scientism of writers such as Steven Pinker[6], who assert that the scientific method provides the only route to political 'truth'. As the late, great political journalist Michael Brooks - a frequent critic of Pinker - wrote shortly before his untimely passing: whereas the left and centre-left *historicise*, the right and centre-right *naturalise*. The left shares an understanding with natural scientists that the state of the world is contingent, its structures and behaviours dependent on the path a society took through history. It is largely thinkers on the right who reify these contingent social structures and hierarchies into transcendental values and laws of nature.

The eighteenth-century Scottish enlightenment philosophy David Hume famously observed that it was 'altogether inconceivable' how a normative statement could be deduced from ordinary reason[7]. We can only prescribe a course of action if we share common goals, and agree on the legitimate methods we may use to obtain them. The disciplines that are most committed to a 'scientific' approach to politics, namely economics and moral psychology, also often smuggle in assumptions about the common ends for which society is established. This is an 'is' book: it offers a descriptive account of the structure of social behaviour while acknowledging the fundamentally subjective and diverse body of beliefs, symbols and norms that, as we shall see, are required to make those structures operate. Readers might continue on to my 'ought' book, "*Politics for the New Dark Age: Staying Positive Amidst Disorder*"[8] after completing this one.

This book is also for would-be socialists and progressives. The Left has

---

5   Turchin (2016) at pg. 35.

6   E.g. Pinker (2018).

7   Hume, "A Treatise on Human Nature" (1739), Book III, Part I.

8   Skews, "Politics for the New Dark Age: Staying Positive Amidst Disorder" Hybrid Publishers (2017).

an uncomfortable relationship with methodological naturalism. They carry the baggage of 'scientific socialism'[9], which was used to justify revolution and dictatorship. They've learned the dangers of Social Darwinism, and to be wary of the perversion of evolutionary theory to justify the murder and enslavement of others. They live under the inhumane and brutal thumb of the invisible hand of the market, as economists and technocrats measure its rate of profit on their spreadsheets and charts. As feminists, they witness every day in homes and workplaces the way meaningless sex differences are abused to construct gender roles that oppress half of humanity. Above all, they innately resist and oppose the conservative appeal to nature that says we live in the best of all possible worlds (see Chapter 17: "The Naturalist Fallacy").

But if socialists can overcome their discomfort with naturalist accounts of social behaviour they may be able to seize upon recent scientific findings which undermine the selfish rational actor model of human nature which dominated the twentieth-century. Nature matters because − rightly or wrongly − people are persuaded by naturalist narratives. The philosopher Karl Popper argued that science cannot prove a fact, merely show that it is not false[10]. But the scientific method is persuasive because it offers the least worst way we have of testing, communicating and disseminating beliefs. Every political philosophy, one way or another, begins with a theory of human nature[11]. Evolutionary socialism may be just one among many possible stories about the origins of cooperation, but it's a compelling story that makes falsifiable claims about the material and social world and which poses an existential threat to one of the foundational myths of capitalism.

Indeed, the construct of the self-interested individual which is axiomatic to contemporary capitalism[12] cannot be justified other than by a certain

---

[9] Ironically, first so named by the anarchist Proudhon, in "What is Property?" (1831).

[10] Popper (1959).

[11] Lewontin (1991) at pgs. 61.

[12] Edgeworth (1881).

reading of natural selection[13]. Naturalistic myths have been embedded in liberalism since its inception: for Hobbes the default condition of mankind was a war of all against all that could only be pacified by the state[14]; for Hume, the *"state of nature is to be regarded as a mere fiction . . . yet [it] deserves our attention because nothing can more evidently show the origin of those virtues . . . [which remedy] certain qualities of the human mind [such as] selfishness and limited generosity."*[15] For John Rawls, *"the fundamental principles of justice quite properly depend on natural facts about men [sic] in society."*[16] Richard Dawkins' influential evolutionary text *The Selfish Gene* is explicitly in this tradition: *"a predominant quality to be expected in a successful gene is ruthless selfishness. This . . . selfishness will usually give rise to selfishness in individual behaviour"*[17]. Dawkins is wrong on the merits, and we will return later to his role in building this false narrative.

Understanding nature matters because if socialists want to shift politics in progressive directions, they also need an accurate model of how society and culture works. The Left can be objective without being neutral. The discipline of economics has begun to move decisively in the direction of recognising that human beings are not purely rational utility-maximisers but bundles of biases and neuroses who frequently act sub-optimally (see Chapter 10: "Mediocre Individuals, Exceptional Species"). Armed with this knowledge, modern capitalism is becoming ever-more adept at manipulating the illusion of choice[18]. Without an equivalent model, progressives have walked into policy cul-de-sacs, failed to bring the masses

---

13 Bowles & Gintis (2011), at pg. 10: "The economists usual defence of the self-interest axiom is that it is self-evident, with the fallback assertion being that natural selection could not have produced any other kind of preferences. But, as the evidence to follow suggests, the assertion is far from self-evident, and simply false."; The same point is made in Cosmides & Tooby (1992) at pg. 327; and Ostrom (1998) at pg. 2.

14 Hobbes, "Leviathan" (1651).

15 Hume, "A Treatise on Human Nature" (1739), Book III, Part II, Section II.

16 Rawls (1971) at pg. 159.

17 Dawkins (1979) at pg. 2.

18 Thaler & Sunstein (2009).

with them, provoked a backlash from powerful constituencies and made it easier for the Right to wind progress back. To make progress resilient and adaptive, socialists need to work with a sophisticated theory of social behaviour – not insist on the Cartesian perfectibility of the individual through education, moral restraint and the cultivation of virtue.

When the entomologist Edward Wilson (more on him later) wrote that *"socialism works, it's just that [Marx] had the wrong species"*[19] he was articulating a common assumption that progressive political ideology is somehow out of step with human nature. The 'survival of the fittest' framework inherently positions socialism as fighting an uphill battle against biology, requiring heavy-handed and paternalistic intervention. Dawkins parrots the dualist view first articulated by Thomas Huxley[20] when he writes that we need to *"teach generosity and altruism, because we are born selfish"*[21]. But an overemphasis on ideological control and self-denial as the basis of social order is counter-productive. It establishes a hierarchy of worth predicated on compliance with social norms, often enforced by violence: whether the Soviet Union or the Catholic Church, regimes which seek to control human nature through virtue have been undermined by vice.

If this book has a singular purpose, it is to dispel once and for all the notion that socialists do not have an empirically rigorous theory of human nature. Since the mid-nineteenth century, socialists have engaged deeply with the evolutionary origin of cooperation, and biologists and social scientists increasingly concur that we are an obligate social and gregarious species. This book takes the view that altruism and cooperation *are part of human nature*[22], and that pro-social outcomes can be spontaneously self-organising and resilient without the use of indoctrination, coercion or force. Moreover, the socialist account of human nature is considerably more empirically grounded than the myth of isolated individuals existing

---

[19] Wilson & Holldobler (1990).

[20] Huxley, "Evolution and Ethics" (1895).

[21] Dawkins (1979).

[22] Wilson (2015).

in a state of nature which underpins our modern philosophy, politics and economics.

Evolutionary politics is therefore not a naturalistic meta-ethics. We're not setting out to find universal, fixed and unchangeable rules for human behaviour in nature. It's about using science and empirical observation to understand the way in which social rules and norms are shaped by evolution, vary by culture, change and adapt over time. While the underlying principles of evolutionary politics are common to all social interactions, the rules, norms and institutions which emerge out of those interactions are diverse, and historically and environmentally contingent. No culture is more or less morally enlightened, much as no plant or animal species is more or less 'adapted' than any other. Moreover, the evolutionary perspective opens the door to seeing the creation of norms and ethics as a process of perpetual and open-ended innovation and adaption.

The book is divided into two broad parts. The first (Chapters 1-8) reviews theories the cultural evolution, multilevel selection and gene-culture co-evolution, beginning with an abbreviated intellectual history. Readers should be forewarned that early chapters of the book employ mathematical terms and techniques. The standard is no higher than secondary algebra, but readers who are entirely allergic may prefer to skip to the overview of these topics in Chapters II & III of my first book, "Politics for the New Dark Age: Staying Positive Amidst Disorder". The second part (Chapters 9 to 18) examine how this evolutionary paradigm can be applied in the social sciences, providing new perspectives on phenomena which underpin significant contemporary political and cultural fissures, including the evolutionary origins of fascism, extremism and political violence.

* * *

Darwin's On the Origin of Species is famously taciturn about the application of evolutionary theory to humans and human society[23]. It was only in

---

[23] Darwin, "On the Origin of Species by Natural Selection" (1859).

his follow-ups, *The Descent of Man*[24] and *The Expression of the Emotions in Man and Animals*[25] that Darwin tackled the social and ethical implications of the evolutionary origins of humankind, focusing in particular on the role of emotion in motivating altruistic behaviour. However pro-sociality originated, Darwin wrote:

"*. . . it is of high importance to all those animals which aid and defend each other, [and] will have been increased through natural selection. For those communities, which included the greatest number of sympathetic members, would flourish best . . .if [a] tribe included a greater number of courageous, sympathetic and faithful members, who were always ready to warn each other of danger [and] aid and defend each other, this tribe would without doubt succeed best . . . . Selfish and contentious people will not cohere, and without coherence nothing can be effected.*" [Darwin, the Descent of Man][26]

Both Darwin and the libertarian philosopher Herbert Spencer (who coined the phrase 'survival of the fittest'[27]) speculated about the evolution of society in language that is eerily similarly to contemporary models of cultural evolution[28]. But both men were also influenced by the reactionary views of 18th century economist Thomas Malthus, and the mathematician and proto-eugenicist Francis Galton. The origin of Social Darwinism, as it came to be later known[29], lies not in the way that natural selection legitimised and licenced *laissez-faire* capitalism and imperialism, but rather how the Victorian and aristocratic milieu of such men was carried into the new branch of science they had created.

Although Darwin himself rejected any teleological reading of evolution,

---

[24] Darwin, "The Descent of Man, and Selection in Relation to Sex" (1871).

[25] Darwin, "The Expression of Emotions in Man and Animals" (1872).

[26] Darwin, "The Descent of Man, and Selection in Relation to Sex" (1871), at pgs. 82, and 162.

[27] Spencer (1852) at pgs. 468-501; Spencer (1864); Johnson (2019) at pg. 18.

[28] Most notably in Spencer's earlier works: Spencer (1851); Spencer (1860); Spencer (1879).

[29] Hofstadter (1955); Hawkins (1997).

his heirs and defenders including Spencer, Galton and Alfred Wallace came erroneously to see evolution as synonymous with Progress (with a "capital-P"): an ideal of the perfectibility of human societies, of which the late nineteenth-century capitalism of the Gilded Age was (of course) the closest possible reflection.

"The fact that Darwin's theory carefully skirted the received relationship between science and politics . . . . left a vacuum in which this connection was left to be re-established by others. In this sense, the emergence of Social Darwinism was due to a sort of ventriloquism that consisted in making Darwin say whatever was needed to justify the existing social order. . ." [Novoa, Social Darwinism][30]

The flaw of the Social Darwinists, and of modern "selfish gene" boosters such as Dawkins and Pinker, is not their mixing of science and politics — that is unavoidable. Rather, it lies in their inability or unwillingness to acknowledge their own social and political biases[31]. The popular version of the evolutionary narrative they have promoted is wrong, and we can now prove using evolutionary game theory and multilevel selection what Darwin only suspected: that altruism and cooperation can be evolutionarily successful, even dominant, strategies. For 150 years the Right has claimed the mantle of nature for itself by propagating a nineteenth century mis-reading of Darwinian evolution. Natural selection does not mandate that every animal is a utility-maximising egoist. Quite the contrary: highly social and cooperative species are often the most fit for their respective ecologies.

Evolutionary socialism is not merely Darwinism applied to the social. Rather, it connects to a broader tradition in philosophy that emphasises the empirical, material and dynamic over the ideal, transcendent and static[32]. In process philosophy, systems are not defined as categories of things but

---

[30] Novoa (2016).

[31] Alford & Hibbing (2004) at pgs. 707-723.

[32] Engels, "Socialism: Utopian and Scientific" (1880).

by processes – – motion, change and becoming. Stability and harmony are mere illusions, sustained by the dynamic tension of sub-structural forces. In the same way that Marxism is the study of economic and political change via dialectical materialism, evolutionary theory is the study of the emergence of social and biological order through the process of natural selection[33].

"[T]he idea of stability which was hitherto attached to everything which man saw in nature, is broken down, destroyed and put to naught! Everything changes in nature, everything is incessantly modified . . .Why should human institutions perpetuate themselves! . . .What we see around us is only a passing phenomenon. . . . we now begin to understand, however vaguely, that revolution is only an essential part of evolution, that no evolution is accomplished in nature without revolutions. Periods of very slow changes are succeeded by periods of violent changes. Revolutions are as necessary for evolution as the slow, changes which prepare them and succeed them." [Kropotkin, Revolutionary Studies][34]

We can find the origins of this perspective in Heraclitus' conception unity of opposites, or Aristotle's view of society as an organism comprised of its citizens and institutions. We can also see it in the historiography of Ibn Khaldun[35] and Machiavelli[36], who put social conflict and institutional learning at the heart of their grand narratives. In process philosophy, the character of subjects flows from the nature of their interactions, not their interactions from their essential character.

Later pre-Darwinian writers such as Comte and Hegel conceived of social evolution [incorrectly] as progress through a series of fixed stages, in much the same way that human evolution might be seen [incorrectly] as a direct road to anatomical and behavioural modernity. Comte directly inspired Spencer, but Hegel's revival of the dialectical philosophy of Heraclitus was

---

33 Engels, "Socialism: Utopian and Scientific" (1880), Chapter 2.

34 Kropotkin, "Revolutionary Studies" The Commonweal (January 1892) at pgs. 2-3.

35 Ibn Khaldun, "The Muqaddimah: An introduction to history" (1378).

36 Machiavelli, "Discourses on Livy" (1531).

taken up and applied by the left Hegelians including, in due time, Marx. All of these writers, in their own way, struggled to reconcile a realist or even harsh view of the natural world with their ideals of social and political progress[37].

Within an evolutionary framework, what are called socialism and capitalism are mere labels for distinct strategy sets which may or may not constitute a stable social equilibrium. Socialism and capitalism are not defined by any fixed economic system, set of institutions or class interests. Rather, as the philosopher Nancy Fraser might say[38], they are archetypes of totalising social relations encompassing both economic and non-economic activity. Both socialist and capitalist economies can exist as 'mixed' equilibria: what matters is the degree to which the dominant social and political strategy set emphasises individual self-help, distrust of others and short-term thinking, or mutual aid, building social capital and an emphasis on ongoing membership in a community. These strategy sets are solutions to the social dilemmas that lie at the heart of all evolutionary systems. In the modern world, we have lost any other names for them but the same paradigms have existed throughout human history because of the common mathematical structure underlying every population of autonomous social agents.

For the purposes of this book, 'socialism' is any belief system predicated on the following three axioms. Firstly, the subject species [e.g. humanity] is social and operates in groups. Secondly, there are cooperative strategy sets which offer equilibrium solutions to persistent dilemmas of social decision-making in groups. And thirdly, cooperative strategies are empirically and normatively superior to non-cooperative or self-help strategies. Whether or not one is a Marxist, these three components should unite all strands of progressive belief. Point one is a biological or anthropological observation; point two is a mathematical theorem, which we will develop in the first

---

[37] "I'm a pessimist because of intelligence, but an optimist because of will." Gramsci, "Selections from the Prison Notebooks" ElecBooks (1999).

[38] Fraser & Jaeggi (2018).

half of this book; point three is a philosophical position that may or may not be valid depending on the particular social dilemma. By temperament, socialists believe that point three is true more often than it is false.

In contrast, capitalist ideology is rooted in the following three axioms: Firstly, that the subject species [e.g. humanity] evolved to be egoistic, utility-maximising individuals. Secondly, that there are competitive (yet non-violent) strategy sets which offer equilibrium solutions to persistent dilemmas of decision-making between individuals. And thirdly, that competitive or self-help solutions are empirically and normatively superior to cooperative ones. Point one is a biological or anthropological supposition with shaky empirical foundations; point two is a mathematical theorem, which *is* sometime true but not exclusively so; and point three – which of course is the central claim of neoclassical economics – is a highly contestable economic or political position but one which right-wingers tend to believe is true more often than not.

While there have always been normative and consequentialist arguments against capitalism, there's also ample evidence that its claims about human nature are flawed or at least not as sweeping as is often assumed. The self-regarding, utility-maximising individuals of the hypothetical species *homo economicus* are not only abstract and ahistorical, but totally absent in nature and largely irrelevant to the way real social agents make most decisions[39]. By-and-large people get by using biologically- and culturally-embedded heuristics (decision-rules) that produce 'good enough' outcomes in most common social environments[40]. Behavioural economics has made great strides in recent decades by studying how heuristics lead to seemingly emotive and irrational behaviour, leading to Nobel Prizes for the likes of Daniel Kahneman and Richard Thaler. But unlike behavioural economics, evolutionary economics offers an explanation of *how* and *why* certain

---

[39] Anderson (2000) at pgs. 170-200; Henrich et al. (2001) at pgs. 73-78; Wilson & Henrich, July 2012; Wilson, February 2013; Rowe (2016).

[40] Simon (1956) at pgs. 129-138.

heuristics evolve and spread throughout a population[41].

Rather than being naturally utility-maximising egoists, human beings generate social structure through their interactions, and are in turn liberated or constrained by those structures. Individuals may act *as if* they are self-interested in some circumstances, but this is because doing so is *adaptively rational* in the context of particular social environments. But it's just as likely that purportedly irrational heuristics can generate fitness-enhancing behaviour when the existence of social life and social structures are taken into account (see Chapter 3: "Adaptive Rationality"). So the evolutionary paradigm sees *populations*, rather than individual actors, as the primary unit of analysis. 'Human nature' consists of being behaviourally flexible, adaptive social agents in an evolving population and adapting one's behaviour to symbolic social norms and rules[42].

So the strongest normative claim evolutionary politics could make is for a liberal democratic society where varied behaviours exist in tension with one another and new 'mutant' social strategies are free to develop and challenge the established order (see Chapter 12: "Norms as Equilibria"). Democracy is a complex adaptive system: it continually produces cultural variants, takes those variants into itself and tests them against existing practices and beliefs. Democracy is also a learning system: it is responsive to changes in the material basis of society and resilient in the face of external threats (see Chapter 11: "The Learning Organism"). Democracy must be defended, preserved and where absent fought for, since without it the cultural selection pressures which lead to cooperative social outcomes cannot be sustained.

The evolutionary socialism laid out in this book therefore self-consciously identifies with that of Eduard Bernstein, the early German socialist and democrat who famously quarreled with Lenin and other orthodox Marxists over the need for violent revolution and a dictatorship of the proletariat.

---

[41] Burnham (2003), at pgs. S113-157; Collins, "Please, Not Another Bias! The Problem with Behavioural Economics" Evonomics, September 2016.

[42] See also Einstein, "Why Socialism?" The Monthly Review (May 1949). "Man is, at one and the same time, a solitary being and a social being."

In his 1899 work, appropriately enough titled *Evolutionary Socialism*[43], Bernstein argued that democracy was a sufficient condition to permit transitions from oppressive to liberated social orders. In contrast to the increasing determinism of the 'scientific socialists', Bernstein recognised that social change was complex and adaptive, and that the political actor had to flexibly respond to institutional innovations he or she had never before conceived of. His central proposition – that the ultimate aim of socialism is nothing, but the movement is everything – succinctly captures the philosophical dichotomy between idealists seeking purity of form, and empiricists interested in the dynamics of change.

Although evolutionary socialism disavows the concept of Progress (with a "capital-P") through fixed stages of development, it holds empirically and normatively that humanity – a socially complex, adaptive animal – -possesses a unique and open-ended potential to cooperate to achieve social ends. Within the democratic tradition, the evolutionary socialist position is liberalism plus structural critique: socialists take seriously the idea that social equilibria are mutually constituted by the behaviour of social actors and that individual outcomes are interdependent with the outcomes of others. As a consequence, it sees society rather than the individual as the target of reform. Socialists do not think progress arises from disciplining individuals; rather, the 'New Man' is the *product* of changes in the structure of society.

* * *

What kind of socialism is this? This book argues that an evolutionary or Darwinian socialist approach sits well within the traditional schools of progressive politics[44]. Both Darwinian socialist and Social Darwinist traditions co-existed in the second half of the nineteenth century, a split which mirrored and prefigured the later divide between ideologies to the

---

[43] Bernstein, "Evolutionary Socialism: A Criticism and Affirmation" (1899).

[44] Pittenger (1993); Hawkins (1997); Weikart (1998); Stack (2003).

left of democratic socialism and to the right of social democracy[45]. It must be remembered that Marx, Engels and Darwin were contemporaries; by one account, Engels owned a first edition of *On the Origin of Species* and Marx attended lectures by Darwin's 'bulldog', Thomas Huxley[46]. In 1872, Marx sent a fan letter to Darwin enclosing a copy of the first volume of *Das Kapital*; the aristocratic Darwin replied with a brief thank-you note[47].

Engels, in particular, was enthusiastic about the use of the natural sciences to expand the scope of the left's materialist analysis of human history.

"We are reminded that we by no means rule over nature like a conqueror. . . like someone standing outside nature – but that we, with flesh, blood and brain, belong to nature and exist in its midst, and that all our mastery of it consists in the fact that we have the advantage over all other creatures of being able to learns its laws and apply them correctly"[48].

Engels was well enough informed to recognise that 'bourgeois Darwinists' like Spencer were smuggling their political values into the new natural science. For such men, he wrote:

"All that the Darwinian theory of the struggle for existence boils down to is an extrapolation from society to animate nature of Hobbes' theory of the war of all against all and of the bourgeois-economic theory of competition. . . . . Having accomplished this feat . . . these people proceed to re-extrapolate the same theories from organic nature to history, and then claim to have proved their

---

[45] See generally Johnson (2019) at pgs. 24-.

[46] Angus (2009); Gerratana (1974) at pgs. 60-82.

[47] Ball (1979) at pgs. 469-483.

[48] Engels, "The Part played by Labour in the Transition from Ape to Man" Progress Publishers (1934)

validity as eternal laws of human society"[49].

The early socialist feminist Annie Besant wrote a response to Spencer and the other earlier Social Darwinists in 1886, showing a clear understanding of the correlation between evolution and socialism:

"I am a Socialist because I am a believer in Evolution. The great truth that organisms are not isolated creations, but that they are all linked together as part of one great tree of life . . .that progress is a process of continued integrations and ever-increasing differentiations. . . . [T]he progress of society has passed from individualistic anarchy to associated order; from universal unrestricted competition to competition regulated and restrained by law, and even to cooperation in lieu thereof." [Bessant, Why I am a Socialist][50]

If this book is to form an intellectual bridge between Darwin on the one hand, and Marx and Engels on the other – and between the moderns science of cultural evolution and the socialist tradition – then no figure deserves as central a place as the exiled Russian prince, anarcho-communist and scientist Pyotr Kropotkin[51]. Kropotkin was a fiery, if idealistic, writer and propagandist. He is also the only anarchist, in my experience, fondly cited by modern biologists[52], geologists[53], economists[54] and social scientists[55].

---

[49] Quoted in Angus (2009). Marx had observed much the same point in his *Poverty of Philosophy* (1847): "[T]he metaphysicians who, in making these abstractions, think they are making analyses, and who, the more they detach themselves from things, imagine themselves to be getting nearer to the point of penetrating to their core – these metaphysicians in turn [say] that the things here below are embroideries of which the logical categories constitute the canvas".

[50] Bessant, "Why I am a Socialist" (1886).

[51] See generally Johnson (2019); Wilson (2019) at pg. 27.

[52] E.g. Gould (1997).

[53] E.g. Ivanova & Markin (2008) at pgs. 117-128.

[54] E.g. Bowles & Gintis (2011), at pg. 7; Nowak & Sigmund (2000) at pgs. 14.

[55] E.g. Chomsky, "Rollback, Part II" Z Magazine, February 1995.

Kropotkin was a naturalist of not inconsiderable renown[56], and his 1902 work, *Mutual Aid: A Factor of Evolution* is the first rigorous articulation of the evolutionary socialist position.

Kropotkin was writing in direct opposition to the Malthusian beliefs of Galton and Huxley, whose pessimism about the 'war of all against all' couldn't be justified by Kropotkin's scientific observations. While there was certainly conflict in nature, there was also mutual aid, mutual support and mutual defence. *"Sociability,"* he wrote, *"is as much a law of nature as mutual struggle."* Moreover, the more social a species, Kropotkin argued, the fitter and better adapted to its environment it was. Whether called cooperation, mutual aid or altruism, he argued that pro-social behaviour in the face of competition was stronger evolutionary force than competition alone. Kropotkin further showed that cooperative behaviour did not require reason, instead it was visible in the behaviour of all categories of mammals, birds, insects and even 'microscopic pond life'[57]. Indeed, some of the defining works in contemporary mathematical biology demonstrate that even the lowliest bacteria is capable of the elementary strategic behaviour necessary to promote cooperation[58]. What place for rational choice when the social agent is incapable of reason? Kropotkin, like Huxley[59] and Edward Wilson, was particularly taken with the complex social organisation among ants – a topic to which we will return in Chapter 1.

Social life, for the early anarchists, did not distinguish mankind from nature but rather confirmed our place in it. In many animals *"sociable life is maintained notwithstanding the quarrelsome or otherwise egoistic inclinations of the individual"*[60]. Much more important than the struggle for survival between individuals was the struggle between groups and their

---

56 See generally: Dugatkin (2011); Adams (2016) at pgs. 49-73.

57 Kropotkin (1902), Chapter I.

58 Axelrod (1984) at pgs. 93-94.

59 Huxley (1878) at pgs. 445-448.

60 Kropotkin (1902).

environment[61]. Social life enables mutual defence against threats, the mutual rearing of children and the cooperative gathering of resources. When environments change, groups or species may fail not because they are conquered, but because they failed to adapt themselves to their new condition. What truly defined natural selection, Kropotkin grasped, was not direct competition but *differential fitness.* Individuals and groups that were more fit would differentially reproduce, driving evolution forward. *"Darwin was quite right"*, Kropotkin wrote, *"when he saw in man's social qualities the chief factor in his further evolution, and Darwin's vulgarisers and entirely wrong when they maintain the contrary"*[62].

Neither the idealistic utopian Kropotkin nor the pragmatic reformer Bernstein were orthodox Marxists but both remained leftists in good standing until their deaths (the former in the Soviet Union in 1922 and the latter in Germany in 1932). Later authors have recognised the similarities in their respective world views[63], even as they found themselves on opposite sides of the increasingly acrimonious splits in the nascent socialist movement[64]. Between anarcho-communism and democratic socialism lies the many other varied and storied traditions of the left, and it is within this broad political tradition that the evolutionary socialism of this book sits.

---

[61] The arguments in this paragraph are taken from Kropotkin (1902), Chapter II.

[62] Kropotkin, "Mutual Aid Among Savages", The Nineteenth Century, April 1891 at pg. 557.

[63] Kinna (2007) at pgs. 67–86.

[64] Kropotkin, ever the accelerationist, supported World War I on the basis that it would bring about the collapse of capitalist imperialism; Bernstein sided with the Spartacus League of Rosa Luxemburg in opposing the war.

I

Theory

1

THE STATE OF NATURE

Key Points

- Any dynamic population with the properties of variation, selection and replication evolves. A trait increases frequency if it causes higher relative fitness than other traits.
- Altruistic traits reduce relative fitness. Kin selection suggests altruism cannot evolve unless the beneficiaries of altruistic behaviour are closely related to one another.
- Selection on genes is only a subset of evolutionary systems in nature. Multilevel selection sees the evolution operating at many levels of variation and replication.
- Multilevel selection offers a general mechanism underlying the evolution of cooperation, with the likelihood of cooperative equilibria dependent on population structure.

If collective decision making in groups is the essence of politics, then its central problem is the disjuncture between group and individual interest: the public good is more than just the sum of individual aspirations[65]. Immanuel Kant identified this at the end of the eighteenth century:

---

[65] Gintis (2017).

"Given a multitude of rational beings who require general laws for their own preservation, but each of whom is secretly inclined to exempt himself from this restraint: how are we to order their affairs and how establish for them a constitution such that, although their private dispositions may be really antagonistic, they may yet so act as a check upon one another in their public relations the effect is the same as if they had no such evil sentiments[?]" [Kant, Perpetual Peace][66]

We shall shortly see that Kant's Problem is indistinguishable from the perspective of modern scholars of cooperation. How can altruistic or pro-social behaviour arise when individuals are presumed to be selfish resource maximisers? As Kant saw, if social structures cause individuals to behave *as if* they were pro-social, then the essence of human nature -- selfish or altruistic – becomes irrelevant. Self-regard and regard for others are not fixed traits, but adaptive behaviours adduced by circumstances. The core problem, therefore, is identifying the circumstances under which pro-social strategies can emerge in evolving systems.

This chapter introduces several core concepts and definitions that the book relies upon to progress further. Most important of these is a formal definition of the evolutionary process. We will also trace the early history of theories of cooperation over the course of twentieth century, including William Hamilton and the great populariser of Hamilton's Rule, Richard Dawkins. We conclude by introducing multilevel selection, which is the contemporary challenger to a purely gene-centric view of selection and evolution. Much of the following chapters will be dedicated to exploring the different population structures that permit cooperative behaviour to be evolutionarily stable.

Darwinian evolution is a subset of the broader study of complex systems comprised of many components which interact with each other as well as their external environment. Complex systems display emergent properties that cannot be reduced down to the behaviour of their individual

---

[66] Kant (1795) First Supplement, Page 154.

components. Life is a complex adaptive system, as are the species that comprise it, the individual plants and animals that form the population of each species and the organs and cells that make up each animal. Human society is also a complex adaptive system, as are the nation-states that rule it, the institutions, firms and associations that comprise those, and their individual members and so on, and so on. Evolutionary thinking is 'substrate neutral': the domains in which evolutionary processes were first observed and described was biological, but the domains in which evolution operates need not be[67].

Evolutionary systems are characterised by the three processes of generalised Darwinism: *variation, selection and (self-)replication*[68]. Let us treat each of them in turn. A population of i agents displays **variation** when every otherwise equivalent agent possesses some property s_i which causes measurably (or 'phenotypically') different interactions with the agent's environment. Every fundamental particle, for example, has identical physical properties and will interact with physical forces in an identical manner. Even molecules as large as proteins have consistent and predictable chemical properties. However, complex polymers (including DNA) can have variable properties while remaining chemically similar enough to treat as a population of interacting agents of a single type[69]. We define $Pr(s_i)$ as the proportion of agents in a population with property s_i, or the *frequency* of that phenotype.

---

[67] Wilson & Sober (1994) at pg. 592; Harrison, "Thinking About the World We Make" in Harrison (ed.) (2006) at pgs. 2-3, 7-8; Harrison & Singer, "Complexity is More Than Systems Theory" in Harrison (ed.) (2006) at pgs. 25-41; Dietl, "Selection, Security, and Evolutionary International Relations" in Sagarin & Taylor (eds.) (2008) at pgs. 90-92; Lustick (2011) at pg. 191;

[68] Hodgson (2013); Lustick (2011) at pg. 191; "To clarify, all that is needed for Darwinian selection are three simple conditions: (1) some amount of variation in characteristics ("phenotypically different"); (2) a process of selection such that some characteristics survive better than others ("differential survival"); and (3) some means of replication so that successful characteristics are passed on to subsequent generations ("survival or reproduction")."; Page & Nowak (2002) at pgs. 93-98; Lewontin (1970) at pgs. 1-18.

[69] Yeates et al. (2016) at pgs. 5030-5035; Dawkins (1982) at pg. 129.

Selection is any process $u(s_i)$ by which an agent in a population with property s_i receives a second property u_i, which we call *fitness*, as a result of an interaction. Fitness can represent any property or payoff, so long as it's acted upon by the third process (replication). u_i can be almost any measurable quantity, defined in any direction: it may represent abstract utility, attractiveness, repulsiveness, warmth, chilliness, income, wealth, poverty, proximity to the colour 'blue', or degree of aural distinguishability from the sound of a malfunctioning vacuum cleaner. The important thing is that fitness is related to the agent's property s_i, which in turn is variable across the population. In other words, the variability of the property s_i generates *differential fitness* u_i. Populations have an average fitness U_P, defined as the sum of the fitness of every possible phenotype weighted by its frequency.

Lastly, **replication** is any process $R(s_i)$ which relates the frequency of agents with the property s_i at time $t+1$ to their fitness u_i at time t, relative to the average fitness of the population U_P. A standard mathematical representation of this relationship is the *replicator dynamic*[70] :

$$\frac{\partial Pr(s_i)}{\partial t} = R\big(u_i - U_p\big)Pr(s_i).$$

The replicator dynamic must be increasing with relative u_i. In other words, if $u_i > U_P$ then the frequency of s_i is strictly increasing. The properties of the replicator dynamic are shared by many processes with different mathematical form but similar effect, including imitation rules by which social agents preferentially copy higher-fitness strategies or where the probability of an agent switching strategies depends on how far they lag behind the rest of the population[71].

---

[70] Taylor & Jonker (1978) at pgs. 145-156; Schuster & Sigmund (1983) at pgs. 533-538; Hofbauer & Sigmund (1998), Chapter 7.

[71] Hofbauer & Sigmund (1998), Chapter 8; Page & Nowak (2002) at pgs. 93-98; Traulsen & Hauert, "Stochastic evolutionary game dynamics" in Schuster (ed.) (2009) at pg. 25.

Fitness is defined with reference to replicator dynamic: if the replication of an agent is increased by lowering its temperature, for example, then we define a reduction in temperature as an increase in its fitness. And while many chemical and nuclear reactions differentially produce output products, only a tiny subset of reactions maintain or increase the population of interacting agents. Auto-catalytic or self-replicating populations that also demonstrate variation constitute the complex system we label 'life'[72].

* * *

Suppose social agents have a property s_i which can take one of two discrete values: C or D. Agents with property D are 'selfish' actors who only increase their own fitness such that $u(s_D)$ is positive. Agents with property C, on the other hand, have altruistic 'virtues' that increase the fitness of *other* agents in the population. Altruism reduces the relative fitness of an agent, such that its frequency in the population decreases after replication[73]. An agent with the property C is said to be *strongly altruistic* if switching to property D would increase both its absolute and relative fitness[74]. An agent with the property C is *weakly altruistic* if switching to property D makes no difference to its absolute fitness while increasing its relative fitness[75]. The presence of agents with property C may increase the average fitness of the overall population (U_P) by providing benefits to others that outweigh the relative fitness loss to themselves.

If agents are rational actors (see Chapter 3: "Adaptive Rationality"), then it's trivial to state that no actor would choose to be altruistic (and would be indifferent to weak altruism). But the same result follows *in an*

---

[72] Maynard Smith & Szathmary (1999) at pgs. 3-7.

[73] Comte, "System of Positive Polity" (1851). The first definition of altruism states it is: "intentional action, ultimately for the welfare of others, that entails at least the possibility of either no benefit or a loss to the actor."

[74] Bowles & Gintis (2011), Appendix A1; See also Bergstrom (2002) at pgs. 67–88; Boyd et al. (2003).

[75] Wilson (1990) at pgs. 135-148.

evolutionary system without conscious agents capable of choice. Since the replicator dynamic depends only on the relative fitness of properties C and D[76], then the proportion of actors with property D will increase in the population even if C is only weakly altruistic. So long as actors with property D are *relatively* better off by some small amount, their proportion in the population will gradually increase and the proportion of actors with property C will decrease.

"[T]he evolution of group-level functional organisation [i.e. cooperation] cannot be explained on the basis of natural selection operating within [groups]. On the contrary, natural selection operating within groups tends to undermine group-level functional organisation." [Wilson][77]

For the first eighty or so years of evolutionary science, Darwin and Kropotkin's qualitative observations about cooperative behaviour in social organisations were largely ignored[78]. To the extent that biologists or social scientists focused on pro-sociality or altruism at all, it was assumed that Darwin had been correct and that behaviours which benefitted the group would be positively selected: a position often termed naïve group selection[79]. But as we have shown here, this is untenable. Even where behaviours benefit a population as a whole, altruistic social agents will be out-replicated by social agents following selfish strategies (See also Chapter 13: "Social Cancers"). Over the course of the 1960s, biologists and mathematicians successfully challenged and undermined the naïve group selection position[80].

---

[76] Wilson, "Reaching a New Plateau for the Acceptance of Multilevel Selection" The Evolution Institute, 22 September 2017.

[77] Wilson (2015) at pg. 21.

[78] One possible exception being Haldane (1932).

[79] For an example, see: Wynne-Edwards (1962); Turchin (2016) at pg. 61; Sober, "Darwin and Group Selection" in Sober (ed.), (2010) at pgs. 45-86.

[80] Represented, for example, Williams (1966); Dawkins (1982) at pgs. 174-178; Borello (2010).

Perhaps humanity has properties that separate our species from the rest of nature; we can be altruistic because we are capable of understanding, knowing and performing virtue. Apparently alone in nature, we are capable of learning and following rules (either secular or religious) that prescribe moral behaviour and as a result learn to categorise good and evil. The capacity to be altruistic, in this view, depends on developing and exercising 'moral Reason' – a talent which is unique in the human species. It's up to empirical naturalists to demonstrate when theorists are wrong, and offer evidence that despite such predictions, altruistic behaviour is common and widespread in nature.

Enter the bees.

The supposition that large-scale social behaviour is found only in humans has a very notable caveat to it, an exception well-known by Darwin[81] and Kropotkin. The social insects -– bees, wasps and termites – live in large colonies consisting of hundreds, if not thousands of individuals. Ants and bees demonstrate a division of labour between individuals, altruistic care of offspring, cooperative foraging and even, in some species, agriculture. Ants and bees fight wars, sacrifice their lives for the hive, and in some species have developed elaborate communication rituals. Social insects are anthropoid invertebrates – separated from humans by hundreds of millions of years of divergent evolution – and, at the individual level, possess reasoning skills that are barely worth mentioning. How is this possible?

Suppose an agent has a choice of behaviours as before (C, D). Switching from the selfish behaviour D to the cooperative behaviour C imposes a relative fitness *cost*, while conferring a relative fitness *benefit* to other members of the community. Any agent that followed the cooperative behaviour, therefore, would be out-replicated by agents following a selfish behaviour, and go extinct. But replication does not necessarily produce

---

[81] Darwin wrote in Chapter 8 of On the Origin of Species that the existence of eusocial insects was potentially "fatal to my theory". See generally: Sober, "Darwin and Group Selection" in Sober (ed.) (2010) at pgs. 45-86.

identical clones of the original agent: many species reproduce by mixing half their chromosomes, and in a cultural evolutionary context, too, there's no guarantee than a child will inherit all of the cultural properties of its parents. So **some fraction the relative fitness advantage conferred on type D may therefore result in the incidental production of agents of type C.**

We define r, the coefficient of relatedness, between two phenotypes as the probability that the replication of one trait will lead to the replication of the other. In biological terms, r is equivalent to the probability that a random gene carried by one agent is also carried by a different agent[82]. If r = 1, agents are identical and do not possess differential fitness. If r = 0, agents are totally unrelated and altruists can never increase their frequency in the population by conferring a fitness advantage on others. But between those values, a co-operator could expect to receive a partial reproductive benefit by conferring a fitness advantage on someone else. Therefore, altruistic behaviours can be positively selected whenever r(benefit) - cost is positive, or:

$$r > \frac{cost}{benefit}$$

This relation is known as Hamilton's Rule[83]. It is the most important, albeit so far incomplete, formula in this book and we will return to variations of it several times[84]. Hamilton's Rule underpins the idea of *kin selection*, which as we shall later see is one of four social structures through which

---

[82] Hamilton (1964) at pgs. 1-16.

[83] Hamilton (1964) at pgs. 1-16; Nowak (2006) at pgs. 1560-1563; Boyd & Richerson (2005) at pgs. 197-198.

[84] The equivalent of Hamilton's Rule with other measures of population structure is discussed by Wilson, "Reaching a New Plateau for the Acceptance of Multilevel Selection" The Evolution Institute, 22 September 2017; For a more academic treatment, see Eshel & Cavalli-Sforza (1982) at pgs. 1331-1335.

pro-social behaviour can be positively selected[85]. While usually thought of as biological relatedness, r can be used more broadly as a measure of social structure[86], and is sometimes technically called the *index of assortivity*[87]. Most abstractly, it represents the likelihood that an agent will receive a fitness advantage by conveying a benefit on another.

In its purely biological manifestation, kin selection does an incredible amount of explanatory work. It underpins the parental investment almost all species show towards their offspring, the risks prey animals take to warn their family group of the approach of predators, and perhaps even the cooperative child-rearing displayed in quasi-social mammals where closely-related individuals invest in the survival of the children of a dominant breeding pair. On the other hand, kin selection also drives the habitual infanticide of cubs whenever a new lion takes over a pride, and has been hypothesised to contribute, in complex ways, to higher rates of child neglect by human step-parents[88]. One question that arises, of course, is how a social agent recognises its relatives -- an ant cannot read the genetic code of another ant. But the 'kin recognition problem' is a minor difficulty: even putting aside the possibility of direct recognition through biochemical markers, viable proxy signals for genetic relatedness may include physical proximity, repeated interactions and even cultural similarity (for example, with whale songs). More on this in Chapter 6: "Order From Chaos".

Kin selection, it turns out, neatly solves the mystery of the ants (and also mole rats, which, through quirk of evolution have evolved a similar social structure)[89]. Many social insects use a unique sex determination system in which the number of chromosomes determines the reproductive role of an individual. As a result, males are typically all children of a single reproducing

---

[85] We condense direct and indirect reciprocity: Nowak (2006) at pgs. 1560-1563; See also Skyrms (2014) at pgs. 55-60; Cederman (2002) at pg. 7299.

[86] Bowles & Gintis (2011) at pgs. 48-49.

[87] Bergstrom (2002); Bergstrom (2003); Bowles & Gintis (2011) at pg. 72.

[88] Although this is, of course, heavily disputed:, see: Daly & Wilson (1999).

[89] Nowak, Tarnita & Wilson (2010) at pgs. 1057-62.

female (the 'queen'), and female workers are strongly related to each other with a potential coefficient of relatedness of up to r = 3/4, depending on the species and hive structure. Because of this system, many invertebrate species have achieved a level of social complexity and adaptability that rivals humans, and have grown to become one of the most successful orders of animal life on the planet.

* * *

Unsurprisingly, it was an entomologist – Edward Wilson, whom we met earlier – who first advocated the idea that kin selection might help explain the existence of cooperation in humans. At first haltingly, in *Sociobiology: The New Synthesis*[90], but later with increasing confidence in *On Human Nature*[91], Wilson argued that human social behaviour could be explained as a result of genes interacting under natural selection. *Sociobiology* generated immense controversy upon its release, and Wilson and his intellectual heirs have in subsequent decades faced the charge, sometimes justified, of biological determinism[92]. Steven Pinker's well-known book *the Blank Slate*[93] was largely written as a defence of sociobiology and critique of Marxism, as was Peter Singer's pamphlet *A Darwinian Left*[94] in 1999.

The kin selection view of social cooperation is powerful, but its formulation in terms of genetic relatedness has generated a misplaced focus on genetic replication as the central evolutionary process[95]. The mathematical argument that a gene or trait will only spread to the degree that it spreads

[90] Wilson (1975)

[91] Wilson (1979)

[92] Allen et al. (1975); Lewontin (1976); Dawkins (1982), Chapter 2; Lewontin (1982); Lewontin et al. (1984); Boyd & Richerson, (2001) at pg. 444; Richerson et al. "An Evolutionary Theory of Commons Management" in Stern (ed.)(2001); Binmore, "s (2005); Laland & Brown (2011), Chapter 3.

[93] Pinker (2002).

[94] Singer (1999); See also Stack (2003).

[95] Birch & Okasha (2014) at pgs. 22-32.

copies of itself lies at the core of what we will call the *genetic essentialist* view of evolution. But kin selection under-explains social behaviour in humans, who clearly habitually cooperate in extremely large social groups with near-zero genetic relatedness[96]. If kin selection were the only mechanism promoting pro-social behaviour, then the Thatcherites could well argue that society consists only of individuals and their families. While re-defining r to cover more abstract notions of relatedness has been scientifically productive, the further the genetic analogy is stretched the less useful it becomes[97].

For the lay reader unfamiliar with this arcane academic schism, 1975 marked the beginning of a divergence between the application of evolution to social behaviour in the broadest possible sense, and a narrower reading that focused exclusively on genes and inheritance[98]. The latter branch is the ancestor of both the Santa Barbara school of Evolutionary Psychology (with a "capital-E" and "capital-P") associated with Leda Cosmides & John Tooby[99], and at extremes the pseudoscientific racism and classism of the likes of Charles Murray[100]. It conceives of natural selection as a biological process that operates exclusively on genes and sees ideas, beliefs and rituals as a set of unnatural deviations from a DNA-centric ideal of what it meant to behave as a human.

But in the more progressive-learning branch of sociobiology – Darwinian socialism – evolutionary sociology is more than merely measuring the influence of genes on social and cultural life. Rather, it recognises that biological evolution is merely a special case of a broader constellation of

---

[96] Dunbar (2014), Chapter 9; Turchin (2016).

[97] Wilson (2015) at pgs. 43-45; Nowak, Tarnita & Wilson (2010) at pgs. 1057-62; Gintis (2017), Chapter 9.

[98] For an overview, see Laland & Brown(2011)

[99] Cosmides, Tooby & Barkow (1992); Minkel, "Psyching Out Evolutionary Psychology: Interview with David J. Buller" Scientific American, July 4 2005; Cosmides & Tooby (2013) at pgs. 201-229; Laland & Brown (2011), Chapter 5.

[100] Hernnstein & Murray, "The Bell Curve: Intelligence and Class Structure in American Life" Free Press (1994).

processes with a common mathematical structure. Culture is also adaptive system which evolves alongside and interacts with biology[101]. While Wilson is an irascible and combative figure, and certainly no friend of the left, he was always more open-minded than the caricature of him[102] and by the late 2000s he had jettisoned the primacy of kin selection and embraced the possibilities of an expanded evolutionary synthesis that includes both genetic and cultural evolution operating at multiple levels of analysis[103].

These ideas are not new. The early evolutionary psychologist James Mark Baldwin[104] anticipated the idea that culture, genes and environment all play a part in the evolution of human behaviour, and that behavioural flexibility and the capacity to learn and adapt to changing environmental conditions offered advantages over the fixed reproduction of inherited biological strategies. Baldwin recognised that the biological and the cultural interact with one another, so that while the former might set the terms for the development of the latter, a cooperative culture could over a sufficient timescale influence a species' biological impetus to competition and selfishness. In modern terms, this is referred to as gene-culture co-evolution (see Chapter 5: "Strategy and Culture")[105].

The genetic essentialist view of evolution has always been robustly critiqued, but rarely as effectively as by Stephen Jay Gould[106]. For Gould, Dawkins' key mistake was to overvalue the linkage between the genes and replication. It's not genotype that generates differential fitness and is

---

[101] Cavalli-Sforza & Feldman (1973) at pgs. 618-637

[102] C.f. Lumdsen & Wilson (1981)

[103] Wilson & Wilson (2007) at pgs. 327-348; Nowak, Tarnita & Wilson (2010) at pgs. 1057-62; Wilson (2012); Wilson (2019).

[104] Baldwin (1896) at pgs. 441-451.

[105] Durham (1991); Gintis (2017), Chapter 1.

[106] Gould (1977); Gould, "Darwinian Fundamentalism" New York Review of Books, 12 June 1997; Gould (2002); Shanahan, "Selfish Genes and Lucky Breaks: Richard Dawkins' and Stephen Jay Gould's Divergent Darwinian Agendas" in Delisle (ed.), (2017) at pgs. 11-36.

selected for by evolution, but rather phenotype or expressed behaviour[107]. Genes are the output of the evolutionary process, but only to the extent that they generate fitness-enhancing phenotypes under a narrow set of environmental and developmental conditions. The somewhat naïve view that every behaviour might potentially be controlled by a single gene – the 'phenotype-to-genotype gambit' – is unscientific and untenable when it comes to complex behaviours: hundreds, if not thousands, of genes contribute in imperceptible amounts to complex chemical processes that shape behaviour, and the activity and expression of those genes is also influenced by the conditions in which the organism grows.

If genes were just 'selfish' agents, as the metaphor holds, then a gene should evolve to promote its own replication at the expense of other genes on the chromosome – after all, why wouldn't competition also operate within the chromosome? While there are certainly genes that behave in this way (i.e. the so-called transposons, or 'jumping genes') most cell nuclei contain ruthless systems to suppress intra-genomic conflict that threatens the viability of the whole cell[108]. Partly as a result of these systems, genes in general behave cooperatively to promote the survival and replication of the whole genome[109], the whole cell and the whole organism, usually in ways that give every gene a scrupulously fair chance of being inherited by the next generations. Genes are not selfish – they are cooperative and altruistic. Within the cell, natural selection favours self-restraint because it gives the population of genes the fitness advantage it needs to compete at higher levels of organisation. A cell or germline containing cooperative genes has higher average fitness than a cell coded with purely selfish ones.

* * *

We must, therefore, introduce the modern form of group selection, or

---

[107] Gould (1977); Hull, "Interactors versus Vehicles" in Plotkin (ed.) (1988) at pgs. 19–50.

[108] Alford & Hibbing (2004) at pgs. 707–723.

[109] Leigh (1971)

as it is more accurately known, *multilevel selection*[110]. A pithy summary of multilevel selection was provided by David Wilson and Edward Wilson [no relation] in a 2007 article re-assessing the theoretical grounding of sociobiology: *"Selfishness beats altruism within groups. Altruistic groups beat selfish groups"*[111]. The key insight of modern group selection is that the selection pressures operating on one level (for example, on the fitness of a gene, a cell, an organism or an individual) can point in a different direction to the selection pressures on another (for example, the fitness of a family group, a tribe or a nation-state). A selfish trait may generate an individual fitness advantage compared to other traits, but lead to an overall reduction in group fitness that drives it extinct in the long-run. A ruthless exploiter who dominates the local tribe goes extinct alongside his or her subjects when overrun by a tribe of effective co-operators.

For an illustration of how this works, we can go back to the British mathematician John Maynard Smith, who offered (and rejected) the first theoretical model of group selection in 1964[112] – later dusted off and promoted by David Wilson[113]. In Maynard Smith's haystack model, small rodents (for example) are reproductively isolated each season (breeding generation) in 'haystacks'. Colonies which by chance have a higher proportion of cooperative rodents will have higher average fitness and produce more offspring that season than Hobbesian stacks with a high proportion of selfish rodents. So although a cheater will do very well for itself in a cooperative stack, cooperative stacks will have more offspring than stacks comprised entirely of cheaters. When breeding occurs and new rodent colonies are formed by the offspring of the previous generation, cooperative

---

[110] Wilson, "Reaching a New Plateau for the Acceptance of Multilevel Selection" The Evolution Institute, 22 September 2017; Wilson & Sober (1994) at pgs. 585–654; Dietl, "Selection, Security, and Evolutionary International Relations" in Sagarin & Taylor (eds.) (2008) at pgs. 93-96.

[111] Wilson & Wilson (2007); Wilson (2015) at pg. 23.

[112] Maynard Smith (1964) at pg. 1145. Maynard Smith concluded that his model did not support the group selection argument, which was then going out of fashion.

[113] Wilson (1975) at pgs. 143-146.

traits may increase overall.

So long as social agents are part of structured sub-populations, and those groups are subject to natural selection amongst themselves, it's at least mathematically possible for pro-social traits to evolve. Each sub-population settles into (or 'fixes') its own equilibrium – it's *group strategy* – and then selection operates between groups to select the most fit equilibria. Formally, this will occur whenever the ratio of inter-group variance to intra-group variance is stronger than the selective pressure on individuals[114] (we derive this relation in Chapter 7: "Evolutionary Games"). Multilevel selection predicts that cooperation can evolve when the selection pressure on individuals is relatively weak *or* when groups are relatively internally homogenous *or* when the variance between different groups is high. So long as there's an internal population structure that coheres co-operators together, altruistic traits may be evolutionarily stable.

The evolution of pro-social norms and behaviours is therefore the result of selection pressures acting at different levels of analysis. When a pro-social norm becomes stabilised (or 'fixed') a group undergoes what Maynard Smith termed a 'major evolutionary transition' and starts to experience new selection pressures at a higher level of organisation[115]. Groups of agents become larger 'meta-agents'. Just as the first organic chemicals organised themselves into chromosomes that replicated together, so too simple single-celled organisms that processed sunlight (chloroplasts) or ATP (mitochondria) for energy started to cooperate in complex cells, and eukaryotes in turn began to associate in colonies, then specialised to form multi-cellular organisms, and individual organisms associated in herds, packs and tribes, and then tribes banded together to form proto-states and empires. The history of life is a story of the dilemma of cooperation being repeatedly 'solved', only to generate new dilemmas for the resulting

---

[114] Wilson (1977) at pgs. 157-185; Wilson & Sober (1994) at pgs. 585–654; Turchin (2016) at pg. 82.

[115] Maynard Smith & Szathmary (1995); Harrison, "Thinking About the World We Make" in Harrison (ed.) (2006) at pgs. 8-9. Dietl, "Selection, Security, and Evolutionary International Relations" in Sagarin & Taylor (eds.) (2008) at pgs. 95-96.

organism (We take this up further in Chapter 9: "The Evolution of Society").

The following chapters will introduce four different mechanisms through which populations can structure themselves in order to generate the conditions for pro-social behaviour to evolve. With kin selection, we have already been introduced to the first of these. We will see that that each mechanism has a similar mathematical structure and that the coefficient of relatedness can be interpreted not only as genetic similarity, but also temporal and spatial proximity, and relatedness of group identity[116]. In each case, what matters is the probability that a co-operator will share in the fitness benefit of helping others.

As we move forward, it's important to not repeat Spencer's mistake and acknowledge the interaction of personal belief and science. Many of the most prominent biologists cited in this chapter, including J.B.S. Haldane[117] (the pre-war originator of inclusive fitness theory), John Maynard Smith, Stephen Gould and Richard Lewontin (an advocate for cultural evolution and strong critic of genetic essentialism) were all committed progressives, if not Marxists, for most of their lives. I've met David Wilson, and while I'm sure he'd object to being labelled a socialist, he's a committed social reformer[118]. There's a strong component of personal psychology in how scientists apply and interpret evolution.

"[I]nclusive fitness theorising leads researchers to think atomistically, while group selection theorizing leads researchers to think structurally. . . . [These] are personal preferences – highly contrasting yet equally useful ways of thinking about society. The correct [approach] is to embrace both atomistic and structural approaches and analyse the corresponding interplay of forces." [Gintis,

---

[116] See: West et al. (2011) at pg. 247; Dunbar (2014), Chapter 9; Wilson (2015), Chapter 3; Villarreal, "From Bacteria to Belief: Immunity and Security" in Sagarin & Taylor (eds.) (2008) at pgs. 42–68.

[117] Haldane, "Marxist Philosophy and the Sciences" (1939).

[118] C.f. Wilson (2011).

Individuality and Entanglement][119].

Progressives should take comfort in the fact although conservative interpretations of Darwinian evolution are better known, many scientists are convinced that evolution supports, and indeed demands, a pro-social approach to political life.

---

[119] Gintis (2017).

2

INTRODUCTION TO GAMES

Key Points

- Social dilemmas are endogenous to the majority of strategic interactions -where the fitness consequences of an action are interdependent with the behaviour of others.
- The Nash equilibrium of a social dilemma is a set of strategies such that each agent believes its actions are the best response to those of others.
- The socialist critique of structure constitutes the search for cooperative solutions to social dilemmas. Asymmetric or hierarchical social structures are far from the only such solutions.

Game theory is the formal study of strategic interaction between social agents[120]. It offers a logic and methodology to describe the condition of *interdependence*, wherein the consequences of an agent's actions are causally influenced by the behaviour of others. Interdependence undermines any simple correlation between means and ends, because the fitness consequences of any agent's choices depend on the choices of someone else[121]. Game theory is best known amongst economists, experimental

---

[120] Von Neumann & Morgenstern (1944)

[121] Harrison, "Thinking About the World We Make" in Harrison (ed.) (2006) at pgs. 9-10.

psychologists and theoretical biologists, but there's a widespread aversion to its methods amongst social scientists[122]. At least in part, this aversion stems from the strict adherence to rational choice methods by economists and mathematicians (addressed in Chapter 3: "Adaptive Rationality"). But the use of game theory by biologists interested in the behaviour of bacteria, insects and other animals shows the assumption of common rationality is unnecessary.

Game theory focuses on the solution of **social dilemmas**: situations created when strategic behaviour that is rational from each individual's point of view leads to outcomes that are unfavourable for all. These are also known as social tragedies or collective action problems. The solution of social dilemmas is the common context of both political decision-making and natural selection.

"Political outcomes do not necessarily reflect the preferences of any one actor, or group of actors, rather they are the product of many actors pursuing their interests [independently]. It is important to take this insight one step further: political actions do not necessarily reveal preferences over outcomes either; at best they reveal subjective beliefs about what actors consider the best response to the expected behaviour of other relevant actors." [Clark, Agents and Structures][123]

Consider again two agents, Player 1 and Player 2, with a choice of two pure strategies (C, D) and fitness payoffs (u_1, u_2). We define strategy as a decision rule or rules that specifies an agent's behaviour given their beliefs about the structure of their [social] environment. When an agent uses one, and only one, behaviour we call this a **pure strategy** (we relax this condition in Chapter 4: "Mixed Strategies, Mixed Populations").

We can display strategic interactions in what is known as the *normal-* or *strategic-form*. Player 1 is the *row* player, and its behavioural options and the resulting payoffs are shown below and to the left; Player 2 is the *column*

---

[122] Gintis (2009); Gintis (2007); Lustick (2011) at pgs. 179-209.

[123] Clark (1998) at pg. 247.

player, and its options and payoffs are shown above and to the right (Figure 2.1). Obviously, the number of strategies can be expanded infinitely, and an N-player game can be represented as an N-dimensional matrix.

		Player 2	
		C	D
Player 1	C	$u_2(C,C)$ $u_1(C,C)$	$u_2(C,D)$ $u_1(C,D)$
	D	$u_2(D,C)$ $u_1(D,C)$	$u_2(D,D)$ $u_1(D,D)$

Figure 2.1: A normal-form game

There are alternative ways of representing strategic interaction, but the normal form is typically used in situations of complete but imperfect information. This terminology can seem confusing, but is actually quite simple. In a complete information game, the identities, strategies options and payoffs are commonly 'known' to all players -- the game structure can be fully described (this condition is relaxed in Chapter 8: "Beliefs and Signals"). In a perfect information game, agents additionally know the actual strategies or moves of the other players. Perfect information games are commonly represented as a sequence of moves, or a decision-tree, because each actor is able to observe the behaviour of the others before implementing their own strategy. For this reason, they are also sometimes called sequential games. The normal form, on the other hand, is best for situation in which agents move at the same time or cannot reliably observe each other's move; they are otherwise called static or simultaneous games.

A normal form game is *symmetric* when the players are identical or equal in every way. That is: $u_1(C, C)=u_2(C, C)$, $u_1(D, D)=u_2(D, D)$, $u_1(C, D)=u_2(D, C)$ and $u_1(D, C)=u_2(C, D)$. A symmetric game is one in which agents start in an initial condition of equality. The standardised two-player, symmetric, normal form game that we'll use for the remainder of this book reduces to

Figure 2.2.

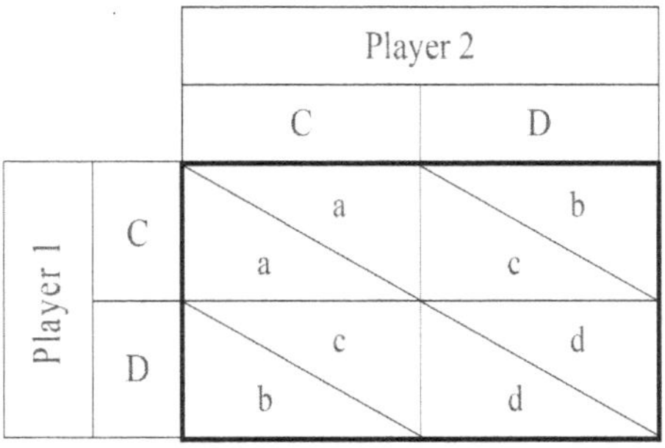

Figure 2.2: The symmetric normal-form game

In this standardised form, a is the 'reward' payoff when both players cooperate (for this reason, it's sometimes represented as R). b is known as the 'temptation' payoff (T), because it represents the fitness advantage a player gains by defecting when one's partner naively cooperatives. c is also called the sucker's payoff (S): it is the fitness value a player obtains by playing a cooperative strategy when one's partner cheats or defects. Finally, d represents the so-called penalty payoff (P), i.e. the score both players receive when both defect from cooperation.

Using this framework, how do social agents solve a strategic interaction to know what choice is optimal? It cannot be simply assumed that an agent will choose the action with the highest payoff, since the outcome an agent receives depends on the choice of their opponent, which is unknown. In other words, aiming for the maximum possible payoff may result in receiving the minimum possible payoff, because agents do not directly control the social structure which mediates between their preferences and payoffs.

A strategy is **strongly** or **strictly dominated** if an agent has no reason to play it *regardless of the strategy played by their opponent*. A strategy is **weakly dominated** if there is at least one scenario in which playing it would make an agent worse off and the agent would be indifferent in all other scenarios. The simplest process for solving normal form games is called the iterated elimination of dominated strategies: each agent removes from its potential strategy set every choice that is strictly dominated. This follows from the observation that every strictly dominated strategy guarantees an inferior fitness payoff[124]. If, as a result, an agent has only one strategy remaining then it will have no reason to vary its behaviour and unilaterally deviate from that strategy.

Let's see how this works by examining the game below (Figure 2.3). This is called the **cooperation** (or **'harmony'**) **game** and it's the simplest scenario possible because both agents have an incentive to follow the strategy that maximises the collective payoffs. Any game in which a > b, c > d and a > d is a cooperation game (i.e.: there's no temptation to defect; an agent would rather be a sucker than suffer from non-cooperation; and mutual cooperation is preferable to mutual defection).

Harmony		Player 2: C	Player 2: D
Player 1	C	3, 3	4, 1
Player 1	D	1, 4	0, 0

Figure 2.3: The Harmony, or cooperation, Game

To check that this is the case, we hold one strategy constant and highlighting (in **bold**, above) the payoff which each agent would prefer. First, for Player 1, we see that they would prefer to play C if Player 2 implements strategy C (3 > 1); they would also prefer to play C if Player 2 implements strategy D (4 > 0). So C is the **dominant strategy** for Player 1. Next, for Player 2 we see that they would also prefer to play C if Player 1 is also playing C (3 > 1), and they would also prefer to play C even if Player 1 plays D (4 > 0). C is also the **dominant strategy** for Player 2.

---

[124] Gintis (2009), Chapter 4.

In the cooperation game, C is the dominant strategy for both players and the strategy profile (C, C) is therefore the pure strategy **Nash equilibrium** of the game – named after the famous mathematician John Nash (of '*A Beautiful Mind*' fame). In a Nash equilibrium, no player has an incentive to vary their strategy because it represents the mutual best response to the other[125]. A Nash equilibrium does not guarantee the highest possible payoff: it delivers the best payoff possible given the existence of other social agents. Nor is a Nash equilibrium efficient in a utilitarian sense: there's no expectation that the distribution of payoffs maximises the collective good. Nash proved that there's at least one Nash equilibrium in every game with finite players and finite pure strategies (the 'Nash Existence Theorem'). In the cooperation game above, each player would prefer to maximise their fitness payoff (4), but because this payoff relies upon the choices of the other player, it is inaccessible.

The cooperation game is trivial because there's no social dilemma: cooperation is incentivised by the structure of the game. However, for a two player symmetric normal form game with two pure strategies, there are a total of four strategic game archetypes (divided into mirrored pairs). These archetypes are known as 'Zeeman classes', and they provide the simplest way of categorising the social structure of dyadic or paired interaction[126]. No matter what the payoffs, any symmetric two-strategy normal form game will simplify into one of these classes. The number of possible archetypes increases combinatorially with the number of discrete, pure strategies, such that there are 20 Zeeman classes for a three-strategy game, and 228 Zeeman classes for four-strategy games, and so on. The remainder of this chapter will be dedicated to introducing the reader to the two-strategy archetypes.

* * *

---

[125] For a formal definition, and critique, see: Gintis (2009) at pgs. 98–100.

[126] Zeeman, "Population Dynamics from Game Theory" in Nitecki & Robinson (eds.) (1980) at pgs. 471–497

The Prisoner's Dilemma

The prisoner's dilemma is the most famous Zeeman class in game theory and the one that a lay reader is most likely to be familiar with. The narrative myth of the prisoner's dilemma goes like this: two individuals are engaged in a criminal enterprise. They are arrested after generating suspicion thanks to minor offenses, and placed in different interrogation rooms. They cannot communicate with each other and thus do not know what the other will do. The authorities offer each offender a bargain: testify and we'll let you go free. But if your co-accused testifies, you'll do time and they'll be the one who goes free. Of course, if both players confess, both end up in jail; if neither does, they both go to jail for some minor infraction. Each prisoner has the choice to testify (D) or not (C), but is unable to communicate with the other and verify their decision ahead of time – this is a game of complete but imperfect information.

The prisoner's dilemma will also be referred to in this book as the **anti-cooperation game**. Any game in which the payoffs are structured such that b > a > d > c is a prisoner's dilemma. Like the cooperation game, the prisoner's dilemma has one dominant pure strategy, and one Nash equilibrium in pure strategies. b > a implies that agents are tempted to defect from cooperation; and d > c requires that actors prefer mutual defection to being a sucker. The relation a > d implies that mutual cooperation is preferable, in terms of payoffs, to mutual defection – – this generates a social dilemma in which there is tension between the collective good and the structural incentives of the game.

Let's check this by the elimination of dominated strategies for the example anti-cooperation game in Figure 2.4. For Player 1, we see that they would prefer to play D if Player 2 implements strategy C (0 > -1); they would also prefer to play D if Player 2 implements strategy D (-3 > -4). So D is the **dominant strategy** for Player 1. Next, for Player 2 we see that they would also prefer to play D if Player 1 is playing C (0 > -1), and they would also prefer to play D if Player 1 also plays D (-3 > -4). C is also the **dominant strategy** for Player 2.

Prisoners Dilemma		Player 2: C	Player 2: D
Player 1	C	-1, -1	-4, 0
	D	0, -4	-3, -3

Figure 2.4: The Prisoner's Dilemma, an anti-cooperation game.

The strategy pair (D, D) is the Nash equilibrium of the anti-cooperation game. The two prisoners will always rat each other out. Even if it delivers the worst fitness payoffs, and the agents would prefer other outcomes, the interdependent nature of their choice means they are unable to satisfy this preference in any scenario in which they do not know the strategy of the other player. This result often seems strongly counter-intuitive to many people, and such intuitions are a credit to the hundreds of thousands of years of evolution which have produced a variety of psychological mechanisms to avoid this exact outcome. This book is, in large part, the story of the evolution of those mechanisms.

In order to accept that (D, D) is the Nash equilibrium of the anti-cooperation game, game theory actually smuggles in some rather significant claims about the nature of reason and knowledge – as we will see in the next Chapter. In order for the iterated elimination of dominated strategies to uncover the Nash equilibria of a game, it's not sufficient for an agent to be a rational actor (see the next Chapter for a formal definition): rather an agent *must also believe that every other actor is also a rational actor, and believe that every other actor believes that every other actor is a rational actor, and so on.* This assumption is known as the **common knowledge of rationality**, and it is the foundational assumption of rational choice game theory[127]. Much of the arcane disputes amongst academics over the value of the game theory

[127] Gintis (2009), Chapter 4.

approach is dedicated to undermining or defending this assumption, and several alternatives or reformulations have been proposed.

Fortunately for us, evolutionary game theory *does not require the common knowledge of rationality*, or any alternative thereto. To see why this is so, consider the payoffs of the prisoner's dilemma in terms of reproductive fitness. It is clear than any actor playing the strategy D cannot go extinct: at worst, they match the fitness of the other player, and if the other player naively cooperates, D players will have *higher* fitness and preferentially reproduce. On the other hand, while the strategy pair (C, C) may be stable if every agent in the population plays C, a single defector (known as a **'mutant'**) will exploit that population, outcompete it and eventually come to dominate the population. We say therefore, that the strategy pair (C, C) is not evolutionarily stable but that the strategy pair (D, D) is. We define these terms and concepts in further detail in Chapter 8: "Evolutionary Games".

Coordination Games

A coordination or 'assurance' game is any game in which a > b and d > c. In other words there's no temptation to defect, but an agent would rather defect than be a sucker. If a > d we can also use the labels 'cooperate' and 'defect' for the two pure strategies as usual. Coordination games have more than one dominant pure strategy, and instead having multiple Nash equilibria. They have the property that agents prefer to play the *same strategy* as their opponent, but are more or less indifferent to *which* strategy that is. In other words, agents prefer to coordinate their actions.

There are two subtypes of coordination games, depending on how the payoffs are structured. A game in which a > b ≥ d > c is also known as a **stag hunt (Figure 2.5),** following the canonical description of the social dilemma by Jean-Jacques Rousseau in his *Discourse on Inequality*[128]. In the stag hunt, two hunters in a state of nature are carefully hunting deer in the forest, a difficult prey but one that offers enough meat to feed everyone well.

---

[128] Rousseau, "A Discourse on the Origin and Basis of Inequality Among Men" (1754).

"If a deer was to be taken, everyone saw that, in order to succeed, he must abide faithfully by his [social role. i.e. cooperate]: but if a hare happened to come within the reach of any one of them, it is not to be doubted that he pursued it without scruple [i.e. defect], and, having seized his prey, cared very little, if by so doing he caused his companions to miss theirs." [Rousseau, Discourse in Inequality]

Games in which a,d > b,c are **pure coordination games (Figure 2.6)**. Games of this type typically involve the selection between two alternatives, both of which are equally good (such as choosing which side of the road on which to drive), as well as games in which each player has different preferences but still prefers a cooperative outcome. In pure coordination games, agents tend not to strongly prefer one equilibrium over the other so long as coordination – and not unilateral defection – is the end result.

Examples of these games, and solutions for them, are shown below:

Stag Hunt		Player 2	
		C	D
Player 1	C	10 / 10	0 / 7
	D	7 / 0	5 / 5

Figure 2.5: The Stag Hunt, a coordination game

Pure Coordination		Player 2	
		C	D
Player 1	C	10 / **10**	0 / 0
	D	0 / 0	10 / **10**

Figure 2.6: A Pure Coordination Game

In games with multiple Nash equilibria, how do agents choose which strategy to implement? Obviously, when a > d, the strategy pair (C, C) is said to be payoff-dominant and has higher relative and absolute fitness. But is this decisive? A population comprised of all C players would be evolutionary stable because it could not be invaded by lone players with the D strategy, but the inverse is also true: a population of all D players is evolutionary stable and cannot be invaded by lone players with the C strategy. The only way for the fitness differential between C and D to have evolutionary consequences is if *groups* of C players compete with *groups* of D players, or if there's some mechanisms by which C and D players can preferentially associate themselves with one another.

Anti-coordination Games

An anti-coordination game is defined as any game in which b > a and c > d. In these games, there's a strong temptation to defect *but* an agent would rather just be a sucker than engage in mutual defection. If a > d we can also use the labels 'cooperate' and 'defect' for the two pure strategies as usual. Anti-coordination games also have more than one dominant pure strategy, and multiple Nash equilibria. They have the property that agents prefer to play the *opposite strategy* to their opponent, but are more or less indifferent to *which* strategy that is.

The classical example of anti-coordination game is **chicken (Figure 2.7)**.

In chicken, two hot-headed youths drive vehicles at each other at great speed in a test of daring and cunning. The driver who swerves (C) first loses pride and respect, while the driver who stays the course (D) wins an increase in their social rank. However, if *neither* youth swerves then both die in a horrible crash (D,D); if both drivers swerve (C, C), both fail to gain social standing but neither dies.

Chicken		Player 2: C	Player 2: D
Player 1	C	0, 0	-1, 1
Player 1	D	1, -1	-10, -10

Figure 2.7: Chicken, an anti-coordination game

In an anti-coordination game, a population comprised entirely of one strategy type is not evolutionarily stable. A population of pure C can be successfully invaded by a single D player, whose aggression will be rewarded with a fitness advantage. But the inverse is also true: a population of all D can be successfully invaded by a single C, whose decision to avoid conflict allows him or her to avoid mutually assured destruction. The only stable equilibrium is a mix of C and D players – some drivers swerve and others don't.

* * *

In symmetric games, there's basic equality between actors: they are functionally identical and the structure of the game is essentially fair. But when social dilemmas are asymmetrical, the players in a game are unequal and one player has **structural power** over the other – defined as a greater capacity to secure a distribution of fitness benefits in their favour (we will take up distributional bargaining more in the next Chapter). The capacity to shape the structure of social interactions, determine who gets to play, and influence the payoffs are the primary dimensions of structural power. We can define a **social hierarchy** to constitute precisely any asymmetric power relation in a social game[129]. Hierarchy may make certain solutions to games more or less likely than they otherwise would have been and may alter the composition and stability of equilibrium population states[130]. However, hierarchy is not the only solution to the problem of generating order – in fact it could be argued it is no solution at all, and merely restates the structure of social dilemmas[131].

Let's re-consider the prisoner's dilemma again, but make the payoffs asymmetric. In this version of the game (Figure 2.8), Player 1 is in a position of social power or authority over Player 2, such that they can impose a (cost-free) penalty if Player 2 rats on them. The structure of this game is shown below

Figure 2.8: An Asymmetric Prisoner's Dilemma

As can be seen here, the defect strategy for Player 2 is now strictly dominated by cooperate. As a consequence, Player 1 freely informs to the authorities and gets out of prison free-and-clear. In other words, if a criminal is in a

---

[129] Nowak et al. label this "structural dominance". Nowak et al., (2010) at pgs. 19-30.

[130] Dawkins (1982) at pg. 119.

[131] Boyd & Richerson (2005) at pgs. 231-235.

position to threaten or punish his or her partner in crime, it's the 'fall guy' who ends up going to prison. In such cases, we say that there is a hierarchy within the society of criminals and that Player 1 has more decision freedom than Player 2.

We said in the Introduction that socialism or progressivism could be described as liberalism plus structural critique. *Structural critique* is often defined as ruthless rejection of asymmetric social structures that are violent, coercive or hierarchical. But this is incorrect. Game theory shows us that social dilemmas occur in three out of the four possible Zeeman classes of dyadic interaction, *even where the foundational liberal position of equality is assumed*. When socialists engage in structural critique, they are noting that even perfectly free, perfectly equal, perfectly rational individuals are constrained by social dilemmas over which they have no control, and that these recurrent dilemmas lead to social outcomes that make everyone worse off. That's why socialism is an essential revision and extension of liberalism.

The evolutionary socialist analysis of structure is grounded at least in part in the identification of equilibrium solutions to social dilemmas. The evolutionary socialist methodology is to ask where we are, how we get here, and how we might move from one strategic equilibrium to another. This requires both good theory and well-grounded empirical social research. But to discover if there are other social solutions that are superior to our current social norms requires that progressive also use their political imagination and break out of the ordinary liberal and capitalist assumptions of selfish strategic conflict.

3

ADAPTIVE RATIONALITY

Key Points

- Behaviours have multiple interacting causes: the motivational drive of individual action; the ontogeny or developmental history of the agent; the adaptive purpose of a behaviour in a given population; and its phylogeny or evolutionary history.
- The mechanisms of agent behaviour are shaped by selection, so an individual's action rules are likely to be adaptively rational in the context of their social environment and evolutionary history.
- Agents may act as if they were preference-consistent, utility-maximisers under some fixed conditions. But instrumental rationality is not required nor expected from social actors.

Selection by consequences 'causes' evolution[132]. That is, interactions among agents with varying phenotypes leads to the production or destruction of some quantity – which we may term fitness, utility, or welfare – which in turn controls the rate at which those phenotypes reproduce. While evolutionary analysis takes as its primary unit of interest the emergent structure of populations as a whole, the German sociologist Max Weber and others

---

[132] Skinner (1981) at pgs. 501-504.

have argued that any social theory must specify the micro-foundations or mechanisms of agent behaviour ("methodological individualism")[133]. Indeed, on a technical level, using computer modelling informed by cultural evolution to examine complex social phenomena requires highly specific, theoretically-informed rules for the behaviour of individual agents[134].

However, whenever selection operates simultaneously at multiple levels of organisation (Chapter 1) causation does as well. Selection at one level of analysis can motivate an agent to behave in one way while selection at a different level of analysis points the other. The Dutch biologist Nikolaas Tinbergen, who shared the Nobel Prize in Medicine for his study of social behaviour in animals, set out an evolutionary framework for understanding causation[135] based in turn on the work of Aristotle and Ernst Mayr[136]. Tinbergen's framework requires us to distinguish between the proximate (or 'individual') reason for an action and the ultimate (or 'social') cause[137]. When most people think superficially about causation, it's the proximate or motivational drive they think of first: an agent moves towards light/food/water in order to obtain the resources it requires to continue functioning. By contrast, the so-called 'ultimate' cause is evolutionary or adaptionist: agents of a particular type move toward light/food/water because groups of agents which acquire those resources reproduce better than those that don't.

Overvaluation of the explanatory power of proximate mechanisms, which is the flaw of the micro-foundation models we will discuss in this Chapter, is as much in error as overvaluation of ultimate causation. Criticism of the Functionalism (with a "capital-F") and the 'naïve adaptionism' inherent

---

[133] Alexander (1987).

[134] Axelrod (2000) at pgs. 130-151; Axelrod, "Introduction" in Axelrod (ed.) (1997) at pg. 4; Rousseau (2005), Chapter 7.

[135] Tinbergen (1952); Tinbergen (1963) at pgs. 410-433; Wilson (2015) at pgs. 62-64; Wilson & Gowdy (2013) at pgs. S3-S10; Stephen & Sulikowski, "Tinbergen's Four Questions" in "The Encyclopedia of Evolutionary Psychological Science" Springer Nature (2019).

[136] Mayr (1961) at pgs. 1501-1506

[137] Binmore (2005), Chapter 1.

in some evolutionary social accounts is valid[138]. The economist who states that the maximisation of wealth explains individual behaviour, because two dollars has more utility than one, is examining only a single method of causation. But so too is the Evolutionary Psychologist (with a "capital-E" and "capital-P") who explains entire system of gender relations in a social species on the basis of its supposed value to the reproductive fitness of a population. It's incorrect to state with certainty that structure causes agent behaviour by offering a narrative or calculation of its supposed evolutionary value to a population.

Tinbergen's innovation was to note that causation is both multi-level and inter-temporal. An organism, agent, or cultural complex is not merely adapted to its current environment, but is the product of an evolutionary chain of adaptions stretching back in time and across different, and dynamic, material conditions. Evolutionary sociology is therefore inherently path dependent or historically contingent: a particular social or behavioural outcome may be accessible or inaccessible to a society depending on its particular population history[139]. As a result, behaviour may not be strictly adaptive to an agent or population's current circumstances (we address these issues in more detail in Chapter 16: "Outside Context Problems"), and we must also consider its phylogeny or evolutionary origins.

As with populations, so too with individuals: the final of Tinbergen's four questions asks about the ontogeny or development of the social agent. What were the conditions under which its biological pathways were forming: was it under stress, or malnourishment, or did it experience resource abundance? What are the lessons the agent learned about social relations, and how fixed are its beliefs about the environment and social structure in which it lives? Through its development, an organism or organisation experiences different conditions that may be either supportive or hostile, and as these vary throughout its life stages they will alter the internal equilibrium of that organism or organisation.

---

[138] For a good overview, see Dawkins (1982) Chapter 3.

[139] Lustick (2011) at pgs. 179-209, especially at pg. 199-; Boyd & Richerson (2005) at pg. 151.

Tinbergen, and those who have relied on his framework, argue that we cannot begin to understand the causes of social behaviour without answering all four questions. Methodological individualism is necessary but not sufficient to 'explain' social outcomes – population-level dynamics may cause behaviours that are inexplicable from the perspective of the individual alone. If a particular social group engages in violence at a higher rate than others, is it because violence is an instrumental choice to acquire necessary resources; or because violence is an adaptive strategy for that group to prevail in a hostile economic environment; or do individuals in that group experience higher levels of childhood conflict, leading to low levels of social trust throughout their life; or is it because of that particular social group's history of oppression and marginalisation? The answer of course is it's all those things at once, interacting in complementary and contradictory ways. Anyone who tells you otherwise, that a single factor is the best way to understand particular behaviour, is lying to you – and probably themselves.

This chapter introduces readers to the standard, 'rational actor' model of individual behaviour. The rational actor selects their strategy on the basis of a comparison of the consequences of their choices; the actor is said to be rational if they do so in a way that reliably or consistently maximises fitness. We already implicitly relied on rational choice models in our analysis of normal form games in the previous Chapter; this Chapter will extend the games presented there to include games with continuous payoffs in which agents can choose how much effort or resources to commit to cooperation. The reader is warned in advance that the rational actor model is merely a simplifying assumption – and not a very good one at that. It cannot be the axiomatic foundation of sociological inquiry. Societies display emergent and irreducible complexities that cannot be explained by the aggregation of the preferences of individuals.

Instead, the illusion of rationality is an emergent property of the life and population history of an organism, and its social and environmental context. As we have already hinted, evolutionary accounts operate perfectly well to describe the population structures of organisms, even complex chemicals, that are incapable of exercising either reason or choice. So long as variation, selection and replication continue to function, individual agents with strategies that reliably produce higher than average fitness will outcompete those that don't, so may appear *as if* those agents are optimising for fitness[140]. A cheetah does not choose to focus on speed, nor a turtle on investing resources in its shell, nor humans in their capacity for social learning and interactions. The cheetahs, turtles and humans that *didn't* optimise for those behaviours have simply gone extinct: out-replicated by those that got better results.

As we shall see (especially in Chapter 10: "Mediocre Individuals, Exceptional Species") optimisation for fitness often produces behaviour that cannot be considered instrumentally rational from the point of view of the individual agent. Indeed, the entire field of behavioural economics exists in order to discover and catalogue these deviations from ideal rationality in humans. A child raised in a time of famine may hoard resources in times of plenty to a degree that is irrational, so too may cultures conditioned by conditions of environmental scarcity. Again, we must reiterate that nothing in social behaviour makes sense except in light of social evolution. So behavioural economics is more than merely an account of the way 'fallen' human beings deviate from the Platonic ideal of perfect rationality; it must be seen first and foremost as evidence that instrumental rationality is not, and will never be, a good approximation for the behaviour of any successful social species.

* * *

When presented with strategic variability, a 'rational' actor would select their strategy so as to maximise or satisfy their *interests* or *preferences*, rather than employ some simpler decision heuristic such as copying others, their own past behaviour, or simply randomising. Agents select a strategy which leads to the expected outcome they most prefer -- where 'expected' simply

---

[140] Harrison, "Thinking About the World We Make" in Harrison (ed.) (2006) at pgs. 9-10.

means the agent's probabilistic estimate of the likelihood of receiving that outcome. It's not sufficient that a rational actor merely have a *reason* for their decision – a reason could be anything! Rather, their reason must connect means to ends and reliably produce what the agent values. Importantly, the rational actor model says absolutely nothing about the content of an agent's preferences: an agent can value frivolous or important things, their own welfare (they may be selfish) or the welfare of others (they may be selfless). In order to rely on rationality to make reliable inferences about agent behaviour, an agent's preferences must merely be *consistent*[141].

Consider a series of fitness payoffs u_A, u_B, u_C etc. A preference ordering amongst these payoffs is considered consistent when it possesses four essential properties[142]. A preference ordering is **complete** if u_A, u_B, u_C etc. can be arranged such that an agent either strongly or weakly prefers, or is indifferent between, every value of u: there is no fitness payoff outside the range of their preferences that cannot be compared to the fitness value of the other fitness payoffs. A preference ordering is **transitive** if $u_A > u_B$ and $u_B > u_C$ then necessarily implies that $u_A > u_C$ i.e. there is a monotonic relationship amongst the complete set of fitness payoffs. A preference order is **continuous** or compensatory if there is always some combination of fitness payoffs u_A, u_B etc such that an agent is indifferent between receiving a combination thereof and payoff u_C: in other words, utility or fitness is measured on a single scale and fully substitutable. Finally, a preference ordering must respect the **independence of irrelevant alternatives**. Given a preference ordering amongst u_A, u_B, u_C etc, then the existence or non-existence of another fitness payoff u_D would not change the order amongst u_A, u_B, u_C etc.

If a preference ordering is consistent, then there will always exist a function [i.e. an equation] U(x) such that agents can be treated as if they maximise its value over the payoff space in which they are choosing. In the language of decision theory, U(x) is known as a utility or payoff function

---

[141] Nozick (1993) at pgs. 139-151.

[142] Von Neumann & Morgenstern (1953); Gintis (2009), Chapter 1.

and much of the day-to-day work in the economic and political sciences involves specifying the shape of this function (often based on empirical observations of human behaviour) and solving by 'maximising utility'.

However, preference consistency – if not treated as axiomatic – has been and perhaps can only be justified on the basis of natural selection[143]. Agents may act *as if* they have consistent preferences because consistently maximising fitness payoffs may be a reliable way to ensure traits are passed down to the next generation. Consistent preferences, if they exist at all, must be adaptive and the shape and specification of utility functions is also subject to natural selection in the context of an organism's material and social environment. There's no guarantee that evolved behaviour will display the four criteria necessary to be consistent. For example, individual agents require multiple material inputs (energy, food, water etc) that are not fully substitutable, and fitness itself is an unobservable, abstract property whose value cannot be calculated by the individual agent.

There are many ways in which the assumption of preference consistency does not hold up to even mild scrutiny. The most justifiably famous errors are **time-inconsistency, state-inconsistency, belief-inconsistency** and **risk-inconsistency**. To start with, the preferences of real social agents in the world are not consistent across time periods[144]. Most humans behave as if, for example, $10 today is more valuable than $20 in a year's time, even though they would prefer $20 to $10 if given the choice right now. Similarly, many people make short-term consumption decisions that will have disastrous long-term negative payoffs, in terms of their health or wellbeing. As a result, economists assume that rational agents discount future payoffs by a proportion –that 'a bird in the hand is worth two in the bush'. We will later see in Chapter 6: "Order From Chaos", that this assumption is not axiomatic either, but emerges naturally from the

---

[143] Gintis (2009), at pg. 8; Robson (1996) at pgs. 397-424; Robson (2001) at pgs. 900–914; Robson & Samuelson, "The Evolutionary Foundations of Preferences" in the "Handbook of Social Economics, Volume 1" (2011) at pgs. 221-310.

[144] Gintis (2009), at pg. 9.

evolution of strategic behaviour in repeated games.

Next, it's also obvious that preferences are not state-consistent. If I am relatively wealthy, or well fed, I might value dedicating personal time to exercise, whereas if I were poor, I would devote that time to extra work in order to afford the essential food, medicine or shelter my family needs. If I am tired, I prefer sleep to activity, and if I desire recreation, I may value consumption of entertainment over saving for a profitable investment. To give an example, it's been suggested that the outcome of criminal sentencing depends on how recently the trial judge ate[145]! These effects are so pervasive that merely verbally priming a person with a particular social framing[146] can change the way they vote and political policies they prefer.

A related finding is that preferences are not consistent given varying beliefs about the state of the world. If I believe that a certain event occurs with a 10 per cent probability, but gives a payout of $100, I should prefer that to receiving $9 with absolute certainty since the expected payout from taking a risk is 0.9 x 100 = 10 > 9. Now, if the probability of receiving a payout was fixed – such as if it were guaranteed odds in a public lottery, a game of cards or generated by a computer program – then such a preference ordering would be consistent. But very few real life events are so predictable. The likelihood of receiving $100 is only a subjective estimate, and if I receive new information that changes that estimate, then my preference ordering would change. Without knowing an agent's subjective beliefs about the likelihood of uncertain events, their preference ordering cannot be specified.

Finally, but not exhaustively, the shape of the utility function often depends on the degree of risk involved. Mathematically, an agent should be indifferent between a 10 per cent chance of a $100 payoff and a one per cent chance of a $1000 payoff, but humans – and most other evolved social agents – are not indifferent between these payoffs and demonstrate a desire for one over the other. An agent is **risk-averse** if they would prefer a certain outcome to rolling a dice for the same expected payoff; their utility shows

---

[145] Danziger, Levav & Avnaim-Pesso(2011) at pgs. 6889-6892.

[146] Tversky & Kahneman (1981) at pgs. 453–58; Thorisdottir & Jost (2011) at pgs. 785-811.

diminishing returns for higher-risk payoffs. An agent is **risk-loving** if they would prefer a probabilistic gamble with a given expected payoff to the certain receipt of the same payoff; their utility function shows increasing return for higher risk payoffs.

The rational actor model does not specify the shape of the utility function; there is no axiomatic assumption that social agents are either risk-averse or risk-loving or some mixture. Empirical studies on human behaviour, by Daniel Kahneman and Amos Tversky[147], have suggested that utility functions in our species depend on context: on average, humans are averse to taking risks when we might lose what we already have, but do entertain risks when we might benefit. In the literature, this is referred to as **prospect theory**. This means that preference ordering is contingent on (beliefs about) the *status quo* state of the world. If a decision were framed in terms of potential loss rather than as a potential gain, a different preference ordering would result even if the fitness payoffs and subjective beliefs about the probability of each payoff occurring were otherwise identical.

Why might risk aversion be adaptive? If we consider payoffs as fitness, falling behind the average fitness of the population is potentially catastrophic for the long-term survival of a phenotype. But so long as a strategy does no worse than the population average, its frequency in the population will remain unchanged. On the other hand, small fitness advantages can reward a strategy that delivers them (even at low probabilities) a permanent increase in their frequency in a population. In terms of raising children, for example, human beings always try to ensure that their kids 'keep up with the Joneses'; but also play the lottery (perhaps metaphorically, by making investments in human or financial capital) to give their family a chance at long-term economic and social advantage.

Whether, given all these limitations, we consider the rational actor model worth saving is ultimately beside the point. Herb Gintis, the left-leaning evolutionary economist, comes down on in favour of the view that preference consistency can be rescued, *if* utility functions are fully specified

---

147 Kahneman & Tversky (1979) at pg. 263; Kahneman & Tversky(1986) 251–278.

with respect to the time, state, subjective beliefs and risk profile of the agent[148]. Within this framework, social agents are only rational within the boundaries set by their knowledge and circumstances – they are *boundedly rational*, in Herbert Simon's words[149].

But requiring so much individualised information, much of it empirically unmeasurable, to consider a model valid or even useful raises legitimate concerns about using it to study behaviour in general[150]. As we've argued repeatedly over the course of this chapter, it's conceptually simpler and much more computationally tractable to focus on the evolution of populations, and consider what kinds of individual beliefs and preferences – rational *or irrational* – are consistent with a given population structure. It may be that preference consistency is a useful simplifying tool for modelling subsets of political problems with fixed conditions. But as the foundational narrative of economic and social life, it's untenable.

The German psychologist Gerd Gigernezer has proposed replacing the concept of the rational actor with the ecologically rational agent, whose decision-making rules are adapted to their physical and social environment – their decisions are 'adaptively ratifiable'[151]. In this framework, social agents are equipped with a toolbox of 'fast and frugal' decision rules that have been subject to selection pressures and which reliably reproduce fitness-enhancing behaviour under a range of plausible environmental conditions. Employing such heuristics may be more efficient than engaging in abstract calculations of utility and probability, because inherited decision-rules contain more information about the success and failures of particular behaviours than any individual social agent could conceivably learn in one lifetime.

---

[148] Gintis (2009); Gintis (2017), Chapter 5.

[149] Simon (1955) at pgs. 99–118; Simon (1957).

[150] Gigerenzer & Selten (eds.) (2002) at pg. 5;

[151] Gigerenzer & Selten (eds.) (2002) at pg. 46-; Gigerenzer (2008) at pgs. 20-29; Gigerenzer & Gaissmaier (2011) at pgs. 451-482; Skyrms (2014) at pg. 58; Gigerenzer (2019) at pgs. 1-19.

Adaptive or evolutionary rationality expands our perspective from methodological individualism. As we know from Tinbergen, in order to consistently model the behaviour of social agents we must also describe their material and social environment, and their population and developmental history[152]. Gintis also refers to this as being 'collectively or socially rational' – making consistent decisions within the constraints imposed by a given population[153]. It's good to have the rational actor model in our back pocket, as a computationally tractable approximation of simple agents in fixed environments. But the world is a more complex, and more wonderful place, than that imagined by economists.

* * *

In Chapter 2, we introduced the four classes of dyadic, symmetrical normal form games. As introduced, the games offered a choice of discrete strategies: the choice of agents is either one behaviour or another, and the fitness payoffs were fixed. Now that we are equipped to rank preferences over a broader range of options, we will introduce versions of those games with *continuous* strategies. By continuous, we mean that the fitness payoffs are variable and can take any real value. In continuous games, the range of strategies is potentially infinite, and the structure of games – and hence the Nash equilibrium – may change. Moreover, by mixing continuous payoffs with strategic choice, we can model situations in which agents must solve either/or (e.g. do I cooperate or do I defect?) and distributional (i.e. how much of a benefit should I expect?) political problems simultaneously.

The ultimatum game

Let's begin with one of the simplest, yet most powerful, games employed in economics and psychology: the ultimatum game (Figure 3.1)[154]. The

---

[152] Adami et al. (2016) at pg. 1; March (1970) at pgs. 570-592.

[153] Gintis (2017), Chapter 3.

[154] Güth, Schmittberger, & Schwarze (1982) at pgs. 367-388.

ultimatum game is an asymmetric, continuous implementation of the cooperation game in which there is a power imbalance between the Players. Its narrative structure is as follows. Player 1 ("the proposer") engages in an interaction with Player 2 ("the responder"). Player 1 is endowed with an amount of a resource. They propose a division of that resource to Player 2, whereby Player 1 keeps a fraction of the resource (c) and Players 2 receives the remainder (1 - c). This is the cooperate strategy. Player 2 has the option to reject the proposed distribution (or defect), in which case both players receive nothing. For the sake of completeness, Player 1 also has the option to refuse to make an offer, in which case both players also get nothing.

Ultimatum Game		Responder	
		C	D
Proposer	C	c ; $1 - c$	0 ; 0
	D	0 ; 0	0 ; 0

Figure 3.1: The Ultimatum Game

It is trivial to show that cooperate is the dominant strategy for both players and that (C, C) is the Nash equilibrium of the game *regardless of the distribution offered by the proposer*. The responder will accept any non-zero offer, because any share of the distribution is better than nothing. Knowing this, the proposer prefers to keep almost all of the resource in their own hands, knowing that any non-zero offer (c < 1) will be accepted. The asymmetry between the two agents is almost total: Player 1 has complete power over Player 2, and therefore has complete decision freedom about the proportion of the resource they offer.

The ultimatum game demonstrates that equilibria in continuous strategies can be thought of as negotiations over the distribution of resources, where the relative power of the two parties reflects the credibility of their threat to defect out of the Nash equilibrium. The minimum that a social agent can expect to obtain in such a negotiation is what they could get through self-help (their 'best alternative' to cooperating[155]), and an agent is therefore only willing to bargain over quantities greater than this. Although Player 2 has the option to withhold their consent from the interaction, and force the 'no deal' option on Player 1, this threat is not credible in the ultimatum game and their expected benefit from the exchange reflects the weakness of their position. In one of the most fascinating results in psychology, human agents playing the ultimatum game offer much higher proportions than game theory would suggest, approaching the ideal of fairness for the society and culture in which they are socialised[156].

To highlight the power of self-help, consider a version of the ultimatum game in which instead of getting nothing by rejecting the proposer's offer, the responder is guaranteed a minimum share of 20 per cent of the resource, perhaps representing a guaranteed social right or entitlement. By the same logic, if the proposer refused to engage in interaction, their resource is 'taxed' away from them and they receive the same 20 per cent guaranteed share. Figure 3.2 below shows this game in normal form.

80/20 Game		Responder	
		C	D
Proposer	C	$1 - c$ / c	0.2 / 0.8
	D	0.8 / 0.2	0 / 0

Figure 3.2: The Ultimatum Game with basic rights

---

[155] Fisher & Ury (1981).

[156] Guth et al. (1982) at pgs. 367-388; Guth & Tietz (1990) at pgs. 417-449; Roth et al. (1991) at pgs. 162-202; Nowak, Page, & Sigmund (2000) at pgs. 1773–1775; Gintis (2017).

What are the conditions for both players to cooperate? The responder will accept any offer such that $1 - c > 0.2$, or $c < 0.8$. By the same token, the proposer must offer $c > 0.2$, such that the grounds for bargaining is the strategy space $0.2 < c < 0.8$. Clearly, the proposer is still in a more powerful position, but less so than before. If the proposer wanted to hold on to more than 80 per cent of the resource, the responder would defect from social cooperation; by the same token, even the powerful proposer will defect if the expectation of the responder is to receive more than 80 per cent of the resource.

The Traveller's Dilemma & Public Goods

Next, we introduce continuous versions of the anti-cooperation game. The **traveller's dilemma** or the 'guessing game' has many variations, but all involve bidding against an opponent under conditions of imperfect information (i.e. we do not know what our adversary will bid). One version goes like this: two identical travellers from the same company attend a conference, and must claim their expenses on their return home. The maximum amount that can be claimed is $100, but company policy says that only expenses necessarily incurred will be reimbursed so only the minimum of the two traveller's bids will be accepted as the true figure. As an incentive for saving the company costs, the traveller(s) who bids the lowest receives a bonus and other bids will be penalised – by let's say $2.

It is easy to show (for example by writing out a normal form matrix in which the possible strategies are integers) that the traveller's dilemma is an anti-cooperation game and that the Nash equilibrium strategy is the minimum bid: in this case, $0 of expenses and a payoff of $2. To see why this is so, we iteratively eliminate dominated strategies. It might be thought initially that both travellers would claim the maximum: $100. But traveller A might reason that they could receive a higher payoff of $101 by bidding $99; Traveller B might then reason that since traveller A is going to bid $99, they would be better off revising their bid downwards to $98, and so on. As a result, both travellers should bid zero if they assume the common knowledge of the rationality of the other – even though both would be better off bidding higher and being a sucker. This basic paradox has been used to study the determination of prices and the value of stocks[157], and can be extended to an arbitrary number of players.

The **public goods game** is a similar continuous implementation of an anti-cooperation game. The public goods game is studied by economists on a large scale, as its dynamics represent the behaviour of agents who must choose how many resources to contribute to a common pool. In the public goods game, a group of agents of size N in possession of [equal] resources choose whether to contribute to or 'invest' in a collective endeavour. In the literature, a common pool resource is rivalrous (i.e. limited) but non-excludable, in the sense that no agent can prevent another from accessing benefits from it. Therefore even when an agent defects and fails to contribute to the common pool, they will receive a share of the benefits. When the resources contributed are added up, it is conventional to multiply the result by r, which is a number representing the additional value generated by combining resources or effort. A synergy ratio of 2, for example, would mean that the invested resources were doubled before being redistributed.

Solving a public goods game requires a little more algebra than the games we've examined so far. At equilibrium, a given agent has the choice to contribute (C) or defect (D). Out of a population of size N, we designate the number of contributors each round as N^C and the number of defectors as N^D. From the perspective of an uncommitted agent, $N^C + N^D + 1 = N$. Given that the agents are identical, we assume that at equilibrium the amount contributed (c) by each will be the same. The payoffs for each strategy are as follows:

$$D: \frac{1}{N}(N^c cr)$$

$$C: \frac{1}{N}(N^c + 1)cr - c$$

---

[157] Keynes (1935).

Thus, agents will contribute if and only if:

$$\frac{1}{N}(N^c + 1)cr - c > \frac{1}{N}(N^c cr)$$

$$cr - Nc > 0$$

$$r > N$$

So if the synergy ratio is larger than the number of players, the public goods game is an N-player cooperation game and everybody contributes. If $1 < r < N$, then the public goods game is structured as an N-player prisoners dilemma where no one contributes is the equilibrium state – the same result holds if contributing is wasteful and counterproductive ($r < 1$).

Let's suggest instead that every agent begins the public goods game with a subjective prior belief that there will be an average contribution c^* by the other players. Repeating the above analysis, we find that agents will contribute if:

$$\frac{1}{N}(N^c + 1)c^*r - c > \frac{1}{N}(N^c c^* r)$$

$$c^*r - Nc > 0$$

$$c < \frac{r}{N}c^*$$

This is a more interesting result. It demonstrates that given *any* prior belief about the contributions by others, a rational agent will only contribute a fraction of that themselves. Moreover, that proportion is determined by the structure of the game: the larger the number of players N, the smaller their contribution: i.e. the larger the size of a society, the greater the benefit from free-riding on the contributions of others. If the public goods game is played over multiple rounds, we therefore might anticipate that the size of contributions will progressively decrease as agents update their beliefs, and the game will once again settle into the *always defect* equilibrium. This is indeed what happens when people in experiments play the public goods game over multiple rounds.

Hawk and Dove

The **hawk-dove game** is an anti-coordination game (similar to chicken) described by Maynard Smith and Price in their seminal work applying game theory to evolution, *The Logic of Animal Conflict*[158]. In the **hawk-dove** game, birds consist of one of two Types with fixed, pure strategies: hawks and doves. When two doves meet, they share a resource benefit (B) evenly between themselves, such that each receives a fitness payoff of B/2. When a hawk meets a dove, the dove backs down and receives nothing, granting the hawk the full resource. When a hawk meets another hawk they engage in a costly battle, with the winner receiving the full value of the resource and the loser paying the full cost (C) of defeat. When the hawks are evenly matched, their probability of victory is one half, so their expected fitness payoff from any encounter is (B - C)/2. This game structure is represented in Figure 3.3 below:

Hawk-Dove		Player 2: Hawk	Player 2: Dove
Player 1	Hawk	$\frac{B-C}{2}$, $\frac{B-C}{2}$	**B** , **0**
Player 1	Dove	**0** , **B**	$B/2$, $B/2$

Figure 3.3: Hawk-Dove, an anti-coordination game

Under what conditions is hawk-dove an anti-coordination game? It is clear that if C > B, birds would prefer to be a sucker and back down from a fight rather than pay the heavy fitness toll of hawk-on-hawk conflict. But if C

158 Maynard Smith & Price (1973) at pgs. 15-18.

≤ B, then a different structure results: an *anti-cooperation* game in which both players might prefer to be doves but will always engage in destructive hawk-hawk conflict[159]. The cost of violence is therefore critical to shaping the structure of social interaction. One of the key themes we will develop in this book is that the threat of consequences is often effective in shaping evolutionary equilibria, and in many cases may be necessary for equilibria to be stable.

* * *

In interdependent interactions, which accounts for the majority of group decision-making in social species, there is no distribution of a resource that can be considered natural or optimal. Instead, the distribution of payoffs reflects the structural power of the participants: *value is allocated by relations of power*. Assuming that the output of a political decision is a collective benefit (as in the public goods game) there's also no guarantee that 'rational actors' will distribute a resource in a way that maximises its supply. From a technocratic perspective, autonomous self-help is inefficient. The only way to ensure that individual strategic decision-making is aligned with collective outcomes is to change the structure of the game – to reduce the power of strong actors, to guarantee the minimum rights of weaker ones, and to use the implicit threat of consequences to shift social equilibria in more productive directions.

Since the minimum that an agent will bargain for is what they can get through self-help, norms and institutions – such as the liberal social contract which establish fundamental rights and an expectation of equal dignity – grant structural power to the otherwise powerless and ensure that minimum standard of fairness are met. Because these norms and institutions are cooperative and altruistic, they must evolve through group selection. Whether we define justice as the optimal allocation of resources,

---

[159] McElreath & Boyd (2007) at pg. 43.

or the satisfaction of basic rules guaranteeing equal dignity[160], the absence of structural coercion and violence is not a sufficient condition for the production of justice. Free but unequal social agents are not truly free – their choices are constrained by the social structures in which they must operate.

As we will see in coming Chapters, evolutionary sociology does not require the rational actor model to be true; quite the contrary: simple evolutionary rules acting on populations of social agents produce behaviours that appear to demonstrate preference consistency in some respects, but not others. Evolution produces the appearance of fitness-maximising behaviour in categories of agent – ranging from the tiniest bacterium to the largest nation-state – that are incapable of exercising rational choice. Maximising for individual fitness is not a strategy for long-run evolutionary success. Gluttony and unrestricted growth can just as easily destroy the ecological whole (see Chapter 13: "Social Cancers").

---

[160] Anderson (1999) at pgs. 287-337.

4

MIXED STRATEGIES, MIXED POPULATIONS

Key Points

- A mixed strategy is randomised combination of pure strategies such that one's opponent becomes indifferent between their available strategic options.
- The Nash Existence Theorem guarantees that every strategic interaction with a finite number of strategies has at least one mixed strategy equilibrium.
- The likelihood of playing a pure strategy in a mixed strategy equilibrium is equivalent to the frequencies of that pure strategy in a large, well-mixed population at equilibrium.
- An equilibrium may be an *attractor* -- the population will return to that state after any perturbation – or a *repulsor* – a population will irrevocably destabilise once perturbed.

In the previous Chapter, we discussed strategies with variable levels of commitment. This Chapter introduces **mixed strategies** that vary the *behaviour* of social agents. That is, an agent engages in pure strategy C some of the time, and strategy D at others. The Nash Existence Theorem does not guarantee that every game possesses a best response equilibrium in pure strategies; but it does guarantee that an equilibrium exists in mixed strategies. Mixed strategies are important because finding the mixed strategy equilibrium turns out to also give us the structure of a mixed population using pure strategies.

Consider a social agent who has a choice of pure strategies s_1, s_2, s_3 etc. We define a *mixed strategy* as a strategy $s_M = (p_1, p_2, p_3 \dots)$ where p_1, p_2, p_3 ... etc. are the *probability* that an agent performs the action s_1, s_2, s_3 etc. We can conceive initially of an agent as flipping a coin, or using a random number generator, to select a pure strategy to implement. The sum of the probabilities of playing each strategy each round sum to one – the agent *must* perform one of the pure strategies in the game.

Solving a game in mixed strategies is a little different to solving one in pure strategies[161]. If an opponent knows what your move will be, they can select their own strategy such as to maximise their own payoffs. The purpose of employing a mixed strategy is to make the opponent *indifferent* between their own strategies, so that no matter what choice they make they cannot improve their payoff. Therefore, we calculate p_1, p_2, p_3 ... etc etc. by finding the combination of probabilities which equalises the opponent's payoffs in pure strategies.

Let's take an example to illustrate how this works. **Matching pennies**[162] is a normal form game in which two social agents must call out one side of a coin, either 'heads' or 'tails' (see Figure 4.1 below). They do so simultaneously, such that this is a game of complete but imperfect information. Player 1 wins both coins if they have chosen the same coin face as their partner (they are playing a coordination game); Player 2 wins both coins if they have chosen the *opposite* coin face to their partner (they are playing an anti-coordination game). Variants of matching pennies are used to model shot choice in tennis, goal kicks in soccer penalty shootouts, and attack-defence dynamics in military simulations. In those applications,

---

[161] Morrow (1994) at pg. 87.

[162] Morrow (1994) at pgs. 85-85; Kydd (2015) at pgs. 49-50.

one player (the 'attacker') chooses to hit or kick the ball left or right, for example, and the defending player can select only one side to defend. Clearly, it advantages the attacker if they choose opposite to the other player, and it advantages the defender to choose the same side as the hitter.

Figure 4.1: Matching Pennies

We can see that neither player has a weakly or strictly dominated strategy, and there's accordingly no Nash equilibrium in the matching pennies game in pure strategies. But what about mixed strategies? How should a person playing matching pennies (or tennis, or penalty shootouts) randomise their plays?

Taking the perspective of Player 1, their mixed strategy is $s_M = (P_H, 1 - p_H))$ where p_H is the probability that they call heads. The expected payoffs for Player 2 are therefore:

$$u_H = 2(1 - p_H)$$

$$u_T = 2p_H.$$

Setting these equal, so that Player 2 is indifferent between their options, we find:

$$2(1 - p_H) = 2p_H$$

$$p_H = 0.5$$

Player 1's mixed strategy in matching pennies is to randomise so they call heads exactly half of the time and tails the other half. If $p_H < 0.5$, then Player 2 would always choose heads. If $p_H > 0.5$, then Player 2 would always choose tails. Only when p_H =0.5 is Player 2 indifferent between their pure strategies.

If Player 1 employs a mixed strategy, Player 2 receives an expected payoff of one – every possible choice is a best reply. Player 2 no longer has decision freedom, because no matter what they do they cannot improve their fitness payoff. Yet we know that if Player 2 were to choose heads every time, then Player 1 would have a strong incentive to move off their own mixed strategy and also choose heads every time; so the strategy pair (s_1, s_2) = ((0.5,0.5), Heads) is not a *mutual* best reply. Therefore, although it's trivial, we must show that Player 2 also has a mixed strategy at equilibrium, also of the form $s_M = (P_H, 1 - p_H)$, in order for Player 1's mixed strategy to be part of a stable equilibrium.

Player 1's expected payoffs are equal when:
$$2p_H = 2(1 - p_H)$$
$$p_H = 0.5$$

If $p_H > 0.5$, then Player 1 would always choose heads. If $p_H < 0.5$, then Player 1 would always choose tails. Only when $p_H = 0.5$ exactly is Player 1 indifferent between their pure strategies. The mixed strategy s_M=(0.5, 0.5) is therefore the best reply to itself, and the mixed strategy pair (s_1, s_2) = ((0.5, 0.5), (0.5, 0.5)) is the Nash equilibrium of the two-player matching pennies game.

Let's consider another example that we'll return to at the end of this chapter, the ancient East Asian children's game of **rock-paper-scissors (Figure 4.2)**. Rock-paper-scissors has three strategies, not two; it is an anti-coordination game because players are incentivised to adopt different strategies, but they would also rather match their opponent (i.e. take the punishment payoff) than be on the losing side of the rock-scissors, scissors-paper and paper-rock conflicts (i.e. take the sucker's payoff). In fact, rock-paper-scissors is one of the Zeeman classes of three-strategy games.

Everyone knows that the only way not to lose at rock-paper-scissors is to choose randomly; if you follow a pattern too obviously, your opponent will detect it and gain an advantage over you. Let's prove that's the case.

Rock Paper Scissors		Player 2		
		R	P	S
Player 1	R	0 / 0	1 / -1	-1 / 1
	P	-1 / 1	0 / 0	1 / -1
	S	1 / -1	-1 / 1	0 / 0

Figure 4.2: Rock-Paper-Scissors, based on an ancient Eats Asian children's game.

Rock-paper-scissors has no strictly or weakly dominated pure strategies. Let's assume that Player 1 adopts a mixed strategy $s_M = (p_r, p_p, p_s)$. Then Player 2's fitness payoffs are:

$$u_r = p_s - p_p$$
$$u_p = p_r - p_s$$
$$u_s = p_p - p_r$$

Making the payoffs equal, we get:

$$u_r = u_p = p_r - p_s = p_s - p_p$$
$$p_r = p_p = p_s = 1/3$$

* * *

What are the mixed strategy equilibria, if any, in the four symmetric Zeeman Games we introduced in Chapter 2? Both cooperation and anti-cooperation games have a single dominant pure strategy pair and lack a unique mixed strategy solution-. However, coordination and anti-coordination games have multiple pure strategy equilibria and at least one additional Nash equilibrium in mixed strategies.

Consider again the **stag hunt** introduced in Chapter 1 (Figure 4.3):

Stag Hunt		Player 2: C	Player 2: D
Player 1	C	10, 10	0, 7
Player 1	D	7, 0	5, 5

Figure 4.3: The Stag Hunt, redux

We know that this is a coordination game with two Nash equilibria in pure strategies (C, C) and (D, D), and that these strategies are evolutionarily stable. Does the **stag hunt** have a mixed strategy equilibrium as well? Suppose Player 1 has a mixed strategy of the form $s_M = (p_C, 1 - p_C)$ where p_C is the probability that they choose to hunt stag. Player 2's utility functions would therefore be:

$$u_C = 10p_C$$

$$u_D = 7p_C + 5(1 - p_C)$$

Setting these equal, we find:

$$10p_C = 7p_C + 5(1 - p_C)$$

$$p_C = 5/8$$

The mixed strategy $s_M = (5/8, 3/8)$ is therefore a dominant mixed strategy. Against this strategy, an opponent can never receive a fitness payoff greater than 6.25. Because the game is symmetrical, we also know that the strategy pair ((s1, s2) = ((5/8, 3/8), (5/8, 3/8)) is a Nash equilibrium for a pair of hunters.

However, any mistake in perfectly calculating or implementing the mixed strategy would rapidly incentivise a shift to one of the pure equilibria. If $p_C < 5/8$, then the pure defect strategy would be the best reply and an evolving population of agents would shift to the (D, D) equilibrium; if $p_C > 5/8$, the pure cooperate strategy is the best reply and an evolving population of agents would shift to the (C, C) equilibrium. The mixed strategy $s_M = (5/8, 3/8)$ is therefore *not* what is sometimes called a *trembling-hand perfect*. It is not impervious to mistakes made through the error of the players[163]. We call an equilibrium formed from such a strategy a *repulsor* because it's is not robust to even the slightest perturbation[164].

Next, we examine the mixed strategies in the hawk-dove game (Figure 4.4):

Hawk-Dove		Player 2	
		Hawk	Dove
Player 1	Hawk	$\frac{B-C}{2}$, $\frac{B-C}{2}$	**B**, **0**
	Dove	**0**, **B**	$B/2$, $B/2$

Figure 4.4: Hawk-Dove, redux

We know that this is an anti-coordination game with two Nash equilibria: (Hawk, Dove) and (Dove, Hawk). Does the game have a mixed strategy equilibrium as well? Suppose Player 1 can implement a mixed strategy of the form $s_M = (p_H, 1 - p_H)$ where p_H is the probability that they play hawk and $p_{DOVE} = 1 - p_H$ is the probability that they play dove. Player 2's utility functions would therefore be:

$$u_H = p_H \frac{B - C}{2} + (1 - p_H)B$$

$$u_D = (1 - p_H)\frac{B}{2}$$

[163] Selten (1975) at pgs. 25-55.

[164] Taylor & Jonker (1978) at pgs. 149-150.

Setting these equal, we find:

$$p_H \frac{B-C}{2} + (1 - p_H)B = (1 - p_H)\frac{B}{2}$$

$$\frac{p_H B}{2} - \frac{p_H C}{2} + B - p_H B = \frac{B}{2} - \frac{p_H B}{2}$$

$$p_{HAWK} = {B}/{C}$$

$$p_{DOVE} = 1 - {B}/{C}$$

We know from Chapter 2 that when C < B the hawk-dove game is structured as an anti-cooperation game and has no unique mixed strategy equilibrium. A mixed strategy solution s_M = (B/C, 1 - B/C) only exists when C > B and the hawk-dove game is a proper anti-coordination game. Because the game is symmetrical, we also know that the strategy pair (s1, s2) = ((B/C, 1 - B/C), (B/C, 1 - B/C)) is a Nash equilibrium, and at equilibrium no player can receive a fitness payoff greater than u_M = B/2 - B²/2C.

What does this mean in practice? As the cost of conflict increases, the frequency of playing hawk decreases and the frequency of playing dove increases. Moreover, the best conceivable fitness payoff from playing a mixed strategy is $u_M \approx$ B/2 (equivalent to the (dove, dove) pure strategy equilibrium), and is only accessible when the cost of conflict becomes very large compared to the size of the resource. As the cost of conflict decreases, the expected fitness payoff approaches zero, which is equivalent to repeatedly playing the (hawk, hawk) pure strategy equilibrium. Deterrence works! By increasing the cost of conflict, we increase the fitness payoffs available to peaceful, sharing social agents. And, more importantly, an aggressive, conflictual population receives the lowest possible fitness.

But what happens if social agents made mistakes in perfectly calculating or implementing the equilibrium mixed strategy? If p_H < B/C then pure hawk is the best reply and an evolving population of agents would shift back towards the mixed equilibrium; if p_H > B/C, pure dove would be the best reply and the population would also shift towards the mixed equilibrium.

The mixed strategy $s_M = (B/C, 1 - B/C)$ therefore *is* trembling-hand perfect and we call a population equilibrium defined by such a strategy an *attractor*, because it's locally robust to irrationality or perturbation[165].

$$* * *$$

There's a certain artificiality to mixed strategies. Although they're mathematically elegant, how would an adaptive agent in a single shot game calculate the required probabilities and then randomise their strategy accurately? Moreover, common knowledge of rationality requires that an agent also be certain that the other player is also capable of calculating and implementing a properly randomised strategy. The empirical evidence, such as it is, suggests that the ability to calculate and implement random strategies is not an emergent trait in evolved social agents: human beings in particular are notoriously bad with probability. We like patterns, even abstract ones, and behaviour with meaning and symbolism (see Chapter 10: "Mediocre Individuals, Exceptional Species").

The so-called 'mixing problem' vexed game theorists for decades[166]. If a mixed strategy is calculated on the basis that an opponent receives the same payoff regardless of what strategy they play, then why shouldn't an opponent facing a mixed strategy simply play a pure strategy? Implementing a mixed strategy is both computationally expensive and carries significant risk of miscoordination. In his unpublished PhD dissertation, John Nash offered two different interpretations of the mixed equilibria that were central to his Theorem[167]. The probabilistic, rationalist account we've already used in this Chapter is the version that went on to become dominant in the field. But there's an alternative, one based in population structure and which explicitly abandons the requirement of individual rationality:

---

[165] Taylor & Jonker (1978) at pgs. 149-150; McElreath & Boyd (2007) at pgs. 43-44

[166] Gintis (2009), Chapter 7.

[167] Kuhn et al. (1996) at pgs. 153-185.

"It is unnecessary to assume that the participants have full knowledge of the total structure of the game, or the ability and inclination to go through any complex reasoning processes. But the participants are supposed to accumulate empirical information on the relative advantages of the various pure strategies at their disposal [i.e. there is a selection mechanism]. [We] assume that there is a population of participants for each position [strategy] in the game, ... [if] there is a stable average frequency with which each pure strategy is employed . . . .[then] the probability that a [pair] of pure strategies will be employed in a playing of the game should [match] the chance of each of the n pure strategies employed in a random playing. . . .Thus the 'mass-action' interpretation lead[s] to the conclusion that the mixed strategies represent[s] the average behaviour in the population [and] form an equilibrium point."

Let's restate this in plain English. The probability p_s in a mixed strategy equilibrium with which an agent is supposed to play the pure strategy s, is identical to $Pr(s)$, the proportion or frequency of a large and well-mixed population that plays the pure strategy s at equilibrium. By well-mixed population, we mean that social agents are unconstrained and free-associating, such that every agent has an equal chance of meeting every other agent in the population. A mixed strategy $s_M(s_1, s_2) = (p, q)$ can be validly interpreted as and is mathematically identical to a percentage (p) of such a population playing only strategy s_1, and another percentage (q) playing only strategy s_2. In the literature, this is referred to as the *purification* of mixed strategies (because mixed equilibria are converted into an equilibrium comprised of pure strategies). The proof is known as Harsanyi's Purification Theorem, following a 1973 article in which Novel Prize winning Hungarian-Australian economist John Harsanyi proved Nash's conjecture[168].

The broad outlines of Harsanyi's proof is as follows[169]. Consider again the Stag Hunt coordination game we examined earlier in this Chapter. Now the

---

[168] Harsanyi (1973) at pgs. 1-23.

[169] See also Gintis (2009), at pgs. 133-135; Govindan et al. (2003) at pgs. 369-374.

hunters form part of a population of similar hunters who have individual preferences about rabbit meat which form a symmetric distribution around the idealised or average payoff shown in the normal-form representation of the game. The variable represents an error or perturbation in the subjective value of rabbit-meat (Figure 4.5).

Stag Hunt		Player 2	
		C	D
Player 1	C	10 / 10	7 + ϵ / 0
	D	0 / 7 + ϵ	5 + ϵ / 5 + ϵ

Figure 4.5: The Stag Hunt, with a perturbation

We know that because the mixed equilibrium in coordination games is a *repulsor*, any perturbation should cause a social agent to prefer their pure strategy such that if is positive an agent would prefer to play D and if is negative, they would prefer to play C against an opponent playing the equilibrium mixed strategy. Two agents from the population are chosen at random to conduct a Stag Hunt together (there's no positive assortivity which would cause agents of the same Type to hunt together) but they do not know their partner's rabbit preference – is private information.

Player 2 will meet an opponent who plays pure strategy C with probability Pr(C), which is the proportion of pure C players in the population. They'll meet an opponent who plays pure strategy D with probability Pr(D), which is the proportion of pure D players in the population. Therefore player 2's utility payoffs are:

$$u_C = 10\Pr(C)$$

$$u_D = (7 + \epsilon)\Pr(C) + (5 + \epsilon)(1 - \Pr(C))$$

Setting these equal, we find:

$$10\,\Pr(C) = 7\Pr(C) + \epsilon\Pr(C) + 5 - 5\Pr(C) + \epsilon - \epsilon\Pr(C)$$

$$\Pr(C) = \frac{5 + \epsilon}{8}$$

As approaches zero, then the frequency of pure strategy C is identical to p_C, the probability that a rational actor would play strategy C as part of mixed strategy. There are other interpretations of what the perturbation actually represents; as we'll see in Chapter 8: "Beliefs and Signals" we can also think of as a prior subjective beliefs about the private payoffs of other players, and think of a mixed strategy as a 'best guess' about their optimal behaviour[170]. But for our purposes, it suffices to note that a mixed strategy equilibrium represents the *proportions* of a population playing particular strategies.

In fact, this is the preferable interpretation of the hawk-dove game. Obviously, birds are not behaviourally-flexible, rational actors capable of changing their Type at will – they can only implement a single strategy. If we define Pr(Hawk) as the probability that a hawk will encounter another hawk, and Pr(Dove) as the probability that a hawk will meet a dove, then Pr(Hawk) and Pr(Dove) are contingent upon the state of the population and at equilibrium Pr(Hawk) = B/C and Pr(Dove) = 1 - B/C. Any mixed binary population of birds (i.e. consisting of two types whose interactions are defined by the stage game) will converge towards this equilibrium. The most important thing to remember is that *population structure at equilibrium is determined by the structure of the social game being played.*

The most famous empirical evidence of this property in nature is the common side-blotched lizard, a small iguana native to North America. The male side-blotched lizard has three potential mating strategies, which are determined biologically, pass down generation-to-generation, and

---

[170] Aumann (1974) at pgs. 67-96.

which have the structure of a rock-papers-scissors game[171]. Orange-throated lizards are the largest and most aggressive males, who fight over large harems of females with large potential reproductive upsides but correspondingly poor survival rates. Blue-throated males are monogamous, selecting and defending a single female partner; blues can lose mates and reproductive opportunities to more aggressive oranges, but breed more reliably overall. Finally, the yellow-throated males imitate the colouration and behaviour of female lizards to implement a 'sneaky' reproductive strategy to infiltrate the harems of orange males and cuckold them – a strategy that is riskier than that of the blues.

As we might expect by now, populations of side-blotched lizards at equilibrium consist of roughly equal proportions of all three reproductive strategies. Moreover, these proportions are evolutionarily attractive, such that any imbalance of the population (and excess of oranges, for example) is corrected by offering enhanced reproductive opportunities for another type (the sneaky yellows). An important rule of evolutionary game theory is that while preferences may or may not be consistently ordered, strategies cannot be. What strategy is best depends on the social context and environment.

This has dire consequences for methodological individualism. Traditionally, since the preferences of social agents are hidden, the only way to empirically measure preferences was to study agent behaviour or strategy. It is often incorrectly assumed that consistent behaviour would be evidence of consistent preferences. But in reality, strategies cannot be monotonically related to one another - strategy A may be better than strategy B under some circumstances, but not others. Consequently, any sociology which relies on observations of individual strategy to reveal the 'true' preferences of the players is doomed to inconsistency.

We can now summarise the key argument of the previous three Chapters. The structure of a population is at least in part determined by the social dilemmas it must solve. A social system where the dominant social interaction has the form of an anti-coordination game, for example, will

---

[171] Sinervo & Lively (1996) at pgs. 240-243.

display different emergent norms and structures than a social system where the dominant interaction has the form of a cooperation game. It's rarely so simple of course – in a modern society, humans play dozens of social games, with potentially very many continuous and discrete strategies, with many different sub-populations and at multiple levels of organisation. Yet even if they are computationally intractable, the principles of interdependence, selection by consequences and dynamic equilibria allows us to make sense of huge swathes of the social and political life of any social species.

5

STRATEGY AND CULTURE

Key Points

- Evolution selects amongst strategies. Adaptively rational strategies are neither instrumentally chosen by social agents nor determined by environmental conditions.
- Replicators store information about the prior fitness value of strategies. Replicators are not directly selected, but are transmitted between individuals based on the fitness value of the behavioural strategies they produce in a particular environment.
- Gene-culture co-evolution or dual inheritance theory suggests both genetic and cultural replicators generate adaptive strategies in complex social species. The cultural transmission of information permits adaption faster than genetic transmission alone.

So far, we've relied (with caveats) on the ontology of choice-centred action in which self-conscious social agents possess causal primacy. We've modelled the strategic options of individual decision makers, and measured success and failure in terms of their fitness. Methodological individualism has historically been counterpoised within the social sciences, particularly on the left, by structuralist explanations which emphasise population-level factors and limitations on individual choice. So, for instance, progressives tend to think we cannot fully 'explain' an interaction between social agents without also considering their race, class or gender, and the ways in which these social positions relate to the population as a whole. Debates between the two perspectives are extensive, and often unproductive.

Evolutionary causality requires us to consider both an agent's motivation *and* the adaptiveness of a behaviour within a population. Neither structure nor agents have ontological primacy. Social agents are not eternal, and all eventually die. But population structure is not eternal either: class, race and gender are not Platonic ideal forms that exist somehow in the aether. Social structures and hierarchies are emergent and constituted dynamically by the interaction of individual agents. This Chapter will argue that *strategy* – the range of behaviour that is physically possible (or 'free', to borrow a term from quantum mechanics) – is ontologically prior to both agents and structures and the central subject of natural selection. In terms of process philosophy, the dynamics of an object shape its properties, not the other way around.

Focusing on strategy allows evolutionary narratives to transcend the tiring agent-structure dichotomy, while drawing on strengths from both[172]. And we can incorporate into our models a whole host of social organisms and organisations that are not instrumentally rational in the classical sense.

"A standard technique in evolutionary theory shift[s] emphasis to strategy . . . .The shift entails a focus not on that which constrains choice (structure) or that which chooses (agent), but on [the behaviour] which is chosen. Adding this perspective means trading the stultifying duality of "structure and agency" for a triplet – structure, agency and strategy." [Lustick][173]

---

[172] "Biologists have been thinking this way ever since Darwin, but it is still news in some fields. Are people products of their societies or are societies products of people? The answer must be "both", but theory in the social science has tended to take one side or the other. . . .Population models allow explanation and real causation at both levels (and more than two levels) to exist seamlessly and meaningfully in one theory." McElreath & Boyd (2008) at pg. 4; See also Fiorini (1996) at pgs. 363-389; Modelski (1996) at pgs. 321-342.

[173] Lustick (2011) at pg. 198.

Population structures, as we saw in the last Chapter, are shaped by the available strategies within that population; the population structure in turn shapes the payoffs of strategies. Strategies are implemented by agents, but the range of possible strategies within a population limits the types of agents that can plausibly survive and reproduce. Figure 5.1 illustrates the complexity of the interactions:

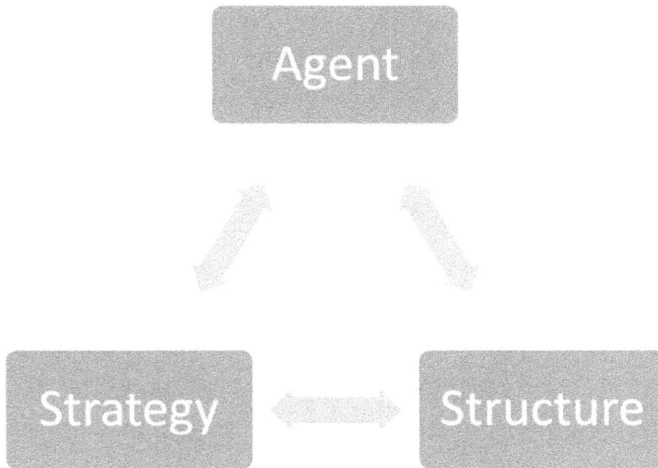

Figure 5.1. Thinking about society requires us to consider agents, structures and strategies

Rather than focusing on the probability of survival or success of individual agents, the evolutionary paradigm considers only the probability of survival or success of strategies [measured by their frequency in the population][174]. We can conceive of this using the biological metaphor. Over evolutionary timescales, the lives and deaths of individual animals are irrelevant – what matters is the likelihood that genes are passed on, and whether or not the behaviours coded by those genes remain adaptive and successful in a changing social and material environment. What defines a society is not its members, but the continuity of its strategies and behaviours over

---

[174] John (1999) at pgs. 39-62

generations. We are members of a particular, tribe, religion or association not because we or our ancestors were original members, but because we engage in the cultural rituals and forms of behaviour which define membership of that community.

"[I]n this setting, is strategies that come to the fore; the individual that implement them on various occasions fade from view. Although the [interactions] that drive evolution are a series of . . . games, the payoffs are determined by what strategy is played against what strategy. The identity of individuals playing is unimportant and continually shifting. This is the Darwinian Veil of Ignorance." [Skyrms, Evolution of the Social Contract][175]

The primary object of study of evolutionary game theory is how the relative frequency of behaviours in a population change over time. The evolutionary approach therefore shares with social constructivism the view that ideas, culture, norms and institutions cause social outcomes[176], but only to the extent that the frequency of ideas is in turn shaped by the past and present strategic environment and how effectively they are reproduced by individuals. In both biological and cultural evolution, the spontaneous emergence of new behaviours creates variation and can perturb even fixed biological and cultural equilibria.

A strategy is a sequence of actions at one level of analysis that produces observable behaviour at another level. A strategy transforms a signal about the world external to the organism, including a null signal, into an act or behaviour of the organism, including null behaviour. Since any given social agent at one level of analysis consists of a system in equilibrium unto itself at another, external signals perturb or select amongst internal equilibria. So when a society goes to war, it signals danger to its members, which in turn changes the neurological signals in their brains, which in turn changes the

---

[175] Skyrms (2014) at pg. 10.

[176] Blute (2010); Harrison, "Complex Systems and the Practice of World Politics" in Harrison (ed.) (2006) at pgs. 184-185.

chemical balance within their cells. So cells produce more stress hormones, which produce emotional and risk-taking behaviour, which produces war enthusiasm, which produces a military capable of fighting and winning an armed conflict. Genes, neurons, cultural expectations and state propaganda work together across multiple levels of organisation to generative adaptive behaviour on a planetary scale.

Evolution takes place as a result of the differential fitness of strategies. The replicator dynamic merely relates the future frequency of strategies to their current relative fitness. Strategies – not individuals, not populations, not genes, and not 'memes' – are the subject in evolutionary ontology[177]. In every domain in which natural selection operates, strategies are the property that vary and generate differential fitness. This is contrary to Dawkins who argued that replication – not selection – was the essence of Darwinian evolution[178]. Genetic essentialists mistakenly believe that the final part of the evolutionary process – the transmission of information from one generation to the next – provides the *telos* for the entirety of that process[179]. That is a heroic assumption, to say the least. There is no particular reason the unit of selection and the unit of replication must be one and the same.

New social agents do inherit a record of the effectiveness of prior strategies in the population[180]. But any stored unit of information – i.e. genes, a psychological trait, cultural practice or institutional form – can constitute

---

[177] See Dawkins (1982), Chapter 7, for an introduction. However, be warned that Dawkins – ever the biological essentialist – rejects this interpretation

[178] Dawkins (1982) at pg. 41.

[179] Jablonka & Lamb (2005); Hull, "Interactors versus Vehicles" in Plotkin (ed.) (1988) at pgs. 19-50.

[180] "[G]ene differences do not cause evolutionary changes in populations, they register those changes." Sterelny (2007).

what Dawkins called a 'replicator'[181]. Natural selection does not act directly on replicators: it acts only on the behaviours or phenotypes ("strategies") they produce in a given social and environmental context[182]. Replicators are differentially reproduced through the selection of strategies and passed on as data to the next 'generation', such that the frequency of successful strategies increases and the frequency of relatively less successful strategies decreases. To invert a piece of Dawkins' own terminology, replicators are vehicles for the transmission of strategies.

Replicators give social agents heuristics based on past learning about the fitness of particular strategies[183]. But, importantly, a replicator does not guarantee a given social agent will perform a particular strategy, especially in complex organisms and in complex polities. Even with a fixed inheritance, variation in individual development generates variation in behaviour and therefore fitness. So replicators are not necessarily adaptive in their own right – they may have neutral, adverse or probabilistic effects on fitness depending on environment. We can't presume that any individual's inherited information makes a net positive contribution to their fitness in their current environment.

This is a complex idea, so let's illustrate it with a well-known biological example. Sickle-cell diseases are a family of blood disorders caused by single nucleotide polymorphisms – variations in the make-up of a single gene that produces haemoglobin. People who carry a single copy of a mutation in this gene, typically with ancestors in malaria-prone parts of the world,

---

[181] Dawkins, "Replicators and Vehicles" in King's College Sociobiology Group (1982) at pgs. 45–64; "The cognitive architecture, like all aspects of the phenotype from molars to memory circuits, is the joint product of genes and environment. But the development of architecture is buffered against both genetic and environmental insults, such that it reliably develops across the (ancestrally) normal range of human environments."

[182] Gould (1980) at pgs. 72-78; Mayr (2004); Dietl, "Selection, Security, and Evolutionary International Relations" in Sagarin & Taylor (eds.) (2008) at pg. 92.

[183] Rosas (2010) at pgs. 450-456. "Taken strictly, talk of strategies and rules in evolutionary game theory makes no reference to the causes of behaviour, neither psychological nor social. . . . However, when it comes specifically to models of human cooperation, rules can be taken to refer to the social and/or psychological causes of behaviour."

fold haemoglobin in a particular way that partially protects them from infection by the *plasmodium* parasite. The genetic mutation itself is not selected: in fact, if a person carries two copies of the mutation they are *more* prone to disease. It's the *effect* of the mutation on an organism, living in a particular threat environment and population structure, that is selected for. The sickle-cell replicator would not be adaptive in a population where everyone carried it and children were guaranteed to carry two copies (which would be catastrophic), or in a population with no environmental exposure to malaria.

$$* * *$$

Evolutionary sociology applies the same lens to cultural evolution that biologists use to study the evolution of biological species. The genetic essentialist view of evolution, in which germline information is the only replicator, is wrong. Both genes and culture carry data about the prior fitness of strategies: both generate behaviour by transforming signals about the environment into motivated action. Whether we talk about genes or 'memes'[184], what matters is the information they contain regarding the differential fitness of strategic behaviours. Pioneering work on the study of cultural evolution has been done by the biologists Cavalli-Sforza & Feldman[185] and Boyd & Richerson[186]; the latter's aptly-named 2005 book, *Not by Genes Alone: How Culture Transformed Human Evolution* is the definitive introductory text on the topic. A framework that incorporates both genetic and cultural selection is termed gene-culture co-evolution, or 'dual inheritance theory'.

As already mentioned, selection occur primarily through testing the fitness of adaptive agents against their environment, rather than directly against one another. For social species, this environment may be social as

---

[184] Dawkins (1982) at pgs. 166-170.

[185] Cavalli-Sforza & Feldman (1973) at pgs. 618-635; Cavalli-Sforza & Feldman (1981).

[186] Boyd & Richerson Press (1985); Boyd & Richerson (2005).

well as material. However, for most biological entities most of the time the availability of sunshine, water, nutrients, liveable temperatures and the presence of predators are the material constraints that determine their relative fitness. Replicators conserve information about the past environment while variation permits new strategies to arise if the environment changes. A replicator is passed down to the next generation because in the context of its environment it produced behaviours that increased, or at the very did not decrease, the fitness of individuals that carried it to reproductive age.

DNA reliably passes information from one generation to the next. But if genetic replication were one hundred per cent accurate, and every generation was in terms of its behaviour a clone of the one that preceded it, then a population would be vulnerable to a changing environment. Sexual reproduction and random mutations in the chemical properties of genes ensures that a population retains variability and thus that natural selection will continue to operate. However, mutations occur slowly. Research estimates of the probability of a point mutation in humans to be of the order of 10^8 per generation[187]. So if human DNA is roughly 3 billion base pairs long, the expected number of base pair substitutions per generation is around 20 to 40 – but the vast majority of these errors will occur in inactive parts of the genetic code, or lead to no substantive difference in cell behaviour.

So long as environmental conditions shift slowly – on the order of hundreds of thousands of years – species adapt and change by altering at a population level the information content of the genetic replicators they pass to their descendants. When environmental conditions shift rapidly, thanks to climate catastrophes, seismic events or the sudden emergence of new predators, many species can't adapt fast enough and might go extinct. Their libraries of genetic data hold no answers, because replicators are solely backwards-looking – not capable of forward planning.

Most animals do have at least some capacity for learning and behavioural plasticity – they aren't entirely slaves to their genetic code. Neurons will grow and respond to conditions as individuals develop, including in the

---

[187] Roach et al. (2010) at pgs. 636-639.

womb, so animal behaviour changes if there's a drought, for example, or intensified sexual competition. Almost any animal can be trained to respond to both positive and negative re-enforcement. But with a few exceptions, learning during an individual's lifetime is not passed down to its offspring, only the *capacity* for learning. Any information that may be passed down from one generation to the next that is *not* encoded in DNA is called *epigenetic* – meaning outside the DNA code.

One of the more interesting discoveries in biological science over the last few years has been evidence that chromosomal epigenetic transmission does in fact occur. To give an extremely simplified example, genes can be switched on and off during development by attaching a methyl group to some amino acids. Historically, it was assumed that DNA methylation was not passed on during reproduction, but we now have several hundred examples in nature of exactly that happening. The rare examples in humans tends to focus on extreme stress: children whose parents have experienced starvation or other hardship inherit metabolic changes to prepare them for a potentially difficult life ahead.

The scope, nature and extent of epigenetic transmission is a contested topic in biology, but there are no difficulties incorporating it into models of evolution that are substrate neutral[188]. Related concepts also include *niche or artefact construction*[189] and Dawkins' *extended phenotype*[190]. A niche or artefact is simply a modification of an agent's material environment that enhances its fitness: typical examples include beaver damns, termite mounds and mammal dens[191], but the concept also includes modifications to entire ecosystems such as the spread of grasslands by browsing herbivores. Organisms can increase or decrease the availability of essential resources in the environment available to other organisms. Niches are passed down to offspring (termites *can* build new mounds but tend to live in those already

---

[188] Maynard Smith (1990) at pgs. 41–53.

[189] Odling-Smee et al (2003)

[190] Dawkins (1982).

[191] Dawkins (1982), Chapter 11.

built by their hive) and form part of the environmental inheritance of the next generation. Niches are also epigenetic information that is *not* stored in a species' DNA.

Niches can also be social. In complex animals with population structure, there may only a certain number of roles that exist and an individual must either adapt to those roles or leave. Kin recognition – which we discussed briefly in Chapter 1 – may work much this way. How does an animal know that is related to another? Well, kinship may require a social structure in which parents raise their offspring in close physical proximity, and siblings are raised together by the same individuals on same food sources. Kinship forms a social structure that conveys relevant information about how an animal should behave and the level of altruism that's fitness-enhancing (in accordance with Hamilton's Rule).

Dawkins' extended phenotype concept includes the idea of niche construction, but also a second strategic element. An animal's behaviour affects not only their material environment, but may also change the behaviour of other agents. The hunting strategies of predators, for example, are shaped by the defensive strategies adopted by prey animals; and the flowering strategies of planets change the feeding strategies of insects. The neoteny of infants produce chemical and behavioural changes in parents that helps ensure their survival. Both niche construction and the extended phenotype are examples of the epigenetic transmission of non-genetic replicators from one generation to the next.

For proponents of gene-culture evolution, none of these labels and distinctions are of great importance. Genes are not the only replicators that generate behaviour, and phenotypes are generated through the interaction of multiple replicators exercising influence through multiple channels. If we wanted to focus on the individual actor, we might pay more attention to their childhood development; if we preferred environmental explanations, niche construction looks important; at the population level, cultural explanations dominate. But ultimately, all forms of adaptive inheritance share common mathematical properties and can be treated as equivalent[192]. The particular framework chosen is ultimately a matter of personal or political preference.

But for the essentialists, genes are the *most significant* replicator that transmits information from one generation to the next[193]. There's variation in the strategic behaviour a particular gene produces, but this variation is 'evoked' by the gene's interaction with other genes on the chromosome, the developmental conditions of the organism's development, and with its material and social environment[194]. In the eyes of an essentialist, we could take any population of humans and put them in a given environment with a certain endowment of technology, and statistically speaking their behaviours would not differ. Their cultures would develop as a result of the interaction of their genes with the environment, and to the extent that any meaningful variation was observed, only genes and random chance would explain the difference.

Not only does the essentialist position naturalise human cultural differences, it's also empirically wrong. Compared to other animals, human beings can survive in a staggeringly diverse range of environmental and economic niches, from the Arctic Circle to the most inhospitable of deserts. Yet if you took a group of people from one such extreme environment to another they would almost certainly perish, or at the very least possess vastly reduced fitness[195]. Even if you provided the new arrivals the tools and technology used by the people who lived there, humans do not innately come equipped with the strategies to adapt to extreme changes in environmental circumstances without copying the behaviours of or being taught by other humans[196].

---

[192] Wilson (1998); Mesoudi et al. (2006) at pgs. 329-347.

[193] Cosmides & Tooby, "The psychological foundations of culture" in Cosmides & Tooby (eds.) (1992) at pgs. 114-115; Minkel, "Psyching Out Evolutionary Psychology: Interview with David J. Buller" Scientific American, July 4 2005.

[194] Cosmides, Tooby & Barkow (1992) at pg. 84; Buss (1995) esp. at pgs. 12-14; Gangestad, Haselton & Buss (2006) at pgs. 75-95.

[195] Boyd & Richerson (2005) at pgs. 21-21; Henrich (2016), Chapter 3.

[196] Boyd & Richerson (2005) at pgs. 29-30, 46-48.

That prior learning simply isn't stored in their genetic code – even with all the impressive behavioural flexibility and capacity for reason humans possess wouldn't be enough for us to survive on our own in most environments. Whether its shipwrecked sailors or colonial mercenaries in the heart of strange continents, history is replete with examples of humans travelling to strange new environments and dying horribly – despite large populations of highly genetically similar people thriving in the same location[197]. Humans travel further and faster than other species, and live in a more diverse range of natural and social ecosystems – in order to adapt, we've had to find ways to store information about our social and material environment outside our physical bodies and transmit that information to other social agents through learning and imitation. This is what we call culture[198].

Unlike the biological determinists, gene-culture co-evolution does not deny that genetic and environmental influences play a role in shaping behaviour. There's plenty of evidence for genetic adaptions to new cultural environments[199], the most famous of which is lactase persistence in multiple, geographically diverse groups of humans who engaged in cattle herding. Humans without that genetic mutation could be taught to herd cattle, but without the biological adaption to digest lactase into adulthood the fitness benefits of doing so would be limited. We could just as easily discuss the adaption to low-oxygen environments amongst Tibetans and Andeans[200], or to long-duration dives amongst the Bajau people in Indonesia[201]. Or to the most variable trait of all: the differential susceptibility to disease amongst human populations who have been geographically separately in different parts of the world for tens of thousands of years. These aren't just examples of our genetic code adapting to relatively recent environmental

---

[197] Henrich (2016), Chapter 3.

[198] Definition taken from Boyd & Richerson (1985).

[199] Fan et al. (2016) at pgs. 54-59.

[200] E.g. Beall et al. (2004) at pgs. 14300-14304.

[201] Ilardo et al. (2018) at pgs. 569-580.

changes, they're genetic adaptions *caused* by changes in human culture.

So too with environmental factors. A person's weight, height and other physical attributes are shaped to a significant degree by the availability of resources during their development. Famously, the 'Flynn effect' shows a significant, sustained increased in human intelligence over the twentieth century – largely as the result of better nutrition and childcare – far larger than the variation in intellectual ability amongst living humans. The social and political value placed on skin colour varies significantly depending on the mode of labour employed by a society and the geographic latitude in which they live. We can't say that these social variations are entirely cultural – but they're not genetic either. They are evoked during development by material changes in the environment.

But culture evolves, and evolves in its own right and not merely as an adjunct to genetic or environmental changes. Studies have been done of different groups of European migrants who moved to settler societies in North America, showing that even when closely related human groups adopted closely related economic patterns of life, variation in their strategic culture persisted so long as it wasn't subject to strong inter-group selection pressures. Similar studies have compared migratory populations in central and eastern Africa, where there has been considerable movement of peoples and transformation in economic life over a relatively short and recent period of time[202]. Culture exists, culture matters and it cannot be reduced to a function of other evolutionary replicators.

The human capacity for culture, that is, accurately passing on information about the adaptiveness of behaviour within a population through means other than genetic transmission, is vast – but not unique in nature. Non-genetic strategic selection is seen in many organisms, including fish, birds, mammals[203] and, importantly for our purposes, also in non-biological organisms such as human tribes, organisations, firms and countries. Paleoanthropologists have ample theories and evidence about the particular

---

[202] Boyd & Richerson (2005) at pgs. 29–30, 207.

[203] Laland (2017).

environmental circumstances which drove the acquisition of this capacity: most prominently, it is thought of as an adaption to a precarious and rapidly changing environment and a social structure that relied on cooperation for parenting and protection from predators.

Culture is important to the evolution of large, complex societies because cultural information changes much, much faster than genetic information or the material condition of the environment[204]. Cultural replicators are gained and lost must more rapidly than genetic ones. Social species with non-biological culture can therefore not only adapt more easily to an environment that changes on the timescale of generations, but also arrange themselves into a wider potential range of social structures than could be organised by genetic mutations. Once human culture got going, not only did we expand to conquer the globe, but developed such a staggering diversity in political, cultural and economic arrangements that we put the rest of nature to shame And all this despite a genetic bottleneck such that every human alive today shares an ancestor within the last 200,000 to 300,000 years. This marvellous behavioural diversity in turn increased the fitness differentials of particular social strategies and intensified the selective pressure on human sub-populations.

* * *

For the German sociologist Max Weber, the defining characteristic of a social action was its intentionality – but in an evolutionary frame instrumental rationality is not a requirement for actors to act consistently to maximise their fitness. All that matters is if an agent's strategy is out of sync with social and environmental conditions, they will *"act inappropriately, fail to achieve their goals, and may be punished."*[205] Social agents inherit a library of culturally acquired information, which produces strategic behaviour with variable fitness consequences, and so their cultural information

---

[204] Boyd & Richerson (2005) at pgs. 42-44.

[205] Harrison, "Thinking About the World We Make" in Harrison (ed.) (2006) at pg. 9.

is differentially reproduced[206]. Behaviours that lead to an increase in individual fitness are likely to spread throughout a population, those that are fitness-decreasing are likely to go extinct.

Rather than calculate the expected utility of every possible strategic behaviour, human psychology is in fact likely organised around 'scripts' or stories[207], in which neural pathways attempt to pattern-match current circumstances to an action-consequence sequence that they either experienced during development or inherited socially. Particularly when decision-making is resource- or time-constrained, individuals will tend to behave in a way that worked before in similar circumstances. Human beings are preternaturally skilled at pattern-matching, inferential deduction and telling stories, rather than estimating probability and assessing risk.

These scripts can be transmitted to others and stored culturally for later use. Cultural information is primarily stored in the brains of individuals, but is also within the shape of artefacts, in a society's architecture and ecology, in its art and, where writing has been invented, in its books and literature. Cultural evolution is therefore cumulative, in the sense that information acquired during the lifetime of social agents is at least partially stored by the population and passed on to the next generation. Cultural evolution is gradual and experimental, driven by new variations in existing norms, laws, and behaviours.

"Isaac Newton famously remarked that he stood on the shoulders of giants. For most innovators in most places at most times in human history, a different metaphor is closer to the truth. Even the greatest human innovators are, in the great scheme of things, midgets standing on the shoulders of a vast pyramid of other midgets. The evolution of languages, artefacts and institutions can be divided into many small steps, and during each step the changes are relatively modest. No single innovator contributes more than a small portion of the total . . . .Individuals are smart, but most of the cultural artefacts that we use, the

---

[206] Boyd & Richerson (2005), Chapter 3.

[207] Schank & Abelson (1977); Schrodt (2004).

social institutions that shape our lives, the languages we speak, and so on are far too complex for even the most gifted innovator to create from scratch." [Boyd & Richerson, Not by Genes Alone] [208]

In the context of a social organisation with continuity beyond the individuals that comprise it – such as a commercial firm, bureaucratic institution or political party – corporate behaviours that lead to success are likely to be written down as stand operation procedures: manuals, training resources, policy guidance (or the autobiographies of corporate leaders). Even after the individuals who innovated successful strategies have moved on, those manuals and policy documents record their strategies for the next 'generation', and some of these in turn are written down as law or taught in business schools. Culture allows us to record evolutionarily-relevant information outside our genetic codes.

Thinking about evolution only in biological terms leads many otherwise intelligent people to reject the cultural evolution paradigm. If replicators – Dawkins' 'selfish gene' –– are what matters for natural selection, then there must be an analogous replicator for complex behaviours (the "meme") residing in the brains of cultural animals that is reliably copied and transmitted[209]. And for some critics of cultural evolution, such as Steven Pinker[210], social behaviours are so irreducibly complex that they could not possibly have evolved piecemeal – in an obvious analogy to creationist arguments about biological evolution. Pinker believes cultural products must be invented out of whole cloth by the conscious will of individual creators and that culture merely records the triumphs of geniuses. Since cultural products cannot change, they are not variable and cannot evolve: a Beethoven symphony is the same today as it was eighteenth century. To the extent that certain ideas do seem to spread in populations in a

---

[208] Piketty (2013); Laland (2017) at pg. 157.

[209] Dawkins (1982) at pg. 166-170.

[210] E.g. Pinker, "The False Allure of Group Selection" Edge, 18 June 2012; See also: Boyd & Richerson (2005) at pgs. 48-50; and Sperber (1996) esp. Chapter 5.

seemingly biological way, Dawkins' heirs tend to see culture as a parasite that hitchhikes on the human symbolic reasoning but which makes no meaningful contribution to social or economic adaptation[211].

From the viewpoint of cultural evolution, the assumption that there must be fixed cultural replicators is wrong[212]. It mistakes the output of natural selection (the replicator) for the whole process (selection on strategies). Cultural replicators are therefore not directly analogous to genes – but then again genes aren't directly subject to selection either! Generalised Darwinian evolution acts on *strategies*, and it does not matter a great deal whether those strategies are transmitted genetically, epigenetically, in books, in practices, in cultural tradition, or in any other form[213]. Evolution is not limited to any particular vehicle of strategic variation, selection and replication.

---

[211] Turchin (2016) at pg. 220; Haidt (2012) at pgs. 291-295.

[212] Boyd & Richerson (2005) at pgs. 83-84, 88-91; Laland & Brown (2011) at pg. 196-197.

[213] Gintis (2017), at pg. 2.

6

ORDER FROM CHAOS

Key Points

· Cooperative strategies can be evolutionarily stable when mutual co-operators have a opportunity to repeatedly interact with one another.
· When populations are structured such that social agents are temporally, spatially or socially proximate, co-operative clusters may emerge even in the absence of social hierarchy.
· In indefinitely repeated social interactions, punishment of cheaters via the withdrawal of benefits or the impositions of costs incentivises cooperation and discourages exploitation
· Reputation – the memory of prior acts – facilitates medium-scale social cooperation. Direct reciprocity occurs when actors remember past dealings with one another; indirect reciprocity occurs when actors inherit data about how potential partners treated others.

This Chapter, we return at last to the problem with which we began: how to sustain cooperative behaviour in social species such as our own when altruism is costly. There's a common view – dating back to Jeremy Bentham[214] and the positivist Auguste Comte – that social order must be

---

[214] Bentham, "Anarchical Fallacies" (1816).

the product of power, hierarchy and hegemony. A social rule, norm or institution comes into being because it serves the self-interest an actor with the power to shape social outcomes and who uses violence to enforce compliance. Typically, conservatives view power and hierarchy as a positive force, and progressives view it negatively. But both sides are embedded in a framework that sees social agents as irreducibly egoistic, self-interested and incapable of spontaneous self-organisation. In the traditional view, social order is produced through of the coercion of individuals (and families) by powerful people and institutions.

The positivist argument about the origins of large-scale social cooperation is wrong. Structured, altruistic cooperation can emerge spontaneously even in the absence of social hierarchies.

"[The g]reat part of that order which reigns among mankind is not the effect of government. It has its origin in the principles of society and the natural constitution of man. It existed prior to government, and would exist if the formality of government was abolished. The mutual dependence and reciprocal interest which man has upon man, and all the parts of a civilized community upon each other, creates that great chain of connexion which holds it together. . . Common interests regulates their concerns, and forms their law; and the laws which common usage ordains have greater influence than the laws of government." [Paine, the Rights of Man][215]

In Chapter 1, we introduced Hamilton's Rule, which proposed that two closely genetically correlated individuals could cooperate with one another without a loss of relative fitness. This Chapter will introduce two further mechanisms which can sustain cooperation (reputation and proximity); the next will introduce the fourth and final (group identity) and demonstrate how these four dimensions of assortivity form the evolutionary origins of cooperation. Their shared, essential feature is repeated interaction: the likelihood that replicating social agents will encounter and interact with

---

[215] Paine, "Rights of Man, Part Two, Chapter I" (1791)

one another on more than one occasion.

In sequential games of perfect information, in which each player's move is observable to every other player, the solution concept employed most often in game theory is the **subgame perfect equilibrium**[216]. A subgame is simply any series of choices which forms part of the overall game. A subgame perfect equilibrium is a strategy set that's a Nash equilibrium of every subgame of the overall game. Every perfect information game has at least one subgame perfect equilibrium. Similarly to the iterated elimination of dominated strategies, the method for finding the subgame perfect equilibrium begins with the smallest possible subgame [i.e. the last decision] and works backwards through the series of progressively larger subgames until the complete game is solved. A player who sticks to a strategy that is subgame perfect is considered 'sequentially rational'. That player selects their strategy for the entire game before it begins, and does not change their overall strategy at any point in the sequence.

Take, for example, the simple sequential interaction known in the literature as the **centipede game**[217]. Two players, A and B, take turns passing a pot back and forward. The pot is divided into a larger share and a smaller share. Each stage, a player has the choice to either pass the pot and allow it to increase, or defect and steal the larger share of the pot for themselves. If the game has a finite time horizon, and both players know this, then the player that is scheduled to move last will defect; knowing this, the other player would defect in the penultimate round, and so on and so on. The centipede game is obviously a perfect information version of the traveller's dilemma or the public goods game (see Chapter 3: "Adaptive Rationality"), and so the player who moves first should defect on the first round, even though both players are better off in absolute terms the longer the game lasts. Real social agents (humans) do not play the centipede game like this, suggesting once again that sequential rationality is not itself adaptively

---

[216] Selten (1975) at pgs. 25-55.

[217] Rosenthal (1981) at pgs. 92-100.

rational[218]. Something else -is going on.

If the strategic choices that agents have each round of a sequential game are identical, with the same payoffs, we can consider them to be playing a repeating or iterative game with a single stage and N rounds rather than a sequential game with N stages. Even if the stage game permits simultaneous moves, players can observe the strategies implemented in the prior round during the next, and thus the subgame perfect equilibrium concept is still employed. Consider again the ultimatum game introduced in Chapter 3 (an asymmetric cooperation game). In a one-shot interaction, the weaker party has no choice but to accept the minimum possible offer proposed to them. But if the interaction were to be repeated a second time, the weaker player could reject low offers in the first round in order to elicit a higher offer in the second[219].

A conditional action rule is a strategy that withholds short-term coopera-tion in order to impose a fitness cost on their partner – **a punishment** –to incentivise cooperation in the long-term. Mathematically, the imposition of costs and the withdrawal of benefits are equally effective as punishments. All iterated games have conditional strategies of some form, with a wide va-riety of implementations[220]. However, in order for the threat of punishment to be credible, a conditional strategy must be subgame perfect whenever common knowledge of rationality is presumed. A threat of punishment that requires a social agent to make a choice that is not itself rational (it is 'off equilibrium') is not credible and cannot therefore influence the behaviour of other players.

But as we shall see, in evolutionary games with strategic variation, selection and reproduction, a strategy does not need to be a subgame perfect equilibrium in order to be stable in the population[221]. Indeed, the evolutionary stability of (irrational) conditional strategies that reject

---

[218] McKelvey & Palfrey (1992) at pgs. 803-836; Nagel & Tang (1998) at pgs. 356-384.

[219] Skyrms (2014), Chapter 2.

[220] Rosas (2010) at pgs. 450-456.

[221] Skyrms (2014), Chapter 2; Gale et al. (1995) at pgs. 56-90.

unfair offers in iterated versions of the ultimatum game has been offered as an explanation of why real human beings play as if fairness was a value that mattered[222]. Humans may have evolved our innate (if culturally conditioned) desire for approximate fairness precisely because we alternate throughout our lives between the roles of proposer and responder in variations of the ultimatum game, and adopt a behavioural heuristic that is robust to changes in our social position.

* * *

Consider the two–round game below in Figure 6.1, in which two agents play a **prisoners dilemma** (a symmetric, anti-cooperation) stage game against each other twice.

---

[222] Guth et al., (1982) at pgs. 367-388; Guth & Tietz (1990) at pgs. 417-449; Roth et al., (1991) at pgs. 162-202; Nowak, Page, & Sigmund (2000) at pgs. 1773–1775

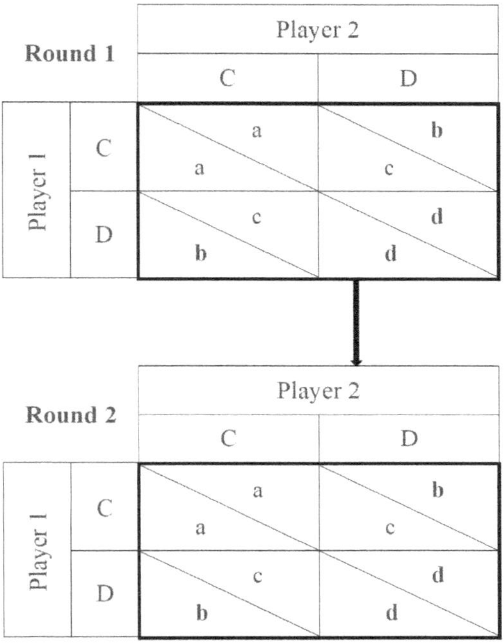

Figure 6.1. A two-stage, symmetric normal form game

A complete strategy for the iterated prisoners dilemma must specify a decision rule for each round, and the scope of possible behaviours increases rapidly with the number of rounds. For example, while the players have the choice of C or D in the first round, in the second round a player's strategy takes the form $s_i = (p_{CC}, p_{CD}, p_{DC}, p_{DD})$ where p_{mn} is the probability that player i implements strategy C, given that they previously played the pure strategy m and their opponent played the pure strategy n. So for instance, if $p_{CD} = 0$ then a cooperative player whose partner previously defected will punish them in the next round.

Employing sequential rationality, the fact that the Nash equilibrium to the second (or final) round is (D, D) suggests that both players will defect in both rounds. Neither player can change the behaviour of the other in the final round, so there's correspondingly nothing they can do in the first round to increase their overall fitness payoff. The same is true regardless of how many iterations are performed, *if the number of iterations is known with certainty at the outset of the game.* Therefore, if a stage game has only a single Nash equilibrium, then there's only a single subgame perfect equilibrium of the finitely repeating version of the game – in the case of anti-cooperation games, this is *always defect.*

Interesting things start to happen, though, when games are indefinitely repeating – i.e. social agents do not know precisely which round is going to be the last one. Since the variety of conditional strategies is literally infinite, how do players choose the strategy that is optimal? Let us define as a player's subjective belief that an indefinitely repeating game will continue for one more round, or to be precise: that interactions with a particular social partner will continue. Therefore the total expected number of rounds is 1/(1 –). When = 0 players believe that the current round of the game will be its last; when = 1 players believe that the game will continue forever – that it is *infinitely repeating.* In an indefinitely repeating, iterated prisoners dilemma, players cannot be certain what their partners will do in the next round, and therefore may be able to influence their actions by their behaviour in the current round.

It's important to note that the *always defect* strategy will always be an evolutionarily stable, attractive equilibrium of the iterated prisoner's dilemma, because defect will always be a best reply to itself. But there are also, it turns out, many stable strategies which *conditionally cooperate,* i.e. will defect only if their partner performed some action in the previous round(s). Let's discuss what those might be.

The maximum punishment that can be imposed in the iterated prisoners dilemma is to defect forever. We define the *grim trigger* strategy as: "Cooperate in the first round; and if the opponent defects, defect forever.". The expected utility of perpetual cooperation in the iterated prisoners dilemma is the cooperation payoff multiplied by the expected number of rounds in the game, or:

$$u_C = \frac{a}{(1 - \partial)}$$

If a player unilaterally defects from cooperation ('cheats') against a player with the grim trigger strategy, they receive the temptation payoff for one round, and then the punishment payoff in every expected round thereafter. Therefore:

$$u_D = b + \frac{\partial d}{(1 - \partial)}$$

Comparing these payoffs, we find that grim trigger players have no temptation to cheat whenever:

$$\frac{a}{(1 - \partial)} \geq b + \frac{\partial d}{(1 - \partial)}$$

$$a \geq b - \partial b + \partial d$$

$$\partial \geq \frac{b - a}{b - d}$$

If players believe that the game will continue for a sufficient large number of rounds (i.e. they are patient), then the grim trigger strategy may be a subgame perfect Nash equilibrium[223]. If they believe the game will be short, they have a greater incentive to defect and take the temptation payoff.

In contrast to the *grim trigger* strategy of defecting forever, the minimum period a player can withhold benefits before resuming cooperation is one round. We define the *tit-for-tat* strategy as: "Cooperate in the first round; in every subsequent round choose the strategy that the opponent played in the previous round." For the *tit-for-tat* player, the expected utilities of

---

[223] McCarty & Meirowitz (2007), Chapter 9.2.

playing against the *always cooperate* and *always defect* strategies are as for the grim trigger strategy – *tit-for-tat* matches the fitness of co-operators and does no worse than grim trigger against habitual defectors. But is *tit-for-tat* a Nash equilibrium with itself? If a *tit-for-tat* player cheats (or makes a mistake) for a single round, the result is oscillation or a 'death spiral' between the temptation and sucker payoffs (i.e. the cheater receives the temptation payoff for one round, but when they return resume cooperating they receive the suckers payoff, because the honest actor is punishing them for their prior defection. The cheater then retaliates the next round and so on).

The expected payoff of a single defection from the *tit-for-tat* equilibrium is therefore:

$$b + \partial c + \partial^2 b + \partial^2 c + \ldots = \frac{b + \partial c}{(1 - \partial^2)}$$

Comparing these payoffs, we find that there will be zero temptation to unilaterally defect whenever:

$$\frac{a}{(1 - \partial)} \geq \frac{b + \partial c}{(1 - \partial^2)}$$

$$a - \partial^2 a \geq b - \partial b + \partial c - \partial^2 c$$

$$\partial \geq \frac{b - a}{a - c}$$

If defection for both one round and all rounds are deterred, then defection for any arbitrary number of rounds is also deterred[224]. Therefore *tit-for-tat* is a Nash equilibrium of the iterated prisoner's dilemma whenever:

---

[224] Morrow (1994) at pgs. 265-266; McCarty & Meirowitz (2007), Chapter 9.3; Axelrod (1984) at pg. 207.

$$\partial \geq max \left\{ \frac{b-a}{b-d}, \frac{b-a}{a-c} \right\}$$

Since the left-hand threshold is shared with the *grim trigger* strategy, *grim trigger* can deter defection in a wider variety of game payoff structures than *tit-for-tat* (i.e. including the range b - d > a - c). In other words, defecting forever [a severe punishment] is a more effective deterrent than retaliating only once[225] [a proportionate punishment]. Generally speaking the higher (i.e. the longer players expect the interaction to continue), the greater the range of conditional strategies that are Nash equilibria[226].

We shall soon see that *tit-for-tat* consistently delivers the greatest fitness payoffs in evolutionary simulations of large populations over long time scales. But *tit-for-tat* is not subgame perfect except under very rare structural conditions, relying as it does on an incredible threat of mutually destructive punishment[227]. Think again of two *tit-for-tat* players stuck in the 'death spiral' of mutual retaliation. Each player can actually *improve* their payoff by defecting from *tit-for-tat* and unilaterally cooperating. Eye for an eye makes the whole world blind. To get along, at some point we have to forgive and forget.

So one way out of the 'death spiral' outcome is *tit for tat with forgiveness*, in which we add to the *tit-for-tat* strategy a small but non-zero chance of ignoring its opponent's defection – this provides an opportunity to break out of the cycle of mutual recrimination and resume cooperation. It turns out that the nicer and more forgiving a *tit-for-tat* rule is made, the better it performs at sustaining a cooperative social equilibrium. So while reciprocal altruism can be outperformed for a round or two, exploitative strategies cannot outcompete it in the long run.

In the early 1980s, all this theory was put to the test through a remarkable

---

[225] Morrow (1994) at pg. 266.

[226] Axelrod (1984) at pgs. 15-16.

[227] McCarty & Meirowitz (2007) at pgs. 257-258; Gintis (2009), Chapter 9.

computer tournament organised by the political scientist Robert Axelrod, which pitted 63 possible strategies built by professional game theorists, economists, psychologists and amateurs against one another in an iterated prisoner's dilemma with 200 expected rounds (i.e. = 0.99654). The results, published first as an article co-written with the biologist William Hamilton (of Hamilton's Rule fame: recall Chapter 1)[228], then later as a full-length book (*The Evolution of Cooperation*[229]), is justifiably famous. Over the succeeding decades, Axelrod's simulation approach evolved into a body of modelling and theoretical work in political science and mathematical biology known as the Theory of Cooperation[230].

Axelrod found that equilibrium strategies for playing social games iteratively should be: *nice*, never being the first to defect; *retaliatory*, punishing defection by others; *forgiving*, resuming cooperation quickly when others do the same; and *clear*, in that it is easy for other players to discover how it is playing[231]. *Tit-for-tat* met these criteria. In head-to-head match-ups against other strategies, *tit-for-tat* obtained the highest average scores; *grim trigger* performed the worst of all nice strategies, but better than any of those that attempted to cheat. Axelrod also implemented a replicator dynamic inspired by Maynard Smith and Hamilton, wherein fitness-enhancing strategies were preferentially replicated in the next generation[232]. In these evolutionary simulations, *tit-for-tat* eventually came to represent the dominant culture of the population, and less fit strategies went extinct.

Axelrod proved three main findings: Firstly, strategies based on reciprocity could survive and thrive against many diverse types of competitor; secondly, that mutual cooperation, once established on the basis of reciprocity, was capable of protecting itself against invasion by exploitative

---

[228] Axelrod & Hamilton (1981) at pgs. 1390-1396.

[229] Axelrod (1984)

[230] Axelrod (ed.) (1997); Axelrod (2000) at pgs. 130-151.

[231] Axelrod (1984) at pg. 54.

[232] Axelrod (1984) at pgs. 49-53.

strategies – no matter how clever they were. In other words, *tit-for-tat* might be evolutionarily stable even though it isn't subgame perfect (see the next Chapter)[233]. Finally, Axelrod discovered that an additional condition necessary for cooperation to emerge spontaneously from anarchy was some clustering of co-operators[234]. Lone *tit-for-tat* players vanish in a large, well-mixed population dominated by cheaters. But repeated interactions amongst like-minded strategic cultures enabled cooperation to gain a foothold in an otherwise predatory world[235]. Axelrod had encountered what game theorists now describe as the necessity for 'correlation'[236] or 'assortivity'[237]: mechanisms which increase the likelihood that two actors with the same strategy will interact again, and which therefore lower their propensity to seek a higher payoff through short-term cheating.

Later, it turned out that *tit-for-tat* was merely a special case of a broader family of so-called 'zero determinant (or ZD)' strategies. In 2012, William Press & Freeman Dyson showed that there exists a set of mixed strategies in the two-player, indefinitely repeating prisoners dilemma which allows a player to limit their opponent's payoff to a set ratio of their own[238]. ZD strategies may be either extortionary (in which the ZD player receives a higher payoff than their opponent, or both defect forever), or generous (in which both players cooperate forever, or the ZD player receives a *lower* payoff than their opponent)[239]. *Tit-for-tat* is neither extortionary nor generous -- it equalises the long-term payoffs of all players. And *tit-for-tat* with forgiveness is the most generous ZD strategy that's also a Nash

---

[233] Axelrod (1984) at pg. 21.

[234] Axelrod (1984) from pg. 65-.

[235] Axelrod (1984) from pg. 145-; See also Riolo, Cohen & Axelrod (2001).

[236] Skyrms (2014) at pg. 55-60; Gintis (2009) at pgs. 40, 142-155; Aumann (1974) at pgs. 67-96.

[237] Bergstrom (2002); Bergstrom (2003); Bowles & Gintis (2011) at pg. 72.

[238] Press & Dyson (2012) at pgs. 10409-10413.

[239] Stewart & Plotkin (2013) at pgs. 15348-15353.

equilibrium[240].

The initial discovery of extortionary ZD strategies suggested that Axelrod's Theory of Cooperation might have been wrong: in a two-player iterated prisoners dilemma, an extortionary ZD strategy can limit an opponent to an arbitrarily low payoff. But it soon emerged that in a large and well-mixed population of social agents, extortionary ZD strategies were not evolutionarily stable: ZD mutants could invade most populations, but because a population of ZD players attempted to exploit one another they were not themselves resistant to exploitation by other strategies[241]. The same is not true of generous ZD strategies: in a large and well-mixed population, generous (or altruistic) ZD strategies are evolutionarily robust. No strategy can outperform *tit-for-tat* in terms of fitness while also being evolutionarily stable – whereas strategies that are more altruistic (i.e. less fit) than *tit-for-tat* are more robust.

* * *

What, then, does represent in evolutionary terms, given that it appears to be the critical value for sustaining cooperative equilibria? Consider an altruistic agent playing the *grim trigger* strategy, which permits cooperation under the widest possible set of conditions. Clearly, b - a is the altruist's opportunity cost for playing the cooperate strategy rather than cheating themselves. By the same token, b - d is the benefit the altruist conveys on their partner, who receives the temptation payoff for one round rather than the mutual punishment payoff by exploiting its altruistic opponent.

We can thus re-write our threshold equation which expresses the minimum value of that can sustain a cooperative equilibrium, as:

---

[240] Akin (2012).

[241] Adami & Hintze (2012); Hintze & Adami (2015); Hilbe, Nowak & Sigmund (2013) at pgs. 6913–6918.

$$\partial \geq \frac{cost}{benefit}$$

The similarity of this expression to Hamilton's Rule (recall Chapter 1) is remarkable[242]. It implies that belief in the continuation of an interaction with a partner () is mathematically analogous to genetic relatedness (r) in terms of its effect on incentivising cooperation.

"Cooperation based on reciprocity can gain a foothold through two different mechanisms. First, there can be kinship between mutant strategies, giving the genes of the mutants some stake in each other's success, thus altering the payoff of the interaction when viewed from the perspective of the gene rather than the individual. A second mechanism to overcome total defection is for the mutant strategies to . . . cluster so that they [have] a nontrivial proportion of interactions [with each other], even if they are. . .a negligible proportion of the [population]." [Axelrod & Hamilton, The Evolution of Cooperation]

While assortivity on the basis of genetic relatedness promotes altruism amongst kin, assortivity on the basis of time [i.e. a higher than average probability of interaction over tiem with like agents] is termed reciprocal altruism, a concept described independently by the biologist Robert Trivers and the economist James Friedman in 1971[243]. Most biologists divide theories of cooperation into these two broad families[244]. The fact that social agents discount future payoffs is therefore not an essential component of rational choice theory. Instead, discounting of future payoffs evolves because agents are uncertain how long an interaction will continue [or whether the chance of meeting a particular agent again is more or less likely

---

[242] Bowles & Gintis (2011) at pg. 60.

[243] Trivers (1971) at pgs. 35-57; Friedman (1971) at pgs. 1-12; Boyd & Richerson (2005) at pgs. 199-201; Laland & Brown (2011) at pgs. 57-59.

[244] See e.g. West et al. (2011) at pg. 236; Bowles & Gintis (2011) at pg. 53.

than any other]. The degree of future discounting evolves adaptively in response to its environmental and social conditions: stressed individuals in many species discount the future at a higher rate, because they are less certain a situation is going to continue (see also Chapter 10: Mediocre Individuals, Exceptional Species).

Reciprocal altruism is predicated on the principle that the likelihood of future cooperative interactions is dependent on whether the other agent has – or is of a Type that has – cooperated in the past. We call information about the prior behaviour of another agent its **reputation**. A population becomes internally structured on the basis of the reputations of its members. When an agent has acquired information about the reputation of another agent through prior interactions, we label their interaction **direct reciprocity**[245]. When a social agent has acquired that information through other means, including inheriting cultural data, we label it **indirect reciprocity**[246]. An agent's reputation may not be therefore limited to private knowledge held by its prior partners, but constitute public knowledge available to the whole population. For this reason, indirect reciprocity is also sometimes considered a theory of partner choice, inasmuch as agents only choose to cooperate with others in good social standing[247].

Indirect reciprocity works because social agents reward good behaviour, on the expectation that they themselves will be rewarded by strangers. Indirect reciprocity also collectivises punishment, by ensuring that habitual cheaters cannot exploit the naivete of agents they've never interacted with before. In the mid-1980s, the logic of indirect reciprocity was formalised by the economists Robert Sugden[248] and Richard Alexander[249]. They defined the 'standing' or indirect reciprocity strategy as: "Cooperate if and only if your partner is in good standing. If you are in bad standing, cooperate

---

[245] Nowak (2006) at pgs. 1560-1563.

[246] Nowak & Sigmund (2005) at pgs. 1291-1298.

[247] Skyrms (2014) at pg. 56.

[248] Sugden (1986).

[249] Alexander (1987).

unconditionally". In this model, an agent changes from good standing to bad standing if it – intentionally or accidentally – defects on a partner playing cooperate. An agent moves from bad standing to good standing if they cooperate unconditionally with a punishing partner. Insofar as societies have institutions to accurately measure and share information about the reputations of others, then cooperation can be sustained on the basis of indirect reciprocity[250]. Cultures can keep a record of the trustworthiness of other groups, and pass this knowledge down to the next generation. We tackle the problem of the reliability of signals about reputation in Chapter 8: "Beliefs and Signals".

Unlike kin preference, reciprocal altruism is relatively rare in nature and firm evidence for its existence only comes from some families of birds, mammals, monkeys and apes (including humans)[251]. Most animals, it seems, are highly impatient and lack the sophisticated cognitive capabilities to track of the reputation of other individuals over time, and so have a low likelihood of cooperating with strangers.

Humans, on the other hand, are remarkably good at keeping track of the past behaviour of specific individuals, even outside our own kin-group: our visual sense is highly specialised for identifying and recalling subtle facial differences. Humans with damage to the part of the brain that processes faces (the *fusiform gyrus*), can have difficulty socialising normally with others. The *fusiform gyrus* is also intimately associated with the making of spontaneous moral judgements about the trustworthiness of others, demonstrating the biological link between fitness-enhancing behaviour and emotive moral responses (see further in Chapter 10: "Mediocre Individuals, Exceptional Species")[252].

As a physically vulnerable genus that engaged in cooperative foraging and child-rearing, ancient humans were already cooperating in groups far

---

[250] Bowles & Gintis (2011) at pgs. 68-70.

[251] For a review of the biological literature, see: Bowles & Gintis (2011) at pgs. 61-64; West et al. (2011) at pg. 238; Boyd & Richerson (2005) at pg. 203.

[252] Sapolsky (2017) at pgs. 80-88.

larger than closely related families[253]. The British anthropologist Robin Dunbar has argued that an increasing neurological capability to keep track of the reputations of group members was one of the key factors driving the evolution of the human lineage, and that this capability topped out at an average of 150 people ("Dunbar's number") around 250,000 years ago – right around the time human physiology became fully modern but prior to the point that cultural evolution really accelerated[254]. In the absence of symbolic culture, a mental library of the honour or reputations of 150 people would be sufficient to support large fission-fusion tribes in which family groups engaged in trading and warfare with other distantly-related individuals across a large geographic range. But it probably wouldn't be enough to sustain social life at the level of the village, town or city.

* * *

Repeated interactions across time provide a route to sustain cooperation in a large, unstructured population, even when doing so is not rational. It turns out, so do repeated interactions across space.

William Hamilton was never as puritanical about the primary of kin selection as many of his successors and boosters became. The quote above from his work with Robert Axelrod amply demonstrated his comfort with alternative theories of reciprocal altruism. Hamilton was sceptical almost from the beginning about whether related individuals would be able to recognise one another well enough for kin selection to work (recall the kin recognition problem from Chapter 1)[255]. He proposed, as an alternative, that in species whose offspring displayed limited dispersal and did not travel far or quickly from their place of origin, a social agent could act *as if* others in

---

[253] Henrich (2016), at pg. 155.

[254] Dunbar (1992) at pgs. 469–493; Boehm (2001); Dunbar (1998); Dunbar (2014), Chapter 9;

[255] Hamilton (1965) at pgs. 1-16, and 17-52; Hamilton, "Innate Social Aptitudes in Man: An Approach from Evolutionary Genetics" in Fox (ed.) (1975) at pgs. 133–155; Hamilton, "Discriminating Nepotism: Expectable, Common and Overlooked" in Fletcher & Michener (eds.) (1987); West et al. (2011) at pgs. 231-262

close physical proximity were genetically related to it. Localised interaction served as a proxy for relatedness.

As we know, Axelrod's computer tournament also showed that cooperative strategies needed to initially cluster in order to successfully invade more Hobbesian populations, and attention soon turned to the role of social structure and landscape effects in supporting cooperation[256]. However it wasn't until the 1990s that teams of computer modellers, most notably including Harvard biologist Martin Nowak, began simulating games on a spatial grid and showed that cooperation was evolutionarily stable under certain structural conditions[257]. Eventually, this work came to be known as 'network reciprocity', although conditionality and reputation are not necessarily involved.

In spatial games, populations are not well-mixed, in the sense that every agent has an equal chance of interacting with everyone else. Instead, populations are structured such that each agent will only interact with a small, fixed number (k) of local neighbours. Their choice of interaction partners is constrained and they cannot move freely throughout their social or physical environment. Assuming that actors play a k-player anti-cooperation game (i.e. a public goods game) and that they reproduce in proportion to their fitness, then cooperation is an evolutionary stable strategy when[258]:

$$\frac{1}{k} > \frac{cost}{benefit}$$

Once again, we have a direct analogue to Hamilton's Rule[259], this time

---

[256] Axelrod & Dion (1988) at pgs. 1385-1390; Axelrod (1997).

[257] Nowak & May (1992) at pgs. 826-829; Nowak et al. (1994) at pgs. 4877-4881; Killingback & Doebeli (1996) at pgs. 1135–1144; Lieberman et al. (2005) at pgs. 312-316.

[258] Ohtsuki et al. (2008) at pgs. 502-505; Bowles & Gintis (2011), at pg. 74.

[259] Grafen (2007) at pgs. 2278-2283; Lehmann et al. (2007) at pgs. 2284-2295.

expressed in terms of the number of neighbours a social agent expects (or chooses) to interact with. As the number of neighbours (i.e. the range of interaction) increases, it's less and less likely that mutual cooperation can be sustained. Although local interaction can be understood as cooperation on the basis of territoriality, this effect is substrate-neutral with regard to whether it refers to geographically-determined population structures, (social) network structure or symbolic proximity of any kind. Spatial proximity is likely to be of only limited importance to humans (reciprocity is far more effective at sustaining mutual aid in large groups[260]) but it's of great importance to many other natural agents.

Once again, it's the likelihood of repeated interaction that's key, and temporal and spatial proximity are both circumstances that increase the likelihood of repeated interaction. Nowak argues that 'spatial selection' is distinct from kin selection, reciprocal altruism and group selection[261]:

"Co-operators prevail because they can form clusters, either in physical space, on networks, in phenotype space or in sets. Individuals within such clusters gain a higher payoff than defectors that try to [exploit] them."

While this categorisation of the mechanisms of assortivity is employed in this book for conceptual clarity, it's important to note that all these formulations are mathematically and conceptually equivalent: spatial proximity equals kin selection in the absence of direct kin recognition while creating clusters that make *tit-for-tat* evolutionarily stable; and neighbours and close relatives are likely to have a higher-than-average belief that their interactions will continue indefinitely. Analytically, the choice of frame depends on the preferences of the scientist and the mathematical tractability of the problem.

But from an evolutionary perspective, each of these mechanisms requires supportive machinery to ensure individual agents detect the population

---

[260] Bowles & Gintis (2011), at pg. 74; Gracia-Lazaro et al. (2012)

[261] Nowak et al. (2010).

structure and perform the adaptively rational strategy. It's likely, albeit unproven, that the story of human evolution is the story of each of these systems bootstrapping one another, such that kin selection supported the evolution of network reciprocity, which supported the evolution of direct and indirect reciprocity, which in turn provided the substructure on which cultural group selection, the subject of our next Chapter, developed.

So while it's certainly possible that modern social and institutional norms that promote cooperation amongst co-workers or combat units could operate remotely, the close physical proximity (and our evolved tolerance of others and aversion to interpersonal violence[262]) that often defines such relationships still likely plays a role in making rules and norms cheaper to sustain. Humans are strongly conformist by instinct[263] and physical proximity enhances those instincts. Starting in the 1950s, social psychologists famously demonstrated that most people conform in groups even when doing do was directly contrary to their own knowledge and preferences, or where the social behaviour serves no rational purpose[264]. These effects occur even among strangers and in the absence of shared group identities – copying the nearest person (who, as a child, is likely your parent or otherwise closely related to you) may just be the simplest learning heuristic to implement if you don't want to be worse off than the population average: when in Rome, it truly is best to do as the Romans do.

Classical game theory predicts that the spontaneous emergence of cooperative behaviour in social dilemmas is difficult, if not impossible. Moreover, it predicts that as populations grow larger and interact more frequently, the speed at which self-interest comes to dominate a population should increase. The results of several decades of research presented in this Chapter demonstrate quite the opposite: that in indefinitely interacting populations

---

[262] Greene (2014) at pgs. 35-39.

[263] Henrich (2016) at pgs. 48-49; Morgan & Laland (2012); Henrich & Boyd (2001) at pgs. 79-89.

[264] Asch (1955) at pgs. 31-35; Deutsch & Gerard (1955) at pgs. 629-636; Cialdini & Goldstein (2004) at pgs. 591-621.

a range of cooperative equilibria are evolutionarily stable. Moreover, the more trusting and generous such cultural strategies are, the better they perform. But the evolutionary theory of cooperation is not naïve or utopian. Instead, altruism emerges spontaneously through the amoral mechanism of natural selection acting on the relative fitness of strategies.

The evolution of social agents is by-and-large the story of the incremental development of mechanisms to sustain cooperation on an ever-larger and more complex canvas. Indeed, to the degree that we are all collections of cells and organic chemicals at multiple levels of organisation, the degree to which selfishness is suppressed in the interests of the whole organism is remarkable (see Chapter 9: The Evolution of Society). But there's one final part of this story, a capability that humans have made into the hallmark of our planetary-scale civilization: symbolic culture and the evolution of group identity.

7

EVOLUTIONARY GAMES

Key Points

- In a dynamic system, a distribution of strategies is evolutionarily stable if a population will return to it when perturbed by an invasion by or the mutation of new strategies.
- Conditional, cooperative strategies may be evolutionarily stable in a population when between-group differences are high compared to in-group differences.
- Group selection is most likely to be evolutionarily dominant when cultural variation generates behavioural differences among otherwise similar groups.
- Group identity is mutually constituted by adherence to expected norms and behaviours, especially when those behaviours are irrational or costly.

Evolutionary game theory is the formal study of iterated games under generalised Darwinian conditions. In evolutionary games, the changing frequency of a strategy in a population $Pr(s_i)$ is determined by a *replicator dynamic* $R(s_i)$, which relates its frequency in time period $t + 1$ to its fitness payoff in a stage game in time t. Evolutionary game theory dispenses with rationality and intentionality altogether and instead treats strategic optimisation as an unguided process of variation, selection and adaption[265]. Such games are *dynamic*, not static: rather than settle into a strategic equilibrium, populations may or may not ever reach a fixed state. An evolutionary game therefore needs to specify not only the structure of the stage game, but the rules under which the replication and mutation of strategies occur.

Evolutionary game theory is largely the product of initial work by the biologist John Maynard Smith, whose built a simple a computer simulation of the hawk-dove game for his 1972 article *"The Logic of Animal Conflict"*[266], which was later expanded into the book *"Evolution and the Theory of Games"*[267]. Maynard Smith developed a solution concept for such games he termed the **evolutionarily stable strategy** (ESS). A population of agents playing an ESS cannot be invaded any other strategy – such a population exists in an equilibrium which is established and maintained purely by natural selection. An ESS is the dynamic equivalent of the trembling-hand perfect strategy, in that it is resistant to any invasion, mutation and mistaken implementation. Formally, an ESS is a strategy s_i such that its payoffs against itself are higher than the payoffs of any other strategy s_j against s_i (or their payoffs are the same, but it scores better against itself than any other strategy scores against itself).

Every ESS is a Nash Equilibrium, but not every Nash Equilibrium is an ESS. Recall, in the previous Chapter, that *tit-for-tat* could be exploited by ZD strategies, but that because ZD strategies exploited one another, they in turn could be outcompeted by clusters of cooperative players (i.e. ZD was not successful against itself). Neither *tit-for-tat* nor ZD strategies are ESS in the iterated prisoner's dilemma under all possible conditions: only the *always defect* strategy is both a Nash equilibrium and an ESS. In evolutionary games there's no guarantee that a game will possess an ESS at all. As a property

---

[265] Adami et al. (2016) at pg. 1; Axelrod, "Introduction" in Axelrod (ed.) (1997); March (1970) at pgs. 570-592.

[266] Maynard Smith & Price (1972) at pgs. 15-18; See also: Maynard Smith (1974) at pgs. 209-221.

[267] Maynard Smith (1982).

of particular strategies, evolutionary stability guarantees a strategy would spread and become 'fixed' in a population regardless of its initial state[268]. As a consequence, if an ESS exists and is carried to fixation, it would destroy the initial variation in a population and cause further evolutionary adaption to cease[269].

We must therefore introduce a related, alternative solution concept: the **evolutionarily stable (or equilibrium) state**[270]. A state is a distribution of strategies in a population. An evolutionarily stable state may be either monomorphic (consisting entirely of a single ESS strategy) or polymorphic (consisting of a mix of different non-ESS strategies). In much the same way that a mixed strategy can be interpreted as a population of agents playing a combination of pure strategies (recall Chapter 4: "Mixed Strategies, Mixed Populations"), a polymorphic state can be evolutionarily stable even though none of the pure strategies that comprise it is itself an ESS. An evolutionary stable state is a *population strategy* that is resistant to invasion or mutation and will return to its prior state if perturbed to a limited degree by an outside force.

Recall the mixed strategy solutions of the coordination and anti-coordination games in Chapter 4. A population of hawks and doves playing pure strategies in proportions given by the mixed strategy equilibrium would be evolutionarily stable, because the mixed strategy in anti-coordination games is an *attractor*. On the other hand, a mixed population of stag hunters is not evolutionarily stable, because the mixed strategy equilibrium in coordination games is a *repulsor* and only populations comprised of either all stag hunters or all rabbit hunters are stable. Speaking generally, if the mixed strategy Nash equilibrium of the game is an ESS then the corresponding population state will be an evolutionarily stable state. The

---

[268] Taylor & Jonker (1978) at pg. 154.

[269] Dawkins (1982), at pg. 31.

[270] Taylor & Jonker (1978) at pgs. 145-156; Maynard Smith (1982); Thomas (1984) at pgs. 49-67; Thomas (1985) at pgs. 105-115; Dawkins (1982) at pg. 185.

mixed strategy in the hawk-dove anti-coordination game is an ESS[271], whereas the mixed strategy in the stag hunt coordination game isn't.

But as the number of strategies increases – as in games with continuous strategies or repeated play – then the likelihood of any particular strategy being an ESS decreases while the number of possible equilibrium population states increases. Most stable states in social games with complex behaviour are therefore polymorphic combinations of strategies[272]. And there are very many mixed strategies which are attractors under some circumstances without being an ESS under all conditions[273]. Every ESS is an attractor but not every attractor is an ESS – an attractor may be essentially a 'local' ESS that is resistant to some, but not all, potential alternative mutations[274]. For every mixed strategy attractor, the corresponding mixed population state is resistant to *some* invasion or mutation. In evolutionary terms, the existence of evolutionarily stable states with diverse internal distribution of behaviour allows a population to develop predictable structure while retaining the internal variance required for selection to continue to function. A population may be thereofre be both *evolutionary stable* and *dynamic* at the same time.

* * *

The replicator dynamics used in evolutionary game theory differ greatly in their design and implementation, and a full treatment is far beyond the scope of this book[275]. Given the field's origins in the biological sciences, most implementations employ a *genetic algorithm* – a mathematical expres-

---

[271] McElreath & Boyd (2007) at pg. 44.

[272] Skyrms (2014) at pgs. 10-22; Thomas (1984) at pg. 52.

[273] Theorem 1 in Zeeman, "Population Dynamics from Game Theory" in Nitecki & Robinson (eds.) (1980) at pgs. 471-497.

[274] Pohley & Thomas (1983) at pgs. 87-100.

[275] Hofbauer & Sigmund (1998), Chapter 8; Page & Nowak (2002) at pgs. 93-98; Traulsen & Hauert, "Stochastic evolutionary game dynamics" in Schuster (ed.) (2009) at pg. 25

sion which simulates either sexual or asexual reproduction[276]. Axelrod, for example, has represented strategies in the prisoner's dilemma as information on digital 'chromosomes' that are split and then recombined in each new generation[277]. Many researchers have concluded that the genetic algorithm is a highly effective tool for simulating dynamic populations in a wide variety of settings[278], even if its parsimony with how strategies reproduce in non-biological settings is low[279]. Arguably, this reliance on biological analogies has held back the adoption of evolutionary game theory in the social sciences, even though the replicator dynamic can be expressed in many formally equivalent ways which do not rely on highly abstracted genetic analogies[280].

Every specification of the replicator dynamic should also include a mechanism by which variation is generated or maintained in the population, such that the full dynamic rule is sometimes called the replicator-mutator dynamic[281]. Mutation may take the form of random errors in the copying of strategic behaviour from one generation to the next; the spontaneous generation of entirely new strategic variants; or rules which permit the occasional invasion of one population of evolving agents by another. The presence of mutants may alter the evolutionary stable equilibrium of a population and may in fact be necessary for an evolutionary stable state to exist in the first place[282].

Consider, for example, an iterated prisoner's dilemma in which the

---

[276] Taylor & Jonker (1978) at pgs. 145-156; Holland (1980) at pgs. 245-268; Adami et al. (2016).

[277] Axelrod (1997) at pgs. 17-21.

[278] Axelrod (1997) at pg. 23.

[279] A critique strongly made by Earnest & Rosenau, "Signifying Nothing? What Complex Systems Theory Can and Cannot Tell Us About Global Politics" in Harrison (ed.) (2006) at pgs. 151-152.

[280] Page & Nowak (2002) at pgs. 93-98

[281] Page & Nowak (2002) at pg. 94; Rousseau (2005), at pgs. 318-319.

[282] Boyd (1989) at pgs. 47-56; Wu & Axelrod (1997) at pg. 33; Bomze & Burger (1995) at pgs. 146-172.

replicator-mutator dynamic ensures a small, but persistent presence of *always defect* mutants. *Tit-for-tat* is not an ESS when playing against *all cooperate*, because it cannot do better than *all cooperate* in terms of fitness. However, when *always defect* mutants are present in the population in some small numbers, *tit-for-tat* will outcompete *all cooperate*, and a population state in turn dominated largely but not exclusively by *tit-for-tat* is resistant to invasion by *all cooperate*. Whether or not a particular state is evolutionarily stable depends on the context of each particular population[283].

Cultural evolution through social learning can also be expressed in the form of a replicator-mutator dynamic[284]. *Social learning* is simply any process through which cultural information is selected and replicated. Individuals can learn on their own, of course, and generate new information on a highly personalised basis – much individual knowledge is created, and subsequently lost, in this way. But for many other purposes, including participating in repeated games, social learning will be faster, more efficient and more effective than individual problem-solving[285]. Social learning would not optimal for a species that needed to adapt to environmental changes occurring faster the lifetime of single individuals – in that setting, evolution would favour agents with highly specialised reasoning abilities because other agents would not be able to convey useful and reliable information about the exploitation of their environment (see Chapter 17: "Outside Context Problems").

As a species for which social learning is our evolutionary niche, humans are astoundingly good imitators. Very young infants are obsessively observational and will imitate adult behaviour many decades before they possess the capacity to use mathematics to solve normal form games. Even adults will subconsciously mirror the body language, speech patterns and

---

[283] Taylor & Jonker (1978) at pgs. 145-156.

[284] For details, see McElreath & Boyd (2007) at pg. 27, and pgs. 206-215; Bowles & Gintis (2011), at pg. 172 and Appendix 7.

[285] Boyd & Richerson (2005) at pg. 111-.

behaviours of other adults (See Chapter 11: "The Learning Orgnism" for more on this topic). In many cases, the fitness risk of deviating from group behaviour simply isn't worth the potential gains of non-conformity.

* * *

In the remainder of this chapter we will formally introduce the theory of cultural group selection, the fourth and final mechanism of positive as-sortivity. In Chapter 1, we provided an overview of the academic controversy over group selection. In the following pages, we will derive the formal mathematical rules governing group selection and discuss whether or not it's a plausible mechanism supporting the evolution of cooperation amongst social species. Remember, the guiding model of group selection is that a population is internally structured into a number of sub-groups, and that there exists an altruistic trait C which lowers the reproductive fitness of individuals that possess it but raises the average fitness of the group of which they are a member. An individual with trait D is not altruistic.

Type C individuals convey a *benefit* (b) on others at a *cost* (c) to itself, such that benefit > cost > 0. When two Type C players meet, their fitness payoffs are *benefit - cost*. When a Type C player meets a Type D player, the Type D player receives the benefit and the Type C player pays the cost without getting anything in return. It's easy to show that this is an anti-cooperation game (Figure 7.1).

Altruism		Player 2	
		C	D
Player 1	C	b-c \\ b-c	b \\ -c
	D	-c \\ b	0 \\ 0

Figure 7.2. Altruism structured as an anti-cooperation game

Assume the population is divided into a number of M sub-groups j = 1,2,3, . . . M comprising proportions q_j of the entire population, each of which is comprised of N individuals i = 1,2,3, . . . N. Let u_{ij} represent the fitness payoff of individual i in group j; u_j the average fitness of group j; and u the average fitness of the entire population. Furthermore, p represents the proportion of Type C in the entire population; p_j the proportion or frequency of Type C in group j; and p_i the probability that member i of group j is Type C[286].

Therefore an individual's expected fitness from an interaction is $u_{ij} = bp_j - cp_{ij}$.

Summing the fitness of each group, we find:

$$u_j = \frac{1}{N} \sum_{i=0}^{i=N} u_{ij} = p_j(b - c)$$

And therefore a group's fitness will vary with the proportion of co-operators such that:

$$\frac{\partial u_j}{\partial p_j} = b - c$$

---

[286] Bowles & Gintis (2011) at pgs. 53-54.

The final relation summarises the effect of the proportion of co-operators in a group on the fitness of group. If b - c is positive, as in altruistic behaviour, then an increasing proportion of co-operators increases the overall fitness of a group, as we expect to find. But if the cost of cooperation is too high, then the proportion of altruists will decrease.

We assume a replicator dynamic in which individuals with fitness higher than the average will preferentially reproduce and comprise an increasing share of the overall population. Under these conditions, the Price equation[287] shows how the frequency of co-operators in the total population will change over time:

$$\frac{\partial p}{\partial t} = \frac{\partial u_j}{dp_j} var(p_j) - c\overline{var}(p_{ij}) = (b - c)var(p_j) - c\overline{var}(p_{ij})$$

Where:

$$var(p_j) = \sum_{j=1}^{j=M} q_j(p_j - p)^2$$

Is the between-group variance, or the expected value of the square of the deviation of each group's proportion of co-operators (p_j) from the mean (p).

And:

$$\overline{var}(p_{ij}) = \sum_{i=1}^{i=N} q_j(p_{ij} - p_j)^2$$

Is the weighted average of the within-group variance.

The Price equation divides the process of replication into two effects. The left hand term represents replication of Type C on the basis of the differential

---

fitness of groups, and the right hand term represents the replication of Type C on the basis of within-group differential fitness. For games where altruism is costly, the inter-group effect is positive and the within-group effect is negative, as we would expect. The proportion of Type C within groups falls over time, but the size of groups with higher proportions of Type C increases, potentially offsetting this effect. Moreover, the Price equation predicts more altruists when *either* the variance between groups grows *or* groups themselves grow more homogenous.

We can re-write the conditions for the evolutionary stability of Type C in familiar terms:

$$\frac{\partial p}{\partial t} \geq 0$$

$$(b-c)var(p_j) - c\overline{var}(p_{ij}) \geq 0$$

$$bvar(p_j) \geq c\left(var(p_j) + \overline{var}(p_{ij})\right)$$

$$\frac{var(p_j)}{var(p_j) + \overline{var}(p_{ij})} \geq \frac{cost}{benefit}$$

Once again, we have recovered an equivalent formulation of Hamilton's Rule, except this time the critical threshold is the *variance ratio*, or the variance between groups as a proportion of the total between-group and in-group variance. The greater this ratio, the more groups are different from one another compared to their internal variation. The variance ratio is expressed in terms of population statistics, but can also be reformulated in terms of the probability of similar agents meeting one another[288]:

$$P(C|C) - P(C|D) \geq \frac{cost}{benefit}$$

In other words, the probability of being paired with another altruist if you

---

[288] Bowles & Gintis (2011), at pgs. 55-56; Aoki (1982) at pgs. 832-842.

are already an altruist (P(C|C)) must be greater than the probability of being pair with an altruist if you are a cheater (P(C|D)). Once again, we see that population structure is critical: it must ensure that co-operators encounter one another more frequently than they encounter defectors. In fact, because of this mathematical equivalency, we can also express kin selection, reciprocal altruism and local interaction in terms of the Price equation under some circumstances. Groups may be physically, genetically or temporally isolated from one another, but the formulae are general enough to describe most population structures.

From the viewpoint of genetic essentialism, group selection imposes very stringent conditions for the evolution of cooperation that are rarely, if ever met in nature. This indeed was the conclusion of Maynard Smith when he first encountered Price's equation and developed his haystack model of group selection[289]. When information is carried by genes, migration of breeding individuals between groups – as occurs in almost all natural species – extinguishes genetic variation between them much faster than mutation generates new variance[290].

Genetic group selection is a particularly poor fit for humans and other higher order primates, who have passed through recent genetic bottlenecks and possess remarkably low genetic variation between groups. Estimates of the genetic variation in human populations produce numbers of the order 0.01-0.04, suggesting that the benefits of in-group cooperation must exceed the costs by a factor of 25-100 times[291] in order to be evolutionarily stable! Even comparisons of the most extreme genetic variation within the entire species only produces estimates only as high as 0.11-0.15[292]; so on a global scale, the variation within any human group is always much larger than the variation between two groups. There are ongoing anthropological and historical debates about whether warfare and group extinction was

---

[289] Maynard Smith (1964)

[290] McElreath & Boyd (2007), Section 6.3.

[291] McElreath & Boyd (2007) at pg. 235.

[292] For example: Esko et al. (2010).

common enough in early human history to make the benefits of cooperation sufficiently high to outweigh this limitation. This debate effective replays the philosophical debate between Hobbes' view of life in the state of nature as bring 'brutal and short' as opposed to Rousseau's 'noble savage'[293].

But the better view is that in order for group selection to be evolutionarily significant, variation, selection and replication can't be limited to genetic mechanisms. Instead, we need an evolutionary system that generates strategic variation between groups much faster than genetic mutation; which offers strong advantages in terms of the exploitation of the physical and social environment; and which is relatively immune to the migration of breeding individuals between groups. Culture fits the bill nicely[294]: cultural variation takes place faster and more stochastically than genetic drift; social learning can offer significant advantages in terms of the exploitation of the natural environment; and although breeding individuals contribute their DNA to the family groups they migrate to, they are highly likely to conform to the culture of their new family group – in other words, their child is guaranteed to receive half an out-group's DNA, but much less of its culture.

For this reason, group selection is often treated as being virtually synonymous with cultural evolution[295], since it is mainly after a social species develops a biological substructure that supports the emergence of culture that sufficient variance develop between groups to make intra-group competition a major or even dominant factor in the evolution of cooperation. If we think of Hamilton's Rule in simple, reductionist terms as applying only to genetic relatedness, then cultural group selection is a theory of the evolution of cooperation based on cultural differentiation.

* * *

---

[293] Turchin (2016); Boyd & Richerson (2005) at pg. 208-209; Sapolsky (2017) at pgs. 305-326; Gintis (2017) at pgs. 30-31.

[294] Cavalli-Sforza & Feldman (1973) at pgs. 781-804; Cavalli-Sforza & Feldman (1973) at pgs. 42-55; Cavalli-Sforza & Feldman (1981); Boyd & Richerson (1985); Boyd & Richerson (2005) esp. at pg. 203-; Scber & Wilson (1998).

[295] West et al. (2011) at pg. 248.

We have now repeatedly encountered situations in which population struc-ture or *positive assortivity* amongst co-operators can make pro-social outcomes evolutionarily dominant[296]. With perfect assortivity, there would a single stable population state consisting entirely of a single strategy Type. But when a population has a measurable internal differentiation, multiple polymorphic population states may be evolutionarily stable[297].

Figure 7.2 summarises the findings of Chapter 6 & 7 of this book. It replicates table 4.1 from Bowles & Gintis (2011)[298], which constitutes the most remarkable set of findings in evolutionary sociology. Each mechanism listed generates positive assortment between altruists, and when certain conditions are met cooperation becomes evolutionarily favoured. Moreover, while each mechanism generates assortivity along a single dimension of relatedness, each one can conceptually be transformed into any other mechanism (i.e. a family represents a group who you are physically proximate to for an indefinite period of time). We see that there is nothing special about the coefficient of genetic relatedness (r); it is merely an estimate of the likelihood that two social agents will share the same strategy.

Figure 7.2. Positive Assortative Mechanisms in Evolutionary Games			
Model	Rule	Interpretation	Assortive Mechanism
Kin selection (Hamilton's Rule)	$r > \dfrac{cost}{benefit}$	r is average genetic relatedness amongst interacting individuals.	Bearer of genetic trait C interacts more frequently with other bearers of the same trait
Reciprocal altruism	$\partial \geq \dfrac{cost}{benefit}$	∂ is the probability that an interaction will continue.	Probability that interactions will be with a partner who previously cooperated.
Local interaction	$\dfrac{1}{k} > \dfrac{cost}{benefit}$	k is the number of partners an individual interacts with.	Chance of interacting with social network is higher than whole population.
Group selection	$\dfrac{var(p_j)}{var(p_j) + var(p_{ij})} \geq \dfrac{cost}{benefit}$	The ratio of between-group variance to total variance.	Probability of interacting with strategy C is higher than meeting strategy D.

Cooperative behaviour will only emerge when it co-evolves with a biological, social and environmental substructure that encourages positive assortment

---

[296] Eshel & Cavalli-Sforza (1982) at pgs. 1331-1335.

[297] Skyrms (2014) at pg. 20.

[298] Bowles & Gintis (2011), at pg. 75.

amongst altruists. For most natural species, genetic relatedness and physical proximity are sufficient; in social animals that live in groups of non-related individuals, the capacity of individual to remember past behaviour and their place in the social hierarchy is critical; finally, to support cooperation at a civilizational scale beyond the capacity of any one individual to keep track of the reputation of its members, reliable markers of group delineation are necessary, and even then, a species must possess sufficient capacity for cumulative non-genetic information transmission and inheritance to generate high levels of inter-group variation. Culture, in other words, cannot support cooperation without the necessary biology evolving first.

The question is then what marks a 'group' for the purposes of cultural group selection? Clearly it cannot be merely genetic relatedness, or living together in physical proximity, or being part of a social network, since all of those effects could be accounted for through other mechanisms and none is sufficient to explain the evolution of cooperation on the scale seen in humans. Altruists have to be able to signal one another reliably that they are members of the same group, in a way that does not leave them vulnerable to exploitation by potential cheaters. The signal of group membership must also be exclusionary, such that members of the group spontaneously exclude out-group members.

Dawkins hypothesised the existence of so-called 'greenbeard' effects: linkages between genes such that the possession of a behavioural trait always generates a second phenotypical trait that serves as a reliable signal of trustworthiness. A gene or tightly linked gene complex that produce cooperative behaviour might have the side-effect of causing a creature to grow [for example] bright green beards that signalled to others that they carry of a copy of the cooperative genotype[299]. Although such effects do exist in nature among single-celled organisms and possibly insects[300], it's unlikely – if not impossible – that genes encoding for both behaviours and

---

[299] West et al. (2011) at pgs. 244-245.

[300] Gardner & West (2010) at pgs. 25-38; West et al. (2011) at pg. 245.

phenotypes in complex species could be reliably selected together *and only together*. Once again, the genetic essentialism is explanatorily insufficient when applied to complex social behaviours.

In cultural systems, markers of group belonging do not need to be encoded genetically: they can be encoded culturally or symbolically[301]. In 2006, Axelrod and the political scientist Ross Hammond performed another simulation of the iterated prisoner's dilemma, except every social agent was arbitrarily assigned (or 'tagged'[302]) one of four different colours[303]. Agents were randomly given strategies that specified what pure strategy to play when meeting every other colour, and strategies were permitted to replicate on the basis of their evolutionary fitness and mutate. Unsurprisingly, cooperative strategies once again ruled the day. But in fully three-quarters of all simulations the dominant strategy was 'ethnocentric', in the sense that it only cooperated with its own colour.

A tag is merely a stable characteristic that is observable by other agents during interactions[304]. Despite the fact the tags in the Axelrod simulations were absolutely arbitrary, and had no effect whatsoever on the payoffs of the game, populations evolved towards states in which a player's tag became the only thing that mattered – precisely because in those simulation such tags, no matter how meaningless, provided a reliable way of signalling group membership. Moreover, the simulations showed the rudiments of inter-group competition, with same-colour groups organising themselves into small clusters and them competing with neighbouring clusters of differently-coloured groups. We will cover this more in Chapter 9: "The Evolution of Society", but this inter-group competition disincentivised cheaters from gaining ground within groups by increasing the rewards of cooperative behaviour.

---

[301] Boyd & Richerson (2005) at pgs. 211-213.

[302] Holland (November 2001) at pg. 441.

[303] Axelrod & Hammond (2006) at pgs. 926-936. Based on earlier work in Riolo, Cohen & Axelrod (2001).

[304] Riolo, Cohen & Axelrod (2001).

This all sounds rather dire, if we consider identity to be something essential or fixed (as were the colours in Axelrod's simulation). Prejudice on the basis of external appearance is one of the more toxic features of human social life, and one that is learned very, very early on in our development. Humans carry with us life-long difficulties in recognising faces with different phenotypes to the ones we were most exposed to with children, and with this recognition difficulty comes affective biases included aversion, fear and even disgust. Skin colour, hair colour, height, body shape, facial features – at one point or another in human history dozens of essentially meaningless physical tags have formed the fault line along which genocidal violence has been committed (see Chapter 14: "The Dark Side of Cooperation").

But humans also have the capability to generate identity variation through cultural artefacts. Language, essential to social life and difficult to learn without long study (from parents, neighbours or repeated partners) is an obvious group marker, but so is clothing, technology, religious symbols, shared stories, beliefs and practices. Think of how we separate ourselves by class on the basis of clothing, the music we listen to and the slightest differences in accents. Posh vowels are the sign of an elite education – hard-to-fake without effort – and the truly cultured can discern the thread count of a suit at a hundred paces. That person on the street with different skin colour, poor quality clothes and using a shopping trolley in a way that no civilized person would is a *stranger* – not be trusted, not to be cooperated with, distrusted, isolated and shunned. We are biologically and culturally predisposed to behave preferentially towards in-group members, and avoid and ostracise those that lack the requisite tags of group membership.

We can't help ourselves: we are machines for the discrimination of difference between ourselves and others and we are very, very good at it[305]. It's of no use moralising this human trait, to see prejudice as inherent vice that must be overcome through education, strict obedience to hierarchies or

---

[305] Boyd & Richerson (2005) at pgs. 221-224; Sandole, "Complexity and Conflict Resolution" in Harrison (ed.) (2006) at pgs. 47-49.

the operation of law. Instead, we have to see what this biological and cultural substructure really is: a tool that allows us to recognise an arbitrarily chosen group of mutual co-operators, and then work with that group altruistically to achieve some collective ends. There's no point in blaming our tools for the terrible ways we behave towards out-groups; rather, it's up to us to decide whether what we have inherited have a finely-honed surgical instrument or a sledgehammer (see Chapter 14: "The Dark Side of Cooperation").

The best kinds of signals are those that convey important information about group membership (high information content) but which are difficult to fake (high salience or quality[306]). Every Muslim in the world could likely acknowledge another by their expression of a shared confession of faith – Islam is a broad, inclusive community. But a declaration of faith is easy to say and religious belief difficult to prove. Some ethnic groups and religious sects encourage circumcision as a costly marker of differentiation. Body modification, in fact, is common in tribal societies and scarification often forms part of the ceremonies that mark the transition from childhood to full member of the community. For the same reasons, members of criminal gangs are often heavily tattooed with symbolic representations of their group membership – markers that reinforce both their membership of the gang and their difference from the rest of society.

But at the end of the day, almost any arbitrary sign might do. Religious groups develop rituals that bind those that participate in them together in a shared practice[307]; some ethnic and religious minorities, including Mormons, anabaptists and orthodox Jews, favour certain kinds of highly specific clothing; secret societies have specific patterns of handshakes, signs and symbols by which their members can recognise one another. In the Byzantine Empire – as in modern Europe! – gangs of sports fans wearing different coloured clothes fought violently in the streets.

---

[306] Skyrms calls these two aspects "informational quantity" and "informational content". Skyrms (2010), Chapter 3.

[307] Sosis & Alcorta, "Militants and Martyrs: Evolutionary Perspectives on Religion and Terrorism" in Sagarin & Taylor (eds.) (2008) at pgs. 105-124.

Political parties around the world encourage their followers to positively associate with particular symbols or colours: in the United States, the red states and blue states look at each other with suspicion, as do the red shirts and yellow shirts on the streets of Thailand. Internet subcultures develop slang words and phrases that allow their members to converse and make jokes only they understand. There are symbolic markers of group identity everywhere[308], and it's probably *homo sapiens'* capacity for symbolic thought that distinguished us from other, extinct members of our genus.

But the fact remains that identity markers can be faked, exploited and undermined[309]. Successful religions gain converts[310]; trendy clothing becomes fashionable and desirable; slang spreads in proportion to the influence of its users. The greater the benefits of group membership, the greater the incentive of individuals to acquire the markers of status – even where that status is costly, painful or difficult to obtain. The middle classes spend vast sums giving their children the right schooling, the right social networks, and the right tertiary degrees, because these things have become the markers of membership of the global elite and the keys to extremely beneficial cooperative networks. But they're in an evolutionary arms race: the more agents gain access to a marker of identity, the more likely it is that sub-groups will develop new distinctive markers of exclusiveness in order to preserve their own cooperative advantage.

While genetically and developmentally-influenced markers of ethnicity such as height and skin colour might seem more difficult to fake, their meaning is also culturally determined. In an entirely fair-skinned pop-ulation, for example, red-haired or green-eyed sub-groups may become marginalised (as in the Anglo-Saxon world), just as height and certain facial features were used by the colonial powers to construct ethnic differences in parts of Africa. What's more interesting is that arbitrary tags employed

---

[308] Boyd & Richerson (2005) at pgs. 211-213.

[309] Boyd & Richerson (2005) at pgs. 211-213.

[310] Wilson (2003).

by humans often correlate with economic modes of production and social behaviour: as the Irish and English converged towards the same system of economic production, the salience of the superficial and arbitrary external markers of difference disappeared – suggesting that [economic and] social strategy, not biological tag, is often the most important marker of inter-group difference.

Consider any well-known sport or game, such as basketball, soccer or chess. In many large cities, there are public venues where strangers congregate to play these games against one another recreationally. Sometimes the people who play together are neighbours or have long histories of playing together, but by-and-large if you're a tourist visiting one of these public places you could show up and join a game and have a reasonable expectation that others weren't going to cheat – much less arbitrarily rob or assault you. *So long as you know the rules of the game*, you're welcome. The community of game-players is comprised of those who respect the cultural traditions by which the game is played, who perform the pattern of behaviour expected of game players in good standing. Sport is just a fantastic unifier across nations and cultures because a North Korean soccer team and a French soccer team play by the same rules.

In game theory, a norm, rule or institution can be treated as correlating device – and a stable population state formed when social agents follow that rule is a correlated equilibrium[311]. This terminology is borrowed from a type of game in which a third player – called a "choreographer" – coordinates the strategies of the players. The choreographer need not be an independent being: its role can be performed by shared beliefs and expectations (see the next Chapter: "Beliefs and Signals"). A social norm specifies the actions and behaviours required in order to be a member in good standing of the group. So for instance, the norm that people in Australia drive on the left-hand side of the road choreographs driving behaviour, selecting between the multiple equilibria in a game of chicken and preventing recurrent head-on

---

[311] Aumann (1987) at pgs. 1-18; Binmore (2005), Chapter 1; Gintis (2009), Chapter 8; Gintis (2010) at pgs. 251-263; Bowles & Gintis (2011) at pgs. 89-90.

collisions! A norm, rule or institution is simply a strategy which performs this correlating function without the presence of an authority to enforce compliance.

Let us consider this formally. We meet another player and want to know if they are Type C or Type D. The other player can send a variety of signals about their Type, but these signals are unreliable and if we make a mistake we may end up exploited. But in a an evolutionary sense, **their Type is just their strategy.** As the other player performs the behaviour that we would expect from the having strategy C, our confidence that they are in fact Type C increases over time. When we reciprocate by also performing strategy C, we increase the other player's confidence that we are Type C as well. There may be a combination of beliefs and behaviours which can become mutually constitutive of a stable group identity even in the absence of specialised signals. Following the rules and norms of a group is itself a credible sign that an actor is a member and that cooperative behaviour should be reciprocated.

Sometimes, the willingness to punish cheaters at a cost to yourself and reward cooperation is a stronger signal than cooperation itself. In a population playing an iterated prisoners dilemma, for example, a polymorphism of tit-for-tat and *always cooperate* players would be stable, because the tit-for-tat player is capable of recognising the *always cooperate* players as suitable cooperation partners. Introduce a sub-population of defectors, however, and things change. Now, the tit-for-tat players can distinguish other tit-for-tat players, because they're engaging in moralistic/altruistic punishment of the defectors. Now the *all cooperate* players essentially become free riders on the punishments performed by the tit-for-tat players, who can now choose to exclude them on the basis of a reliable signal as to their Type.

The logic of constitutive group norms has important consequences for our understanding of adaptive rationality. For a society in which group identity is an important assortive mechanism, the fitness of a strategy may not be the same as in a large, well-mixed population. If membership of a group is fitness-enhancing, then compliance with group norms and behaviours may be prioritised even if those norms and behaviours are unrelated to fitness and may be costly for the individual. Sociologists call this the 'logic of appropriateness': group identity determines the strategy or behaviour that is appropriate for members of the group[312]. It is adaptive for social agents to comply with appropriate behaviour regardless of their individual calculation of utility, because group membership is overall fitness-enhancing.

Secondly, a behaviour may be favoured in a structured population because the performance of that behaviour, no matter how irrational, serves as a signal of group identity. As we've noted already, being seen to punish out-group members may be more valuable than actually doing so. This constitutes what is called "performative rationality": an action is performatively rational not because of its direct consequences, but because of the information it conveys to a potential audience about the performer's Type. In other words, the fitness value of an action varies with the social composition of the potential audience: with no audience we might be free to act as egoistic utility-maximisers, but when an audience is present our behaviour changes radically. Psychological studies on humans have demonstrated that being watched dramatically increases pro-social behaviour[313] – indeed any symbolic stand-in for human eyes, including cameras or eyes drawn on walls, can have a measurable impact on individual behaviour[314].

We cannot say that norm-following behaviour is ever irrational – even if the norms in question are entirely symbolic, scientifically unjustifiable or individually costly. Rather, they are adaptively rational from the point of view of the group, because if they enhance or are merely neutral vis-a-vis group fitness, then they will assist the group to thrive in a hostile environment against other groups. Religious charity, for example, may be individually costly or even ruinous – but religions which are successful at concentrating the resources of their members may have a cultural advantage over religions that don't[315].

---

[312] March & Olsen (2011).

[313] Ariely et al.(2009) at pgs. 544-555; Burnham (2003) at pgs. S113-157.

[314] Van der Linden (2011); Dear et al. (2019) at pgs. 269-280.

[315] Wilson (2003)

In summary, the human tendency towards groupishness and xenophobia is not selected for directly, but *assortative strategies in general are.* A group-rational strategy specifies the external signals which serve as reliable markers of identity, but it's the strategy that is subject to selection and adaption on the basis of its fitness. There is nothing special about the identity markers themselves. This is where an evolutionary perspective offers the possibility of transcending the essentialism of identity: because strategies evolve over time in response to a changing conditions whatsignals group identity will also change. *Group identity is not fixed and unchanging, rather it represents a best response to the strategies employed by the other groups in a structured population.*

8

BELIEFS AND SIGNALS

Key Points

- Under conditions of uncertain information, populations at equilibrium develop a self-reinforcing set of common beliefs and mutual expectations.
- A signal is an interaction carrying information which alters the content and level of confidence of an agent's beliefs; Bayes' Theorem relates new information to new beliefs.
- Given social dilemmas arising from mimicry and exploitation, assortivity between agents with the same signalling strategy supports the evolution of pro-social equilibria.

In previous Chapters, we've encountered situations where social agents needed to signal one another about their Type [, or what biologists call a phenotype]. Whether it's kin recognition, reputation mechanisms or group identity, the evolution of cooperation relies on accurate mutual signalling – in social agent's confidence in or 'belief' about their partner's Type (). Since the fitness payoffs from a social interaction depend on an opponent's Type, which is uncertain, such strategic interactions are games of incomplete information. The study of incomplete information interactions is sometimes called epistemic game theory, because the distribution of knowledge and information is fundamental in the same way that population structure is fundamental to evolutionary game theory[316]. This Chapter introduces the final set of mathematical formalism in the book; for readers who are satisfied with the qualitative description of equilibria in evolutionary games from previous Chapters, this one can be skipped and readers should feel comfortable moving on to the second half of the book.

We know from our discussion of Harsanyi's Purification Theorem (recall Chapter 4), that a mixed strategy Nash equilibrium can be treated as *either* the group strategy of a population at equilibrium, *or* an equilibrium in the beliefs (of social agent about their partner's Type[317]). A stable *mutual* equilibrium in beliefs is known formally as a Bayesian Nash equilibrium (for reasons that will soon be clear). Much as every complete information game has at least one Nash equilibrium, every incomplete information game has at least one Bayesian Nash equilibrium[318]. A Bayesian Nash equilibrium is a set of strategies for each Type of player, such that each Type has no incentive to unilaterally deviate from their strategy given their beliefs about the Type of the other(s)[319].

In an incomplete information game, a strategy is dominated for a Type if social agents of that Type would receive a higher fitness payoff by switching strategies (to a different Type). A strategy that is dominant only for a single opponent Type is weakly dominant; a strategy that is dominant regardless of the Type of the opponent is strongly dominant. For this reason, strategies which are able to essentially ignore Type and operate under what John Rawls would have called a veil of ignorance may have an evolutionary advantage over strategies which are reliant on accurately assessing the Type or quality of other players. If such an equilibrium is accessible, it could potentially out-compete strategies which rely on the detailed categorisation and delineation of other social agents.

---

[316] Gintis (2009), especially Chapter 8.

[317] Gintis (2009), at pgs. 138-141; Morrow (1994), Chapter 6.

[318] McCarty & Meirowitz (2007) at pgs. 168-169; Morrow (1994), at pg. 176.

[319] McCarty & Meirowitz (2007), Chapter 6; Osbourne (2004) at pgs. 278-.

Recall the **stag hunt** game from Chapter 3. We know that the symmetric stag hunt is a cooperation game with two Nash equilibria in pure strategies and one mixed strategy equilibrium. In our discussion in Chapter 4, we permitted a hunter's fitness payoff for hunting rabbits to vary by an amount –– representing either variation in satisfaction of their individual preferences. We postulate a population of stag hunters divided into two Types $_i$ = (A, B): Type A is the average hunter, and they have the standard game preferences. Type B, however, is a rabbit hunter with a variation in payoffs from the population mean of = 4. In other words, they really quite enjoy rabbits. (Figure 8.1)

Let us suppose that Player 2, who is an average hunter, is invited to go on a one-shot stag hunt with Player 1. However, they do not know Player 1's Type and Player 1 cannot (yet) send a reliable signal to Player 2. This is an incomplete information game, and the payoff structures are shown in the matrices below. The dashed lined is the standard representation of Player 2's uncertainty about which opponent they are facing.

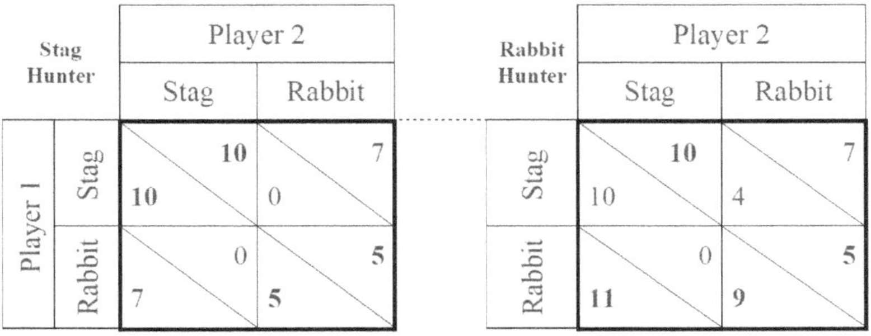

Figure 8.1: A game of imperfect information based on Rousseau's Stag Hunt

If Player 2 is playing against a standard hunter opponent, the game has the usual stag hunt equilibria (the left-hand matrix). However, if Player 2 is up against a rabbit hunter opponent, then the payoffs are structured as an anti-cooperation game which has only a single Nash equilibrium (the right-hand matrix). Player 2 has a belief 0 ≤ ≤ 1 that Player 1 is the same

Type as itself (i.e. $_1$ = A). In other words, is Player 2's subjective estimate of the probability that they are in the world of the left hand matrix, as opposed to the world of the right-hand matrix (which they estimate occurs with probability 1 -).

If Player 1 is a standard player, we know from past experience they have three Nash strategies: pure stag, pure rabbit or a mixed strategy with a probability of hunting stags of 5/8, and a probability of hunting rabbits with a probability of 3/8. If on the other hand they are a rabbit hunter, they will always hunt rabbits because hunting stag is a strictly dominated strategy for that Type. But what should Player 2 do at equilibrium, given their uncertainty about Player 1's Type? We will need to find an best response for Player 2 against every potential opponent they might come up against. Each strategy set will constitute a Bayesian Nash equilibrium.

Player 2's expected fitness for hunting stag is:

$$\omega(10) + (1 - \omega)(0) = 10\omega, \text{ if Type A is pure stag.}$$

$$\omega(0) + (1 - \omega)(0) = 0, \text{ if Type A is pure rabbit.}$$

$$\omega\left(\frac{5}{8}(10) + \frac{3}{8}(0)\right) + (1 - \omega)(0) = \frac{25\omega}{4}, \text{ if Type A mixes.}$$

And their expected fitness for hunting rabbit is:

$$\omega(7) + (1 - \omega)(5) = 5 + 2\omega, \text{ if Type A is pure stag.}$$

$$\omega(5) + (1 - \omega)(5) = 1, \text{ if Type A is pure rabbit.}$$

$$\omega\left(\frac{5}{8}(7) + \frac{3}{8}(5)\right) + (1 - \omega)(5) = 5 + \frac{5\omega}{4}, \text{ if Type A mixes.}$$

Let's examine each of these opponents in turn by setting the payoffs to be equal.

Against a pure rabbit hunter Type A, Player 2 will also always hunt rabbit $(1 > 0)$.

For the case in which Type A mixes their behaviour, Player 2 will hunt stag whenever:

$$\frac{25\omega}{4} > 5 + \frac{5\omega}{4}$$

$$\omega > 1. \text{ (i.e. never)}$$

In other words, against an opponent who randomises, Player 2 will always hunt rabbit; their uncertainty about Player 1's Type selects between the available equilibria in the traditional stag hunt – indeed, it pushes Player 2 into the less optimal of two potential outcomes of the hunt.

Against a pure stag hunter, Player 2 will hunt stag if and only if > 5/8, since:

$$10\omega > 5 + 2\omega$$

$$\omega > \frac{5}{8}$$

So hunting rabbit is Player 2's best response if either: a) Type A hunts rabbits, b) Type A mixes their strategy, or most importantly if c) Type A hunts stags *and* Player 2's subjective belief is that they will encounter a Type A player less than 5/8 of the time. In other words, the only condition under which mutual stag hunting is an equilibrium is if Player 2 believes they will meet stag hunters more than 5/8 of the time. So the accessible equilibrium state depends on Player 2's beliefs about the composition of the population; if their beliefs change, so will their strategy.

One implication of the Bayesian equilibrium concept is that in social interactions under conditions of imperfect information, the population states which are stable depends on the subjective beliefs of the agents in the population about the structure of their society. A population with different beliefs may settle into a different evolutionarily stable state, even when playing the same stage game with identical payoffs. If beliefs are transmitted culturally and subject to variation, selection and replication, then two groups can arrive at different evolutionarily stable population strategies under the same material conditions. Beliefs, then, matter just as much or perhaps even more so than environmental constraints. It does not matter if a particular social strategy is more efficient, if we cannot mutually constitute one another's beliefs in such a way as to make it sustainable.

* * *

A signal is merely any interaction between social agents that carries information from one to another[320]. In the modern era, we may intuitively think of signals as electromagnetic waves carrying bits of information, but a signal can be literally any interaction that transmit information. It may be an agent's colour, shape or size (it's 'tag'), a smell or pheromone it emits, the sound it makes or the way it behaves. Every one of these things, even physical characteristics locked in place during an social agent's development, is a signal and if that signal can be received and processed by another social agent then it forms part of a signalling strategy. A signal may be quantitatively described by the magnitude and direction of its effect on the beliefs of the recipient (in much the same way that photons transmit information between charged particles and change their states)[321].

The mathematical rule that relates new signals to new beliefs is known as Bayes' Theorem[322]. The Theorem is used extensively in probability theory and economics and indeed as the basis of an entire branch of meta-philosophy known as Bayesian epistemology. In short, Bayesian acolytes argue that estimates of probability do not measure 'true' facts about the physical universe, but only the subjective beliefs of an observer. Bayes' rule provides a way for social agents to be justified and consistent in their beliefs, since it provides a mathematical formalism for updating beliefs based on new evidence. But overreliance on formalism cannot free us from our everyday social constraints, and in my experience Bayesian epistemology is

---

[320] Gintis (2009), Chapter 8.1.

[321] Skyrms (2019), Chapter 3.

[322] Morrow (1994) at pg. 160.

often used by pedants justify their pre-existing biases. No matter. An stable equilibrium in beliefs may or may not be 'justified', 'true' or 'consistent' in any kind of deep philosophical sense, but it can be *useful*.

Bayes' Theorem is commonly represented as follows:

$$\Pr(A|B) = \frac{\Pr(B|A)\Pr(A)}{\Pr(B)}$$

Expressed in words, this reads: "The probability of A being true given that B occurs is equal to the probability of B occurring if A is true, multiplied by the probability of A being true, divided by the probability of B occurring." For our purposes A is our estimate of our opponent's type, and B is the signal received. Reconsidered like this, $_t$ = Pr(A) is our prior belief about our opponent at time t, and $_{t+1}$ = Pr(A|B) is our posterior belief about our opponent having received a signal at time t + 1.

The effect of a signal in terms of change of beliefs is causes is therefore:

$$\frac{\omega_{t+1}}{\omega_t} = \frac{\Pr(B|A)}{\Pr(B)} = \frac{\Pr(B|A)}{\Pr(B|A)\Pr(A) + \Pr(B|A')\Pr(A')}$$

Where A' is simply the probability notation for "not A" or "A is not true". So we divide the likelihood of receiving the signal B by the sum of the likelihood of receiving the signal if A is true *and* the likelihood of receiving the same signal is A is not true (in other words, a 'false positive').

Let's see how Bayes' Theorem works in practice. Let's say there is a 10 per cent chance that an hospital patient develops cancer. Patients can be examined for cancer through a test that is ninety per cent accurate if the patient has cancer; or in other words, only misses real cancers one time in ten. On the other hand, the same test gives a false positive at about the same error rate. So ten per cent of patients without cancer will receive a positive signal. If a patient receives a positive result, what is our posterior belief that they are actually sick?

Well, we can plug these numbers into Bayes' Rule to find out.

$$\frac{\omega_{t-1}}{\omega_t} = \frac{\Pr(B|A)}{\Pr(B|A) + \Pr(B|A')} = \frac{0.9}{0.9 \times 0.1 + 0.1 \times 0.9} = 5$$

So if our patient's chance of having cancer (given by 'Nature') is 10 per cent, then after receiving a positive test our new estimate that they have cancer is still only 50 per cent. We've gained a considerable amount of confidence in our diagnosis, but are not yet certain. Depending on how severe and risky the treatment is, we may or may not decide that the cancer risk is high enough to take action. Indeed, partially for this reason, in recent years the medical profession has begun to discourage too-frequent testing, because the rate of false positives leads to over-diagnosis and over-medicalisation of patients.

You might fairly ask where these probabilities come from. In most game theory applications, the prior probabilities are given by 'Nature', an independent third party whose information is always accurate and available to all parties[323]. By now, we know that 'Nature' is just a correlating device, and the same role can be performed by shared beliefs, norms and expectations. Bayesians commonly talk in terms of 'common priors', or beliefs about the probability of events that are ubiquitous in a community or population and which serve to anchor everyone's posterior beliefs. But how do we know if common priors are justified: why would we trust beliefs we inherit from the population? Whereas conservatives would tend to naturalise these beliefs and create 'just-so' stories to justify them, Darwinian socialists should historicise them. These beliefs are the product of a the particular path a complex society has taken throughout its history: we must recognise that we are not in the best of all possible worlds, but we can understand how we got to this world from a previous one. See Chapter 17: "The Naturalist Fallacy" for more.

For the purpose of evolutionary game theory, it does not matter at all if beliefs are true or justified. A certain belief may spread to fixation in a population through processes of variation, selection and replication. Or a

---

[323] Gintis (2009), Chapter 8.1.

distribution of varying beliefs in a population could be locally stable until disturbed by a particularly robust shock (think of the effect 9/11 had on the previous balance in liberal democracies between individual rights and collective security). What matters for our purposes is that, at equilibrium, the signals sent and received as part of each social agent's Bayesian strategy have the net effect of sustaining the pre-existing belief structure of the population. If a new belief were to arise and perturb the existing information structure, then beliefs would shortly return to their equilibrium position.

* * *

Our final piece of theory is to incorporate a signalling framework into our strategic games. Consider again the **stag hunt** we used earlier in this Chapter. How would we design a game such that prior to setting out, Player 1 could send a signal that changed Player 2's subjective beliefs? Perhaps if the stag hunt were iterated, and they hunted stag in the first round as a show of trust, they might be more likely to access the stag-hunting equilibrium in future (by changing Player 2's posterior belief about the proportion of stag hunters in the population). Or if, in a **prisoners dilemma**, two prisoners could signal one another prior to being interview by police whether or not they were trustworthy? To generalise, we might think in terms of sequential or iterated games where a player's move in one round signals their Type to the other players – reputation, in this interpretation, is simply a justified belief about another player's Type. In signalling games, the signal does not necessarily have to be a separate action –– an agent's previous behaviour can be a reliable signal. If you previously followed the rules of chess, for example, you are signalling that you are a cooperative fellow chess player.

In iterated or sequential games, the solution concept used by game theorists is the Perfect Bayesian equilibrium. This is the most complex, and final, solution concept we'll use in this book and it relies heavily on ideas we introduced in earlier chapters. A Perfect Bayesian equilibrium is a set of strategies *and beliefs* that is sequentially rational given each player's beliefs, *and* where players update their beliefs between moves using Bayes'

Theorem (their beliefs are consistent)[324]. A strategy is sequentially rational if it is an agent's best response in every information set of the game[325]. Because these are games of incomplete information, an information set is broader than a subgame: it consists of *every subgame an agent might be in* and their beliefs about how likely each subgame is to occur.

Let's see how this works with an very simple example. The game in Figure 8.2 is a version of the Lewis Signalling Game[326], a generic extensive form game commonly used to explore the dynamics of sequential games of incomplete information[327]. We have partially populated this particular game with the payoffs from matching pennies (recall Chapter 4). Subgames come in two Types $_1$ = (C, D): the first Type (C) is a coordination game and players profit if they select the same strategy; the second Type (D) is an anti-coordination game and players profit if they select the opposite strategy to their opponent.

At the beginning of the game Nature (N) selects the subgame to be either Type C with probability or Type D with probability 1 - . Alternatively, Player 2 has a prior belief that they will encounter subgame C with probability and a or subgame D with probability 1 - . Player 1, on the other hand, knows the state of the world accurately.

Player 1 tosses a coin and then sends a signal about which way up the coin has landed to Player 2. This signal may be either accurate and truthful or inaccurate and deliberately deceptive. Subsequent to receiving a signal and updating their beliefs, Player 2 then chooses to either trust the signal and select the matching strategy (M), or distrust the signal and select the opposing face (D). The must do so uncertain about the payoffs that both players will receive as a result of this choice. This signalling game is written out in extensive form as Figure 8.2 below. Dashed lines represent Player 2's

---

[324] McCarty & Meirowitz (2007), at pgs. 210-214; Morrow (1994), at pg. 170-.

[325] Morrow (1994), at pg. 174.

[326] Lewis (1969).

[327] McCarty & Meirowitz (2007), Chapter 8.2; Gintis (2009), Chapter 8.2; Morrow (1994), at pgs. 222-.

uncertainty about which node of the game they are in.

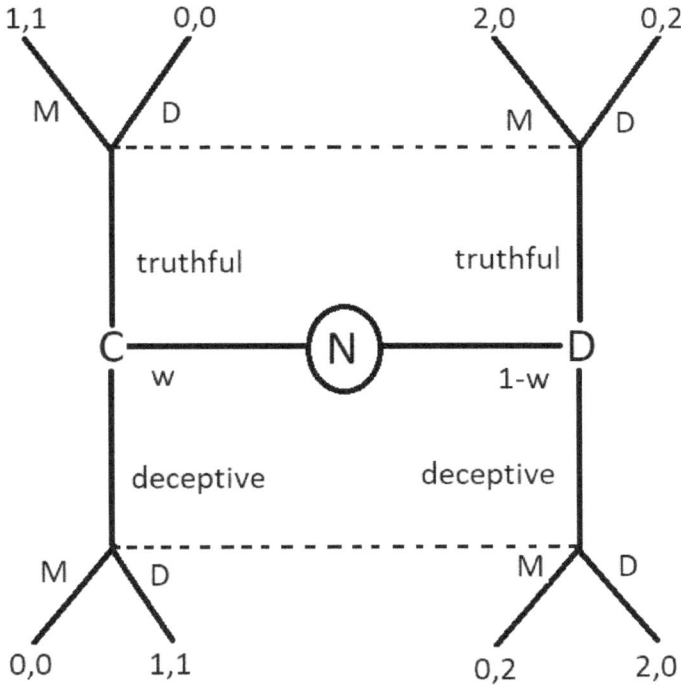

Figure 8.2: A Lewis Signalling Game, a game of incomplete information

Speaking generally, signalling strategies fall into one of two archetypes: **separating strategies** and **pooling strategies**. Separating strategies are such that players of different Types send different signals – signals convey accurate information about Type. Pooling strategies are such that players of the different Types send the same signal – signals carry zero information about the Type of the sender. Separating and pooling strategies are the Bayesian equivalent of pure strategies; we can also conceive of mixed or 'partial' strategies in which Types randomise the signal they send. For the sake of simplicity, we won't deal with partial strategies here.

Let's begin with the separating strategies. If $s_1 = (s_C, s_D)$ is a subgame-dependent strategy, then Player 1 being truthful in subgame C and being deceptive in subgame D (truth, lie) is a separating strategy, as is lying in subgame C and telling the truth in subgame D (lie, truth). Separating equilibria are relatively simple to solve when there are only two signals and two Types: because each Type only sends a single signal, the posterior probability of knowing the opponent's Type is one (i.e. the game is no longer an incomplete information game). If only Player 1 is truthful in subgame C and only deceives in subgame D, then Player 2's best response is always match the call made (M:1 > 0, and 2 > 0). Knowing this, does Player 1 have an incentive to unilaterally deviate from their strategy? Yes! If I'm in subgame D, I would be much better off also telling the truth about the coin toss, because then my partner would match me incorrectly and I could get the anti-coordination payoff.

So what about the (lie, truth) separating strategy, where co-operators lie about the coin toss and cheaters signal honestly? In this case, Player 2 always mistrust the signal they receive (D:1 > 0, and 2 > 0). Now the situation is reversed, and Player 1 has an incentive to deceive in subgame D and pretend to be in subgame C. So there are no separating equilibria to this game. Types cannot accurately signal to one another without the risk of being exploited.

Now let's consider the pooling strategies (truth, truth), and (lie, lie). Updating beliefs in pooling equilibria is also relatively straightforward. Since the signal received by Player 2 carries no information about Player 1's Type, Player 2 does not update their beliefs and their posterior belief is the same as their prior. In the (truth, truth) equilibrium, Player 2 is uncertain which of the two upper nodes of the game they are situated in. Given this, their expected payoffs are as follows:

$$u_M = \omega + (0)(1 - \omega) = \omega$$

$$u_D = \omega(0) + 2(1 - \omega) = 2 - 2\omega$$

This suggests something interesting about Player 2's behaviour. If their prior belief < 2/3, they will *always* defect in this pooling equilibrium. They will only match the true signal received if their estimate that they are playing the coordination game > 2/3. They will implement a mixed strategy, randomising between M and D if and only if = 2/3.

Does Player 1 have an incentive to unilaterally defect from this equilibrium – i.e. to sometimes lie? Their expected payoff if Player 2 defects is precisely zero; they could certainly do better if they sent a false signal. So for beliefs below the critical threshold, the pooling equilibria is not stable. However, this is not true if > 2/3 and Player 2 always matches. In this case, Player 1's expected payoff if they sent a false signal is zero and they would also prefer to follow its strategy and send a true signal. In other words, if players have sufficient confidence they are playing a coordination game, then Player 1 always has an incentive to be truthful and the pooling equilibrium is stable – but if and only if the common prior belief > 2/3. Putting this in population terms, as the frequency of Type D [selfish] players increases, then cooperative equilibrium becomes less likely (see also Chapter 13: "Social Cancers").

Similarly, in the (lie, lie) equilibrium, Player 2 is uncertain which of the two nodes of the game they are situated in. Given this, their expected payoffs are as follows:

$$u_M = \omega(0) + 2(1 - \omega) = 2 - 2\omega$$

$$u_D = \omega + (0)(1 - \omega) = \omega$$

This is clearly simply the inverse of the prior pooling equilibrium. If Player 2's prior belief < 2/3, they will *always* match in this pooling equilibrium. They will only disregard the signal received if their estimate that they are playing the coordination game > 2/3. By the same logic as above, the (lie, lie) pooling equilibrium is also stable if and only if the common prior belief > 2/3.

What have we seen by going through this example? Firstly, it's quite challenging to come up with a strategy that accurately conveys one's Type to other players. In most common signalling games, there's almost always an incentive to mimic the signals sent by other players, in order to access the fitness benefits available to another Type. So the fitness cost of trusting signals is high. Physical mimicry is extraordinarily common in nature, especially amongst parasitic and prey species. And remember the iterated prisoner's dilemma: the strategies that performed best against tit-for-tat were those that imitated its behaviour and only occasionally revealed their hand by trying to exploit it.

Brian Skyrms has pointed out that in games with multiple types of signals, the risk of exploitation decreases as computational requirements increase[328]. Where multiple signals can be transmitted and received, each combination acts as a sort of code or cipher that is more difficult for cheaters to fake. The more mistakes that mimics make in trying to imitate the correct cipher, the worse they will do in evolving populations and the more likely that separating equilibria will be stable. We can even perform simulations where ciphers are allowed to mutate and evolve against one another, much like Axelrod's strategies in the iterated prisoner's dilemma. As with the evolution of arbitrary ethnocentrism, we also see the evolution of arbitrary signalling systems: a population of simulated players with no pre-programmed language can evolve an arbitrary pro-social signalling system through natural selection.

Given that social agents have an incentive to mimic one another and send the same signals, the stability of their social structure is critically dependent on how forgiving a game they are playing. The higher the fitness stakes – the greater the reproductive loss from strategic mistakes – the more critical common prior beliefs become. In order to trust the signals they receive, social agents must believe that games are fair – in a Darwinian sense – more often than not. This contains an important lesson: the more egalitarian the dominant social beliefs are the less important that signals of status are to maintaining social equilibria. But the higher the social status differential, the more attuned that social agents will be to difference – even to arbitrary tags such as race, gender and sexuality that convey no useful

---

[328] Skyrms (2010), Chapters 1 & 4.

information about social role. As mentioned earlier, strategies that are dominant regardless of the Type of opponent are more likely to be adaptive than strategies which rely on accurately assessing the quality of others.

* * *

A Bayesian population equilibrium is characterised by a set of common beliefs and practices that constitutes what Antonio Gramsci would have labelled a cultural hegemony (see the next Chapter). These determine the boundaries of acceptable behaviour amongst members of the community in good standing, and their function is to perpetuate the current distribution of fitness benefits in that community. However, contrary to naïve sociological position, this hegemony is not the conscious creation of social actors at the top of a hierarchy of power, but arises spontaneously as a result of the interaction of strategies and beliefs in an evolving population. It is not necessary that a cultural hegemony exist for the benefit of any particular actors or class, but rather each hegemony is a system from which no one in the population is willing or able to deviate.

As strategic interactions, signalling games are subject to social dilemmas. In an evolving population where differential fitness controls the future frequency of a strategy, strategies that fake their Type, that mimic the successful and exploit the unwary will out-compete with those that trust, are honest about their own type and deal fairly with others. Trusting other people is altruistic, in the sense that it is personally costly or risky, and conveys a benefit on others in the population. Fortunately, the same kinds of solutions that work for other strategic interactions also work for signalling games[329]: mechanisms which increase the positive correlation – including kin selection, reputation, network proximity and group membership – can make cooperative signalling population states accessible via natural selection. We might paraphrase Wilson and speculate that 'deception beats honesty within groups; but honest groups beat dishonest ones'.

---

[329] Skyrms (2010) at pg. 70.

So, unsurprisingly, we find assortative mechanisms in the interpretation of signals in both nature and culture. We are more likely to believe close family members and relatives than we are distant strangers. We are more likely to trust in a signal of another social agent's quality if we've either dealt honestly with that agent in the past or if society establishes a common prior belief that their reputation is impeccable. We are more likely to be honest and open in close physical proximity, than when we are communicating anonymously over the internet. And resting on top of all that, signals themselves can serve as complex signifiers of group identity, such that sending the correct sequence of signals of group membership can unlock access to the substantial benefits of membership and cooperation.

Altruism is an example of what is commonly called in the literature a *costly signal*[330]. A signal is more likely to be considered true if generating it carries a fitness cost to the sender. So we might think of education from an unrelated adult as carrying more reliable information because – if they are not being deliberately deceptive – they are suffering a relative fitness loss by giving it. Especially if, for instance, they've undertaken years of prior training to even get in front of a classroom in the first place. Since less fit strategies cannot make the investment required of a costly signal, the expense or risk of a signal can be taken to indicate its quality or reliability. A local leader who is generous with their food and supplies, offering gifts to the community at their own expense, gains a certain amount of cultural cachet when they are later making suggestions on where and when to fight[331]. The same goes for the general who physically risks their own life in the fighting.

Costly signals are especially effective as signifiers of group membership. As we've already discussed, cultural and religious practices which impose considerable expense on members – including charitable giving, body modification and clothing that signals ostracism from the rest of society

---

[330] Zahavi (1975) at pgs. 205-214.; Grafen (1990) at pgs. 5187-546; Gintis (2009), Chapter 8.4.

[331] Boone (1998) at pgs. 1-21; Bowles & Gintis (2011) at pg. 71.

– can be a reliable marker of group identity and trustworthiness[332]. The more that individuals must sacrifice to be recognised as members in good standing of a group, the larger that group can grow without worrying about admitting potential cheaters and deceivers. And the ultimate costly signal, the ability to persuade members to commit violence, to risk their lives and to die in the name of a group or cause, often serves to increase rather than decrease the attractiveness and longevity of cultural strategies that engage in such violence (more on this Chapter 14: "The Dark Side of Cooperation").

Putting this all together, social groups that develop stable intra-group signalling strategies are likely to outcompete groups that lack such strategies. Inter-group selection applies selective pressure on the signalling equilibria of each group, and favours the survival and reproduction of groups with more cooperative and robust signalling strategies[333]. When political scientists speak of human beings living in 'imagined communities'[334] they are being quite literal: a community is defined by the shared strategies of the individuals who comprise it, the signalling systems by which they signpost their membership, and the common beliefs (or 'priors') which coordinate and choreograph their behaviour.

---

[332] Tuzin, "Ritual violence among the Ilahita Arapesh: the dynamics of moral and religious uncertainty" in Herdt & Keesing (eds.) (1992); Sosis (2000) at pgs. 223-244; Sosis & Alcorta, "Militants and Martyrs: Evolutionary Perspectives on Religion and Terrorism" in Sagarin & Taylor (eds.) (2008) at pgs. 105-124.

[333] Bowles & Gintis (2011) at pg. 72.

[334] Anderson (1983).

II

Application

9

THE EVOLUTION OF SOCIETY

Key Points

- A society is a structured population characterised by patterned regularity in the beliefs and practices of its members – in social species, this
  pattern forms a cultural hegemony.
- When a population transcends the dilemma of social cooperation and
  develops specialised institutions to suppress internal competition, a
  major evolutionary transition occurs and it begins to act as if it were a
  unitary agent at a higher level of selection.
- Hegemony is catalysed by a coalition or group of actors gaining a fitness
  advantage over other coalitions or groups in society by cooperating
  more effectively.

A society is more than a population of randomly interacting actors. A society
is constituted by patterned or *structured* regularity in the behaviour of the
agents that comprise it – taking the form of evolutionarily stable strategic
equilibria. A social species is a special class of agents which have adapted
to life in a society and lack the tools to flourish outside of one. In a society,
agents possess stable beliefs and expectations about social behaviour which
are enforced by mechanisms of positive assortivity that ensure repeated
interaction between mostly similar agents. A society is thus defined by a

characteristic, self-organising order which we term a cultural or strategic hegemony. Its conceptual opposite is Hobbesian anarchy, in which there is a war of all against all and the only stable strategies are either egoistic self-help or domination of the many by a powerful few.

For definitional purposes, order is not limited to the presence of hierarchical authority and is not necessarily maximised when a single strategy set becomes fixed to the exclusion of all others. On the contrary, order can emerge spontaneously from the interaction of roughly equal social agents and can produce an evolutionarily stable state characterised by multiple strategy sets in dynamic equilibrium with one another. While self-interest and kin selection can generate locally altruistic behaviour, a social species has no such limits and may form a society of the whole on the basis of a common symbolic culture. This Chapter sketches an outline of how this occurs at the population level; the following Chapter outlines the ways social agents are individually adapted to life in a society.

In 1995, the theoretical biologist John Maynard Smith, whom we've met before, proposed a history of *major evolutionary transitions* in the story of life on earth[335]. Maynard Smith attempted to explain something unexpected about biological systems: that their level of maximum complexity appears to have increased over time. As we've seen, evolutionary stable strategies can spread rapidly and become fixed such that replicators effectively cease further adaption (until and unless the material environment changes or new mutations arise). We might superficially expect, therefore, that once life evolved the ability to replicate itself indefinitely by absorbing external energy and minerals, evolution would have come to a halt – a sort of biological 'grey goo' scenario[336].

That, of course is not what we see. Even discounting human civilisation, the upper limit of life on this planet is significantly more complex today than

---

[335] Maynard Smith & Szathmary (1995) at pgs. 227-232; Maynard Smith & Szathmary (1995); Maynard Smith & Szathmary (1999). Maynard Smith borrowed the idea from Margulis (1970). Wilson, Ostrom & Cox (2013) at pg. S24-S25.

[336] Drexler (1986).

it was in the deep past[337]. Over hundreds of millions of years, the maximum complexity of biological organisms, the variability in their behaviour, and the overall quantity of genetic information appears to have increased. Natural selection operates today at more levels than it did during the origin of life. On average across the whole biome, life today is not significantly more complex than in the Cambrian Era; but the most complex organisms today have few earlier parallels. It appears that life's behaviour space or strategic freedom increases over very long time horizons. Evolution is a learning system in which population-level knowledge about how to exploit the natural environment accumulates slowly but seemingly inevitably.

Maynard Smith proposed that, although measuring complexity was difficult, several broad stages or transitions could be hypothesised on the basis of theory and the paleontological record. First, self-replicating polymers formed populations of self-replicators; then some polymers joined together, forming complex nucleic acids which replicated as a single unit; then those replicators specialised further into enzymes which do the work of replication and chromosomes which only store information; then cell differentiation occurred, with populations of specialised molecules working together within a single semi-closed chemical environment; then sexual replication arose, in which reproduction was split into separate functions which must necessarily recombine; then groups of cells began working together and specialising their function to form multicellular organisms; then lone organisms began to associate in family structures to aid survival and reproductions; until finally groups of unrelated individuals developed language and cultural replicators so that they began to operate as recognisable societies[338].

As applied to the social life of complex species, we can think of the evolution of large-scale states and empires as a series of staged increases in the size and scale of cooperation. The exponential increase in the complexity

---

[337] For a fuller treatment of this topic, see Sterenly (2007), Chapter 11.

[338] Taken from Maynard Smith & Szathmary (1995) at pgs. 227-232; and Maynard Smith & Szathmary (1999) at pg. 17.

of social organisation in each instance relies on new biological and cultural technologies to catalyse positive assortivity amongst co-operators and generate communities of common interest that could go on to conquer, contend with or absorb other groups. Implicit within both biological and cultural evolution, it seems, is a sense -- however slow, halting and prone to reversal -- of "capital-P" Progress, the very idea that 19th century Victorian philosophers used to bastardise Darwin's theory.

For Maynard Smith, approaching the problem as an evolutionary game theorist, the implications of major transitions in the evolutionary record was even worse[339]. In order for molecules, cells, and individual organisms to specialise in function and begin to operate as a unitary agent at a higher level of complexity, life would have to have 'solved' the dilemma of cooperation – over and over again throughout deep time. The first chromosomes were vulnerable to exploitation by selfish genes that promoted their own replication at the expense of the whole. Cells must cooperate throughout their life to specialise and send the correct chemical signals to support the growth and survival of the whole organism: but cells which break this compact can consume the body's resources and grow exponentially (see Chapter 13: "Social Cancers"). Social animals which live in stag hunting groups will always be vulnerable to the lone opportunist who prefers to catch rabbits. In a multi-level framework, selection pressure at a lower level of organisation will always pose a threat to successful replication at a higher level of organisation[340]. But evolution hints repeatedly that altruistic cooperation dominates selfishness.

Altruism and cooperation *must have evolved in each instance to make an evolutionary transition possible.* We are speaking here of altruism in the game theoretic sense: there can be no suggestion that genes, cells, or most animals are egoistic, rational fitness-maximisers. Instead, we are

---

[339] Maynard Smith & Szathmary (1995) at pgs. 227-232; and Maynard Smith & Szathmary (1999) at pgs. 19-22; Corning (2005); Dietl, "Selection, Security, and Evolutionary International Relations" in Sagarin & Taylor (eds.) (2008) at pgs. 93-96.

[340] Maynard Smith & Szathmary (1995) at pg. 227.

speaking of behaviours that confer a fitness advantage on other agents at a fitness cost to themselves. Complex cooperative behaviour is not exclusively a phenomenon which takes place in human communities: instead, it is an recurrent organising principle that is embedded in the history of life itself. Large-scale sociability is not the exclusive preserve of humans, with our high-level cognitive abilities and capacity for morality and reason. Rather, *morality and social reasoning* are themselves simply the highest-order expression of an apparent mathematical dominance of altruistic strategies in evolutionary games.

Maynard Smith identified a number of features that define a major evolutionary transition. Firstly, major transitions are characterised by role specialisation and a 'division of labour' amongst social agents. Individuals cooperating together in defined social roles can achieve a higher fitness payoff for the group than everybody being in it for themselves -- as we see repeatedly in the structure of human social, political and economic communities. Secondly, at the moment of transition the individuals which comprise a population lose the capacity to independently self-replicate. In a human sense, we can imagine how precipitously human life expectancy would drop if the structures of social life were dissolved – recall our earlier discussion of the disastrous consequences that follow when human beings are isolated in alien environments. Thirdly, Maynard Smith noted that major evolutionary transitions were characterised by the codification of a method of controlling defection, such that any selfish, exploitative behaviour was strongly suppressed [although never completely eliminated][341]. It is these common features which will form the central focus of the remainder of this Chapter.

* * *

In 1986, the political scientist Robert Axelrod published a follow-up to his

---

[341] Wilson, Ostrom & Cox (2013) at pg. S24-S25.

famous simulation of the iterated prisoners dilemma[342]. Axelrod argued in now-familiar terms that strategies (or 'norms') determine the structure of social life, and that stable norms could evolve through either biological or cultural evolutionary processes. A social norm is simply a rule or principle that specifies how agents *should* behave. In Axelrod's norms game, a player who defects for individual advantage can be punished by other players, at a rate set by their *vengefulness – an adaptive trait*. Punishment is effective in reducing the fitness advantage of defection, but is costly to the punisher [i.e. punishment is altruistic].

We have already seen behaviour similar to this in the iterated prisoners dilemma (recall Chapter 6). Punishment is simply a conditional action strategy that triggers altruistic behaviour on the basis the of the actions of others. A rational player would never choose to punish defectors. Axelrod indeed found that in a large, well-mixed population rates of *vengefulness* tended to evolve rapidly to zero – altruistic punishment was not individually rational[343]. The same result is seen when real people play economic games requiring altruistic punishment[344]. The evolutionary stable strategy was also the Nash equilibrium (recall that tit-for-tat is not a Nash equilibrium because of the incentive to unilaterally forgive). And in the absence of any punishment, "everyone defects" usually became the dominant population state.

Axelrod theorised a number of mechanisms to escape this dilemma, including the existence of fixed social networks, reputation and other assortative mechanisms with which we are now very familiar. But the central theoretical issue he identified were the relative plausibility of either hierarchical authority (or 'dominance') or spontaneous self-organisation. In versions of the norms game where some social actors possess dispropor-tionate power over outcomes, those actors can punish at little relative cost to themselves, selectively punish only that that oppose their interests, and

---

[342] Axelrod (1986).

[343] Dunbar (2014) at pg. 312.

[344] Fehr & Gachter (2000) at pgs. 980-994.

withhold beneficial cooperation from hold-outs. There's an abiding debate in political science as to whether every social norm on is the product of coercion by powerful actors. Are hierarchy and inequality necessary social order? Or in other words, is every social or cultural hegemony inherently hierarchical?

Most work applying Axelrod's model employs some variant of the public goods game (which we first met in Chapter 3) as the basic model of social life. The public goods game is simply an N-player anti-cooperation game, in which a group of agents choose whether to contribute to a collective endeavour. No agent can prevent another from accessing public benefits [they are non-excludable] so that even when an agent fails to contribute to the common pool, they will receive a share of the public good. Such players are labelled free-riders, and this particular social dilemma is often called the free-rider problem.

The free-rider problem lies at the core of Garret Hardin's tragedy of the commons[345], which must rank among the foundational myths of modern capitalism (although Hardin was superficially an environmentalist, he was also a Malthusian, a genetic essentialist and a promoter of social Darwinism – an 'eco-fascist'). If the cooperative provision of public goods inevitably collapses, then the only alternative is for individuals to dissolve their society and divide common resources into private property, with the boundaries of that property enforceable through Hobbesian violence or by the coercive institutions of the state. Rather than a community ruled by common norms, each property owner becomes a sovereign unto themselves, responsible only to self-regard, no longer a social being at all.

In the standard hegemonic picture[346], which owes its development to the economist Mancur Olson[347], norms supporting the provision of common pool resources evolve only when they take the form of a 'club good'. A club

---

[345] Hardin(1968) at pgs. 1243-1248; Sethi & Somanathan (1996) at pgs. 766-788; Greene (2013), Chapter 1.

[346] Harsanyi (1969) at pgs. 512-538; Kindelberger (1973); Gilpin (1981).

[347] Olson (1965); Olson & Zeckhauser (1966) at pgs. 266-279; Ostrom (2000) at pgs. 137-158.

good's benefits are available only to certain individuals (hence a 'club') and not the community as a whole. Would-be hegemons – either dominant primates, feudal warlords or powerful nation-states –– form alliances to establish their rule over a population, and then distribute benefits to their supporters to maintain their allegiance. The establishment of social norms by the hegemon, even norms that materially benefit other actors, are ultimately a selfish expression of hegemon's ability to seize and maintain political power. They punish other actors who did not support their rise by excluding them from the 'club'. But these kinds of regimes have high information and monitoring requirements, and are potentially rigid and unstable as power shifts and alliances change. Dominance hierarchies tend to be unstable and ephemeral – just ask a chimpanzee.

Early in his career, the game theorist and international relations scholar Duncan Snidal showed that powerful actors should be willing to unilaterally supply public goods at a cost to themselves in each of the four Zeeman games if doing so maximised their *relative* payoff[348]. That is, weaker social actors might gain from free-riding on the hegemon, but so long as the hegemon remained relatively more successful the social order they provided could be self-sustaining. From an evolutionary sociology, why this should be so is intuitive: it is the relative fitness that determine a strategy's reproductive success via the replicator dynamic. It's in the fitness interest of a would-be hegemon to establish social orders and through cultural selection, these cooperative regimes can stabilise.

Most public goods models in political science tend to build-in the role of powerful actors like this, be they hegemons, 'elites', or 'political en-trepreneurs'. These actors are considered a categorically different Type of social agent and have access to a unique strategy set that permits them to select the terms of a social order and enforce that order through punishment. So for instance, Fearon & Laitin's model of in-group policing includes an authority who carries the cost of monitoring their own community and

---

[348] Snidal (1985) at pgs. 579-614; Snidal (1991) at pgs. 701-26.

who is able to identify and punish bad actors[349]. Bhavnani's model of inter-group violence ascribes political extremists disproportionate social influence and more opportunities to influence other actors[350]. And Stone et al.'s general iterated public goods game allows a hegemonic player to declare a 'punishment' round if and when contributions fall below a specific level, withholding their own provision of collective goods in order to reduce the fitness of free-riders[351].

On the other hand, the biologists Hintze & Adami have developed an iterated public goods game in which the decision to punish is democratised[352]. In other words, every player can choose to punish independently [the strategy of every agent includes a version of Axelrod's *vengefulness*] regardless of their level of resources, and there are no categorically different Types of players (i.e. no baked-in hegemons). They showed that even in the absence of a single dominant social actor, a *coalition* of cooperative players who positively associate with one another can trigger a phase transition from the *all defect* to the *all cooperate* population state (and vice-versa: a sufficiently large group of defectors working together can trigger a transition in the other direction – see Chapter 13: "Social Cancers"). In other words, vengefulness does not *necessarily* fall to zero if altruistic punishers can associate with one another.

In scientific parlance, a phase transition occurs when a material's properties change rapidly from one state into another. When liquid water evaporates into steam, the molecules remain the same but the properties of the substance suddenly change. Strategic change in the behaviour of social agents happens in much the same way. The players in the game are the same, but once a critical threshold is crossed their behaviour and that of the population as a whole is radically different. Biological evolution sometimes

---

[349] Fearon & Laitin (1996) at pgs. 715-735.

[350] Bhavnani & Backer (2000) at pgs. 283-306; Bhavnani (2006) at pgs. 651-669.

[351] Stone et al., (2008) at pg. 335-.

[352] Hintze & Adami (2015); Adami et al. (2016) at pg. 1. See also similar work in Ye et al. (2011).

operates similarly – think of Gould's theory of punctuated equilibria[353]. Mutations accrue gradually and the genetic content of a new species is, at least at first highly similar to that of its forebears, but changes in its behaviour and body plan can emerge comparatively suddenly. The politics of social species display phase transitions between strategic equilibria – for long periods of history, nothing seems to change very much, then suddenly, everything changes all at once[354].

Hintze & Adami's model also demonstrated that a widespread expectation of democratic punishment lowers the payoff thresholds for beneficial cooperation to emerge, so that populations can self-organise under a wider variety of environmental circumstances. The threat of punishment acts as a sort of 'normative potential field', incentivising the alignment of social actors in a cooperative direction[355] – even when material conditions change and a population should in theory flip into Hobbesian anarchy.

Under ideal conditions, very few social agents actually have to follow through and pay the cost of punishment as the mere possibility of punishment – even as a pure threat – is sufficient to deter would-be free-riders. Demonstrative punishments, performed occasionally and selectively against defectors, sustain the belief that all future cheating will be punished, even if in reality mass spontaneous rebellions could not possibly be adequately suppressed (as many hegemons discover, to their chagrin). An expectation of punishment reverses the collective action problem, such that it is *defectors* who must cooperate to achieve their aims. So long as cheaters do not comprise a sufficiently large share of the population, or are not networked together in such a way through kinship or relations of proximity which permit them to work together effectively, social norms may therefore be evolutionarily stable without widespread coercion.

---

[353] Gould & Eldredge (1977) at pgs. 115-151.

[354] A quote attributed to C.S. Lewis: "Day by day nothing changes, but when you look back everything is different".

[355] Hintze & Adami (2018)

What these models all show is that the evolution of cooperation is histori-cally contingent and path-dependent. In a large, well-mixed population, we could not guarantee its evolutionary dominance. Strategic randomness is likely to inhibit the evolution of altruistic social orders *unless* altruists are initially grouped together by some mechanism, as Axelrod found in his initial work on the iterated prisoners dilemma. The evolution of cooperation relies on stochastic events bringing together altruistic actors of sufficient size and influence to catalyse the transformation of the rest of the population into the cooperative equilibrium[356]. But after such a major evolutionary transition has occurred, a cooperative strategy becomes 'annealed' and robust to some later shocks, unless they are of a truly significant scale. Large scale social organisation is difficult to achieve, but once it evolves it provokes a whole series of changes in the environment that make it difficult to reverse.

This body of work neatly brings together several unrelated observations about the nature of cultural hegemony. The political scientist Robert Keohane had already argued that 'coalitions' – sub-groups of co-operators brought together by other factors including cultural similarity –– could act to maintain a social order[357]. And we know from evolutionary game theory that a population structure that generates positive assortivity amongst co-operators supports the evolution of stable cooperative population states. Once a cooperative coalition of sufficient size has formed, evolutionary pressures between sub-groups in the population will favour those that cooperate within themselves most effectively – including via altruistic punishment. Indeed, in some senses we can think of dominant would-be hegemons as a kind of individual-as-coalition: the genes of the alpha animal, and the institutions of the imperial state, work together more effectively and control more resources than those of their competitors.

There's compelling evidence of the power of coalitional behaviour in our

---

[356] Boyd (1989) at pgs. 47-56; Wu & Axelrod, "How to Cope with Noise in the Iterated Prisoner's Dilemma" in Axelrod (ed.) (1997) at pg. 33.

[357] Keohane (1984).

own species' evolution. Amongst many animals, including our own closest relatives, dominant individuals use violence, alliances and intimidation to established social orders that are stable until another individual of comparable strength, brutality and policy savvy comes along[358]. Anthropological evidence, however, strongly suggests that early human populations did not work this way – that humans tended to band together to overthrow potential tyrants and punish or ostracise those who disturb the communal peace[359]. Our unusual shoulder joints, seemingly adapted for throwing, provided a way for less physically powerful members of a group to use stones and other weapons at range to safely challenge and dispose of would-be tyrants – in a likely example of cultural behaviours helping in part to shape our physical capabilities[360]. Throwing weapons made early hominin societies less hierarchical and more egalitarian, reducing the importance of physical strength and inter-personal violence, and incentivising the kind of coalition-building that stabilised group cooperation.

In summary, the establishment of a hegemonic social order catalyses evolutionary transitions to ever-higher levels of organisation. This hegemonic order is generated by selection among different social coalitions, with their differential degrees of internal organisation and self-cooperation leading to differential coalition fitness. Democratic politics in the modern nation-state can be understood in precisely these terms. Hegemony may be established by particularly powerful individual agents acting alone, but is far more likely to consist of groups of individuals brought together by assortative social mechanisms operating at a lower level of organisation – including kinship, or social or geographic networks. Each potential coalition self-organises its affairs, and those coalitions which are most fit collectively can spread their norms and practices to others in the population.

* * *

---

[358] Turchin (2016), Chapter IV.

[359] Boehm (2001); Witt & Schwesinger (2013) at pgs. S33-S44.

[360] Gintis (2017) at pgs. 26-29, 35.

The democratisation of punishment – in which every member of society participates in the disciplining of rogue members – is effective but inefficient at scale. Looking at the various forms of human social organisation, we see democratic punishment only in relatively rare situations: amongst pre-modern peoples, among the society of nation-states which lack institutional mechanisms to restrain aggression, in communities where the rule of law has broken down and in relatively small-scale social groups such as informal associations, small workplaces and democratic gatherings. In all these situations, everyone must act to punish strategic deviance because otherwise the cooperation necessary for the group to continue to exist would cease to function. What these situations have in common is their small population size and the relative ease of detecting cheaters.

What we see in larger-scale societies, however, is something different. Cheaters are potentially more likely to positively assort with one another than potential punishers. So instead of democratic punishment, we find specialised institutions engaging in social monitoring and enforcement of strategic cohesion. By *specialised*, we simply mean they perform a unique strategic variant. An institution is a specialised norm – not defined by a particular building, a particular form of internal-organisation or, *contra* Weber, a particular form of authority. An institution, like a norm, is a strategy – but one that performs a unique social role. A social species which develops a norm against interpersonal violence could, in theory, enforce that norm through democratic punishment. But a sufficiently large-scale society can develop a specialised institution – a group of social actors with a characteristic strategy set – with a comparative advantage in the investigation and punishment of violence. Moderns call this the 'police'.

Specialised institutions are probably necessary to solve the dilemma of cooperation in large populations. We've seen, for instance, that reputation mechanisms can catalyse cooperation in populations whose size exceeds the cognitive capacity of group members to memorise the reputation of every individual. Beyond that cognitive limit [Dunbar's number in humans], institutions can monitor the behaviour of members of the group and disseminate signals about their social standing. Institutions are the veins through which information flows in large populations whose members cannot possibly be acquainted with one another. Institutions can also possess the power to categorise Types, specifying the strategic behaviour to be expected of certain actors in certain situations and doling out punishments for those that deviate from their role[361]. Institutions establish the ground rules for bargaining games, and shape the distribution of resources by guaranteeing certain minimum rights or maximum relative individual advantage.

An institution, and the social actors who constitute it by demonstrating the characteristic behavioural strategy of membership, exist as part of a wider evolutionarily stable population[362]. A society may only need a small number of specialised criminal investigators, but the presence of those investigators renders the overall population more fit. As with any strategy in an evolving population, the existence of a given institution depends on whether its replication is evolutionarily favoured in the presence of alternative strategies. An institution must not only replenish itself by socialising new members into its practices, but must inhabit a strategic environment that is supportive of its social role (for example, education, media and/or propaganda) and where potential rivals (for example, corrupt norms that favour kin or close personal networks over the universal and impartial enforcement of laws) are weak.

Institutions fit into Maynard Smith's schema of evolutionary transitions, in the sense that each is a specialised body which is not capable of reproduction outside the context of the population of the whole. An institution is both literally and figuratively an organ of the social body. Once a society is characterised by an interlocking system of institutions such that that the population operates as a cooperative whole and is largely resilient to external shocks, we can say that a major evolutionary transition has

---

[361] Jenkins (2000) at pgs. 7-25.

[362] "Institution" is just a name we give to certain parts of certain kinds of equilibria". Calvert, "Rational actors, equilibrium, and social institutions" Knight & Sened (eds.) (1995) at pgs. 22-23.

occurred.

$$* * *$$

While there are many institutional forms which may be evolutionarily adaptive under particular forms of social organisation and material circumstance, this book is primarily interested in those institutional forms which solve collective action problems. Perhaps the most importance economist of the last fifty years was the woman who first answered this question, and in doing so decisively demolished Hardin's tragedy of the commons. Elinor Ostrom, a game theorist, founder in the field of institutional economics and the only woman to so far win the Nobel Prize in that discipline, convincingly demonstrated using both theory and extensive fieldwork in real communities that the tragedy of the commons was in fact relatively easy to solve, even in the absence of private property rights, and that many human groups in diverse geographic and social settings were able to establish social institutions to manage common pool resources for the benefit of every member their community[363].

Ostrom argued that there were at least eight 'design principles' characteristic of successful collective action strategies[364]. There have been various formulations of these principles, but an indicative list includes the following:

1. Strong and clearly defined group identity, specifying who is permitted to access benefits of community membership;
2. Economic production is adapted for local environmental conditions; in game theoretic terms, the synergy ratio (r) delivers a return on investment sufficient to catalyse cooperation;

---

[363] Ostrom, (1990); Sethi & Somanathan (1996) at pgs. 766-788; Ostrom (2000) at pgs. 137-158; Waring & Smaldino (2017) at pgs. 524-532.

[364] Adapted from Ostrom (2000) at pgs. 137-158; Ostrom (2010) at pgs. 1-33; Ostrom & Janssen (2010); Wilson, Ostrom & Cox (2013) at pgs. S21-S32; Wilson (2015) at pg. 12.

3. Institutions exist for collective choice, which permits wide participation in decision-making;

4. Local self-determination, in the sense that decisions are made by those most closely affected by them and in possession of the best local knowledge about the environment.

5. Effective monitoring of the community and the accurate identification of cheaters;

6. Graduated punishment of defectors, up to and including banishment from the community;

7. Institutions for conflict resolution that are cheap and easy to access; and

8. Effective coordination between different institutions and in nested networks across different levels of social organisation.

Ostrom's design principles are intriguing to interpret in light of evolutionary sociology. In Rule 1, we see the need for positive assortivity amongst co-operators, in Rule 2, the necessity for material constraints to support a particular mode of economic production. Rules 3 & 4 argue for the evolutionary dominance of something like the fundamentals of democracy, whereas Rules 5-7 set up something approaching the modern idea of an executive government, criminal and private law. In other words, the democratic nation-state represents the highest level of organic social organisation yet achieved by life on Earth. Through cultural evolution we have developed well-adapted principles for the collective management of collective action problems at the scale of tens or hundreds of millions of citizens; the modern democratic state represents the most recent major evolutionary transition in cosmic history.

The state is not a separate institution, or tool of elite oppression. The state is an organism consisting of a set of interlocking social institutions that cooperate with one another at least effectively enough that the state's population see themselves as part of a single community with a single fate (and by corollary that citizens of other states are outside that compact: see

Chapter 14: "The Dark Side of Cooperation")[365]. By employing specialised organs of internal governance and suppressing potentially harmful competition within itself, the state is able to act as a unitary actor in competition with other states. That selection between states in turns generates selective pressures on state institutions, compelling them to work together more efficiently or else see the whole organism defeated and collapsed. The strategic reproduction of every norm and law, of every individual, group and institution depends on the evolutionary adaptiveness of the whole – their individual behaviours can no longer replicate themselves outside the body of the community. As a consequence, individuals are not free to pursue solely their own selfish interests – they must adapt to social life and learn to cooperate with others, or go extinct. In the nineteenth century, the early sociologist Emile Durkheim presciently called such a social order 'organic solidarity.'[366]

We might thus conceive of the evolution of society as (randomised and historically-contingent) progression through a series of abstracted modes of internal self-organisation. A body of agents constitutes a *system* when it becomes a defined population interacting under conditions of strategic interdependence. It becomes a *regime* when a regular order is established which delivers a specified set of benefits to a restricted set of beneficiaries, typically organised around a specific hegemon or hegemonic coalition. A *society* is a complex organism with specialised roles and a characteristic social structure that is evolutionarily stable, deviation from which is controlled by the threat or expectation of punishment. Finally, a *community* is a society in which social agents take the characteristic social strategy as their identity and comply with social norms performatively rather than out of mere self-interest.

It is important to note that thanks to multi-level selection these developments may be partial and evolve at different rates in different part of the social organism. For instance, in a society characterised by a fully

---

[365] Harrison, "Thinking About the World We Make" in Harrison (ed.) (2006) at pgs. 8-9.

[366] Durkheim, "The Division of Labour in Society" (1893).

developed shared communal identity, the distribution of economic goods may take place under a legal regime with specified beneficiaries. In the same society, a kin or spatial networks may share the burden of maintaining public spaces ard participants in a market may be bound to common rules through self-interested adherence to economic forces. Each institution's fitness is determined by both its own internal organisation and how it fits into the broader structures of the social organism. Social institutions may even collapse and fail, if challenged by a sufficient number of cheaters or if its own interral processes were not effective in controlling defections. Institutional failure will only affect society as whole if other institutions are unable to adapt to its absence; so we find that a certain degree of turnover in the corporate sector is healthy, ensuring that only the most fit producers survive, whereas on the other hand the collapse of banks, the healthcare system or the police can presage a broad societal collapse.

In a community, order (patterned regularity in behaviour) is a public good and its spontaneous generation has three core distinctive criteria. Firstly, the provision of public order is indivisible, in the sense that no member of the community is excluded from enjoying its benefits. Individuals who are not so entitled (for instance: tourists and other visitors) are by definition outside the community. Secondly, social agents collectively supply order on the basis of diffuse reciprocity. We have already discussed direct reciprocity (in which we treat others on the basis of the way they have treated us) and indirect reciprocity (in which we treat others on the basis of their social standing) before. Diffuse reciprocity goes one step further by encouraging a default position of trust and cooperation with everyone, even strangers and even those who reputation is poor or unknown, on the basis that this is only way in a large population to ensure the rough equivalence of benefits for all actors in all time periods[367].

Thirdly, and perhaps most importantly, spontaneous order is characterised by the shared expectation that force (violent self-help) will not be employed in the ordinary course of events. Violence and force may indeed

---

[367] Alexander (1987).

form part of a social order – indeed, in some sense, they must: nature does not allow us to accept the idea of uncritical pacifism. But its usage is controlled by public institutions who employ force only in accordance with a defined rule. Social agents must expect that any resort to force outside those contexts authorised by society will result in punishment.

"[W]hat counts is some kind of stability [and] the nature of the forces that secure it. . . Given certain assumptions specifying a reasonable human psychology and the normal conditions of human life, those that grow up under [certain] institutions acquire . . . a reasoned allegiance to those institutions sufficient to render them stable. Expressed another way, citizens' sense of justice, given their traits of character and interests as formed by living under a social structure, *is strong enough to resist the normal tendencies to injustice [self-interest]."*[368] [Rawls, Political Liberalism].

A liberal philosopher like Rawls would say that a social order to which people consent is legitimate but in the context of adaptive rationality our notions of consent and freedom need refinement (see Chapter 18: "Freedom is Scary"). Citizens can choose to withdraw their consent and rebel against the existing order if they really want to. But for most people, most of the time, social compliance is implicit and constructed through performance of expected social roles.

In this way, Marxists and other radical progressives have had a better understanding of culture and its role in social organisation than liberals. As Thomas Paine wrote: *"[M]an is so naturally a creature of society that it is almost impossible to put him out of it."*[369] Marx theorised that the only way to change culture in the long term would be to transform the so-called 'base' of society: its environmental conditions, material basis and mode of production[370]. Changing the beliefs and practices of a society meant changing its material

---

[368] Rawls (1993) at pg. 142.

[369] Paine, "Rights of Man, Part Two, Chapter I" (1791).

[370] Marx, "A Contribution to the Critique of Political Economy" (1859).

conditions. For Marx and the scientific socialists, cultural adaption to changing modes of production was inevitable: as capitalism transformed modern societies, it was laying the seeds of its own inevitable demise by eroding the institutions that legitimised and reproduced it. Later socialist theorists have grappled with the failure of this transformation to occur in the way Marx foresaw.

The Italian communist leader Antonio Gramsci, who died imprisoned by Mussolini's fascist regime, recognised that hegemony was *both* direct domination of society by a small group *and* the spontaneous consent granted by the population to the general direction of social life[371]. Gramsci was somewhat critical of Marx's determinism, and saw social evolution as a path-dependent and historically-contingent process. Since the mode of production is itself a social construct, reliant upon particular patterns of social relations, legal regimes and the threat of force, the base and superstructure tend to evolve and adapt together as a part of a cohesive social whole. Neither changing material conditions nor changing minds alone is sufficient to catalyse evolutionary change – instead, each adapts to the other in a way that is generally anti-fragile and will tend to return its equilibrium point if perturbed[372].

Gramsci argued that it was insufficient to overthrow the domination of the powerful and transform the political and economic institutions of their rule. Existing cultural practice as embodied in the identity and 'common sense' of ordinary people would persist. Similar forms of social order would re-emerge spontaneously, and possibly in forms inferior to, less efficient and less cooperative than those previously overthrown. Indeed, what the twentieth century witnessed was the continual adaption of liberal capitalism even as its economic base shifted radically beyond the industrial world familiar to Marx. Cultural evolution has accompanied technological change, and capitalism has fed its relentless need for more workers and consumers by incorporating previously marginalised groups. Evolutionary socialists

---

[371] Gramsci, "Selections from the Prison Notebooks" ElecBooks (1999).

[372] Taleb (2012).

can recognise this outcome as an adaptive system at work, even as they seek to find ways to shift its course.

If the central problem of social organisation is how we sustain cooperation at large scales, then evolution demonstrates that this problem can be readily solved. Only by building inclusive communities and egalitarian institutions of governance can a group or population sustain the altruistic social behaviour necessary for it to survive in competition with other groups. People are not inherently self-interested, utility-maximising rationalists – they are socially-adapted animals whose practices and beliefs develop through social interaction. Selfish behaviour is adduced through social structures which promote its development – and altruistic behaviour also depends on the erection of supportive cultural norms and institutions. The mechanics of those adaptions forms the subject of our next Chapter.

10

MEDIOCRE INDIVIDUALS, EXCEPTIONAL SPECIES

Key Points

- Human cognitive capacities are adapted to generate pro-social behaviour in a species living in interdependent societies – they do not maximise for individual utility.
- Behaviour which appears irrational, biased or emotionally-motivated may in fact express strategies that are meta-rational in an evolving population.
- Although interpersonal violence is rare in social species, moralistic aggression motivates agents to respond forcefully when their expectations of social behaviour are violated.

In the film *Men in Black*, Agent K [Tommy Lee Jones] remarks "A person is smart. *People* are dumb, panicky, dangerous animals." It's a throwaway line, but it reflects a dominant worldview in liberal philosophy which elevates "capital-R Reason" in opposition to the emotive, animal and sensual[373] – the world of the masses. The liberal plan for social change [and a noble plan

---

[373] Haidt (2012), Chapter 2.

it generally is] is to provide sufficient knowledge capital such that everyone is able to optimise their decision-making like a proper game theorist. Collective welfare comes about through each individual maximising their own utility. But as we now recognise, individual pursuit of self-interest may lead us into social equilibria that are neither stable nor desirable. In fact, the elevation of Reason has historically led to collective action problems, exploitation, warfare, eugenics and atrocity. Agent K had it backwards. Left to their own devices, a single person isn't particularly smart or effective at getting what they want. And Reason is a often a poor guide for managing a complex society.

Humans are a truly remarkable species, unique in nature and as far as we know, the cosmos. The sole survivor of an extinct group of hominins, humans have truly become the planet's apex organism, reshaping the ecological and material composition of the planet to suit our needs. Our waste products transform entire ecosystems and define the geological epoch in which we live. We build enormous cities where millions of strangers live together in relative peace, transform other plant and animal species to feed a population of billions, build monuments and skyscrapers, great canals and space stations. The only other genus that comes close to this level of environmental impact is the ants, also a social species[374]

"We often wish that people could work together better, but actually human beings are astonishingly good at cooperation. We are better at it than any other creature on the planet. And herein lies a profound puzzle, because according to the standard evolutionary science, we shouldn't be able to cooperate very much at all. We do and we did." [Turchin, Ultra-Society][375]

This chapter will look at the evolution of social species, and ask what kind of creature we might expect to be biologically and culturally adapted to social life. It will also ask why individual members of the only social species we

---

[374] Henrich (2016) at pg. 10.

[375] Turchin (2016) at pg. 3.

know of capable of complex cultural evolution are so often poor, irrational decision-makers. It will turn out, unsurprisingly, that these are one and the same question. The reason individuals are such bad "capital-R Rationalists" is the very same reason why we've been so stunningly successful as a species. What economists think of as biases and deviations from their transcendental standard of utility-maximising behaviour, the evolutionary sociologist sees as biological and cultural adaptions to a historical process of natural variation, selection and reproduction.

What are the traits that we might expect a creature adapted to social life to possess in order to solve evolutionary games? Let's compile an initial list, based on our discussions in previous Chapters.

- Discounting of future payoffs, on the basis that interactions will not continue indefinitely.
- Aversion of relative loss and preference for relative gain, to maximise strategic survival under the replicator dynamic.
- A general aversion to interpersonal violence[376], even when it would be advantageous to do so.
- Preferring egalitarian or 'fair' social outcomes, even when it would be advantageous to cheat.
- A desire to punish social deviation, even where doing so is socially costly ('vengefulness')[377].
- The ability to rapidly recognise and follow behavioural patterns.
- Copying the behaviour of nearby others, even when there's no reason for it ('conformity bias').
- The capacity to judge and keep track of the social reputation of others, and be aware when our own social reputation is being tracked.
- Bias in favour of those in a trusted in-group[378], including a tendency to trust in the reliability of signals received from trusted others and to

---

[376] Greene (2013), at pgs. 35-39.

[377] Greene (2013), at pgs. 41-42.

[378] Greene (2013), at pgs. 48-55.

attribute harmful actions by them to mistake or misperception.

- Stereotyping of out-group others based on external markers of differ-ence or tags, and the development of labels and affective categories for Types or Roles.

Game theory suggests that all of these traits can be adaptively rational under certain limited conditions, where an agent is able to calculate the costs and benefits of strategies in particular social contexts. But such calculations are mentally costly and, apart from extraordinarily simplified models, effectively unsolvable. Rather than an aptitude for probability calculations and abstract reasoning, we find instead in humans a set of intuitions and biases which operate largely subconsciously, in specialised areas of the brain. Human actions are not the product of abstract Reason, they're the result of a process with a much greater learning and information-storage capacity: the accumulated knowledge about the prior evolutionary adaptiveness of certain behaviours stored as genetic and cultural replicators by a population.

Emotions – both pleasant and unpleasant, inciting and calming -- represent our conscious awareness of biologically-evolved and culturally-conditioned responses that are taking place in our brains without our knowledge or direction. Our biases and intuitions are adaptive mechanisms for the purposes of fitness-maximisation, yes, but that maximisation takes place as part of a population strategy that is overwhelmingly cooperative and pro-social, and has been for hundreds of thousands of years[379]. We get angry in response to certain stimuli because our ancestors were motivated by it to keep fighting for survival; we get depressed because in times of stress shutting down our emotional responses and hyper-focusing on the source of our pain pushes us to struggle on; and we experience happiness when we perform an action which improves the welfare of ourselves and our community, even it is costly to ourselves to act altruistically.

Before we continue, a quick reminder on gene-culture co-evolution.

---

[379] Damasio (1995); Bowles & Gintis (2011), Chapter 11.

For "capital-E, capital-P" Evolutionary Psychologists associated with the 'Santa Barbara school' of Leda Cosmides & John Tooby[380] human cognitive biases are biologically grounded, genetically transmitted and are adaptions to the human way of life *prior* to the origin of culture – the 'environment of evolutionary adaptiveness' (or 'EEA')[381]. The EEA is a hypothetical point in human evolution where the evolution of our genetic traits essentially stopped. The EEA is not a scientific concept [it's unfalsifiable], but it's generally written of as a time greater than 50,000 thousand years ago, when all humans were anatomically and behaviourally modern, but before culture began to profoundly change human behaviour. To summarise the EP argument, our biases provided a reasonable guide to behaviour under pre-cultural conditions, but are a poor guide for behaviour in modern times.

For Evolutionary Psychologists, the ills of the modern world arise because of a mismatch between biologically rooted behaviours and the cultural beliefs and practices that have 'hijacked' human societies since our essential nature as humans became fixed[382]. And indeed, biological traits that were adaptive in previous environment contexts may indeed be maladaptive in the context of a modern culture (see Chapter 16: "Outside Context Problems"). But Evolutionary Psychology significantly underestimates the way culture mediates how behaviours are expressed, and often fails to recognise that culture may, under the pressure of multilevel selection, produce behaviours that are themselves adaptive. The genetic essentialists hold that if there's variation in human behaviour, it must 'evoked' by differences in the environment and its effect on each agent's ontogeny or development[383], a theory we previously encountered in Chapter 5. The better view is that:

---

[380] Cosmides, Tooby & Barkow (1992); Minkel, "Psyching Out Evolutionary Psychology: Interview with David J. Buller" Scientific American, July 4 2005; Laland & Brown (2011), Chapter 5.

[381] Bowlby (1969, 1973); Burnham (2003), at pgs. S113-157.

[382] Burnham (2003), at pgs. S113-157.

[383] Cosmides, Tooby & Barkow (1992) at pg. 84; Buss (1995) at pgs. 12-14; Gangestad, Haselton & Buss (2006) at pgs. 75-95.

"Basic and social emotions are expressed in all human societies, although their expression is affected by cultural conditions. For instance, in all societies, one may be angered by an immoral act, or disgusted by an unusual foodstuff, but what counts as immoral or disgusting is, at least to some extent, culturally specific."
[Bowles & Gintis, A Cooperative Species][384]

Disgust is a highly adaptive, biologically-rooted response to environmental dangers such as rotting food or other dangerous biological matter[385]. But disgust can be culturally conditioned, associated with some foods and not others depending on what was available during childhood, and even with social behaviours. So we find that social conservatives, for example, often cultivate a disgust reaction to same-sex activity or sexual activity in general, whereas other social strategies employ that same emotive reaction to social and political behaviours which harm minorities, animals or the environment. Only the *capacity* to feel disgust is innate. The adaptiveness of a behaviour or strategy can only be considered in the context of the culture in which it is expressed.

So in some instances, cultural practices bring out or exaggerate a particular biological bias under specific conditions. Other cultural practices exist largely to suppress biological biases and intuitions that are harmful in a large-scale population that has emerged much faster than our genes could adapt. Most cultures inhibit inter-personal violence even in conflict situations where the emotional parts of our brain still think it might be justified, but we also have specialised institutions (the military) where these violent instincts are honed and brought out under controlled conditions. It's likely that cultural evolution sharpens some biological instincts, increases the selectivity of others, and suppresses yet others – and which particular combination of biological and cultural traits is adaptive will have changed over time alongside cultural and material conditions.

Because genetic essentialists do not see cultural systems as evolutionary,

---

[384] Bowles & Gintis (2011) at pg. 187.

[385] Curtis et al. (2004) Haidt (2012), at pgs. 70-71, 170-177; Askew et al. (2014) at pgs. 566-577.

they dismiss mechanisms in which behaviours and culture are selected together on the basis of their combined effects. A cultural trait must represent, in some sense, a deviation from the ideal biological form which was fixed at the time of our most recent common ancestor. Some Evolutionary Psychologists therefore unsurprisingly tend to support conservative notions of sex and gender roles, express hostility to universalist and cooperative symbolic ideologies they see as incompatible with human nature, and attribute to cultural practices responsibility for every behaviour that is harmful, irrational or destructive. The preferable view, that of gene-culture co-evolution, is that strategies are the ontological subject of natural selection, and that genetic and cultural replicators reproduce together on the basis of their combined fitness effect.

The Evolutionary Psychologists do have at least one thing right, though.

As mentioned previously, many animals have generalised intelligence and problem-solving ability, because they're likely to encounter situations and environments over the course of their life that either change too quickly for replicators to record the success of strategies, or which are so varied and complicated that replicators are not able to reliably generate adaptive behaviour for every eventuality. Humans have the greatest capacity for this kind of general problem-solving in nature, but the difference is one of degree, not kind[386]. Chimps perform as well as young children on most cognitive tests of abstract reasoning – it is only when social learning, imitation and cumulative knowledge are added to experiments that human children pull well ahead[387]. Our working memories are also not especially impressive, and we become easily confused when trying to keep track of large quantities of information[388].

Biology, economics and neuroscience are well and truly moving away from a model in which the brain is seen as a general purpose computer, to a model in which we are seen as having unusually strong general intelligence

---

[386] Henrich (2016), at pgs. 13-17.

[387] Hermann et al. (2007) at pgs. 1360-1366; Hermann et al. (2010) at pgs. 102-11.

[388] Inoue & Matsuzawa (2007) at pgs. 1004-1005.

but otherwise operate like any other creature. In this model, the brain is conceptualised as a series of overlapping 'modules' which evolved at different times in our past to solve particular social and environmental dilemmas[389]. No module was ever or will ever be a perfect adaption: environments change, new functions are jury-rigged on top of old ones and the evolution of new mental faculties changes the relationships amongst those already extant. Most animals are effectively slaves to these intuitions, their behaviour governed by biological replicators coding their brains for particular behaviours in response to particular stimuli. We can train some animals to ignore some of their instincts or promote others, but free of such conditioning animal behaviour is an adaptive response to the environment of its ancestors. And without culture, they cannot transmit new information to their heirs.

General intelligence, or executive function, mediates between these specialised cognitive capabilities, picking and choosing behaviours on the basis of the emotive and energetic priority each organ generates within the brain. Self-control over its instincts requires an animal to focus and have patience, to limit its impulses, to conceptualise the relationship between means and ends using its working memory, and be open to novel behavioural solutions. But exercising this executive control is extremely energy-intensive and cannot be sustained for long periods. For most people, most of the time, biologically-evolved and culturally-conditioned intuitions provide a speedy and efficient set of behavioural heuristics that are 'good enough' to get by and free up cognitive capacity for other priorities.

Although several researchers have advanced and promoted this 'dual process' approach to understanding social behaviour, including Jerry Fodor, Cosmides & Tooby, and Jonathan Haidt[390], the psychologist most associated with the modular view of sognition is its great populariser, Daniel Kahneman. Kahneman, who shared the Nobel Prize in Economics for co-creating the field of behavioural economics, classifies human cognition into

---

[389] Cosmides & Tooby (2013) at pgs. 201-229.

[390] Fodor (1980); Haidt (2001) at pgs. 814-; Haidt (2012), Chapter 2. Greene (2013), at pg. 120.

two broad families: "System 1", which is fast, instinctive and emotional, and "System 2", which is slower, requires significant mental effort, and which is conscious and calculating.

Rationalists, such as the psychologist Joshua Greene[391], tend to see "System 2" thinking as a superior tool for resolving social dilemmas. In this view of human sociability, good things happen when we slow down, engage in careful problem solving, and limit the influence of emotional stimuli. This perspective tends to take for granted that 'human nature' is selfish and competitive, and 'reason' is moral, or at least justifiable. Such people tend to see our instincts as irrational and potentially harmful, if they put us at odds with other solution sets that would produce greater utility. On the other side, Intuitionists such as Jonathan Haidt tend to see our emotional responses as generally well-suited to guiding behaviour in social situations. In other words, our instincts may make us cooperative and altruistic where narrow self-interest would preach competition and self-help. As Hume famously said in the eighteenth century, "Reason is, and ought only to be the slave of the passions"[392], for our intuitions provide time-tested responses to social complexity any individual, no matter how clever, could never fully understand.

It's unnecessary for the evolutionary socialist to take a firm aesthetic position – both System 1 and System 2 are clearly evolutionary products, so *both* must play some role in enhancing human fitness. It's largely a scientific question, not a normative one, as to which circumstances favour the application of Reason and which favour the application of Intuition – and an ideological question what social goals are desirable in the first place. And it may be that the potential scope of application of System 2 thinking has expanded over time, as the urgency of meeting basic human physical needs has receded[393].

But it's also likely that at least some of the adaptive function of System

---

[391] See generally Part 3 of Greene (2013).

[392] Hume, "A Treatise on Human Nature" (1740), Book 2.

[393] We might term this process "The Enlightenment".

2 thinking in humans was not to improve decision-making but rather to generate *persuasive justifications* for behaviour, using our capacity for language and symbolic communication to send signals which modify the emotional reactions of other social actors[394]. As we discussed in Chapter 7, it matters less whether a belief is justified than whether a signal can persuasively or usefully influence it. Abstract problem solving may not have been subject to strong selection, but social problem solving ("Machiavellian intelligence") likely was. We may, for example, have an intuitive revulsion of harming others, but if we can persuade others that violence is justified – that we followed the applicable laws, that our actions were authorised by proper authority, that it was necessary to prevent greater harm, or that our victim was themselves an outsider unworthy or moral regard – then we can alter their responses and avoid punishment.

* * *

Let's begin with something simple. We saw in Chapter 6 that time-inconsistency in preferences – which is irrational under a strict definition of instrumental utility – arises organically in evolutionary game theory as the social agent has to reckon that interactions will at some uncertain point in the future come to an end. In effect, they become impatient to pursue the selfish strategy because they may be able to obtain a fitness advantage by cheating – if they choose the right moment. This conclusion is so foundational that both rational-choice and behavioural economics include a time discount factor () in their models – though it cannot be justified as an axiom other than as a subjective belief about when the game will end[395].

Time discounting was first shown quantitatively among animals in

---

[394] Haidt (2012) at pgs. 38, 50-52; Mercier & Sperber (2011) at pgs. 57-111.

[395] As even the hardline Austrian economists admit: Reismann (1998) at pg. 795.

the 1960s[396], and later demonstrated among humans in a plethora of different experiments. Interestingly, humans do not display consistent time-discounting, but rather preferences which drop off sharply in the short term but then remain relatively consistent over long time horizons[397]. We might have strong preferences about whether we receive our paycheck this week or next week, but when discussing the same time interval and the same dollar amounts a year from now, we are relatively indifferent. This suggests we anticipate one-off interactions are short-term and unlikely to be repeated, but also that the same *kinds* of social interactions will recur over long time horizons.

But time-discounting is not a behaviour fixed in our genes, despite its deep evolutionary roots. Individuals will adapt their level of time discounting based on both the circumstances of their personal development and the social environment in which they find themselves. It's well established that the greater stress that individuals are under, the more likely they are to make decisions favouring short-term payoffs. Wilkinson & Pickett have conclusively demonstrated that risk-taking behaviours such as inter-personal violence, criminal activity and unsafe sexual practices are the inevitable by-product of living at the bottom of a highly stratified society[398]. These strategies deliver short-term fitness payoffs, in terms of higher social status and reproductive opportunity, at the expense of long-term, patient investment in personal development. Criminal and anti-social behaviour is not irrational — it's a best response to a society that puts you at the bottom of the social totem pole.

Entire populations will develop cultural behaviours that shape the expression of time discounting depending on its cumulative learning about

---

[396] Herrnstein (1961); Chung & Herrnstein (1967); Ainslie & Herrnstein (1981); Ainslie (2015) at pgs. 261-275.

[397] Thaler (1981) at pgs. 201-207; Laibson (1997) at pgs. 443-491; Ainslie (2015) at pg. 262; Grune-Yanoff (2015) at pgs. 675-713; Bowles & Gintis (2011) at pgs. 191-192; Gowdy et al. (2013) at pgs. S92-104.

[398] Wilkinson & Pickett (2009), especially Chapters 9-10.

its economic and social environment[399]. Cultures which tended to avoid uncertainty more on other measures also display stronger time discounting than cultures which are more open to risk. In a 2016 paper, Turkish researchers argued that cultural differences in the time discount factor could be understood as adaptions to local agricultural and climatic conditions which determined the availability of food resources and the length of time investment required in farming[400].

Early research on time-discounting showed further divergences from classical utility theory, in that the way in which humans discount future payoffs varies by both their current level of resources (the endowment effect) and whether decisions are taking place in the domain of gains or losses[401]. Humans are generally willing to pay less to gain a good or service than they are willing to accept in payment for the same[402]. Possession changes an agent's valuation of a resource, and indeed many species are highly possessive and will defend their territory or mates at great cost, even if others are available. Some economists have even gone so far as to argue that the endowment effect represents the natural origin of property rights, although as Brian Skyrms and others have argued, the endowment effect is just as likely to be an evolved strategy for selecting amongst equilibria in anti-coordination games[403].

Recall the **hawk-dove** game from earlier in the book. In the classical interpretation of the game, neither bird is in possession of the resource at the start of the game. But if one bird is randomly allocated the resource (perhaps by coming across it first), then the best response strategy may be to play hawk (i.e. be willing to fight) if the resource is yours and play dove (live to fight another day) otherwise. Loss aversion provides a way of breaking the symmetry in a player's strategic choice and selecting between

---

[399] Wang et al. (2016) at pgs. 115-135; Henrich et al. (2005) at pgs. 795-855.

[400] Galor & Ozak (2016) at pgs. 3064-3103.

[401] Ainslie (2015) at pgs. 255-266.

[402] Knetsch (1989) at pgs. 1277-1284; Kahneman, Knetsch & Thaler (1991) at pgs. 285-100.

[403] Skyrms (2014) at pg. 77-80; Gintis (2017), Chapter 8.

the available equilibria – whereas rationality provides no guide on how to choose a strategy in pure anti-coordination games. Like teenagers playing a game of chicken, the only way to win is to be guided by irrational emotions such as attachment, fear, shame, and pride.

The flip side of prospect theory is that while humans are averse to taking risks when we might lose what we already have, we do entertain risks when we might benefit[404]. If decisions are framed in terms of potential fitness loss rather than as a potential gain, people make difference choices even if the payoffs are otherwise identical. People care about relative losses because their preferences have been shaped by the operation of the replicator dynamic So long as a strategy does no worse than the population average, its frequency in the population will remain unchanged. Only by understanding strategic evolution as part of an evolutionary process can we make sense of the seemingly irrational outcomes it produces.

* * *

Human beings have a staggering capacity for mass violence. But that violence is usually a collective affair, carried out for collective ends (although see Chapter 15: "Extremists Amongst Us"). On an individual level, most people have strong intuitive inhibitions against directly hurting another human being[405], so much so that doctors and soldiers must be culturally conditioned to override their impulses. Rather than, as Steven Pinker argues[406], the relative peacefulness of modern times representing our success at self-domestication, the strong biological roots of this aversion suggest rather the opposite. For most of human evolutionary history, we lived in relatively small groups of people we were either related to, lived in close proximity to, or knew the social reputations of. Under

---

[404]Kahneman & Tversky (1979) at pg. 263; Kahneman & Tversky (1986) 251–278; Ainslie (2015) at pgs. 265–266.

[405]Greene (2013), at pgs. 35-39.

[406]Pinker (2011).

these conditions, intra-group violence would have been corrosive to the cooperation necessary for group parenting, hunting and cultural learning.

Even today, there are many situations in which the unilateral resort to force might theoretically offer a fitness advantage – imagine if the workplace operated like chimp societies where gym-goers could physically maul their boss in order to take over the enterprise! Organised crime operates in much this way - short-circuiting the normal rules of commerce to seel excessive profits through the resort to violence and intimidation. So opportunistic violence is thus clearly an available strategy (see Chapter 13: "Social Cancers") – why has it not spread to fixation in the population as a whole?

Every human society since the dawn of time has understood that unautho-rised interpersonal violence was a threat to social cohesion, and developed specialised organs to suppress and punish violators. So yes, humans torture and murder perceived criminals, we rebel violently against tyrants and we fight wars alongside members of our in-group against members of other groups. But in each instance, violence must be learned, in the sense that it is nurtured, guided and generated by cultural norms, scripts and institutions that evolve in response to changing circumstances. The evidence on the willingness of soldiers throughout history to actually fight on behalf of their commanders is mixed[407], but we're clearly getting better at socialising soldiers into violence over time. Thanks to the increasing sophistication of military training, the modern soldier, pilot or drone operator may be less likely to engage in selfish, criminal violence – but more likely to fire upon an enemy combatant when ordered to do so.

In fact, the most common form of violence employed and encountered by human beings is punishment for violations of social norms – or 'moralistic aggression'[408]. Even at the interpersonal level mediated solely by emotions, we become highly charged when we perceive we've been wronged[409]. Self-

---

[407] Grossman (1996); Engen (2011).

[408] Bowles & Gintis (2011), at pg. 193; Trivers (1971) at pgs. 35-57

[409] Greene (2013), at pgs. 41-42.; Henrich (2016), Chapter 11.

defence is a licence for an escalatory, punitive response because justified violence is cathartic. But our capacity for tit-for-tat vengefulness expands far beyond interpersonal wrongs to also cover *social* wrongs – actions which do not harm us directly but which violate our expectations about social behaviour. Even very young children become angry in experiments where adults do not behave as expected[410], and growing up is a process by which we learn which behaviours are governed by enforceable rules and which are not.

In societies without specialised institutions of social control, *vengefulness* and the punishment of deviance is democratised, as we saw in Chapter 9. Anthropological studies have shown that in many parts of the world, social deviance is punished by an escalating pattern of social sanction (as Elinor Ostrom would expect), beginning with gossip about a violator's reputation, moving to an absence of social reciprocity, and lastly ostracism or violence[411]. Victims of selfish crime in such societies are largely those who are already in poor standing with the community – a selfish, exploitative attack against norms violators will not itself attract punishment by the community – and indeed being forced to operate outside the protection of the usual social norms is often punishment enough to control deviant behaviour. Even in more complex societies, exploitative criminal strategies often target those outside the protection of the community, such as drug traffickers, sex workers, migrants and other minority groups.

These emotional reactions are closely linked with our moral categorisation of others. Terrorists and criminals are *bad* people against whom almost any retaliatory violence seems justified (no matter the social rules that would ordinarily apply or the negative utilitarian consequences of doing so). Psychological studies have shown that infants as young as nine

---

[410] Schmidt & Tomasello (2012) at pgs. 232-236; Schmidt, Call & Tomasello (2012) at pg. 325-333.

[411] Henrich et al. (2001) at pgs. 73-78; Henrich & Henrich, "Fairness without Punishment: Behavioural Experiment in the Yasawa Island, Fiji" in Henrich & Ensminger (eds.) (2014) at pgs. 225-258; Bowles et al. (2012).

months make distinctions between justified and unjustified violence[412]. Most people's self-conception as *good* people is linked to their dutiful performance of expected social roles.

The norms and social expectations which define membership in good standing of a group become part of the identity of the members of this group. The literature often referees to this as *internalisation* – the process by which an external or other-regarding value becomes incorporated into the preferences of the individual[413]. But this dichotomy between the social and the individual is false: the values of individuals are *constituted* by the social practices into which they are socialised and norms spread on the basis of their success in reproducing behaviour. The psychological literature demonstrates that this process is automatic, instinctual and intimately tied in with the emotional centres of the brain. We do not make rational decisions about the violation of social norms: we feel immense anger when our expectations are violated by others, and shame which restrains us from violating them ourselves.

Further evidence of our evolved cognitive predisposition towards monitoring and keeping track of our social standing is the vast behavioural changes that take place when humans think they're being observed. Humans who're aware they're being watched behave more morally, according to the standards of their culture. They are more likely to cooperate in social games and prefer a more equitable distribution of resources. Notably, this effect operates when the 'observation' is abstracted, so that paintings of other people or even symbolic representations of eyes (including, notably, camera lenses) can render individual behaviour more pro-social[414]. The omniscient, ever-watchful god sits at the heart of many highly successful religions[415].

---

[412] Hamlin & Wynn (2011) at pgs. 30-39; Hamlin et al. (2011) at pgs. 19931-19936.

[413] Gintis (2003) at pgs. 407-418; Bowles & Gintis (2011) at pg. 173-185; Richerson & Henrich (2012); Gintis (2017) at pgs. 123-26, Chapter 10.

[414] Haley & Fessler (2005) at pgs. 245-256; Fehr & Schneider (2009); Ernest-Jones et al. (2011) at pgs. 172-178.

[415] Wilson (2003); Dunbar, (2014) from pgs. 323.

This strategic switching is autonomic and unconscious, and unrelated to any rational assessments of its cost and benefits. We have all felt the flush of emotion when we realise too late that our selfish or deviant behaviour was, in fact, observed by other people after all.

In most animals, including primates, the emotion that is homologous with human shame is a collection of intuitions and behaviours designed to signal submission to another dominant individual[416]. Shame still has residual applications in humans, certainly: between parents and children, and often in the workplace and other hierarchical groups. But in a social species such as our own, the deep roots of the shame response have been tended and adapted in the direction of motivating compliance with culturally-determined social norms[417]. Indeed, one of the primary characteristics of anti-social individuals is their inability to be self-limited by the shame response (see Chapter 13: "Social Cancers".).

The other major element of our instinctual understanding of moral standing is 'justice as fairness'[418]. We noted in earlier Chapters that real human beings do not distribute goods how the rational actor theory suggests they should: when people play the ultimatum game, they routinely offer a fair division of the resource, even in single-shot interactions when they know there is no chance that exploiting their partner will have consequences for themselves[419]. People routinely share resources and contribute to the provision of public goods, even when doing so is irrational. Moreover, this behaviour is easy, quick and instinctive – the definition of System 1 thinking. In fact, in most experiments in which people are asked to play very simple economic games, they have to be *taught* the instrumentally rational strategy, and in many cases have to put in a great deal of cognitive and emotional

---

[416] Henrich (2016), at pgs. 198-99; Bowles & Gintis (2011), at pgs. 192-193.

[417] Bowles & Gintis (2011), at pgs. 186-187; Gintis (2017) at pgs. 121-123.

[418] Rawls (1985) at pgs. 223-251; Rawls (2001).

[419] Ainslie (2015) at pg. 266.; Henrich et al. (2005) at pgs. 795-855; See generally Skyrms (2014), Chapter 2; and Haidt (2012) at pgs. 158-161

effort to actually follow through[420]. Under stress and time pressure, people are more likely to be trusting and cooperative than not.

Importantly, anthropologists have demonstrated that what counts as 'fair' depends on the cultural context. After two hundred years of liberal socialisation, Westerners will tend to default to a position in which everyone is treated with equal dignity, but other cultures can vary in a wide range (sharing anywhere from 20-60% of a resource) – some cultures habitually share more with others, and others tend to share less by default[421]. As with all examples of gene-culture evolution, it's likely that environmental and social context plays a strong role in how the fairness instinct develop in each individual. It's perhaps telling that the great universalising religions, and political liberalism, are cultural systems which stress the inherent equality of all members of the community – the cultivation of a bias towards fairness has been highly successful in evolutionary terms. In fact, one could easily make the argument that major political fault-lines surround precisely the question of what is 'fair' – how do different definitions of equality serve different interests and which ideology is best able to promote its definition to the next generation? We can also imagine how the lived experience of material inequality might undermine these beliefs, and damage the social trust necessary for large-scale social cooperation to be sustainable.

* * *

As a social species, evolved to operate in social groups characterised by shifting and variable patterns of behaviour, humans are exceptional pattern matchers – even when it would be irrational to be so. Indeed, there's a plausible argument that pattern matching, rather than Reasoning, is at the essence of all cognition[422]: every animal's senses, most notably its vision, operate on the basis of autonomic instincts which generate data on the

---

[420] Henrich (2016) at pgs. 193-196.

[421] Skyrms (2014) at pg. 40.

[422] Margolis (1987); Schrodt (2004)

basis of inferential observations. Specialised sense processing modules are typically one of the largest parts of any living creature's brain, and from our own susceptibility to optical illusions and other tricks of the eye, we know that this processing largely takes place below our level of awareness – it takes significant effort *not* to see such illusions.

Human perception of social behaviour is likely based in part on similar mechanism. Rather than deductive logic, most people most of the time rely on matching the current moment to past situations – and selecting behaviour on the basis of what was successful before. Importantly, most of the time this recall is autonomic, drawing upon mental stories or schema about events that we observed in childhood, or which were drilled into us during our education and socialisation, or which constitute cultural narratives and examples learned from popular entertainment. We use the divergence between current events and our [potentially inaccurate] memories of past events to decide if our current strategy is appropriate (in case the divergence is low) or inappropriate (in case the divergence is high)[423]. We can never be totally confident our strategy is the rational one, but by relying on prior learning – including cultural learning – at least we'll do no worse than others have in the past.

Most people, most of the time, behave in accordance with a set of rules which dictate the appropriate behaviour for a given social context (the 'logic of appropriateness'). The human propensity to believe things that are untrue or irrational – to believe myths and gossip, to follow ritual and ceremony -- arises because most of the time it costs us little in fitness terms to believe and act as others do, and avoid investing the mental time and energy required to critically challenge oneself. Truly novel social situations can be challenging – and lacking experience in a particular social setting or choosing the wrong behavioural rule can generate anti-social behaviour. Human actions are so often irrational and socially maladaptive because the rules we've learned can't be neatly matched to new social structures – this is a problem that can get worse the more we age and the less exposure we've

---

[423] Schrodt (2004) at pg. 50-.

had to other cultures and societies.

Confirmation bias – the tendency of people to interpret new signals in ways that strengthens their confidence in their existing beliefs – is largely a product of this pattern-centric social cognition. Encountering new evidence that challenges our existing beliefs is mentally and emotionally difficult because it temporarily disables the subconscious processes which we rely on to get through everyday life. As Ibn Khaldun observed in the 14th century, *"if [we are] infected with partisanship for a particular opinion . . . [we] accept without a moment's hesitation the information that is agreeable to it. Prejudice and partisanship obscure the critical faculty and preclude critical investigation."*[424] So we prefer to seek out information that does not require critical investigation, which like sugary food, is easier to digest.

The flipside of confirmation bias is backlash. Just as signals that reinforce our existing beliefs are calming and reassuring, signals that threaten those beliefs can activate negative emotions and instincts for moralistic aggression. For a hominin ancestor on the savannah, knowing how the grass moved in the wind would be reassuring – but noticing grass moving in an irregular or unexpected way could represent a potentially fatal danger. Seeing people with the same external tags as ourselves and who perform behaviours the way we'd expect costs very little mental energy – but our brains react to strangers with fear and concern, warning us of a potential threat: an unexpected variance in the pattern[425]. Backlash is more than mere reaction to a threat: it is rapid, emotional, irrational hostility towards other individuals that do not meet our expectations of the social role they are performing.

Beyond the obvious associations with implicit racism and xenophobia, this emotional reaction to difference operates in our daily life on a far more regular basis than anyone would like to admit. Schools, workplaces, sports teams and other human social groups all operate according to rules which are constitutive of membership of those communities. Individuals

---

[424] Ibn Khaldun, "The Muqaddimah: An introduction to history" (1378).

[425] Sapolsky (2017) at pgs. 388-390.

who don't – or simply haven't learnt – those rules can very rapidly become ostracised and find their social standing damaged, even if no one is consciously trying to exclude them.

Backlash against women and minorities who have made impressive strides for equality over the last several decades arises in part because of the socialisation of a generation of men to believe that their place atop the social pyramid was the natural order of things[426]. These men are angry because others appear to be violating social norms that are constitutive of their self-identity – and are incapable of seeing themselves as anything other than moral and virtuous, no matter how poor their own behaviour. It takes most people genuine cognitive effort to reflect upon minority perspectives, and even when we try our best we all struggle to give strangers the same consideration we'd give those more similar to ourselves.

To conclude, human beings are not instrumentally-rational, utility-maximising robots. Not because we have fallen short an abstracted ideal state or rationality, nor due to some Cartesian conflict between our System 1 physical bodies and our System 2 minds. Rather, the integrated human being is adapted for life in a society and inherits strategies from their biological and cultural replicators that generate fitness-enhancing behaviour under most common environmental and social conditions. The evolutionary view takes our intuitions as 'meta-rational' in the context of natural selection. That is, our biases and heuristics deliver decision-making that proved 'good enough' for prior generations. Our mental machinery is neither innately irrational nor accidental – although it may sometimes appear to be both. We have innate beliefs and preferences because they generated effective solutions to the sorts of complex social decision-making that we as a social species are most likely to confront. Such a dynamic system is potentially wiser and more information-rich than abstracted, utilitarian reasoning.

---

[426] See e.g. Faludi (1991).

11

THE LEARNING ORGANISM

Key Points

- Social species are behaviourally flexible. They must solve the omnivore's dilemma by balancing their openness to novelty against the safety and security of the known.
- Social learning transmits strategies within social species through teaching and imitation. Social species preferentially copy behaviours that signal prior fitness.
- From the perspective of multilevel selection, evolving populations constitute a 'collective brain' which stores information about the fitness of strategies within them.

Evolving systems are learning systems. Selection generates new information about the relative fitness of strategies in the context of their environment, and if information reproduces faster than it's lost through error, mutation or extinction, it accumulates over time and leads to increasingly sophisticated exploitation by an organism of its environment. In purely biological systems, new information is generated, transmitted and stored chemically, through the mutation, deletion or re-arrangement of amino acids within DNA. Any individual animal is a biological experiment; and experiments which produce good – or at least, not bad – fitness pass those results on to the next generation. Within social species, non-genetic information flows are just as or arguably more important, and this Chapter will explore how individuals and groups acquire new beliefs and behaviours from their surrounding culture.

Many animals have very limited diets – they tend to exploit only a small proportion of the resources in their environment, and indeed may become highly reliant on a particular food source. The organism has limited choice about how to survive: if they can eat it, it's more than likely safe to do so. Primates, including humans, are among those animals which are *omnivorous*: we can digest a wide variety of different food sources, and more importantly, we want to do so. This dietary flexibility grants us the capacity to survive in both new environments and old environments when conditions change. We can exploit resources unknown to our ancestors, and occasionally luck out and discover new sources of nutrients or energy.

But being omnivorous comes with a risk. For a koala, eucalyptus leaves are always safe to eat – because koalas almost always eat eucalyptus. But for an omnivore there's a non-zero chance that a new food source is toxic or even fatal[427]. The price we pay for a better chance of group survival is carrying a higher risk of individual mortality – there's a classic evolutionary tension between individual and group interests. This generates a strategic dilemma between two behavioural strategies – neophilia [or love of the new] and neophobia [fear of the new]. In an omnivorous species, a behavioural equilibrium will arise such that there's some openness to new food sources, but not *too much* lest the fatalities from organisms merrily ingesting everything they encounter becomes too high. The payoffs of short-term safety and long-term adaptability balance one another out[428].

For the individual animal, this strategic tension generates subjective anxiety when encountering choice – the so-called 'omnivore's dilemma'[429] – and the management of this anxiety by individuals produces an equilibrium

---

[427] Rousseau (2005), at pg. 318.

[428] Haidt (2012) at pg 172.

[429] Pollan (2006).

in behaviour across the population as a whole. Sometimes, we'll adopt a pure strategy: it's always safest not to eat food that we know is fatal; and it's usually safe to try new foods recommended by our kin network and friends with good social reputations. Other times, we might randomise our choices so that we select from the menu by 'flipping a mental coin', which takes an anxiety-inducing choice out of our hands.

Importantly, humans are not merely dietary omnivores. We are also *behavioural omnivores*: we're usually comfortable practicing behaviours socialised into us from a young age, which we inherit from a combination of our genes and culture. But we're also behaviourally flexible, capable of learning novel strategies we've not previously encountered. This flexibility comes with risks and costs, including elevated levels of anxiety when prior learning provides no guide to future behaviour (see also Chapter 18: "Freedom is Scary"). But this anxiety is merely our conscious awareness of the competing signals sent by different biological and cultural heuristics: some modules in our brain will scream that novelty is dangerous and to be avoided, others promise rewards for trying new things. Genetic, developmental, cultural and environmental forces will strengthen some impulses and weaken others. The balance between those forces in each individual will depend on all of Tinbergen's four causal mechanisms.

In the previous Chapter, we noted that the emotion of disgust likely evolved to drive humans and other animals away from potentially dangerous biological material – toxic foods, decaying meat, the sick, waste products etc. Psychologists have shown that in social species, disgust is modified by culture to become what Jonathan Haidt terms 'sanctity' – a conditioned response to see some behaviours as good, clean and safe and others as bad, unclean and unsafe[430]. Many people have the same emotional response today to socially deviant behaviour that their ancestors might once have had to coming across a diseased or dead member of their tribe: they are physically sickened, can't stand to be around it, and act out in irrational ways. The desire to minimise these unpleasant emotions can generate avoidant

---

[430] Haidt (2012), at pgs. 170-177.

behaviour, for example food and sexual taboos, opposition to vaccines and anxieties over who defecates where.

The mental module most frequently counterposed with the disgust/sanctity mechanism is 'openness to experience', one of the 'Big Five' personality traits[431]. An individual who scores more highly for openness will display a greater range of novelty-seeking behaviour more often; they are more likely to try new foods and new social behaviours, and to be willing to copy or learn behaviours from a wider range of exemplars. On the other hand, a person with low openness will tend to avoid new experiences, to prefer the way things have previously been done, and learn only from 'safe' cultural models such as parents, those who share the same identity tags, and those higher in the social hierarchy.

Unsurprisingly, there's a strong correlation between these psychological predispositions and political predisposition: conservatives tend to have higher sanctity scores and lower openness, whereas progressives have higher openness but are less triggered by sanctity violations[432]. Indeed, we can understand politics as an mechanism in which these different adaptive strategies compete against one another and find equilibrium. The distribution of traits across a population which provide solutions to the omnivore's dilemma – how 'tight' or 'loose' its culture[433] – will tend towards an evolutionary stable state where some are constantly exploring new behaviours and others hew closely to the strategies of the past.

Let's think about these mechanisms operated in human history. Imagine you're a sceptical cattle herder in a quasi-agrarian society. You have a short lifespan, in no small part because there's a one in three chance of dying from smallpox. One day, someone from a neighbouring village comes through and describes a behaviour in which people in his village take pustules from infected cows and rub them on the faces or wounds of their healthy children.

---

[431] Jost (2006) at pgs. 651-; McRae (1996) at pgs. 323-.

[432] Jost et al. (2003) at pgs. 339-375; Jost et al. (2009) at pgs. 302-337; Thorisdottir & Jost (2011) at pgs. 785-811; Jost & Amodio (2012) at pgs. 55-64.

[433] Gelfand (2018); Harrington & Gelfand (2014) at pgs. 7990-7995.

He or she swears they haven't had a smallpox fatality in years. Do you imitate this behaviour, knowing that sick cows usually also mean sick children, and given your strong emotional disgust at the idea of exposing children to disease? Of course you wouldn't! You'd think the stranger and their village were mad. And you might be right: another village nearby sacrifices their elderly to the sky-god and claims the same results, and that's obviously nonsense.

And yet, without knowing how or why, the village that practices variolation is correct. Over millennia, they will live longer, healthier lives: have more children, herd more successfully and eventually come to dominate the local cattle-herding economy. Your village of more close-minded sceptics can't compete. You either imitate their behaviour or go extinct. Those who are most comfortable with novelty adapt the quickest. Over time, the behaviour becomes fixed in the population: scientists investigate and confirm the germ theory of disease; institutions are established to subsidise vaccinations and punish those that don't comply. Ritualisation may even set in, such that compliance with the norm becomes a reliable signifier of group identity. Openness to experience was an adaptive trait.

Now flip the script. You're a parent who lives in a society that practices widespread vaccination and regularly signals that vaccination is safe and effective. But one day, you encounter a signal on Facebook that tells you the opposite: somehow a crank theory or conspiracy, a bad scientific study or new religious belief has penetrated through the cultural fog and established an information paradox. What is the behavioural omnivore to do? Here's the thing: were the new information stating that vaccines are dangerous correct [it's not], the fitness-increasing decision would be to accept the new strategy and refuse to vaccinate your children despite the risks. Over a lifetime, your child would be statistically fitter and healthier and may achieve a higher social status. But of course, the opposite is true. The same openness to novelty which is adaptive in one set of conditions is maladaptive in the other. Open-minded people can be just as irrational as close-minded conservatives. A dynamic society needs both in order to adapt to changing circumstances.

* * *

To critics of cultural evolution, human learning is a fundamentally different process to the evolutionary dynamic of variation, selection and replication. Our capacity for sophisticated reasoning, foresight and empirically-grounded science means humans can solve social problems in the abstract, instantly leap-frogging our instincts to arrive at the strategic choice which is most "capital-R Rational". To the extent that not everyone who attempts such calculations arrives at the same conclusion, well, says the liberal wringing his or her hands, only a tiny fraction of the population are properly equipped to Reason. To the extent that humans follow fads and fashions, it demonstrates their fundamental irrationality and unreadiness for self-rule. Because the ESS solution to a social dilemma is potentially discoverable by reason, it should immediately spread to fixation in a properly educated and led population, displacing prior practices and prevent natural selection from playing any further role in human culture.

There are several problems with this critique, the least of which is that humans are not nearly as smart as we like to think we are. If we want to solve an engineering or physics problem, reason and experimentation are fantastic tools. But in complex systems, the connection between cause and effect is obscured, and critically dependent on both stochastic events and the strategies of other players. Every choice is made *under conditions of uncertainty*: we have imperfect information about the outcome of the selection process and so our knowledge about the likely fitness payoffs of our choices are irrevocably grounded in prior population and cultural-level beliefs. Our capacity to conduct meaningful empirical studies on human societies is very limited; even tiny changes in environment and culture can change the outcome, and we only ever get to observe each unique social process once.

One way to reduce this uncertainty might be to conduct millions of computer simulations, using a model of society sufficiently empirically rigorous that it generates accurate – albeit probabilistic – inferences about the outcomes of particular political and social strategies. But the social agent doesn't have the benefit of approaching life decisions as a multi-generational simulation. They make choices which reduce their individual anxiety in the moment, relying on inherited heuristics. Most of us trust what we learned from our parents, who clearly performed well enough to survive to reproductive age and raise us to adulthood. We attribute high status to professionals and the advice they offer and we are at least partly responsive to the directives of social institutions. No matter how well these systems function, nor how clever the individual reasoner, the individual cannot know if their strategy will maximise fitness.

Cultural evolution requires both the transmission of information (replicators) within a population and the selection of strategic variants based on their consequences. The community of the whole is in some sense a collective brain, testing the relative fitness of available social strategies.

"The secret of our species' success resides not in our individual minds, but in the collective brains of our communities. Our collective brains [represent] the synthesis of our cultural and social nature . . .the striking technologies that characterize our species . . .emerge not from singular geniuses but from the flow and recombination of ideas, practices, lucky errors and chance insights amongst interconnected minds and across generations. . . . Innovation . . . depends more on our sociality than our intellect, and the challenge has always been how to prevent communities from fragmenting and social networks from dissolving." [Henrich][434]

The same insight underpinned Friedrich Hayek's views on markets as organic machines for the calculation of efficient prices. But the evolutionary analysis goes beyond capitalist economics to see *all* social relations as a spontaneously self-generated order.

"Civilization advances by extending the number of important operations we can perform without thinking about them. If it is true that the spontaneous interplay

---

[434] Henrich (2016), at pgs. 5-6.

of social forces sometimes solves social problems that no individual mind could consciously solve, or even perhaps even perceive . . . they thereby create an ordered structure which increases the power of individuals without having been designed by any one of them." [Hayek, Studies on the Abuse and Decline of Reason][435]

Social learning provides more strategic options to the individual decision-maker than they could spontaneously invent on their own. Boyd & Richerson refer to the standard theory of rational-choice optimisation as *(self-)guided learning*, in which strategic variants are generated non-randomly by actors[436]. But the social and cultural transmission of information occurs more often through teaching and imitation, i.e. copying of the strategies of others. Imitative learning spreads adaptive strategies when self-guided learning is difficult or costly to acquire, as it often is in social, political and economic life[437]. In Hayek's free market economics, for example, simple price signals allow traders to exchange goods and services without knowing the society-wide supply and demand of every commodity.

Most social learning is therefore *biased*[438], in the sense that actors preferentially select strategies on the basis of some adaptive heuristic proxy for their fitness[439]. Biased social learning rules may preferentially imitate strategies that performed well the previous round (content-bias), or the strategy with the highest frequency in the population (frequency-biases[440]), or which are performed by other social agents of higher social status (prestige-bias). Learning strategies which copy the most common behaviour in the population are conformist – they operate on the basis of 'social proofs'. Strategies which preferentially copy less common strategies

---

[435] Hayek (2010), Chapter Nine.

[436] Boyd & Richerson (2005) at pg. 69.

[437] Boyd & Richerson (2005) at pg. 117.

[438] Boyd & Richerson (2005), Chapter 3;

[439] Boyd & Richerson (2005) at pgs. 79, 119 .

[440] See also McElreath & Boyd (2007), at pg. 38.

are non-conformist. Social agents may also employ some other heuristic, such as preferentially copying actors who are part of one's own kin or identity group.

What's important to note is that learning rules do not *optimise* for fitness – they *satisfice*. They are adaptive heuristics which employ low-cost proxies for fitness under conditions of uncertainty[441]. From the perspective of gene-culture evolution, it's unsurprising that some generalisable learning heuristics (such as respect for the elderly, or imitation of one's own parents) are universal (including in non-human species) and may be controlled genetically, whereas others (the instructive roles of different genders, or the rituals and clothing which designate certain individuals are respected members of their profession or religion) are culturally adaptive, unique to humans and only acquired through social learning.

Humans are exceptional behavioural imitators, and often copy one another subconsciously without realising they're doing so[442]. For example, we tend to sit or position ourselves instinctively in the same way as those with high social standing, and in one study people were more willing to cooperate with an individual who had earlier mimicked their style of sitting than someone who had not done so[443]. This sort of imitation is autonomic and unconscious: emotional states and their consequent behaviour can be transmitted through a population rapidly, without individuals being consciously aware of the instrumental motivation of their own behaviour.

Cultural selection between social strategies is subject to two additional replication rules[444]. Firstly, behavioural variants compete against one another for limited cognitive resources, such that rules that are easier to learn will more likely result in the replication of behaviour. Secondly, inherited information must have an effect on behaviour in order to be transmitted by imitation. Knowledge which is inherited but which does

---

[441] Simon (1955) at pgs. 99–118; Durham (1991); Boyd & Richerson (2005) at pgs. 71–72.

[442] Henrich (2016) at pgs. 48-49, 124-126.

[443] Muller et al. (2012) at pg. 891.

[444] Boyd & Richerson (2005) at pgs. 73-77.

not change a social agent's strategy will not be replicated if it is not relevant to the generation of the action. So the beliefs, reasons and motivations for cultural strategies can be easily lost, such that what once was a rational strategy becomes ritual, superstition and habit after a few generations.

The reliability of signals is of particular importance in social learning. We earlier noted studies in which chimps and human children performed equally well in some tests of problem-solving that lacked a social element. It turns out that human children (and dogs) sometimes perform *worse* at problem-solving when that social element is deliberately manipulated to provide wrong or incorrect information[445]. Humans will copy the behaviour of others even when it is irrational to do so. We will often copy unnecessary or irrelevant components of an action that has been taught to us even after being told that the extra step serves no purpose[446]. Again, chimps do not suffer from this bias when it comes to fitness-enhancing behaviour – they will adopt the most efficient strategy to get a resource[447]. Although our closest relatives have some of the rudiments of culture, it has clearly not played as large a role in their evolution as ours.

The spread of fads, rumours and myths is sometimes too fast to be subject to either natural or cultural selection unless it has truly disastrous fitness consequences – what we have inherited is the *instinct* for imitation and we blindly copy many behaviours that have no fitness consequences. Over thousands of generations, replicating social behaviours broadly must have been worth the trade-off of the occasional mass suicide – or mass fashion disaster[448]. So heuristics which induce us to preferentially copy strategies which are common in the population, or performed by certain high-status individuals, do not necessarily lead to improved fitness under *all* circumstances.

---

[445] Henrich (2016) at pg. 20.

[446] Henrich (2016) at pgs. 108-109.

[447] E.g. Horner & Whiten (2005) at pgs. 164-181.

[448] Henrich (2016) at pgs. 49-50.

* * *

Humans, of course, do not copy totally randomly. Unsurprisingly, given what we've learnt so far, we're far more likely to copy those we are pre-disposed to trust due to positive assortivity: kin, those who are physically close to us, those with high social standing, and members of our own cultural group. People will instinctively mimic those of higher social status to themselves, including how they hold themselves, their mode of dress, and their vocal tics. The power of celebrities and other high-status individuals to market goods, services and lifestyles to us – including in knowledge domains remote from their area of success – shows that our brain is adapted to imitating those who signal prior success[449]. People who signal high social status – including by sending false signals – have an innate advantage in encouraging others to not only cooperate with them but to copy in turn their own strategies.

A prestigious appearance – the right clothes, the right connections, the right name – opens a doorway to cultural fitness and faking it can be a highly successful exploitative strategy. The middle-class family who consumes beyond their means is hoping to exploit the deference and cooperativeness of others – purchasing a new car or a large home may be economically irrational but socially extremely sensible. But this exploitative strategy is subject to collective action problems – if it spreads to fixation in the population, then the signal will no longer carry any unique information content. Indeed, one of the ways in which social hierarchies constantly reinvent themselves is by innovating new and hard-to-fake signals of prestige that are not yet widely accessible to others.

Following the successful may sound a lot like hierarchy, but the psychologist Jo Henrich argues that prestige-based imitation is an entirely different mental mechanism[450]. Coercive dominance does not alter the motivation

---

[449] Henrich (2016) at pgs. 124-128; Foulsham et al. (2010) at pgs. 319-331. Cheng et al. (eds.) (2014); Witkower et al. (2020)

[450] Based on studies reported in Cheng et al. (2013) at pgs. 103-125; Henrich (2016), Chapter 8.

of subordinates: behaviour is externally enforced by the hegemon. The dominant emotional responses to force or the threat of force are fear, shame or anger – generating behavioural change through self-interest. On the other hand, individuals with lower social status do not feel fear or shame around prestigious individuals, rather they feel *awe* – a complex emotion which dissolves their individuality and encourages them to submit their self-interest to another. Being in a coercive hierarchy is stressful and unpleasant – humans avoid such situations wherever they can. But we'll actively seek out leaders to follow and pattern our lives around – be it parents, teachers or other cultural role-models, forming relationships that are free of coercion. Prestige imitation is how the replicator dynamic functions in a cultural setting.

The biologist Kevin Laland, among others, has argued that the evolution of teaching and language amongst humans permitted cultural evolution amongst humans to accelerate exponentially[451]. The higher the fidelity of signal transmission in a population, the longer that culturally advantageous knowledge will persist against the risk of cultural drift and behavioural mutation with deleterious fitness effects. In order for culture to be truly cumulative – for technological progress to occur and new information added to the collective knowledge base – – people should on average be able to trust the reliability of the information they receive, and this generates a presumption in favour of honesty. Humans are phenomenal imitators, even without formal instruction. But alongside symbolic communication and language came something extremely rare in nature: *altruistic teaching* by non-related adults[452].

Teaching, after all, consists of a long series of signals about the effectiveness of particular social strategies which increases the relative fitness of non-related children. Even when learning is carried out through pure observation and imitation, students and juveniles need to ensure that the instruction they are receiving is in their best interest and not an effort

---

[451] Laland (2017), Chapter 7; Muthukrishna et al. (2018).

[452] Laland (2017) at pgs. 158-166.

to exploit them. Teachers, obviously, are first introduced to children by their parents – a transfer of symbolic kinship to other non-related adults. And teachers [generally] enjoy strong social reputations and high status, reinforced by society-wide common beliefs about their valuable social role. Teachers themselves reinforce their role by performing socially expected actions, including the free dissemination of information, caring for their students, and establishing discipline when necessary[453]. Each of these mechanisms is built on a complicated scaffold of biological and cultural processes: what likely began millions of years ago as cooperative parenting in response to prolonged childhood amongst hominids[454] is now a global institution that provides generally good baseline socialisation to hundreds of millions of children every day.

Teaching is an altruistic strategy because it conveys a fitness-advantage on other members of the community. The association between altruistic behaviour and high social status is common in humans. Anthropological studies of many pre-modern societies have shown that leadership does not fall to the best hunter or most talented weaver in a community. Instead, leadership falls to those who share their wealth, often at great personal expense[455]. In these cases, the cultural advantage of serving as a role model to the rest of the community more than offsets the fitness cost of the material goods given up.

Of course, teachers, leaders and other authority figures have strong incentives to exploit group cooperation, so managing these power relationships has emerged as one of the primary social dilemmas for cultural evolution to solve, once human societies grew larger than could be managed on the basis of kinship and reputation alone[456]. The role of leadership in social species, therefore, is typically associated with strict expectations about behaviour and performance that can lead to violent backlash if not met.

---

[453] Laland (2017) at pg. 168; Boyd & Richerson (2005) at pgs. 53-154.

[454] Henrich (2016), at pgs. 307-311.

[455] Henrich (2016), at pgs. 137-139.

[456] Stoelhorst & Richerson Vol. 90S (2013) at pgs. S45-S56.

Teachers, leaders and individuals in positions of pastoral responsibility are held to a higher standard with regards to those in their care than as between two random individuals. Laws, norms and institution evolve to weld the disparate parts of the community together into a cohesive social organism – the subject of our next Chapter.

* * *

Once we have a firm notion of how individual social agents learn, the logical next step would be to examine how groups and societies acquire new information. But from the standpoint of multi-level selection – which is agnostic as to our level of analysis – we have in the most important sense already answered this question. Every individual is a multitude – a vast population of genes, cells and organs working together cooperatively and in equilibrium with itself. When a social agent acquires a new signal which leads them to adopt a new behaviour, what has occurred in practice is *selection among equilibria* in the organism. Whereas previously the agent was in an equilibrium state outputting strategy A, after learning they have shifted into an equilibrium state outputting strategy B, or outputting strategy A less often, or outputting strategy B under some circumstances.

Nation-states, the largest social organisms on Earth, therefore learn in much the same way as individuals. Kenneth Waltz, the father of modern realist statecraft, wrote in his definite *Theory of International Politics* that states learn by copying those more successful than themselves. States that fail to learn are vulnerable, and may be eliminated from the international system:

"A self-help system is one in which those that do not help themselves, or who do so less effectively than others, will fail to prosper, will lay themselves open to dangers, will suffer. . . . .[International politics] requires neither assumptions of rationality or of constancy of will on behalf of all [state] actors. The theory says simply that if some do relatively well, others will emulate them or fall by

the wayside."[457]

Waltz argued in terms that are familiar to the evolutionary game theorist, that the population of nation-states tends to converge on an equilibrium set of strategies -- forming a balance of power or hegemony:

"The close juxtaposition of states promotes their sameness through the disadvantages that arise from a failure to conform to successful practices. It is this 'sameness,' an effect of the system, that is so often attributed to the acceptance of so-called rules of state behaviour." [458]

What is true of genes within the cell, is true of neurons in the brain, is true of individual in society and even larger social organisms. Natural selection adjusts the population's equilibrium state depending on the group's differential fitness compared to others. Observed behaviour is the product of these multiple layers of equilibria – both constructed for the individual by their genes and culture, and by the individual as part of their contribution to the equilibrium of the community of the whole.

What forms does this inter-group competition take? When we discuss cultural group selection in humans, it is often [mistakenly] assumed that inter-group competition must take the form of violent conflict between groups, in much the same way that chimpanzee troops raid one another's territory, murdering any vulnerable individuals they find (Chapter 14: "The Dark Side of Cooperation"). There's a robust debate among anthropologists about the level of inter-group violence in pre-modern human societies[459] – with perhaps the best we can say at the moment being that absolute deaths from organised warfare were probably low until humans developed the

---

[457] Waltz (1979) at pg. 118.

[458] Waltz (1979) at pg. 118.

[459] E.g. Ferguson & Whitehead (eds.) (1992); Ferguson, "Pinker's List: Exaggerating Prehistoric War Mortality" in Fry (ed.) (2013) at pgs. 112-131; Fry & Soderberg (2013) at pgs. 270-273.

institutional tools to channel individual aggression for collective ends, but that given small population sizes even a small number of deaths might have represented an important selective pressure.

Warfare and group extinction clearly *can be* an important generator of differential fitness: modern nation-states would not exist if not for centuries of territorial conquest and consolidation by warlords and proto-states. Similarly, in the capitalist market, firms can and do go bankrupt and dissolve if they fail to compete profitably against other firms. But we do not need to go so far as the Charles Tilly and Peter Turchin, who have argued that war is the driving engine of creation and destruction that drives the evolution of society[460]. Thinking about natural selection in terms of these violent tropes – of nature 'red in tooth and claw' – limits horizons. Natural selection would operate on groups of differential fitness *even if the social agent was completely pacifistic and inter-group violence impossible.*

Inter-group competition can occur through at least four other mechanisms[461], although this is simply an indicative list. These include: differential group survival without conflict; differential migration; differential reproduction; and prestige-based cultural transmission. Even in the 19th century, Kropotkin argued that the most important aspect of the struggle for survival was the struggle against nature itself. A group which adopts strategies and behaviours which allow it to use resources more effectively, to adapt to changing environmental conditions and exploit new economic niches will probably outlast groups that fail to develop such strategies[462]. When groups can exchange members between themselves, groups which exert a stronger immigration pull will attract more new members, whereas those that drive members away will suffer from reduced prestige and power. And groups which adopt behaviours that facilitate social reproduction – the generation of new members of the community – will expand and grow whereas those that inflict on their population conditions of life that make

---

[460]Tilly (1975); Turchin (2016), Chapter 6.

[461] Henrich (2016), at pgs. 167-168.

[462]Smaldino, Schank & McElreath (2013) at pgs. 451-463.

social reproduction difficult will weaken and lose resilience.

Finally, because cultural replicators are not bound inside the bodies of individual agents and can be transmitted between groups, societies which signal their success and prestige will attract imitators *inside other groups*. Developing states will usually copy the norms and institutions of the hegemonic state of the day, and in doing so they might copy the form of an institution without understanding the history and social structure which makes a social institution stable in a particular population[463]. As with all forms of cultural imitation, irrational fads and fashions – for particular modes of dress, particular rituals or deities to worship – are just as likely to spread as strategies that would enhance group fitness.

A socialist is an individual who believes that the cultural norms and institutions generated and transmitted by cultural selection will tend – in the long run and on average – to take the form of cooperative and egalitarian social strategies which knit individuals together into a community of the whole.

"Different groups cultural evolve different social norms [and institutions]. Having norms that increase cooperation can favour success in competition with other groups that lack those norms. Over time, intergroup competition can aggregate and assemble packages of social norms that more effectively promote such success, and these packages will include social norms related to cooperation, helping, sharing, and maintaining internal harmony." [Henrich][464]

Which strategy or combination of strategies emerges as the equilibrium state in any particular historical moment is a question of empirical circumstance. There are certainly some durable social institutions in egalitarian societies which are decidedly non-egalitarian, such as law enforcement and the military[465]. And there may be times in which the social and material

---

[463] Henrich (2016) at pgs. 168–169.

[464] Henrich (2016) at pg. 167.

[465] Gelfand (2018) at pgs. 150–151.

environment changes so rapidly and the threat of group extinction is so high that the entire social equilibrium shifts in the direction of greater social conformity and rigidity[466]. Plenty of societies have strived to create strict social orders – some have even thrived, for a time. But most went extinct, and few are still extant. Social and material circumstances change slowly, but they do change, and populations which too strongly specialise in a particular mode of social and economic reproduction often find themselves maladapted when environments change

On the other hand, democratic institutions channel the dynamic tension of cultural selection with astonishing flexibility and resilience. Democratic societies are learning organisms. Over the long run, democratic institutions can adapt to changing circumstances, store more information about the fitness of a larger variety of strategies, and can switch between equilibria at lower cost. This offers an evolutionary advantage over other forms of large-scale social organisation. A free and open society does not merely provide an academy wherein elites can Reason freely provide all the answers to our social and political problems. Democracy is not defined by the ends it produces, or its capability to produce 'good policies'. It's defined by its robust *process* of selecting among potential internal equilibria in response to changing circumstances.

---

[466]Gelfand (2018), Chapter 4.

12

NORMS AS EQUILIBRIA

Key Points

- A social norm is an evolutionary stable group strategy sustained through a combination of social conformity, the internalisation of norms by individuals and the threat of punishment.
- Any social agent's normative beliefs and practices are the output of conscious and subconscious processes shaped by genes, environment, development and culture and must only be treated as descriptive of those processes.
- Normative beliefs and practices are a product of cultural evolution acting in the context of a particular population's material and social environment and mode of production.
- Universal political and social systems condition cooperation on a single marker of group identity – species status – laying the basis for a major transition in social organisation.

This book warned at the outset that evolutionary theory tells us nothing about how social agents *should* behave. Population behaviour is an emergent property of a complex system governed by relatively simple mathematical rules of interaction. And yet the median human being is utterly convinced some actions are *correct, moral* and *good*, and other actions are *incorrect, immoral* and *evil*. Those words have had no significant resonance so far in this book, but they are clearly important to how people make decisions and organise social structures. So are we mere evolutionary agents, or something more? People certainly act *as if* norms and values are real and significant factors in their decision-making. So how and why might self-conscious social agents evolve moral senses, and what adaptive purpose do norms play in social evolution? This Chapter is concerned with the relationship of moral and political philosophy with evolutionary theory, and how we should think about the role of social norms. By norms, we simply mean the rules and expectations that regulate social behaviour.

Compared to humans, almost every evolutionary agent we know of has weaker capacity for cognitive control over its intuitions. Even highly social animals are on the whole genetically, rather than culturally, adapted and significantly more strategically inflexible than humans. Individual animals and plants can be conditioned to favour some instincts over others, but this would have to be maintained for very many generations to have any impact on a species' intuitive behaviours (i.e. domestication). But the self-conscious social agent faces a unique cognitive paradox: awareness of alternative social behaviours and sufficient cognitive control and behavioural flexibility to select between them.

Humans alone – as far as we know – can conceive of different actions with different consequences. Only when a social agent is free to choose, and is *aware* of that freedom, is it possible to say that they experience 'right' and 'wrong'.

"[N]orms and normative laws can be made and changed by man [sic], and it is therefore man who is morally responsible for them; not perhaps for the norms which he finds to exist in society when he first begins to reflect upon them, but for the norms he is prepared to tolerate one he has found out he can do something [different]. . . .Nature consists of facts and of regularities, and is in itself neither moral nor immoral. It is we who impose our standards upon nature, and who in this way introduce morals into the natural world. . . .[R]esponsibility, decisions, enter the world of nature only with us." [Popper, the Open Society and Its

Enemies][467]

And what are the strategies that free agents choose between? Social agents are constrained from acting as purely hedonistic welfare maximisers by the need for their actions to be broadly acceptable to others – in the sense of allowing them to continue participating in social life. A social agent is free to the extent that they can select from strategies which vary from the average population norm [as they have received it][468]. Vary too greatly from those norms, and a social agent faces ostracism, punishment or even death. An agent can of course just choose to follow the group strategy but that choice is only free when they *could have chosen to do otherwise.* In a true totalitarian society, in which behavioural deviation from social expectations is impossible, humans beings are not in any sense free.

So only a behaviourally flexible, social species can acquire 'moral' sensibilities. In a state of nature, an individual has no need of them and may act as their impulses direct.

"Imagine a man endowed with the most inspired powers by nature, cast out from all human society into a desert since infancy. If he does not miserably perish, which is the most probable result, he will become nothing but a boor, an ape, lacking speech and thought. . . [Man] is above all a social animal. Only in society can he become a human being, that is, a thinking, speaking, loving, and wilful animal." [Bakunin][469]

There's no 'good' and 'evil' in nature until social agents enter into interdependent relations with one another and develop beliefs and expectations which define their membership and role in a society. We cannot therefore speak of the 'natural rights' of individuals as the early liberal philosophers

---

[467] Popper (1947), at pg. 61.

[468] Dennett (1984); Dennett (1995).

[469] Bakunin, "Three Lectures to Swiss Members" in Cutler, "The Basic Bakunin: Writings 1869-1871" Prometheus Books (1992)

did. A person alone in a state of nature has no claims to make on another, and therefore no claims by others to be protected against. All norms are social norms and all rights are social rights[470].

"Man completely realizes his [sic] individual freedom as well as his personality only through the individuals who surround him . . . Society, far from decreasing his freedom, on the contrary creates the individual freedom of all human beings. Society is the root, the tree, and liberty is its fruit. . . . Man becomes conscious of himself and his humanity only in society and only by the collective action of the whole . . . . the isolated individual cannot possibly become conscious of his freedom." [Bakunin, Man, Society & Freedom][471]

For most people most of the time, instincts and intuitions are if not determining what they should do then at least weighting the decision-making process in particular directions[472]. Humans are behaviourally flexible, yes, but not behaviourally unconstrained. Some courses of action are simply easier than others.

* * *

In moral philosophy, "capital-I" Intuitionism is an epistemological argument that moral intuitions provide true knowledge about the correctness of behaviour. Classical Intuitionists, such as Richard Price[473] [who posthumously published the work of Thomas Bayes] were 'naturalists'. They thought that an intuition about a particular action was a way of knowing some moral quality of the material universe. Most people even today approach moral and ethical questions in this way – they deduce the existence of universal laws from their own gut instincts about the correct

---

[470] Kymlicka (2002), Chapter 6, at pg. 244-.

[471] Bakunin, "Man, Society and Freedom" (1871).

[472] Damasio (1994); Grant et al. (2018) at pgs. 490-501.

[473] Price, "A Review of the Principle Questions in Morals" (1758).

course of action.

More empirical Intuitionists – including 19th century British 'sentimentalists' like David Hume and modern moral psychologists such as Jonathan Haidt – reject the idea of transcendental moral laws, but nevertheless hold that intuition is a valid method of discovering pragmatic knowledge about the world. In this view, emotional reactions provide a reliable guide to the correctness of behaviour – if a mental module [such as pleasure] evolved in all humans to generate a particular behaviour, then that behaviour is *good* for all humans, and if a mental module [such as pain or disgust] has evolved to prevent a particular behaviour, then that behaviour is *bad* for all humans. One can immediately detect the naïve adaptionism inherent in such a viewpoint: to the extent that our mental modules are the product of biological evolution, cultural socialisation and personal development, our moral senses will only offer guidance on the basis of past collective learning. Contemporary social and ethical dilemmas may be largely similar to past ones, but they may very well not be (see Chapter 16: "Outside Context Problems").

The core problem with Intuitionism is that in an evolutionary system the diversity of social agents is a given. Potential variation in individual emotional subjectivity and expression is vast – everyone's moral senses critically depend on the course of their individual development, and the sorts of social problems they confronted in childhood. Worryingly for the philosophers, different cultures cultivate the moral senses in systematically different ways, often for 'irrational' or historically-contingent reasons. No individual, society or culture can assert that it produces moral knowledge superior to others. We cannot rely on innate or intuitive virtue because we are socialised in the context of our particular culture and environment. No society is no more or less moral than any other because no society is no more or less adapted. They merely differ in scale, environment and complexity. Each rests at its own moral equilibrium.

One approach to developing normative politics from intuition, therefore, might be to empirically drill down to those moral senses which are shared [biologically] by all humans, regardless of culture – this is largely the work of the field of moral psychology in which Haidt operates. Haidt argues that some moral senses are biologically-rooted, shared across our species and pre-date the behavioural fragmentation brought about by the development of culture – these 'moral foundations', including an aversion to violence and a basic sense of fairness, are sufficiently ubiquitous as to constitute universal moral laws. And indeed, Haidt's moral foundations provide a good, barebones set of heuristics for solving simple social problems. John Rawls would recognise this approach as searching for the 'overlapping consensus', his own solution to the problem of ethical relativism[474].

Of course, this lowest common denominator technique gives you, at best, a set of behaviours that ensure the survival of hominins living in largely isolated family groups in a pre-agricultural environment. Such behaviours likely wouldn't be fitness optimising today, and may in fact harm the individuals and groups that try to live by them alone. Moral intuitions which are subject to genetic controls only convey a tiny fraction of the wisdom that has been accumulated by our species over hundreds of millennia about how to live together. Much more useful information is stored in our culture, and by ignoring that inheritance the moral foundations approach studies a moral animal no less abstract and unreal than the rational utility-maximiser of the economists.

The *reducto ad absurdam* of the Intuitionist approach is hedonistic utilitarianism[475] – premised on the minimisation of suffering and the maximisation of wellbeing. This may seem odd, since most "capital-R" Rationalists would also endorse some form of utilitarianism, which is seen as less emotional, more deliberative and more 'System 2'. Yet to see pleasure and pain as granting moral knowledge gives undeserved ethical precedence to primitive behavioural triggers that drive an organism to take actions that will aid their survival. Suffering and wellbeing are meaningless guides to behaviour because they're simply signals for an agent to either do a certain action again, or not do a certain action again. Pleasure and pain are certainly

---

[474] Rawls (1993).

[475] See generally Kymlicka (2002), Chapter 2, esp. pgs. 13-.

subjectively desirable, or undesirable. But since what we desire is the product of natural selection, developmental conditions in childhood and our cultural ecosystem, they tell us nothing about the correctness of decisions other than satisficing the bare minimum necessary for individual survival and reproduction – and even then only in particular contexts.

The meta-ethical approach which therefore best embodies the epistemology of cultural evolutionary theory is Emotivism or Expressivism. Both Rationalism and Intuitionism, broadly construed, are philosophies of moral realism. They suppose that there exists a choice, behaviour or strategy which is *correct, right* or *good* and concern themselves with how the self-conscious agent can figure out what that is. On the other hand, Emotivism holds that putatively normative beliefs are merely descriptive of subjective agent motivations[476]. So, for example, the statement that "murder is wrong" does not express a true proposition, but merely conveys a signal – which may or may not be accurate – regarding the speaker's aversion to the act and disgust at the thought of it being performed.

Emotivism therefore takes a position of moral anti-realism. Emotivists agree that is empirically accurate that humans select behaviour largely on the basis of subconscious intuitions, and that these intuitions likely evolved to aid their survival in the context of group selection. But intuitions do not provide knowledge of moral facts – which do not exist – only a description of the individual's own conscious and subconscious cognition (i.e. their internal equilibrium). Any statement containing the word *should*, or which makes claims about the *correctness, rightness* or *goodness* of behaviour, is either a mere description of a subjective preference, or a signal which is attempting to modify the emotional state of others, or both.

The human tendency to describe their behavioural options in normative or moralistic ways is best understood as a product of our capacity to consciously and unconsciously weigh the differential desirability of different courses of possible action in light of prior evolutionary learning by our forebears. We can then communicate our choices using verbal and non-verbal signals

---

[476] Ayer (1936); Nietzsche (1886) at para. 187.

to other members of our community. As discussed earlier, it's plausible that our capacity for moral reasoning was selected for because signalling emotional states was an important mechanism for maintaining group cohesion, enforcing pro-social behaviour and winning in competition against other groups. In a Machiavellian sense, the capacity to manipulate the emotions of others by normatively justifying one's own behaviour must have been a highly successful strategy for exploiting social dilemmas.

* * *

Emotivism provides a framework for understanding both the subjective moral experiences of individuals and the way they are expressed. But evolutionary sociology is ontologically centred on the population as a whole, with the preferences of individuals formed during the course of their development and socialisation. So what the evolutionary sociologist should be most interested in is the *distribution* of norms and beliefs in the population. What moral beliefs occur and with what frequency in the population?

We can only approach moral philosophy descriptively and from *within* the context of a particular population or social group. A shared norm, moral or ethic lays out expectations of correct and incorrect behaviour for community members in good standing. "When in Rome, do as the Romans do." Such an approach is sometimes termed ethical pragmatism, and has antecedents as far back as Aristotle. It meets all the criteria for an evolutionary approach to norms: it locates moral principles in the population as a whole, not the individual; it permits ethical standards to evolve and adapt over time; and it warns us against belief in fixed moral truths[477]. Unlike our ancestors, perhaps, every modern person recognises that ethical standards can shift quickly and will continue do so.

"What then is truth? A mobile army of metaphors, metonyms, and anthropomorphisms . . . which have been enhanced, transposed, and embellished poetically

---

[477] LaFollette, "Pragmatic ethics" in LaFollette (ed.) (2000) at pgs. 400–419.

and rhetorically, and which after long use seem firm, canonical, and obligatory to a people. Truths are illusions about which one has forgotten that is what they are . . . to be truthful means using the customary metaphors – in moral terms, the obligation to lie according to fixed convention." [Nietzsche, On Truth and Lies][478]

Pragmatic ethics, much like Darwinism, has traditionally been associated with reactionary and mistaken ideas about moral progress. For some naïve pragmatics, once a society develops a norm that 'works', that norm constitutes a universal goal towards which all other societies should also converge. Liberals tend to think this is true about liberalism, and socialists about socialism: indeed, modern development assistance to poor nations is often predicated on the belief that implementation of the normative and institutional structures of richer nations will lead to economic and social progress.

But the evolutionary perspective does not allow us to think of adaption as operating in this way. It may be that cultures with similar modes of life and economic production converge on similar normative beliefs, in much the same way that genetically-divergent species with the same ecological niche converge on similar body plans and behaviours. We cannot say the norms and institutions of a society are superior to those of another simply because its population is larger, or because it exploits resources in particular ways, or because of its relative social complexity. The woodpecker and the fungi simply exploit different ecological niches – one is not more 'evolved' than the other. In the same way, city-dwellers have different norms to hunter-gatherers *because they are city-dwellers and have to solve different social problems*, not because the city-dweller is in some sense culturally 'more advanced' – or vice-versa.

Moral and political philosophy is therefore primarily an investigation into the social and ecological conditions of a community. Shared group norms are a population-level strategy which responds to a particular material

---

[478] Nietzsche, "On Truth and Lies in a Nonmoral Sense" (1873).

and social environment, mode of social organisation and production. A community's values and ideals shape the behaviour of its members, but only dialectical and dynamic theories can even attempt to explain why and how a community comes to possess some norms and not others.

"[W]e do not set out from what men [sic] say, imagine, conceive, nor from men as narrated, thought of, imagined, [or] conceived . . . . We set out from real, active men, and on the basis of their real life-process we demonstrate the development of the ideological reflexes and echoes of this life-process. The phantoms formed in the human brain are also, necessarily, sublimates of their material life-process, which is empirically verifiable and bound to material premises. Morality, religion, metaphysics, all the rest of ideology and their corresponding forms of consciousness, thus no longer retain the semblance of independence. . . . Life is not determined by consciousness, but consciousness by life." [Marx, the German Ideology] [479]

In a game theoretic sense, a norm can be treated as an equilibrium position in a social game[480]. A norm is a strategy, or combination of strategies, that is a best reply to itself. A social norm is also an equilibrium in beliefs, because when people follow it consistently they ratify the beliefs of other social agents with the same strategy. A social norm becomes evolutionarily stable when it provides social agents who follow it relative fitness no worse than other agents who follow the norm, and better than social agents with alternative strategies. A collection of social norms constitutes an implied social contract – all members of the community have legitimate expectations about one another's behaviour and can resort to sanctions when those expectations are violated.

For example, in coordination and anti-coordination games with multiple accessible equilibria, social norms can coordinate between the possible solution sets – a social agent may have no rational preference for one

---

[479] Marx, "A Critique of The German Ideology" Progress Publishers (1968), Part 1.A.

[480] Gintis (2017) at pgs. 121-123.

outcome for the other, but deviating from the social expectation (or acting in a way that was morally incorrect) would be potentially catastrophic[481]. In some countries we drive on the left and in others in the right – a choice that as virtually no consequential difference in outcome until the moment we deviate from it. Language operates in precisely this way: there is an infinite number of sounds we could use to symbolically represent four-legged canine companion animals, but calling one a 'dog' will ensure you're understood. Moral anti-realism does not suppose that all equilibria are equally likely – the structure of the game may make some equilibria more accessible than others – but all potential states are theoretically available.

Moral beliefs, therefore, are simply conventions which a population has evolved and which provide adaptive heuristics for re-solving social dilemmas common to its community[482].

"The core idea in the [norms]-as-equilibria approach is that it is ultimately the behaviour and the expected behaviour of others rather than prescriptive rules . . . that induce people to behave (or not to behave) in a particular way. The aggregated expected behaviour of all the individuals in society, which is beyond any one individual's control, constitutes and creates a [social] structure . . . this structure motivates each individual to follow a regularity of behaviour in that social situation and to act in a manner contributing to the perpetuation of that structure."[483]

The philosopher Christina Bicchieri[484], one of the leading proponents of a game theoretic approach to norms, argues that the stability of a particular social norm reflects a combination of three influences: firstly, the empirical frequency of a norm within the population (i.e. what fraction of the

---

[481] Lewis (1969).

[482] Lewis (1969); Sugden (2004); Gintis (2017) at pg. 125.

[483] Greif & Kingston, "Institutions: Rules or Equilibria?" in Schofield & Caballero (eds.) (2011) at pg. 25.

[484] Bicchieri (1993); Bicchieri (2006).

population is believed to carry the strategy); secondly, the effectiveness of a particular norm in being internalised by other social agents (i.e. the likelihood that another agent will comply with the norm even when it is not in their self-interest to do so); and lastly, the strength of the expected punishment for deviating from the norm. What matters is not that *everyone* in a community conforms to a particular norm, or that *everyone* agrees that a particular action is the right thing to do, or that punishment will *certainly* follow wrong-doing. What matters is that these factors taken together render a social norm stable.

Social norms exist for a given community even if they are occasionally violated. And social norms continue to exist even if the particular political and legal authorities do not punish deviance, or if those authorities themselves cease to exist. An intuitive sense of 'right' and 'wrong' are merely heuristics that ensure that individual decision-making is good enough maintain the community most of the time. Our awareness that no one shares 100 per cent of their morality with everyone else, and that 'evil' deeds will not necessarily be punished, creates social anxiety about normative behaviour and the space in which free will exists (see Chapter 18: "Freedom is Scary"). Traditionally, structuralist social theories de-emphasise free will (they are deterministic). Under an evolutionary paradigm, however, social agents have constraints on their behaviour but can challenge those constraints by dynamically changing strategies – a position moral philosophers label 'compatibilism'.

* * *

Social norms develop through cultural evolution, and cultural evolution is subject to the same mathematical laws and structures as every other form of natural selection. So any normative system is likely to feature the mechanisms of positive assortivity game theory requires for cooperative strategies to evolve. Which mechanism predominates will be a function of the population's need to maintain cooperation at the relevant scale. If we look at the smallest-scale human communities, we should expect to see moral systems that centre on kinship or simple hegemonies. Whereas larger-scale societies with denser populations and more frequent interactions with non-kin should employ more symbolic strategies for generating positive assortivity, including reputation networks and constitutive group identities.

The cultural evolutionary tradition treats religions, in the sense of collections of cultural norms, beliefs and practices, as semi-coherent normative equilibria[485]. For a social norm or practice to become constitutive of a cooperative group identity, it's not necessary that the beliefs that underpin be empirically true in any meaningful sense (in scientific terms, that they be falsifiable), nor that the rituals and behaviour that signal group membership have rational cause. Preparing food in a particular ritualistic manner may carry a small cost, but the social benefit of ritual in terms of generating social cohesion may far outweigh it. It's only necessary that adherence to the norm, belief or ritual provides a community a relative fitness advantage compared to other groups[486].

Cultural evolution proceeds through the differential success of populations, and therefore groups which generate more efficient cooperation will outcompete groups with less or more costly internal cooperation. It's not hard to imagine that early communities which were bound together by ancestor cults or localised gods might have traded, fought, and produced more reliably than communities which lacked common beliefs. Moral systems which require, for example, human sacrifice or encourage wanton destruction can of course emerge through cultural experimentation, drift and mutation. But communities which develop such systems are less likely to survive and be imitated, such that over historical time belief systems which generate cooperative, pro-social behaviour become more common.

During the Axial Age – a period corresponding to the middle of the first millennium BCE – new forms of religion emerged alongside new forms of social production including iron working, coinage, and global trade[487].

---

[485] Wilson (2003).

[486] Wilson (2015), Chapter 6.

[487] Jaspers (1949); Christian (2004); Graeber (2011); Turchin (2016), Chapter 9.

The Buddha, Zcroaster, and the ancient Greek and Chinese philosophers likely all lived within a few generations of one another. In relatively short order, the religious and philosophical systems they founded and inspired dominated the cultural and political lives of most of the human population, and underwrote a sufficient degree of inter-cultural understanding that large multiethnic and multilingual empires came to dominate human social and political life. Unlike earlier social contracts, which had tied religiosity − and citizenship − to people living in particular places, or as part of particular family and social networks, or of a particular ethnic heritage, the new belief systems were predicated on a single identity marker − adherence to the forms and rituals of the religion. The most successful of the new cultural complexes − Christianity, Islam and Buddhism − in theory opened membership in the community up to anyone. *"[A]ll of the [major] religions known in the world are founded, as far as they relate to man, on the unity of man as being all of one degree"* [Paine, the Rights of Man][488]

Beyond kinship, beyond social networks and beyond imagined religious communities we find the truly universal ideologies: sets of beliefs and rules which promote cooperation between all social agents regardless of the arbitrary tags carried by individuals and groups. Into this category belong the secular political ideologies including enlightenment liberalism. Universalising ideologies and religions share an information structure where ignoring superficial identity markers is the most important thing; where different classes, races and beliefs can work together so long as they send the correct ritual signs of mutual respect. They are a kind of pooling strategy because they encourage social agents to disregard all other signals of another person's Type other than their shared humanity. Agents of every Type have the same behaviour, and this is sufficient to sustain cooperation regardless of Type.

The political and social struggles which define the universalist social systems are struggles to be recognised as human as such − a person must be recognised by others as a social subject, entitled to equal regard by

---

[488] Paine, "Rights of Man, Part One" (1791).

both the law and other citizens, before the equal dignity promised by the liberal social contract can be claimed and granted. The first liberal regimes of Western Europe were, by-and-large, as racist and patriarchal as the *ancien regimes* they replaced. The fraternal liberty among property-owners ignored medieval markers of difference and positioned them as a potentially hegemonic coalition within the population as a whole. But their relative success encourage others outside their narrow cliques to imitate their rhetoric and adopt the same egalitarian social ethos. The message of a universal citizenship which liberal elites used to signal membership of the community of the Enlightened *philosophes* could be copied and sent back to them by women, working people and racial, religious and sexual minorities.

It turns out that by incorporating other groups into itself, liberal democracy proved far more fit than any prior social, economic and political system. The social hierarchies present within early liberalism turned out to be unimportant – and in fact a long-term drag on its success. And as the liberal European empires set about conquering vast swathes of planet, colonised people also found in the rhetoric of their conquerors the cultural tools they could use to throw off the foreign yoke and claim their right to self-government as equals. Gandhi, Nkrumah and the other products of a colonial education re-established the sovereignty of their peoples in terms recognised, albeit begrudgingly, by the imperial metropoles.

Of course, liberalism's adaptability also means that when environmental conditions allow it can respond by *excluding* parts of society from itself, tightening social hierarchies and establishing ideological hegemonies. In other words, democracies can swing right as well as left, depending on environmental and historical conditions. The political and social immune system of liberalism permits a significant degree of behavioural omnivory but also exposes the body politic to exploitation by parasitic and cancerous beliefs and practices which can exploit liberal tolerance to undermine and destroy it (see the next Chapter: "Social Cancers").

No matter the gap between the rhetoric of liberalism and the reality, it is only from *within* the normative framework of an existing society that we can begin to discuss how we *should* behave as social agents. In this regard, symbolically denoted, universal liberalism forms the invisible ideological structure into which almost everyone in the West and beyond is socialised. It is the air we breathe, the guiding hand behind our actions and our beliefs and defines the boundaries within which almost all modern human life and behaviour is contextualised. By granting personhood to the entire species qua species, humanism contains within itself the potential for an ever-expanding circle of inclusion and cooperation.

Universalism defines the limits of the normative community, but not the rules that guide behaviour in every situation. People might still act as if they owe more to relatives than to strangers, to neighbours than to strangers, to friends than colleagues, and to members of our own in-group to those in an out-group. It's widely accepted that we owe special moral duties to some people[489]. An entire set of social, cultural and legal taboos regulates family relationships, and we are permitted to voluntarily give up rights in contractual relationships that others are ordinarily not permitted to violate. The guilt that even 'virtuous' individuals we feel at favouring our own family over helping those worse off is simply our conscious awareness of these mental mechanisms resolving their relative priority.

Universal symbolic humanism only operates at the broadest level of cooperation – the community of the whole. Within that community, different groups and sub-groups of individuals will be constantly coming together under various social and cultural arrangements to form short- or long-term associations to solve unique social problems. The potential mechanisms that govern such associations, under multilevel selection, are the same as those that govern co-operation on every other scale. Some groups will organise themselves on the basis of kinship, others reputation, geographic networks, biological or cultural markers, or symbolic ritual beliefs. And there may be dynamic tensions between the norms which govern some parts of the community and the norms of others.

Indeed, some sub-groups within a nominally universal community which cooperate more effectively with one another could theoretically gain a

---

[489]Parfit (1984); Kymlicka (2002) at pgs. 22-26.

relative fitness advantage – for both good and ill. Liberal and Confucian social systems have historically developed elaborate legal and punitive systems for the suppression of kin-preference and networks of reciprocity (a.k.a. 'corruption), at least amongst strata with a large political and cultural influence. And they also tend to establish systems of rights and duties that limit the potential range of outcomes for individuals and family, thereby suppressing intra-population conflicts. The forging of a universal political community is largely a question of how well the political organism suppresses internal competition that is harmful to the whole (see the next Chapter, "Social Cancers"). But by permitting largely unrestricted cultural and social experimentation, the strategy space available to liberal democracies is larger than other forms of social organisation.

$$* * *$$

The socialist tradition represents the culmination of the same evolutionary process by which liberal norms developed. Socialists carry forward the idea that a universal community of cooperation is not only possible but desirable. We pick up after liberalism, not only in insisting on full civil and political rights for all citizens regardless of race, sexuality or gender, but by seeking to guarantee social and economic equality to all, regardless of class, wealth or income. The socialist position is that more egalitarian social and cultural norms will produce societies that are more tolerant and inclusive, and potentially economically and culturally more successful than competitor societies.

"[Socialists] do not want to destroy [liberalism], [we] want to sublimate it. That is, [socialists] want to take all that is good in it, and go beyond it. Liberalism is a profound democratic position . . . critical to any possible good future. But liberalism points beyond itself." [Harrington][490]

---

[490] Quoted in Gorman (1995) at pg. 71.

Nevertheless, the granting of community membership and the possession of fundamental rights and privileges to *homo sapiens* only is an arbitrary rule. In relying on the social species concept, we reject recognition of personhood on the basis of divinely-granted status, or some distinctive biological trait or characteristic. There is no single physical or cognitive capacity which we could demonstrate, without exception, was possessed by every human regardless of their mental or physical health and not possessed by any other category of social agent. It's an interesting hypothetical scenario how liberalism might have adapted itself, if in some alternative history our Neanderthal and Denisovan cousins still walked the Earth, but that's not a question we're asked to answer here.

Proponents of animal rights tend to believe that since suffering is common to both social and non-social species, then moral wrongs against animals are of the same category as moral wrongs against humans. Earlier, we noted the weak grounding of moral claims based on the prevention of suffering. But the evolutionary approach to social norms provides other bases for dismissing the alleged moral interests of non-human animals. In order to be part of a society, a category of being has to be capable, under ideal developmental conditions, of recognising and being recognised as performing the symbolic behaviours establishing social trust – of being a social species. Since we cannot directly observe the subjective consciousness of others, mutual recognition of ethical value serves as a universal 'Turing Test' – we can only react to signals which increase or decrease our belief that others have moral status.

With a handful of notable exceptions, very few living beings are capable of symbolically reciprocating human social behaviour. We may be able to hijack the kin preference of some animals to act as surrogate parents and herd-mates, and we may be able to develop bonds of trust based on reciprocal grooming and feeding. But non-social species cannot parse human behaviours for symbolic meaning and lack the physical, mental and behaviour abilities to reciprocate in kind with unfamiliar individuals. Certainly many cultures value the domestic dog, which have been selectively bred over tens of thousands of years to fit into human social structures and which, arguably, instinctively trusts humans and understand our symbolic communication – but others do not. Some cultures recognise and respect the moral value of other highly social mammals with the rudiments of symbolic communication – notably the great apes, elephants and cetaceans – but others do not.

"I can feel free only in the presence of and in relationship with other men [sic].
In the presence of [another] species of animal I am neither free nor a man,
because this animal is incapable of conceiving and consequently recognizing my
humanity." [Bakunin, Man Society and Freedom][491]

In order for group selection to generate adaptive pressures which promote the evolution of cooperation, we must draw the boundaries of the political community somewhere. Given that we are yet to undertake a major transition where we treat all human everywhere with equal moral regard (see Chapter 14: "The Dark Side of Cooperation"), it seems as yet unjustifiable to include non-human animals within our social contract – although some communities and sub-communities may do so in various culturally-specific ways. Such norms are no different than religious beliefs or aesthetic preferences in terms of their claim to moral truth - the personhood of a non-human species is a non-scientific question. But regardless of irrationality, respect for certain animals may have a fitness-enhancing effect it becomes an salient marker of group identity for a particular group. We may say, with some small foundation, that how a culture treats animals can signal how they treat other social beings within their own community.

---

[491] Bakunin, "Man, Society and Freedom" (1871).

13

SOCIAL CANCERS

Key Points

- A cancer is a pathology that occurs when part of an organism replicates selfishly, unconstrained by the mechanisms that ordinarily keep it in check, so as to exploit and ultimately destroy the organism.
- Fascism is a social cancer that undermines the norms and values that sustain cooperation in liberal societies. Since the usual mechanisms of liberal social control cannot detect and eradicate it, democratised ostracism of fascist beliefs and practices is necessary.
- Market extremism also attacks the egalitarian social values which are necessary for a liberal social contract society to function and, when adopted by elites with access to power, poses a threat to ongoing survival of democratic societies.

We've covered a great deal of theoretical ground so far, from the mathematics of simple two-player games all the way to meta-ethics and epistemology. This Chapter is a pivot point; from this point forward, we'll start to consider how the evolutionary perspective generates insight about everyday social and political phenomena. These include some of the big challenges that all complex political communities face: the limits of tolerance, the nature of citizenship, the origins of political violence the function of cultural conservatism and the drivers of political change. We'll approach these issues from the perspective of the social organism developed in previous Chapters, that is: a symbolic-denoted population, capable of ongoing cultural experimentation and adaption, with specialised social institutions and norms to choreograph individual behaviour.

If we think of a political and economic community mechanistically, then when something goes wrong we'll search for solutions by consulting the instructions: we can always restore the *status quo ante* by removing and replacing the broken part. But if were to think of our communities as living organisms, then this mechanistic theory of reform would be too simplistic. Such direct intervention against dysfunctional social elements may be worse than the disease. Doctors don't replace limbs at the first sign of trouble: they first try to aid the body to heal itself. Living beings can break down when attacked by an external pathogen; they can suffer either trauma or chronic injury from their environment; or can suffer from reduced fitness owing to the particular combination of replicators they inherited from their ancestors. It's the same with social organisms: political communities can decline when attacked, when afflicted by natural or economic disaster, or by simply by being outcompeted by other social groups with a different mode of social organisation.

Cancers are a special category of pathology. Although they can be triggered by physical trauma or external attack, what makes a disease cancerous is when a part of the organism turns against the whole. A cancer is not a foreign organism: it is a group of the organism's own cells that have broken free – through various means – of the 'rules' expected of cells in a multicellular organism. As a result, cancers undergo selfish growth and replication, hoarding of the body's resources and abandoning functions essential for the rest of the organism to survive.

Cancers are an almost ubiquitous threat to all multi-cellular organisms because when a population of cells undergoes a major evolutionary transition to multi-cellularity, selfish behaviour is only suppressed, not eliminated. Genetic and behavioural mutation is inevitable, even outside germline DNA, and so every organism has mechanisms in place to ensure that cells which develop harmful behaviour, or otherwise stop performing their function, are eliminated and replaced. Any organism that lacked such a mechanism would be driven extinct by the selfish actions of its sub-components. But every now and again, a mutation will spontaneously occur which gives some cells an immense fitness advantage over their neighbours and which the organism's ordinary mechanisms of punishment and repair cannot deal with. The new behaviour spreads rapidly, collapsing intracellular cooperation and causing the death of the organism. A cancer genome of course does not 'know' that by doing so it typically[492] also kills itself – it only knows that its relative fitness is suddenly much greater than its peers. The dynamics of natural selection do the rest.

If we think of cancer in game theory terms, then this characteristic life cycle has obvious analogues in other evolutionary systems. Cancer is a perturbation of a population of co-operators by a small population of mutated, selfish exploiters; these exploiters, if left unchecked, make the existing equilibrium unstable and instigate a phase transition to the 'all defect' state, the war of all against all. The body's specialised mechanisms for the punishment of cellular deviancy are thus equivalent to the *vengeful* strategy in iterated games – but we know that the *vengeful* strategy can be defeated by a selfish coalition of sufficient size or relative fitness advantage.

This Chapter is about the phenomenon of *social* cancers. Do cultural organisms face the same pathologies as biological ones? Of course – they are governed by the same evolutionary laws! By a direct analogy, social cancers are pathologies of the community not caused by an invasion or an attack on the body politic by an outside force. Rather, a social cancer arises when part of the social organism turns against the rest, adopting behaviours and strategies that benefit itself at the expense of the viability of the community as a whole. This point bears repeating: social cancers are *us*. They are what happens when self-interest, greed and exploitation

---

[492] A small percentage of cancers are capable of ongoing survival outside the body of their original host. Such transmissible cancers are better known among other animals than humans, but several cases of cancers being transmitted between human organ donors have been reported. Dingli & Nowak (2006) at pgs. 35-36.

are allowed to spread unchecked in the social organism, undeterred by the social norms and institutions which ensure the healthy functioning of the community. If left untreated, social cancers can completely overwhelm their host, causing its death and replacement by something altogether new.

Let's look at the defining characteristics of cancer, and see what they tell us about social cancers:

- Firstly, a cancer is defined by its *unrestricted and unlimited growth*. Cancer cells reproduce without limit, seizing the available resources of organism to promote their own growth at the expense of the survival of the organism. By analogy, a social cancer is an individual or group of individuals who exploit others and defects from mutual cooperation in order to acquire resources and relative social advantage without limitation.
- Secondly, a cancer is characterised by its *unresponsiveness to the organism's ordinary mechanisms of control*. More than being merely exploitative, a cancer can escape punishment for its selfishness: cancer cells grow and divide beyond the limits of their usual specialised role, and are able to confuse or defeat the body's normal immune response. Social cancers are similarly free from the constraints established by social and cultural norms and can outcompete, confuse or defeat specialised institutions of social control.
- Thirdly, cancers enjoy the *absence of self-limitation* – in other words, they are free of internal as well as external constraints. Ordinarily, our body's cells are programmed to automatically destruct under certain conditions[493], most typically when the cell is damaged; cancers almost always have ways to escape this self-limitation. When speaking of social cancers, we are speaking of individuals and groups which lack the psychological or institutional motivation to comply with social

---

[493]Villarreal, "From Bacteria to Belief: Immunity and Security" in Sagarin & Taylor (eds.) (2008) at pgs. 42-68.

norms[494]. So an individual may lack the capacity to feel shame at their actions, or a social group may deliberate cultivate this by generating in-group norms which override those of the community.

- Fourthly, cancers construct an *alternative infrastructure* to support their own growth and reproduction at the expense of the organism as a whole. Lone cancers that do not cooperate with themselves are unlikely to survive to defeat the immune system. But cancers often form large bodies [tumours] of cooperating cells, with their own blood supply and internal differentiation. Social cancers are similar: the lone sociopath may lack self-limitation and escape the notice of law enforcement for some time. Dangerous, yes, but not a threat to the ongoing viability of society. But a community of such people, who cooperate to build an infrastructure of safehouses, financial networks and corrupt law enforcement officers will survive and reproduce, threatening the viability of the community as a whole.

- Finally, a cancer is characterised by its *invasion and destruction of other parts of the organism*. A benign tumour leaves the other parts of the body alone. But a cancer seeks to acquire unlimited resources. A social cancer is implacable hostile towards the strategies and behaviours that define the community; it will not rest until it has converted everyone else to its way of life, or destroyed them. We can imagine them as extremist religious cults that see society as irredeemably impure, revolutionary political movements that see the current order as beyond saving, and economic modes of production that demand the elimination of all competitors for the labour and natural resources of society.

Equipped with this set of definitions, we can clearly see what is *not* a social cancer. Routine behavioural variation and mutation is not in and of itself dangerous to the survival of the social organism. As we saw in previous Chapters, individuals and groups will constantly experiment with

---

[494]"In such cases, self-regarding actors who treat social norms pure instrumentally will behave in a socially inefficient and morally reprehensible manner." Gintis (2017) at pg. 122.

new behaviours, new social and sexual norms, new religious beliefs and new modes of economic organisation. For the most part, these groups and individuals remain a part of the community: variant, yes, but also laying claim to the same rights and privileges as others, engaging in ordered social life on more-or-less regular terms. Indeed, the presence of such variation is positively necessary for the population to continue to evolve.

Minority social groups may have to fight to be recognised[495], to convince the metaphorical 'immune system' of the body politic that the way in which they differ from social expectations poses no threat. This may not happen without conflict and strife, but we know they have been successful when society adopts a new equilibrium in which a behavioural tag which previously triggered a social backlash is rendered irrelevant and the membership in the community is made more universal. Under conditions of cultural selection, the incorporation of new organs into the body politics improves the fitness of the whole, or else it fails entirely.

Another category of social deviance that is not necessarily dangerous are the cultural equivalent of benign tumours: groups which develop unique behaviours and stop cooperating with the body as a whole but which do not imperil its survival. We can think of these as cults, communes and convents who reject prevailing social and cultural norms and create isolated utopian communities. Individuals who participate in these projects prefer to interact only with one another, but the group as a whole does not seek to exploit the rest of society. Examples of these kinds of variant sub-groups include the Anabaptists in North America, Ultraorthodox Judaism, New Age cults, revolutionary communes, and quietist *salafis*. Such groups may increase or decrease the population's average fitness, and they may over long periods act as laboratories for the types of social rules the rest of society might either seek to emulate or avoid. But for the social organism as a whole, it's [usually] safe to adopt a live-and-let live attitude. Attacking an otherwise benign group may intensify competition and turn them cancerous.

---

[495] Taylor, "Multiculturalism: Examining the Politics of Recognition" in Gutmann (ed.) (1994) at pgs. 25-73.

* * *

What sets a social cancer apart is its implacable incompatibility with the prevailing social order. This can be self-conscious, as with political movements that have as their objective the overthrow of the existing political structure. But a social cancer can also be constituted by any set of behaviours which sees the norms, beliefs and practices of society as large as a legitimate target for exploitation and encourages aggressive, selfish behaviour in every social interaction. Remember that a society's foundations are the mechanisms of positive assortivity which encourage trusting, cooperative behaviour with other co-operators. Social cancers build an alternative infrastructure which identifies only other social agents of their own type as friendly and every other agent as a target for exploitation.

Let's take a look at a couple of types of social cancer, to see how this operates. As we discussed in the last Chapter, religious beliefs and rituals are one of the main ways in which human groups organise themselves into communities of shared meaning. Even in liberal, secular societies many social agents are motivated to engage in political activity by their religious beliefs and do so successfully without threatening the ongoing viability of the community. This is as true of the Christian Democrats in Germany, as it is of Komeito in Japan, the BJP in India, or the Muslim Brotherhood. However, many religious movement give birth to fundamentalist or puritanical offshoots, which reject the mixed equilibria of mainstream society. But even so, fundamentalism alone poses no threat the whole and if adherents merely remove themselves from mainstream society, they tend to form utopian communities that quietly go extinct.

The line demarking malignancy is crossed when, and only when, a fundamentalist group adopts a policy of hostility and aggression towards the broader community. Radicalisation is not an easy or inevitable process. It involves *re-socialisation* of individuals to the new, pure community – with the adoption of new rituals, beliefs and symbols of membership[496]. It also

---

[496]Bialas (2013) at pgs. 3-25; Kuhne, "Nazi Morality" in Baranowski et al. (eds.) (2018).

involves their *de-socialisation* from all of the symbolic beliefs and practices which make them part of mainstream society – such that what previously were received as signals of inclusion become triggers of a threat response and backlash. When a social cancer has reached the point of encouraging exploitation and violence against others, with no distinctions as to the normally sanctified categories of pro-sociality, then it becomes a terrorist group which poses a dire potential threat to the political community.

Terrorism exists at a nexus of group and individual behaviour. There are a potentially huge number of ideologies and beliefs which tacitly approve of violence towards outgroups. And society always features a large pool of disenfranchised or poorly socialised young people whose attachment to the ordinary mechanisms of social control are attenuated and who are capable in some situations of violence. But a social cancer only emerges when the two combine to produce self-sustaining radicalisation. Extremism attracts converts: it successfully overrides routine socialisation, and encourages individuals to commit acts which spread the message of the group and starts the cycle all over again. When a terrorist group can reproduce itself in this way, and defeat the institutions which aim to stop it, it becomes a social cancer. We should not be surprised that the subjective beliefs and goals of many terrorists are confused or unclear: what matters is that the *strategy of violence they perform is self-replicating*[497].

It hardly needs to be said that social cancers prosper best when society is at its weakest: following defeat in war, after a major economic depression, or in periods of intense social polarisation. At such times, not only is the number of disaffected social actors highest, but the social immune system which would ordinarily detect and defend against extremism is weak, divided or distracted. This pattern is as true of the rise of the Islamic State – a cancerous proto-community – as it is of Bolsheviks in St Petersburg in 1917 and the Freikorps of Germany in 1919. Social cancers can arise in any place, at any time – but they grow and thrive best in the immuno-compromised

---

[497] Lafferty et al., "The Infectiousness of Terrorist Ideology: Insights from Ecology and Epidemiology" in Sagarin & Taylor (eds.) (2008) at pgs. 105-124.

social organism.

Of all the types of cancer which prey on the liberal social organism, fascism is the most common and fatal threat. There's no absence of religious fundamentalists in the cultural West, and left-wing revolutionary movements have also gone through phases of violent radicalism (c.f. the anarchist terrorism of Blanqui, Bakunin and the People's Will in nineteenth century and the Weather Underground and Red Army Faction in the twentieth). But while left-wing extremists may see the norms and institutions of liberalism as weak, corrupt, or a limit on the creation of their perfect society, fascists reject those norms as norms. Fascists oppose the idea of individual rights, the rule of law, and the subjection of political and economic power to limitations that lift up the weakest. They institute a regime of domestic militarism and violence in place of a regime of domestic peace. They reject the idea of the universal citizen and in its place substitute group belonging on the basis of superficial markers of identity – usually, but not always, racial tags. And they reject the egalitarian dignity of all citizens in favour of rigid hierarchies and obedience to a hegemonic leader or party. Fascism is not an ideologically coherent program: it is liberalism's anti-ideology.

Fascist ideas and fascists practices are always present on the margins within liberalism, because they demarcate the liminal boundaries of its community. Liberal states often behave barbarously towards foreign peoples and migrants, precisely because this barbarism contrasts with the dignity owed to members of the domestic political community. The tactics of fascism are therefore honed abroad, or on indigenous lands or in prisons hidden deliberately partitioned off from social norms. But liberal societies draw a veil that ordinarily prevents these strategies from operating in the metropole. It's only when these behaviours are deployed inwards on the community itself that we say that a social cancer has emerged.

The rise of fascism at home is most likely under conditions of internal stagnation and external challenge: fascism in Europe was an inevitable reaction to the Great War, the Great Depression and the weakness of the bourgeoisie democracies, much as Putin was a response to the collapse of the USSR and Trump to the liberal failures of the Iraq War and the Great Recession. In these times, the idea that prevailing liberal norms are themselves responsible for the community's declining relative fitness gains purchase, alongside the rising populations of marginalised and disaffected people ready to be converted to the cause. Fascism is literally liberalism in decay[498].

Because they arise from within liberalism, fascists are adept at falsifying the signalling strategies liberals use to maintain social norms. Fascists do not care about freedom of speech, the right to protest or democratic elections and upon obtaining political and social power would abrogate these rights for everyone. Yet liberals are unable to distinguish between genuine democrats and fascists who wear the clothes of democrats. Fascism uses the tools of liberalism to undermine and destroy it in the same way cancers use the lymphatic system of the organism to travel freely and ultimately destroy it. Fascists implement their exploitative signalling strategy by re-socialising adherents with an alternate set of beliefs which emphasises that liberal social norms are merely a performance. Modern fascists refer to this as 'red pilling'. For most people most of the time, the performance of an action and belief in its moral correctness are one and the same. But for malignant social agents, instinctive norm-following is replaced by a gleeful willingness to exploit the pro-social intuitions and biases of others. Violence and exploitation become moral actions for the individual fascist.

Fascist signs and signals thus have two audiences and two sets of effects. For the ordinary liberal, fascist signals appear within the realm of permissible social behaviour – defence of fringe opinions signals membership, even enthusiastic membership, in the liberal community. But for those already sympathetic to cause, the fascist signal is a separating strategy – it marks the speaker out as a person 'in the know' and open to further cooperation against society-at-large. Fascism is able to defeat the social defences of liberal societies. And the more common its deceptions become, the less reliable ordinary social signals which reinforce social order become. No one

---

[498]Adapted from a quote by Lenin, "Imperialism: The Highest Stage of Capitalism" (1914).

can be sure who really believes, or how far the cancer has spread. For the average liberal, the anti-fascist criticising the licence of fascists to organise freely and openly seems a more obvious threat to the social order. And to the victims of fascism, the liberal's defence of the right of the fascist to speak and organise looks like collaboration. Citizens look to the choreographers of social order to see how they should respond, and receive no hint of danger.

Because the social immune system of liberalism is vulnerable, combatting fascism must therefore be democratised, with individual social agents speaking and acting out against fascist beliefs and behaviours rather than relying on the routine institutions of social order. Specialised security norms and institutions may be able to protect us against foreign and criminal social threats with clear behavioural tags, but we cannot rely upon them to save us from social cancers that threaten us from within. Anti-fascist organising is a spontaneous altruistic response to the threat of a social cancer; individuals pay the personal cost of opposing fascism because pointing out the threat, and ostracising its adherents, is the only way to get the broader social immune system to activate. No doubt, this will often increase levels of social conflict and mobilise the institutions of state oppression. But like the body using a fever to rid itself of infection, temporarily activating the body's defence mechanisms might succeed in holding the threat at bay – if it doesn't kill the patient first.

For the philosophers John Rawls and Will Kymlicka, liberalism presupposes a certain social structure, in which all social agents are genuinely committed to individual freedom, equal rights for all and universal solidarity amongst the citizenry – liberty, equality and fraternity. Because liberalism is a best reply to itself, society reproduces the ideology and the ideology reproduces the social structure. But for liberalism to be evolutionarily stable, citizens in good standing cannot be neutral towards social agents who would undermine those structures[499]. Tolerance breaks down in the presence of fascist ideologues – who aim to push society onto an entirely different equilibrium.

---

[499] Rawls (1971) at pgs. 220; Kymlicka (1995); Donnelly (2013), Chapter 4.

Popper's famous paradox of tolerance is therefore an unavoidable result of an evolutionary understanding of liberal political and social life. Every ideology, no matter how broadly accepting and universal in its aspirations, must be willing and able to use force against threats to its survival.

"If we extend unlimited tolerance even to those who are intolerant, if we are not prepared to defend a tolerant society against the onslaught of the intolerant, then the tolerant will be destroyed, and tolerance with them. I do not imply . . . that we should always suppress the utterance of intolerant philosophies; as long as we can counter them by rational argument and keep them in check by public opinion, suppression would certainly be unwise. But we should claim the right to suppress them if necessary even by force; for it may easily turn out that they are not prepared to meet us on the level of rational argument, but begin by denouncing all argument; they may forbid their followers to listen to rational argument, because it is deceptive, and teach them to answer arguments by the use of their fists or pistols. We should therefore claim, in the name of tolerance, the right not to tolerate the intolerant." [Popper, The Open Society and Its Enemies][500]

* * *

Recall that in the Introduction, we defined the axioms of capitalist ideology in an evolutionary framework. Capitalism's characteristic belief is that competitive strategy sets offer equilibrium solutions to persistent social dilemmas. And that these competitive or self-help solutions are empirically and normatively superior to cooperative ones. Game theory-derived models are typically employed in economics to show that under market conditions competitive self-help produces an efficient allocation of social resources at equilibrium. The 'collective wisdom' of market institutions allows prices for goods and services to find their optimal level, with competitive selection punishing producers who set prices too high or too low and consumers who

---

[500] Popper (1947) at pg. 265.

bid for goods and services too low or too high.

As we know, the structure of a social dilemma determines which strategies are dominant, and we can define a market dilemma as any iterated social game in which a competitive self-help strategy is evolutionarily stable. So for example, a group of traders who exchange goods and services on terms that maximise their individual utility in each interaction may produce a spontaneous social order – a market – that is able to out-compete other modes of economic organisation. Even so, a market order is very likely to include elements of both competition and cooperation: those traders will be operating in a social context in which their property is respected and where contracts are binding; they will likely have developed specialised institutions to standardised weights, measures and standards of payment; and consented to some form of coercive apparatus to resolve disputes among themselves. Ideologues who have extolled the advantages of competition, from Adam Smith to Friedrich Hayek, have in the main recognised that the social domains which in selfish strategies dominate are limited.

Putting aside the many and manifold ways in which market competition produces inefficient outcomes (covered in my other book, "Politics for the New Dark Age: Staying Positive Amidst Disorder"), we can specify the general boundaries of the tolerated economic order, to which most contemporary political actors from social democrats to neoliberals would agree. In such an order, cooperative strategies are dominant in some aspects of social life, and competitive strategies are dominant in others. Selfishness is the norm in some activities, and trust is the norm in others. In the way, a population maximises its overall fitness by maintaining a mixed equilibrium in which specialised institutions adopt the most efficient behaviour for its particular social function. And more importantly, the *interaction* of these institutions forms an important part of the social balance, so that competition amongst producers is limited by the cooperative raising of children, the socialisation of health and risk, the equal rights of all in courts of law, and the equality of all citizens. Societies may allocate social spheres to either competition or cooperation differently, or move dynamically over time between them, but the range of permissible variation defines the boundaries of the liberal cultural world.

It must be added that although market competition may (or may not) be economically efficient, it does not emerge spontaneously among humans in the absence of cultural evolution. Biologically, humans are social creatures who live cooperatively in groups, and anthropologists have repeatedly noted that competitive self-help behaviour must be learned. For most of human history, traders did not engage in one-shot market transactions, but rather borrowed goods and services from other members of their community, mediated by mechanisms of social assortivity including kinship and reputation[501]. Bartering was an activity only engaged in with total strangers, and to expect upfront payment for the supply of necessary goods and services was seen in many cultures as an unethical act. Market structures as we know them today are a product of cultural evolution, and rest in large part on the existence of broader symbolic communities which encourage diffuse rather than direct reciprocity among strangers.

Selfish social strategies produces relative gains for some actors and losses for others. Over time, economic production may become more efficient overall, but the distribution of resources in the population will change. So the growth of inequality under conditions of self-help competition is inevitable – and multilevel selection would indeed predict this outcome: remember, selfishness beats altruism within groups. Within groups, exploitative individuals – the innovative financial trader, the ruthless CEO, the charismatic con-man – will gain fitness, status and resources, and thanks to this will come to enjoy dominance in their community. Power will grant them the ability to shape the distribution of payoffs for other social agents, to choose the rules of the game and who gets to play.

But when we look at things from the perspective of the group, rising inequality has negative effects on fitness. Excessive intra-group competition *lowers group performance*. In an often-cited study of chicken breeding performed in the 1990s, hens were chosen for breeding on the basis of the number of eggs they produced, with the best egg producers often being

---

[501] Grief (1993) at pgs.525-548; Grief (2006) at pgs. 221-236.

the most aggressive[502]. However, within a few generations, egg production plummeted in a population of hens that came to be dominated by aggressive, selfish traits – a population of selfish breeders could no longer live with one another successfully. In order to maximise productions, breeders had to select not the hens that laid the most eggs, but the hens that were most social.

Indeed, the corporate firm can be exactly understood as a cooperative social group. What many observers of capitalism have noted is what while competition between producers occurs as a matter of theory and practice on the basis of ruthless self-help, inside the firm there is equally ruthlessly enforced cooperation. The firm is usually structured as a strict hierarchy, with clearly defined standard operating procedures, internal punishments and mechanisms to ensure that workers act in the interest of the firm as a whole. The world's largest corporations act as centrally-planned and controlled institutions. But firms which attempt, for ideological reasons, to apply the principles of market competition to their *internal* organisation fare less well in the long run (e.g. the US retail giant Sears, whose CEO Ed Lampert was a dedicated acolyte of Ayn Rand, and which collapsed after implementing Lampert's free-market ideas). Competition and selfishness undermine the social trust and cooperation necessary for the group as a whole to continue to function in an environment characterised by natural or cultural selection.

Machiavelli, in his *Discourses on Livy*, noted that the institutions of the Roman Republic developed piecemeal, in response to social conflicts that arose between different social orders. Rather than letting the selfishness of the elites rip the Republic apart or force it towards a despotic oligarchy, the Romans responded by developing democratic institutions that increased the political and economic power of those disenfranchised by its cut-throat politics, and began to implement the rudiments of a welfare state so that at least some of the economic gains enjoyed by the aristocracy were taxed and

---

[502] Muir (1996) at pgs. 447-458; Goodnight & Stevens (1997) at pgs. s59-s79; Wade et al. (2013) at pgs. 453-465; Muir et al. (2013) at pgs. 1598-1606.

shared with the urban plebeians. More despotic and unequal societies tend to fail in competition with healthier communities which put limits on the relative fitness advantage of selfishness through progressive taxation and redistribution. In the regulated capitalist state, selfishness is advantageous but *not too advantageous.*

But there's always a risk that some political actors can break free of these constraints. If, by some luck or happy accident, a person comes to acquire vast economic resources then the ordinary mechanisms of limiting their behaviour – law, opprobrium, shame – may no longer operate effectively. Elites need not control vast capital directly; sometimes they gain social and economic power through their institutional role as the heads of large companies or governments that aggregate the labour of hundreds of thousands of workers. But whether because they lack internal self-regulation (e.g. Donald Trump), were trained to operate outside the law (the *siloviki* in Russia), or can simply buy or cajole their way out of trouble, elite cooperation with social norms is in essence voluntary.

As Joseph Stiglitz has so persuasively argued[503], elites who are able to corrupt legal and moral constraints on their behaviour to preserve their own privilege and pass it on to their descendants have a corrosive effect on the norms and institutions which are supposed to govern a liberal social and economic order. By re-writing the rules of the game, elites minimise the cost to themselves of taxation and thereby limit the amount of redistribution that occurs; they choke off intergenerational mobility and weaken labour laws that limit their dictatorial powers in the workplace. They arrange it so that communal resources – land, social services and infrastructure – end up under their control. As monopolists, they set prices to bleed consumers dry and prevent the emergence of competitors from among the ranks of small business. And given their high social status, the behaviours and goals of elites are likely to imitated and normalised by many in the population with corrosive effects on social cooperation. A lone billionaire is essentially a fluke; a group of politically active billionaires is an existential threat to

---

[503] Stiglitz (2012), esp. at pg. 216. See also: Michels (1911).

the liberal order.

Peter Turchin provides another example of how selfish strategies employed in specialised institutions can break their limits and overthrow egalitarian social norms[504]. War-fighting organs – the military – are typically organised differently from society-at-large, with their own specialised social norms and rules which focus on the calibrated use of violence and obedience to authority. This makes the military an effective tool of organised defence. But in a failing state, or in a stable state with a hyper-successful and privileged military, military elites with military values may seem like attractive alternate rulers. The institutions of the Roman Republic could not stop Caesar or his many imitators[505].

Managing elites socialised by competitive institutions like the market or the military is a challenge for any liberal democracy, but I don't believe these institutions meet the definition of a social cancer in their own right. Elites are not implacably hostile to the existing social order – quite the contrary: it has facilitated their rise and they rely on it to maintain the legitimacy of their authority. And most elites, at least those of the first generation, remain self-limited by their socialisation – they can still feel shame and a normative sense of obligation to their fellow citizens. It's hardly surprising that the ostensible culture of the ultra-rich, from Andrew Carnegie to Bill Gates, so heavily emphasises charitable giving and *noblesse oblige* – it's the only way the egalitarian liberal order and the vast wealth and power of billionaires can be mutually intelligible.

So just as fascist and terrorist groups need both individual exemplars *and ideology* to become a self-replicating social cancer, malignant capitalism needs more than a few elites to destroy liberal democracy – it needs to promulgate an alternative set of norms, behaviours and values. Throughout recent history a small but growing proportion of the ultra-wealthy have attempted to preserve and entrench their class privilege by erecting a political, economic and normative structure in which mistrust and the

---

[504] Turchin (2016) at pg. 159-.

[505] Turchin (2016) at pg. 164.

selfish accumulation of resources is seen as *social good*. Rather than arguing that competitive self-help is merely economically efficient in some spheres of human activity, they promote the idea that egoistic competition is a virtuous behaviour in *every sphere of economic life*. Rather than millionaires being temporarily embarrassed egalitarians, ordinary citizens should behave as temporarily embarrassed millionaires[506].

We shall call such views 'market extremism' or 'market fundamentalism', and although they had been circulating among economists of the Austrian school since Ludwig von Mises, they rose to sudden and dramatic prominence in the Anglo-Saxon political world in the 1980s. When Margaret Thatcher said there was "no such thing as society", she was justifying a new political narrative in which the pro-social norms, behaviours and institutions which made liberal society possible were seen as anachronistic restraints on the freedom of the masters of the world.

Taken as a pure strategy, we might define this malignant form of selfishness as anarcho-capitalism, following the terminology of Murray Rothbard, but as a set of belief and behaviours we also see market fundamentalism as a current amongst both right-libertarians and neoliberals. It's far more dangerous among the latter group, because the neoliberal desire to capture the institutions of state power and use it to protect the market against democratic rule[507] robs liberalism of its collective defences against cancerous movements that would subvert it. Like fascism, market fundamentalism deprives liberals of their capacity to distinguish norm-following behaviour from norm-breaking behaviour, because in rhetoric and behaviour it uses many of the same signals. Unlike fascism, market fundamentalism presents itself as the ultimate perfection and culmination of liberty, non-violence and the sanctity of property even if in practice it enslaves the vast majority of the population in an unequal and structurally violent economic system in which they have no say over the decisions that affect their lives. This contradiction between the ideal of liberty and the

---

[506] Wright (2004).

[507] Slobodian (2018).

reality of wage-slavery is the dialectical engine of modern socialism.

Market fundamentalism is a social cancer. It arises when elites use their social and cultural power to spread and enforce a new social strategy in which competition determines the moral and ethical fabric of a society. It requires a cultural complex in which young people are actively socialised into this new way of thinking, in which acting selfishly in pursuit of individual power is seen as a moral act, and failure to rise to the top as seen as the product of moral failure and degeneracy.

"The disposition to admire, and almost to worship, the rich and powerful, and to despise, or, at least, to neglect persons of poor and mean condition . . .[is] the great and most universal cause of the corruption of our moral sentiments." [Adam Smith, The Theory of Moral Sentiments][508]

Market fundamentalism inverts the social norms that normally permit social cooperation – it erects a virtue of inequality and hierarchy, and strips social and economic rights away those that cannot defend themselves. Under market fundamentalism, there is no right to health, education, work or a living wage – and an individual's inability to secure those rights proves their lack of social and moral value. Possessing more resources than one could ever conceivably need is seen as a righteous act granting high social status and wide opportunities for social reproduction.

Liberal democracy cannot defend itself against market fundamentalism. It's a cultural cancer whose very existence is incompatible with the norms and institutions of a cooperative society. The rise of this particularly virulent strain of capitalism in the global West since the 1980s has led to rising economic instability, declining satisfaction with democracy and growing social conflict. For a species biologically adapted to living in cooperative social groups, life under modern capitalism is stressful, alienating and cruel – fuelling increases in mental health problems, anxiety and suicide[509]. As

---

[508] Smith, "The Theory of Moral Sentiments"(1759), Section III, Chapter III.

[509] Fisher (2009).

the existing social equilibrium becomes unstable, elites reach for alternative symbols to provide order, include imperial expansion abroad and pogroms against domestic enemies. And in the face of this self-induced crisis, the hand that reaches out to offer the oligarchs salvation is that of the fascist.

And here we return full circle. An strong, egalitarian society would be able to defend itself against the rise of the market extremists and fascists. But under attack from one, societies often find themselves at the mercy of the other. The market fundamentalists look to the fascists to defeat the social immune system that inhibits their spread – fascists often start out as the foot soldiers in campaigns to smash unions, murder progressive activists and destroy socialist political parties[510]. But they also serve as a bogey man – under violent attack from within, the liberal society may double down on the steady hand of rule by an undemocratic elite and the liberal values of individualism and private property. The alliance between fascists and capitalists is natural, but unstable. Together they can destroy, but not create.

How can socialists hope to stand up to such forces? Clearly, strengthening social defences against illiberal and undemocratic ideologies by defending liberal values and institutions plays an important role. And since social cancers can be triggered by external and environmental shocks, we must stop those practices that increase the risk of pathogenic beliefs spreading – ending foreign wars and imperialism, stewarding the natural environment and stopping climate change, and fighting for a more equal and just society. But there is no cure or perfect prophylactic for cancer, and no way to make our social organisms completely immune. There'll always be a background risk of spontaneous cultural mutation, and we have to be ready to identify and fight against those mutants when we perceive that they may become malignant (see Chapter 16: "Outside Context Problems"). There is only perfecting the treatment – developing better and more effective machinery for the suppression of exploitation in all its forms.

Perhaps we should draw some small comfort from the fact that the most

---

[510] Szejnmann (1999)

common treatments for biological cancers – chemo- and radiation-therapy – involve exposing the organism to extremely hostile environmental conditions. Healthy cells, working together cooperatively, are stronger and more resilient than cancerous ones. Although the body may suffer and some parts of the whole may be lost, the organism's ability to compensate for the damage caused by tumours and go on living is a testament to the evolutionary strength of cooperation in the face of exploitative pathologies that seek to destroy it.

14

THE DARK SIDE OF COOPERATION

Key Points

- For group selection to drive cultural evolution, social species develop behaviours which condition cooperative behaviour on group identity. If altruism evolves, it must be parochial.
- All humans have biases which make it cognitively simpler to trust and empathise with members of their own group, and which generate fear and distrust towards outsiders.
- Identities which are integrative, solidaristic and permit diverse participation in a community or movement are compatible with universalism; identities which are disintegrative and exclusionary are not.

We have defined evolutionary socialism as any political and philosophical program which shares three key insights. Firstly, the subject species must be social and operate in groups. Secondly, cooperative strategies offer evolutionarily stable solutions to persistent dilemmas of social decision making in those groups. And thirdly, cooperative strategies are empirically and normatively superior to non-cooperative or self-help strategies. Socialists make a virtue of pro-social cooperation and altruism. Moreover, using cultural group selection, we have a parsimonious account of the evolution of these social strategies and the role they play in our social and political life. Progressive social movements promote doctrines of inclusive – even universal – trust in the benign intentions of others.

But cooperation has a dark side. We do not see, in nature, universal and unconditional trust towards others. Social bonds do not form automatically among complete strangers and individuals only rarely sacrifice for the good of humanity as a whole – note our appalling failures to cooperate to prevent the climate from changing. There are a variety of ways of explaining this, of course: behavioural variation means a small percentage of social agents will always be tempted by the payoffs from social exploitation. But there's a systematic pattern in the interactions in which humans and other social agents are cooperative and the interactions in which they are exploitative. We are generous, trusting, reciprocal, kind and altruistic with others we see as members of our own group. But we are often stingy, distrustful, exploitative and cruel towards those we perceive as being different. While we avoid violence in our everyday lives and find it relatively easy to treat everyone with equal dignity, as a species we are also capable of mass atrocities and can easily dehumanise and instrumentalise outsiders.

The tension between the universal altruism anticipated by humanist philosophy and the reality of evolved in-group preference is the subject of this Chapter. These phenomena – our capacity for both extraordinary social cohesion and awful genocidal violence – are inexplicably linked. Kropotkin called this the *"double conception of morality"* and it was as central to his theory in 1891 as it is to us today[511]. The existence of war and cruelty does not negate the fundamentally cooperative aspect of human nature, in fact they confirm it. One cannot exist without the other. Cooperative instincts evolve through a process of multilevel selection dominated by inter-group competition. We are thus adapted to make judgements about who, precisely, are inside that group and who are outside it. Towards our in-group, we experience feelings of affective warmth and closeness, we attribute them positive traits and intentions, and we rate their social value and reputation highly. And towards out-groups, our evolved instincts and

---

[511] Kropotkin, "Mutual Aid Amongst Savages" The Nineteenth Century, April 1891 at pg. 559.

emotions promote behaviours that are decidedly non-cooperative. We see outsiders as cold and alien, attribute them negative traits and evil intentions, and perceive them as having low social value and status[512].

If human beings lived in a universal communitiy in which every person had an equal probability of interacting with everyone else, large-scale cooperation could never have evolved[513]. It's only because social life is structured so as to increase the probability of interaction between more-similar agents that cooperation could have evolved. For this reason, altruism and other cooperative social strategies are *parochial* – favouring some interaction partners over others. In humans and other social species with biologically-grounded instincts, this parochialism is often generated through subconscious biases that regulate our affective response towards others. But in abstracted terms, what matters is that a strategy is capable of distinguishing the group affiliation of interaction partners and conditioning behaviour upon it.

Game theorists have developed several models of the development of parochial altruism, including Axelrod's colour tag model we discussed in Chapter 7[514]. Samuel Bowles has presented a model in which social agents have two traits – altruism and parochialism – with independent effects on behaviour and which evolve separately[515]. There are thus four potential pure behavioural archetypes: universal altruists, parochial altruists, universal exploiters and parochial exploiters. In this model (which we will use again in the next Chapter, "Extremists Among Us"), social agents can interact across group boundaries in either a trusting or hostile manner. The model was simulated thousands of times, over long timescales and using population structures and reproduction rates informed by anthropological studies of

---

[512] Sapolsky (2017) at pg. 393.

[513] Bowles & Gintis (2011) at pgs. 134-135.

[514] E.g. Yamagishi et al. (1999) at pgs. 161-197; McElreath, Boyd & Richerson (2003) at pgs. 122-130; Axelrod & Hammond (2006) at pgs. 926-936.

[515] Choi & Bowles (2007) at pgs. 636-640; See also Lehmann & Feldman (2008) at pgs. 2877-2885; Bowles & Gintis (2011), at pgs. 135-138.

early human populations. Regardless of their starting point, simulated populations tended to settle into one of two equilibria: universal exploiters or parochial altruists. In the latter equilibrium, violence is large-scale and organised but populations are overall more fit than in the world of universal exploiters. Unstable mixed states are also possible – but universal altruism and parochial exploitation were virtually never observed[516].

The dynamic mechanisms by which this occurs should by now be clear. In populations that are more parochial than average, conflict with members of different groups is more likely and cross-boundary cooperation is less rewarding. Because of this intensified inter-group selection, multilevel selection generates fitness pressures which increase the payoffs of in-group cooperation. Even though there's no feature of the model that requires positive assortivity amongst parochial altruists, this behaviour emerges spontaneously through cultural group selection. It is sustained even with levels of inter-group conflict far below those that archaeologists and anthropologists estimate for real populations.

For cooperation to evolve at all, it *must* be parochial. The boundaries of the social community are explicitly defined by who is excluded from it. And the fact that parochial altruism is indeed the behaviour set most observed in humans, with both biological and cultural mechanisms of action, is perhaps the strongest evidence we have that group selection played a leading role in the evolution of our species. Without the capacity to divide a population into groups with differential fitness, to police those boundaries through the selective application of violence, and a bias towards social conformity with members of our own group, cultural selection would not have exercised such an influence on human evolution and it is highly likely that social cooperation could never have become evolutionarily stable.

* * *

Human beings have intuitive in-group biases. We form judgements about

---

[516] Choi & Bowles (2007) at pgs. 138-142.

group affiliation rapidly and easily, below the level of conscious aware-ness[517] – the surest sign of Kahneman's "System 1" thinking. In the by-now well-known implicit association tests, people are asked to associate faces with positive and negative words and phrases. Respondents are given only a fraction of a second to assess each face, and their responses are timed. The tests consistently show that associating positive values with high status members of one's own group is faster and cognitively easier than associating positive values with low status individuals or members of an out-group. Brain scans show that when asked to violate our social expectations about group membership in this way we activate parts of our frontal cortex – an act of "System 2" thinking that is slow and energy intensive[518]. This effect operates regardless of the subject's own conscious views – no matter how woke or "capital-R" Reasonable the individual, the brain's subconscious modules, honed by hundreds of thousands of years of cultural group evolution, are constantly trying to lessen the cognitive burden by making rapid and autonomic assessments of character based on superficial group identity markers – even when we don't want it to![519].

These biases are deep rooted in our evolutionary history. Scientists have shown that social monkeys demonstrate group biases in implicit association tests[520]. And human children develop stereotypes and biases early in their development[521] – the ability to distinguish members of one's own cultural group is expressed in infants as early at six months of age[522]. Psychological studies of people playing basic economic games has shown that humans more trusting, generous and cooperative with members of their own group than others – even in one-shot interactions in which there's no possibility

---

[517] Sapolsky (2017) at pg. 388.

[518] Sapolsky (2017) at pg. 388.

[519] Greene (2016), at pgs. 199-205; Efferson, Rafael & Fehr (2008) at pgs. 1844–1849.

[520] Mahajan et al. (2001) at pg. 387-.

[521] See the studies cited by Sapolsky (2017) at pgs. 391-394.

[522] Kinzler et al. (2009) at pgs. 623-634.

of reputation and reciprocity playing a role[523]. We are intuitively more empathetic towards members of our group – we have a better appreciation of their emotions and make an effort to understand their motivations.[524] And our tendency towards mimicry and imitation is strongest in the presence of those most like ourselves.

On the other hand, the categorisation of another social agent as 'other' activates an entirely different set of intuitions. Our brains more rapidly process the faces of out-groups as showing hostility and aggression, initiating a fear a response that conditions our behaviours to be more violent and exploitative. The disgust trigger is also involved – we are more likely to view members of out-groups as dirty and unclean, and carry those judgements on to our views about their food, culture, religion and moral beliefs[525]. 'Others' have simpler emotional lives, fewer conscious motivations and greater capacity to endure pain and suffering. The *barbaroi* aren't just different – they're inhuman monsters.

The construction of group identities and the attachment of stereotypes and labels to them is a core function of adaptive cognition. In-group bias affects every intuition we have: the aversion to interpersonal violence is strongest towards the in-group and weakest towards the outgroup; we are more likely to treat fairly with the former and cheat on the latter; and we a more likely to be vengeful against members of an out-group while forgiving the mistakes of those in our own group. Systematic discrimination is endemic even in Rational, liberal societies, because it's implausible to expect that all people at all times will be able to exercise the cognitive effort to override it . Whenever we are tired, stressed, distracted, intoxicated or simply in a rush, our evolved heuristics will take over the processing burden and produce snap judgments that perpetuate micro-fractures in what is supposed to be a universal community.

Where migration takes place amongst different regions, superficial

---

[523] Levine et al. (2002) at pgs. 1452-.

[524] Sapolsky (2017) at pg. 395.

[525] Sapolsky (2017) at pg. 398-399.

external tags such as skin colour or mode of dress can become associated with socially constructed hierarchies of difference. In other communities, religious practices and modes of worship can become cleavages, as can economic mode of production, height, dietary preferences or almost any other characteristic of individuals. Remember Axelrod's computer programs, who learned to discriminate based on arbitrary colours that had no inherent meaning. In the 1950s, the psychologist Muzafer Sharif documented outbreaks of violence between boy scouts divided into arbitrary 'clans' for the summer[526]. The next decade, schoolteacher Jane Elliot famously demonstrated that her students would form vicious, competitive groups if told that children of one eye colour were superior to another.

Our brains are primed to categorise, to stereotype, to decide who to trust and who not to trust. Consistent with our broader talent for pattern matching, the tags our brain decide are important for making that distinction are often subtle, irrational and prone to cultural manipulation. Consistent signals from respected social exemplars that a certain social cleavage is a salient marker of group identity can generate sub-groups from a population where none previously existed. Humans are clannish and innately xenophobic, yes, but that particular form and function that xenophobia takes in any given time and place is historically and culturally contingent. And as easily as we can learn to generate group differences, we can unlearn those cleavages when they are no longer salient –– unlike every other animal, who are locked into assertive mechanisms on the basis of genetic and physical proximity, humans have the unique ability to indefinitely modify and expand the circle of cooperation, should we so choose.

So although identity is of high importance to the way humans behave and how we structure our societies, we cannot and should not see identity categories as fixed and unchanging – even though we may subjectively experience them in that way. In a single population, every social agent is a member of multiple diverse communities and the tags and markers of

---

[526] Sherif, et al. (1961) at pgs. 155–184; Whitley & Kite (2019) at pgs. 325–330.

identity that are salient will vary depending on their social and cultural context. Humans mix-and-match different assortative mechanisms in different social contexts – the simplest markers of identity such as biological sex and skin colour are only salient when other forms of cultural identity formation fail or are absent. Amartya Sen has written that we all participate in multiple performances depending on our current social and cultural environment: we don't have a single identity but rather a complex matrix of social roles[527].

"A Hutu labourer from Kigali may be pressured to see himself only as Hutu and incited to kill Tutsis, and yet he is not only Hutu, but also a Kigalian, a Rwandan, and African, a labourer and a human being. Along with recognition of plurality of our identities and their diverse implications, there is a critically important need to see the role of choice in determining the cogency and relevance of particular identities which are inescapably diverse". [Sen, Identity and Violence][528]

Every social agent has multiple identities, each of which may constitute an in-group or an out-group for others depending on social context. While acknowledging the critical role that group identity plays in shaping and conditioning human behaviour, we must always be cognizant that identity is *intersectional*[529] and that any judgements we make about the moral and normative value of other human beings are always dependent on relations between different groups in society. So our ability to make group distinctions should be treated as a scalpel, not a sledgehammer. How a population choose to hone that tool is far more important to the lives of everyday individuals than the fact that biological evolution bequeathed it to us in the first place.

---

[527] Sen (2006); See also Sapolsky (2017) at pgs. 405-.

[528] Sen (2006) at pg. 4.

[529] The Combahee River Collective Statement (1977); Crenshaw (1989) at pgs. 139-167; Crenshaw (1991) at pgs. 1241-1299.

* * *

Group identity is highly motivating for social agents. Human beings crave identity, and suffer physically and emotionally when forced to operate as alienated individuals. We form groups easily based on seemingly arbitrary and superficial distinctions, and can be primed to hate and fear others just as easily. Although we don't have another communicative social species with which to compare ourselves, it's plausible that identifying as part of a group would be a endemic feature of all complex social life. Reckoning with the political consequences of identity is therefore a core concern of every political actor and any account of human social and political life must tackle the role played by group affiliation.

Not all identities have the same salience. Humans tend to form affective groups at every level of organisation, from the family unit to the nation-state, and every group defines its own rules for mutual recognition of affiliation. Identity is therefore never categorical; no social agent could or should ever be considered merely an abstract vehicle for the average behaviours of their group. Within limited allowance for environmental and genetic diversity, every lion is a lion and every bear is a bear – most organisms transmit information primarily through their genes. But in a cultural species such as our own, individuals pass on not only genetic information but also cultural replicators corresponding to every group of which they are a member. With every generation, we inherit code not just for being human, but for being of a certain gender, for example, a certain sexuality, and a citizen of our parent's ethnicity and socio-economic class, among many, many other potential identities.

From the capitalist perspective, identity is often irrelevant. Identities compatible with the market are those which encourage selfish behaviour that maximises individual fitness in market interactions. It cares little for identifies that operate outside market games. Some of capitalism's most impressive social advances have come precisely through the erosion of other group identities: cultural, religious and group behaviours that got in the way of the maximisation of utility have been swept away, as is – at least in theory – any discrimination based on gender, race or sexuality in public spaces. All are equal in the marketplace of self-interest. In fact, hostility from conservatives towards capitalism has always come in large part from the way in which liberal universalism has weakened or dissolved other social bonds.

Socialists and other progressives face a trickier challenge. We start from the proposition that human beings are fundamentally social animals with social needs, and that the formation of cooperative groups is fundamental to political and economic life. Indeed, from the anarcho-communist tradition of Kropotkin and other libertarian socialists, we have inherited a sense in which our 'ideal society' would in some sense be based on the free association of individuals into self-organising collectives, free of all pre-existing hierarchies. So unlike liberal capitalists, socialists do not seek the dissolution of all prior group identities, nor deny that identity should play a role in the public sphere.

An identity is consistent with a progressive or socialist political program if it expands the circle of potential co-operators and supports pro-social behaviour towards other social agents in ways that maintain group fitness. Unlike conservatives, we do not valorise forms of identity simply because they are already existing in the community. Organising for social justice on the basis of race, class, gender, sexuality and even religion – and not just as a group of self-interested individuals – is a fundamental component of the progressive strategy. Socialists and progressives *form new communities* which cross the lines that would otherwise divide us. What socialists add to the principles of liberty and equality is *solidarity* – the view that at least some group identities are pro-social, integrative and worth preserving within the body politic.

Speaking generally, socialists distinguish between the positive and negative aspects of identity in the following way. Identities that are integrative, solidaristic and mutually intelligible with broader social values of the political organism are encouraged both in the community and in our own movements. Identities that are disintegrative, exclusionary and which are incompatible with the ongoing viability of the social organism are discouraged. Any group which can point to its *de jure* or *de facto* exclusion from the social contract, or its unequal material condition, and which lays claim to no more and no less rights than those enjoyed by the community of the whole deserves our solidarity. Social groups which seek to exclude others from the social contract, or to impose upon them unequal conditions of life, and which seeks to exclude others from the right to equal membership of the social contract must be opposed.

"We realize that the liberation of all oppressed peoples necessitates the destruction of the political-economic systems of capitalism . . . [but] a socialist revolution that is not also a feminist and anti-racist revolution will [not] guarantee our liberation. . . . We need to articulate the real class situation of persons who are not merely raceless, sexless workers, but for whom racial and sexual oppression are significant determinants in their lives." [The Combahee River Collective Statement][530]

Although a universalising socialism which focuses on a single social identity to the exclusion of all others is theoretically possible, non-intersectional socialism is almost by definition exclusionary and authoritarian in practice. Every socialist must, to count themselves progressive, also be a feminist. Gender categories are probably one of the first group identities human culture constructed; cultural notions of gender are often based on superficial physical tags that we're at least partially biologically pre-disposed to be sensitive to. It's credible that differentiated gender roles serve as the model for all other social hierarchies: reproductive labour was the original means of production and control over it a source of power and authority.

For largely the same reasons, socialists have historically made common cause with all marginalised groups, including racial and sexual minorities, sex workers, the disabled, indigenous and colonised peoples. From time to time, and varying from place to place, these identities can and have taken on significant meanings for large groups of people – and norms control-

---

[530] The Combahee River Collective Statement (1977).

ling them have led to significant de-humanisation and marginalisation. Wherever a minority is engaged in a struggle to be recognised, to be treated as equal under the law, or to redress material and economic inequalities – socialists and progressives have been natural, if not always reliable, allies to their cause. And when socialists themselves gain political and institutional power, we cannot be blind to the way in which our own organisations can marginalise and alienate supporters with diverse identities and affiliations.

All of this brings us to the vexed question of national identity or nationality. By nationality, we mean an individual's most expansive level of symbolic social and political identification *which falls short of either religious or secular universality*. The historical reality is that many egalitarian leaders have been nationalists first and socialists second. Ho Chi Minh, Simon Bolivar, Napoleon Bonaparte, Tito and Kwame Nkrumah self-consciously created and cultivated a sense of symbolic national identity in order to advance their nation-building projects. The evolution of national identities, through the entirely arbitrary and superficial creation of a shared national history, language and myths, is one of the core tools of state-builders and an important underpinning to the modern nation-state. This is true regardless of whether a new nation is forged from a collection of smaller political and cultural entities, or whether national identity is cultivated in order to encourage a subject or colonised region to break away from imperial control in pursuit of its own self-determination.

Socialists are internationalists and cosmopolitans by disposition. We aspire to a universal cooperative community consisting of all humanity and encourage all social agents to voluntarily form affective bonds across national and other group boundaries. But socialists are not committed to internationalism for its own sake. If 'cosmopolitanism' means British, Hapsburg, American or Russian hegemony without the democratic consent or participation of subject populations, then integrative nationalisms which are more inclusive and democratic can and should seek an independent road. In truly egalitarian and democratic multinational states, unlike empires, there's no tension between the enjoyment of group identity and participation in the community of the whole, because -- as with identities based on gender, sexuality, race or class – national affiliation would have no effect on the enjoyment of full citizenship and causes no differential fitness between groups. Every citizen of the EU has [in theory] all the social and economic rights that accompany that status while remaining French, German, Italian or otherwise. With clear imperfections, every Australian or American citizen can in principle maintain their ethnic, religious or cultural traditions while still enjoying full social and political rights.

On the other hand, nationalisms which are disintegrative or exclusionary must be opposed. Within a liberal and democratic multinational democracy, ideologies which seek to assert an exclusive nationalist identity can become cancerous and lead to the disintegration of the community of the whole. By privileging cooperation with members of the in-group, and adopting a hostile, violent or exploitative attitude towards members of out-groups, disintegrative nationalism seeks to generate fitness differentials across so-ciety that will, in time destroy it. In the same way, imperialist nationalisms which tolerate diversity but which grant to certain ethnic or cultural groups a chauvinistic right-to-rule are barely disguised hegemonies. They are not evolutionary stable, because changing fitness relations will lead to the collapse of social structures which rely on the privileged cultural position of some groups over other. Only social strategies that are best replies to themselves – such as liberalism – are robust to such perturbations.

For progressives, the human desire for community offers both immense political promise and risks. On the one hand, if we can organise people to trust one another and act collectively, we can form robust political formations that do not rely on coercive domination to generate social order. But on the other, activation of people's intuitive biases against out-groups is just as easy (see the next Chapter: "Extremists Among Us"). Throughout history, conservatives and authoritarians have used 'the outsider' as a symbol of threat and fear in their quest to re-write existing institutions and norms, tighten social cohesion and limit the range of permissible behavioural variation within the community. At the dawn of the 21st century, as right-wing and even fascist movements grow in power across the liberal democratic world, hostility towards the 'immigrant other' has become the most potent political weapon the right possesses. It turns out that even nominally liberal societies are willing, and indeed eager, to embrace a level of brutality and dehumanisation against immigrants – only to learn too late that the institutions of oppression that they licence are later turned against themselves (recall Chapter 13).

We noted earlier than even humanist liberal societies have a thin civic identity, which grants impressive egalitarian solidarity to most but tends to systematically exclude those on the margins, most notable indigenous and colonised peoples, from full civil rights. Because citizenship of the liberal social contract state is predicated on the performance of a minimal – but normatively significant – set of rituals, liberal societies largely treat migrants from other cultures no better than societies with thicker and more exclusionary national identities. Migrants are readily 'otherised' – with superficial and arbitrary tags such as skin colour, religion and language constructed as barriers to citizenship – while the citizenship status of existing residents is elevated to sacred virtue, abstract values carried as a trait by those born into the community, or speaking a certain language, or with a certain skin colour. The reality of culture – that its symbolic rituals are easily transmitted and learned – is ignored. Put simply, migration between cultures is unlikely to extinguish cultural variation. Many successful multicultural states have shown that migrants readily adapt local culture and over time become behaviourally indistinguishable.

The free and unlimited movement of people, an ideal held by many utopian thinkers, is predicated on the existence of a universal human community that does not yet exist. We have not yet evolved the norms and institutions to govern a population of billions; nor undertaken a major evolutionary transition in which regionalised identities can be tamed or suppressed while maintaining the liberal and democratic character of the whole. The unsteady and fragile democracies of the European Union and the Republic of India show that there are significant challenges to undertaking such an organisational leap with our current set of cultural tools and institutions.

So long as this is true, the category of national *citizen* will continue to carry political and cultural weight, much as we wish it did not. Socialists recognise that no human being is illegal, and all are entitled to a broad set of rights on the basis of our recognition of their common humanity, including freedom from arbitrary detention and punishment, to have their status adjudicated by a court of law, and to an adequate standard of living. They would extend these same rights to everyone, everywhere – we may no more arbitrarily and indefinitely detain a foreigner than we should our own people. Human rights are granted on the recognition of each other as social beings. But recognition of and behaviour towards non-citizens remain of a categorically different sort than recognition and behaviour towards citizens.

When a migrant arrives in our communities, they might lack the symbolic papers that would automatically lead our institutions to recognise them as citizens. But as we well know, there are other assortative mechanisms which generate pro-social cooperation in social species. When a migrant is linked to a community by bonds of kinship; or, when they are physically proximate by being present in a community; or participate in repeated social interactions and participate in reciprocal altruism, people readily and successfully include migrants in their local social networks. It is perhaps revealing that the communities which most oppose immigration are usually those with the least day-to-day interaction with them. Non-citizens, in other words, can easily become productive members of a society without meeting the strict requirements of symbolic citizenship.

The immigration policies pursued by the political right seem aptly designed to prevent the growth of precisely this organic solidarity. A detainee in a prison camp is not your neighbour or part of your social network. They are not buying and selling goods in your community, helping pick up your kids from school or caring for your grandparents. They have no proximity, they have no reciprocity, and they can develop no reputation in the community. Because they're prevented from forming cooperative bonds with mainstream society, migrants have been successfully 'othered' on the basis that they lack the right papers, the right language, and the right symbolic culture. The only way the political left can fight back against the intensification of inter-group conflict is precisely to reverse these policies: to permit the immigration of those with family ties to the community; to allow potential migrants to live and work in communities, at least while their status is being determined, and develop the ties of affection and friendship which will, in time, lead to their acceptance. So long as national political boundaries continues to exist, we must fight to ensure they remain permeable to the possibility of mutual cooperation and collaboration.

There are those that would oppose these cross-boundary interactions, however.

They form the subject of our next Chapter.

15

EXTREMISTS AMONGST US

Key Points

- When population membership is ambiguous, group identities can be maintained through the punishment of social actors who engage in cooperative interactions with outsiders.
- Extremists individuals and institutions are highly motivated to engage in the third-party punishment of social deviance by others.
- Extremist social punishments are in principle selective but in practice often indiscriminate. Information asymmetries render extremism prone to error and exploitation.

No population is an entirely closed system. The boundaries of a community can never be perfectly defined, especially in a species capable of doing so with flexible and symbolic behaviours. The characteristic behaviours of social membership are variable, and so community boundaries are subject to at least the possibility of revision. Different assortative mechanisms can change in prominence depending on the needs of the community and the individual. The same ambiguity applies to the sub-groups, specialised organs and identities which make up the community of the whole. This Chapter will take up the question of how social group identities and boundaries are enforced and maintained – and by whom.

As we learned earlier, porous group boundaries and the migration of individuals can potentially extinguish the differential variation required for group selection to drive pro-social adaption. But this does not require totally closed societies: only that the average between-group variation remains large compared to the average within-group variation. Inter-group migration is routine, and helps mitigate the most destructive effects of in-group bias. Moreover, migration of individuals into more successful groups is one of the non-violent methods through which differential group fitness is favoured by cultural selection. So social agents can expect to have repeated interactions with individuals from out-groups or members of their own population with divergent social, economic or political behaviours. Adaptive populations are likely to inherit shared norms governing those interactions.

Game theorists who study this behaviour use models with multiple, porous populations. Every social agent has an interaction probability with members of their own group and a separate interaction probability with other groups or sub-groups. In some models, the likelihood of interacting with an outsider varies with an agent's position in a social network or location on a geographic grid, so that social agents on the physical and organisational boundaries of a community are more likely to interact with outsiders. As we briefly noted in the last Chapter, a social agent in these games can typically choose to either cooperate or defect against outsiders in the same way as against members of their own group.

However, there's a tension between individual- and population-level interests, setting up a social dilemma. A social agent who interacts with an out-group may build up mutually beneficial cooperative relations (e.g. on the basis of network or direct reciprocity) and thereby increase the fitness of themselves and their partner (e.g. in terms of trade, mate selection or knowledge exchange). But this comes at a cost to the fitness of their own group, the cohesiveness of its identity markers and ability to differentiate group members from non-group members. The mutually beneficial social and political alliances that form on the social margins between migrants, communists, sex workers, radicals, the working poor, anarchists and homosexuals have always been seen as a threat to the established social order.

A social agent who instead withholds their cooperation from members of out-groups performs an 'altruistic punishment' of outsiders on the basis of mismatched identity markers. But this behaviour is potentially costly. Over time, social agents with more flexible choice of partners and a marginally weaker in-group bias may gain a fitness advantage over those who enforce group membership more strictly. It's therefore possible that less choosy co-operators come to comprise an increasing share of the overall population. Eventually, a sufficient proportion of the group will no longer see outsiders as strangers at all; the populations in effect merge and a larger social and political community comes into being. Good for humanity – not so good for group selection and the evolutionary stability of cooperation.

If we conceive of in-group bias as a social norm, who or what ensures that norm is enforced? In other words, who punishes the punishers? Axelrod termed norms that enforce other norms 'meta-norms'[531]. A meta-norm prescribes social penalties for those that fail to enforce other social norms, and may establish rewards for those that do comply. So if a social norm prohibits cooperation with outsiders, then a meta-norm may prescribe ostracism of those that *do* cooperate with outsiders. In the same way that only a small proportion of the population has to be willing to enforce a norm in order for the threat of punishment to be a credible belief, an even smaller proportion of the population must be willing to be 'doubly altruistic' and pay a personal cost to punish those that have transgressed against the group by failing to enforce its rules.

This is a Chapter about extremists. By extremists, we mean individuals and institutions that are highly motivated to carry out moralistic aggression: punishment of deviance in their community and the maintenance of social norms at almost any price. Extremists correlate with authoritarian political personality types on both the right and left which are highly distrustful of the autonomous self-determination of other social agents, and who are willing to use coercion to enforce social discipline. Extremists are not social

---

[531] Axelrod (1986); Axelrod (1997), Chapter 3.

cancers, because like an over-active immune system they have the goal of preserving the social organism as such – not its destruction. But the existence of extremists is a consequence of cultural group selection with often deleterious effects on the political life of a social species. Extremists must be understood by the evolutionary sociologist as integral to the political process, and not treated as irrational outliers.

Definitionally, extremism may or may not be stretched to include the ordinary institutions of law enforcement in the modern democratic state. Conceptually and structurally, the police and pre-modern mechanisms of social control share obvious similarities. But the rule of law means that the enforcement of social norms in liberal societies is itself subject to strict institutional oversight, and so we might chauvinistically exclude modern law enforcement on that basis. Extremists carry out social control and enforcement function in populations and sub-populations *which lack other specialised institutions to do so* – they are a democratic form of meta-norm enforcement that our biological and cultural evolutionary history has ensured emerges organically in all cultures and societies. Definitionally, extremists carry out social punishments that are unlicensed or illegitimate from the perspective of the liberal social contract.

The extremist individual or institution does not direct their – often violent – punishment towards outsiders. They aggression is directed inwards, towards members of their own group. The extremist does not engage in tit-for-tat behaviour: the individuals they target for punishment have not wronged them directly but rather have infringed upon the shared norms of the society. For these reasons, the phenomenon of extremist violence is often referred to in the literature as 'third-party punishment' and also 'in-group policing'[532]. Extremist behaviour is strictly speaking irrational from the classical utilitarian perspective – the extremist in essence has private payoffs in which enforcement of social norms is highly individually rewarding. This may be experienced, for example, as an expectation of divine reward for righteous conversions or social status and job satisfaction

---

[532] Fearon & Laitin (1996) at pgs. 715-735.

for members of law enforcement agencies.

Third-party punishment has long been studied by anthropologists[533]. In the early 2000s, the Swiss-German psychologists Ernst Fehr & Simon Gachter conducted a series of economic experiments employing the by-now familiar public goods game[534]. They showed that in randomised and anonymous social groups (i.e. lacking shared identities) without the ability to punish defectors, unilateral contributions to public goods fall rapidly to zero – the free-riding strategy was dominant. However, whenever players could pay a price in order to punish free-riders, most groups established and sustained a norm of cooperation in which everyone contributed resources to the common pool. So whereas 'everyone defects' is the only evolutionarily stable strategy in the absence of punishment, 'everyone contributes' was also evolutionarily stable with a norm of punishment.

In general, players adapted their behaviour to the threat of punishment without having to receive a punishment first, and the penalty imposed by altruistic punishers was proportionate to the degree to which a particular player was free-riding. As we would expect if the behaviour of social agents evolved to operate under a replicator dynamic, players were mostly concerned about relative gains by their peers, and were indifferent to players who stuck to the average contribution of the group[535]. Twenty per cent of players free-rode no matter what – but such free-riders received a 15 per cent smaller payoff in the presence of punishment (which may seem a surprisingly small difference but remember free-riders in a public goods game still benefit from the contributions of others). Overall, groups that established a norm of punishment received a 20 per cent higher payoff than those that didn't – giving strong support to the idea that altruistic punishment can have significant positive fitness consequences for group selection[536].

---

[533] Barth (ed.) (1969); Banton (1983); Laitin (1995) at pgs. 31-57.

[534] Fehr & Gachter (2000) at pgs. 980-994; Fehr & Gachter (2002) at pgs. 137-140.

[535] Fehr & Gachter (2000) at pgs. 990-992.

[536] Fehr & Gachter (2000) at pg. 993.

In follow-up studies, Fehr & Gachter found that more than four fifths per cent of players would engage in altruistic punishment sometimes, but roughly ten per cent of players did so always[537]. This minority of 'super-punishers' represent individuals with the social strategy we label 'extremism'. The researchers cross-referenced the behaviour of players with their subjective emotional experience, and found that punishment was strongly correlated with subjective feelings of anger and resentment towards free-riders – consistent with the idea that altruistic punishment is an irrational, "System 1" behaviour. Neurological imaging has also shown that third-party punishment is associated with parts of the brain the play a role in regulating anger, fear and disgust[538].

There may be a reason why in English we colloquially label extremist social, political and religious movements 'hate groups'. An important practice of such groups and institutions is the methodical cultivation of anger, fear and disgust towards others in the community they see as degenerate or deviant (the 'dispassionate' training of law enforcement thus provides another grounds on which to distinguish them). The manipulation of these emotional triggers can be highly selective – hate groups may be compassionate, even loving, towards community members who comply with their strict social standards. But extremist institutions also licence individuals to hate their neighbour, a level of emotional arousal which has the intended effect of motivating them to take action without explicitly being directed to do so.

Two conclusions suggest themselves. First, that extremist behaviour is more likely among social agents with poor emotional regulation, or who are facing social stressors that limit their cognitive controls. Strong third-party punishers also score highly on tests for other personality disorders, including Machiavellianism and antisocial personality disorder[539]. Secondly, because all social agents share a common emotional architecture, the

---

[537] Fehr & Gachter (2002) at pgs. 137-138.

[538] Spitzer et al. (2007) at pgs. 185-196.

[539] Spitzer et al. (2007) at pgs. 185-196; Buckholtz et al.(2008) at pgs. 930-940.

awareness of the possibility of triggering moralistic aggression in others is likely a strong factor motivating compliance with norms. We might therefore expect rule-breaking to be more likely when social agents are atomised and less sensitive to one another's emotional states. And that more tightly bound communities would be more norm-abiding overall[540].

These estimates of third party punishment have been replicated in a number of other experiments, including the prisoners dilemma and ultimatum games. Approximately two thirds of people will consistently punish other players who cheat, and act as though two thirds to four fifths of their own interaction partners might punish them if they cheated. Moreover, a small percentage of people will always engage in vengeful punishment; and players report that they expect anywhere from 10-20 per cent of their partners to be irrational extremists[541]. Notably, this pattern of third-party punishment develops in human children relatively late (at around six years of age)[542] and is absent in chimpanzees and other animals[543], suggesting that it's characteristic only of cultural species such as our own with high levels of inter-group competition and frequent migration.

So third-party punishment is a ubiquitous component of life for a social species. For most societies most of the time, the punishment of rule-breakers is a distributed affair and behavioural mutants are kept in check by the threat of some of their partners punishing them some of the time. However, the mixed social equilibrium tolerates, and indeed may require, that a small but persistent proportion of the population act in a highly irrational manner, and *almost always* punish deviance. This may manifest either as a form of neurodiversity in the population, or as hate and anger explicitly cultivated by evolutionarily stable institutions which appoint themselves as guardians of social norms. The fear of this small population of extremists can have a disproportionate effect on the behaviour of the

---

[540] Gelfand (2018).

[541] Fehr & Fischbacher (2004) at pgs. 63-87.

[542] McAuliffe et al. (2015) at pgs. 1-10.

[543] Riedl et al. (2012) at pgs. 14824-14829; Raihani et al. (2012) at pgs. 288-295.

population as a whole. The threat of mob justice only subsides when a society develops institutions which constrain the actions of individual extremists, while simultaneously rationalising and regularising their role in society.

* * *

One of the great unanswered questions of the study of political violence is why terrorists, *genocidaires* and other mass killers murder such large numbers of people from their own population. Before implementing the final solution throughout Europe, the Nazis spent years honing their tools of extermination against communists, homosexuals and German Jews. The perpetrators of the Rwandan genocide killed tens of thousands of Hutu civilians, including their own political leaders and, especially, those who had intermarried with Tutsis[544]. During the Iraq War of the early 2000s, at least a third of the civilians killed were victims of local insurgents and militias. And since 9/11, the vast majority of the victims of Islamist extremist violence have been Syrian, Afghan and Iraqi civilians. Wherever we find violent ideologies that pose a threat to international peace and security, we find that their primary target has first and foremost been 'traitors', collaborators, appeasers and moderates within their own population.

In the late 1990s, the political scientists Fearon & Laitin developed an agent-based model of in-group policing in which populations organically develop strategies to identify and punish individuals who violated group norms regulating relations with outsiders[545]. While the purpose of their model was to prove that in-group policing could sustain cooperative relations between ethnic groups, they conceded that *"the same in-group institutional structures used to identify and sanction members who offend against the other group can just as well be used to sanction members who seek to establish ties with ethnic others or who refuse to fight against them."*

Ravi Bhavnani (a doctoral student of Axelrod) noted that extremism

---

[544] Prunier (1995); Bhavnani & Backer (2000) at pgs. 283-306.

[545] Fearon & Laitin (1996) at pgs. 722-733.

could therefore be seen as a the 'dark side' of in-group policing[546] – a phenomenon that drives the construction of strong group identities and exacerbates inter-group conflict. As such, he and his co-authors simulated populations in which social agents possessed varying levels of a trait they labelled 'extremism'. Extremists would punish those who refuse to ostracise outsiders – they construct a meta-norm of group conflict[547]. Simulations showed that the distribution of extremist traits played a key role in mass violence – populations with more extremists and stronger meta-norms were more likely to perpetrate genocidal violence *even though extremists only directed their violence at members of their own social group.*

These models are instructive. Levels of *inter-group conflict* depend critically on the intensity of *in-group policing* and third-party punishment. To understand mass violence, the *internal structure* and cohesion of each group is more explanatory than the structure of relations *between* groups[548]. In order for mass violence to emerge as a group norm, intra-group punishments must be severe. A small coalition of extremists can trigger a phase transition to a meta-norm of group conflict by substantially raising the anticipated costs of collaboration with outsiders. The evolutionary account of extremism is therefore dynamic and critically dependent on population structure – inter-group conflict is not a 'primordial' or fixed part of human nature. Rather it is an emergent behaviour that occurs under specific conditions even between populations with no prior history of mutual hatred and violence as a result of changes in their internal composition.

The evolutionary account of extremism has several implications for understanding terrorism and extremist violence. Inter-group conflict is rarely driven purely by political leaders and ambitious would-be tyrants – so eliminating figureheads is likely to be pointless unless accompanied

---

[546] Bhavnani & Backer (2000) at pgs. 283-306; Bhavnani (2006) at pgs. 651-669; Bhavnani, "Agent-based Models in the Study of Ethnic Norms and Violence" in Harrison (ed.) (2006) at pgs. 121-136.

[547] Bhavnani & Backer (2000) at pg. 292.

[548] Bhavnani (2006), esp. at pg. 662-.

by a systematic effort to undermine the social status and prestige of their ideology. Extremism drives social violence 'from below' – a democratic and participatory process in which the community responds to pressures generated by third-party punishers. The existence of inter-group tensions is far less important than the existence of norms that legitimise harsh in-group policing. The more puritanical and hateful a group's internal norms, the more like it is to direct violence outwards at others.

In the same way, we should not expect hate and extremist groups to operate a centrally directed hierarchies with strict rational-legal authority and clear chains of command flowing downwards from a single leader. Terrorism and other forms of social violence are stochastic: leaders can construct narratives, emotional triggers and permissive environments for others to take action, but who commits third-party punishment, and when, is left to chance. Perversely, the more random an act of third-party punishment, the more effective the extremist group has been at motivating ordinary members of society to enforce their preferred group norm. Leninist organisations with strict hierarchies such as Al Qaeda, ironically, are much less effective in generating social conflict than ISIS or white nationalists who insist that it's everyone's responsibility to confront the outsider threat.

* * *

One of the key predictions evolutionary sociology makes about extremist violence is that it should be *selective* and *conditional* – each victim is punished by a specific perpetrator for a specific reason[549]. Whether we're talking about lynchings in the American South, the Spanish Inquisition, trans- and homo-phobic hate crimes, violence by religious extremists or counterrevolutionary terrorism in Latin America and elsewhere, the perpetrators and victims of extremist violence are, in principle, knowable one another. Mass violence is an intimate, participatory activity in which neighbours become enemies – often after long periods of peaceful co-

---

[549] Kalyvas (2006) at pg. 6.

existence[550]. Whether for consorting with foreigners, cross-dressers, communists or trade unionists, the targets of extremists must be perceived to have violated a group norm *and this knowledge must somehow make its way into the hands of extremists individuals and groups.*

This creates a puzzle. Mass political violence often appears to be arbitrary and indiscriminate – it is inconceivable that every Muslim victim of Islamist extremist violence was a known apostate, or that the tens of thousands of victims of political violence across Latin America were actual communists. When observers can't make sense of *why* terrorists or extremists have targeted a particular group or individual, they tend to make up 'just so' stories that explain away mass violence on the basis of superficial identity tags. They hate us because of our freedom, or the colour of our skin, or because of the mode in which we worship. Extremist violence is irrational. But these convenient fictions often disguise complicated narratives. Even lone killers frequently target communities they know intimately, and large-scale political violence can often be traced back to family feuds going back generations.

It turns out that the information structure of society is vitally important to way in which extremism plays out[551]. Extremists are not omniscient – they must identify rule-breakers *somehow.* Signals identifying potential targets must be sent and received, and information asymmetries create opportunities for exploitation, especially when extremist groups or institutions lack institutional power and authority.

"A notable characteristic of the [Cultural Revolution] that ravaged the Chinese countryside was the close link between political victims and their tormentors. Rural society was not a passive universe helplessly rocked by political campaigns launched from above. What the political campaigns did was to unlock a Pandora's box, pushing the local agents of the state into the hunt for concrete targets at the grassroots levels, in pursuit of the "perpetual revolution" envisioned by

---

[550] Kalyvas (2006), Chapter 10.

[551] Kalyvas at pg. 174.

Mao. At the centre of thousands of villages were local collaborators trying to manipulate these campaigns to their own advantage. In many cases, they were motivated by long-standing hostility between individuals, families, or local factions. More often than not, their victims were neighbours, childhood playmates, or even immediate relatives by blood or marriage." [Jun Jing, The Temple of Memories][552]

In his book, *The Logic of Violence in Civil War*, political scientist Stathis Kalyvas posits that the enforcement of group norms is a *joint* action between local actors and extremists: the latter requires the former to identify outsiders and deviants within the population; the former relies on (and exploits) the latter to perpetuate their private feuds and vendettas. Kalyvas' model thus combines a structural theory of political violence with an analysis of individual acts of terror[553]. The key social dilemma that prior theories of extremism had missed was *collaboration*: the process whereby civilian actors 'denounce' neighbours to extremist actors or authorities – identifying who should be targeted for punishment – and thus become active participants in political conflict themselves[554].

"Individuals have strong incentives to exploit the informational asymmetries of civil war in order to reap all kinds of benefits, including settling accounts with personal and local enemies. . . . While political actors "use" civilians to collect information and win the war, it is also the case that civilians "use" political actors to settle their own private conflicts. Put otherwise, civilians may effectively turn political actors into their own private 'contract killers'" [Kalyvas, The Logic of Violence in Civil Wars][555]

In Kalyvas' model, social agents interact knowing that at any time their

---

[552] Jing (1996) at pg. 87.

[553] Kalyvas (2006) at pg. 10; Kalyvas (2003) at pgs. 475-494.

[554] Kalyvas (2006) at pg. 14.

[555] Kalyvas (2006) at pg. 14

partner could denounce them to a political authority which would impose a heavy or even fatal penalty upon them for defection. The stronger the extremist authority, the more credible the threat of denunciation becomes. But there's a trade-off. The stronger the extremist's local presence, the more likely they are to have their own intelligence and the ability to detect false signals. So when extremist control is imperfect and the demand for intelligence is high, Kalyvas predicts that civilians will exploit this asymmetry and provide misleading or false information[556], leading violence to become more intense and arbitrary. But in areas where extremists have one-sided control, the need for private information on the population's loyalty, and thus the rewards for collaboration, are reduced. And with it the likelihood of arbitrary violence.

Of course, this creates a social dilemma for the extremists. Extremist groups, at least the successful ones, are often highly cognisant of the risk of exploitation by false denunciation, and establish internal rules and procedures to authorise targets – and may even develop institutional mechanisms which resemble intelligence and security agencies. The more effective an extremist is at assessing the accuracy of denunciations, the more selective their violence will be and the more efficient their quest for political and cultural hegemony. On the other hand, groups with poor internal discipline, or which have only weak local control, or which are under significant external pressure are likely to be far more indiscriminate and brutal in their use of violence. States which occupy foreign populations often face the same issue, with local communities providing vast but unreliable intelligence on the allegiance on their neighbours. Good counterinsurgency relies on sorting the accurate intelligence out from the chaff – the risks of triggering a backlash through the indiscriminate application of punishments is significant.

Kalyvas' model anticipates that extremist behaviour should be structured – with the scope and accuracy of social punishments dependent on localised patterns of information and authority. Studies of the Greek and Spanish

---

[556] Kalyvas (2006) at pg. 178.

Civil Wars, the Balkan Wars, communal violence in Colombia[557], Israel-Palestine[558], and Iraq[559] have gathered evidence that real-world conflicts largely follow this model[560]. Figure 1 illustrates Kalyvas' basic framework, featuring two political authorities which are at odds over the enforcement social norms (the status quo incumbent and revolutionary insurgent). Revolutionary forces are attempting to shift group behaviour; counter-revolutionary forces aim to prevent this by strict third-party punishment in support of existing social norms. Moving across different parts of the population, levels of incumbent and insurgent control vary, and so does the nature of political violence.

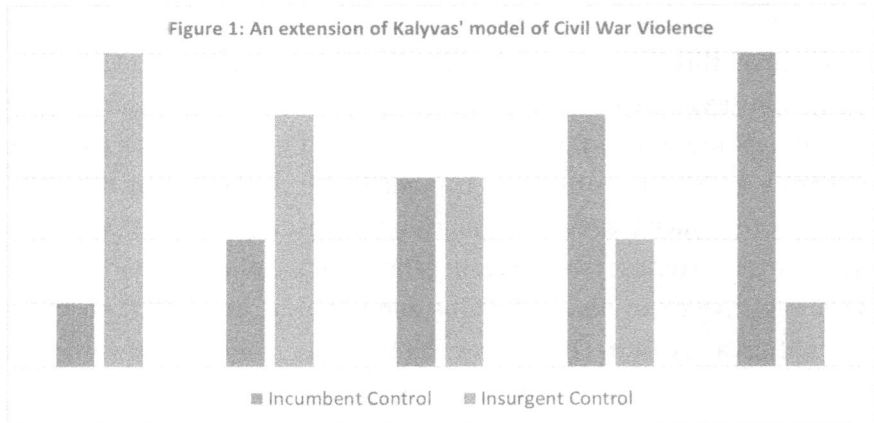

Figure 1: An extension of Kalyvas' model of Civil War Violence

■ Incumbent Control   ■ Insurgent Control

In territory, or over those parts of the population, where extremist authorities exercise strong control, they can be highly selective about their targets, 'disappearing' domestic opponents and perhaps even covering their actions with the veil of institutional legitimacy. Terror can be highly selective and thus effectively invisible in authoritarian states – Augusto Pinochet, for

---

[557] Vargas (2009) at pgs. 110–132.

[558] Bhavnani et al. (2011) at pgs. 61–80; Bhavnani et al. (2012) at pgs. 133–158.

[559] Kalyvas & Kocher (2007) at pgs. 183-223; Green & Ward, "The Transformation of Violence in Iraq" in "The Criminology of War" Routledge (2017) at pgs. 123-141.

[560] Kalyvas (2012) at pgs. 658-668.

all his regime's sadism and crimes against humanity, murdered only a few thousand people between 1973 and 1990. The number guillotined by the Jacobins in Paris in 1793-1794 was similar. In both cases, the Terror was efficient because most of those targeted were either already in state custody or known to authorities. This selectivity contrasts strongly with *La Violencia* in Colombia from 1948-58, or the French War in the Vendée of 1793. In both those cases, hundreds of thousands of civilians died as metropolitan authorities contested power in rural regions where their level of local control and access to reliable information was poor.

In totalitarian political regimes, which place a high premium on social conformity and compliance with group norms, the phenomenon of mutual denunciation reaches its zenith even as the value of denunciation is near-zero. Everyone becomes, in effect, a *de facto* extremist because social norms and institutions create an expectation of denunciation. Failure to inform on one's neighbours can just as easily lead to being informed upon. For such a state, violence can be highly selective – the number of political prisoners need not be high. But the *expectation* of state violence is all consuming and all encompassing. So much so that social agents are often expected to inform on themselves in ritualistic sessions of self-criticism, establishing their credibility as rule-followers by putting a figurative knife to their own throat. Ironically, in a totalitarian regime Terror is highly democratised, because no social actor is willing to extend anyone else even a modicum of tolerance for deviance.

In zones where extremists have virtually no local presence and extremely poor information about the local population, revolutionary or counter-revolutionary violence is most likely to be indiscriminate – taking the forms of random bombings and terror[561]. At the nadir of their influence, the only option for such movements is to assume the entire population is hostile and thus a legitimate target for punishment. Lacking local supports, they have little to fear from a backlash. Terrorist groups thus often lash out indiscriminately in the homeland of the 'far enemy'. Whereas Timothy

---

[561] Kalyvas (2006) at pg. 206.

McVeigh and other white nationalist militia in the United States bombed government buildings because they saw the workers inside as traitors and collaborators, ISIS aspires to the mass murder of Western civilians in public spaces wherever and whenever they can. The only way the violent Islamist extremist can conceive of Westerners is as an undifferentiated mass of support for their enemies, all of whom deserve punishment for participating in a system they perceive as a hostile to the kind of world they want to build.

Kalyvas' model predicts that the most deadly political violence should occur in zones of mixed control, where an authority has sufficient control to effectively carry out punishments of the local population and contest for power but where asymmetries in information environment permit local actors to provide false or misleading signals of group affiliation and behaviour at little risk. This can occur either as an insurgent or revolutionary group begins to grow in strength, or an established authority finds its grip starting to weaken. Denunciation fuels counter-denunciation and selective violence spirals out of control[562]. *La Violencia* and the Indonesian purge of the communists in 1965 demonstrate the sheer scope of the carnage that can be produced when existing authorities feel their grip on a country threatened by a potentially viable challenger. The War in the Vendée, the Killing Fields of Cambodia and the Russian Civil War demonstrate that the opposite is also true – that insurgent and revolutionary movements that are on the verge of taking power can also act indiscriminately in the course of disciplining civilian populations to accept the new order.

In this model of political violence, extremists with conflicting social and political goals rarely, if ever, fight one another directly. The true battle is for the allegiance of the civilian population and violence is directed inwards in order to condition its obedience. Conventional armed conflict between competing authorities, with forces fighting one another directly, is relatively rare and – perversely – safer for the civilian population. When two sides are finely balanced, neither would provide the other an advantage by taking the risk of acting on bad intelligence and persecuting a part of

---

[562] Kalyvas (2006) at pg. 194-195.

the local population that they may rely upon for critical support. In war, collateral damage to civilians is not just a tactical cost of doing business: it's a potentially catastrophic strategic mistake that could erode your long-term capacity to win.

* * *

Extremist individuals and institutions that seek to control the behaviour of members of their own society are likely to form part of the strategic equilibrium in any social species. The threat of third-party punishment plays an important role in maintaining social cohesion and generating the differentials in group fitness that are required for cultural group selection to function. But there's an unavoidable feedback loop between social cohesion and large-scale political violence, and those societies with the strongest internal enforcement of norms are also likely to be those most willing and able to engage in atrocities against their perceived enemies at home and abroad.

Progressive and tolerant societies therefore have valid reason to be concerned about the internal organisation of other societies. The greatest single predictor of whether another population is preparing for conflict is the intensity of its internal controls – the anticipation of greater conflict is almost always preceded by violence directed inwards, a reduction in the range of internally tolerated behaviours and limitations on the scope of legitimate opposition. And societies which respond to the increasing levels of globalisation and commerce by turning inwards, strengthening xenophobia and domestic cohesion, are a potential threat to the society of states because such behaviours signal that they anticipate elevated levels of inter-state competition, and may act offensively to secure their relative advantage.

16

OUTSIDE CONTEXT PROBLEMS

Key Points

- When individuals and groups encounter novel strategies, many social agents will intuitively interpret their current strategy as being adaptive or fitness-enhancing and the alternatives as maladaptive or harmful.
- Political and cultural conservatives display naïve adaptionist thinking: the presumption that existing social norms, rules and institutions have necessary social or political functions.
- Evolutionary thinking provides us with a variety of alternative hypotheses for the origins of social structures, and expands the range of tolerable social strategies.

Previous Chapters have addressed three of the disintegrative forces in the life of social species that are explained by the evolutionary account of social behaviour but not by most other political philosophies. The final set of Chapters will address another significant social force: conservatism – what it is, where it comes from, and how it is expressed. Conservatives are social agents with a set of heuristic biases which include scepticism of novelty and emotional attachment to social order. Earlier, we touched briefly on 'adaptionism' – the naïve idea that natural selection adapts behaviours for a "capital-R" Reason or gives them a "capital-F" Function. This

Chapter builds the foundations of an argument that cultural and political conservatives display, adopt and promote adaptionist thinking, and sets out the arguments for why the adaptionist – and thus the conservative – approach to managing social ambiguity is often wrong.

Speaking very simply, a social behaviour may be either *adaptive* (reliably increasing or maximising individual fitness[563]), *maladaptive* (reliably decreasing individual fitness) or *nonadaptive* (have no or unreliable effects on fitness). By-and-large, biologists agree that evolution does not require that every behaviour is adaptive: adaptiveness is *"special and onerous concept that should not be used unnecessarily"* [Williams][564]. Many behaviours will have existed in at least one prior generation and been carried into the present by selection without going immediately extinct. But other strategies in the population will represent mutations – novel behavioural variations that arise by chance. Some [perhaps many] mutations will inevitably have negative relative fitness payoffs.

This Chapter is concerned with the question of how social agents decide whether a behaviour outside their current social context is adaptive or maladaptive. While individuals in a closed society may only encounter others with the same behaviour as themselves, in open and liberal societies encounters between individuals with different strategies and behaviours are inevitable. As technology accelerates the rate of interaction and cultural innovation over time, managing exposure to novel behaviours becomes a key cultural and political challenge - particularly if we want to prevent the strengthening of the extremist forces encountered in the last Chapter. The cultural balance between openness or novelty-seeking and conservative or tradition-seeking strategies is how stable populations manage this challenge.

Routine socialisation, as well as the threat of backlash and third party punishment of deviance, primes a significant proportion of social agents to avoid the unfamiliar. There may be good evolutionary reasons for these

---

[563] Buss et al. (1998) at pgs. 535-536.

[564] Williams (1966) at pg. vii.

biases – a risk-averse social agent who upholds the prevailing social norms can be reasonably confident that they'll be no less fit than the social average. We cannot know whether novel mutations might grant a positive fitness advantage given that the payoffs of any course of action depend on the distribution of strategies in the population – which has now changed. On the other hand, social and political progressives may still seek out unfamiliar social strategies – they are often emotionally rewarded by novelty-seeking behaviour. But there are risks attached: adopting an unproven social strategy generates a risk of lowered biological and cultural fitness. Openness to experience is an evolutionary gamble that may lead to either social and political advancement – or ruin.

In 1979, the biologists Stephen Jay Gould and Richard Lewontin wrote a landmark paper critical of what they called the 'adaptionist' thinking they saw in early sociobiology and as represented by genetic essentialists like Richard Dawkins. The *Spandrels of St Marco* paper[565] provides the standard definition of adaptionism as a way of thinking: an organism's behaviour is atomised into a collection of traits, with each trait being assumed to be optimally adapted by natural selection to perform a particular biological or social function. And to the extent that any trait can be demonstrated to be sub-optimal, then the inferiority of any given trait or behaviour is an altruistic contribution to the best possible design of the organism as a whole. So although there may be trade-offs between different behaviours, overall the fitness of the replicating organism is maximised[566]. The null or default hypothesis is that an extant behaviour is *adaptive*[567].

Although Gould & Lewontin were critiquing bad science by some reactionary biologists, their model of adaptionism applies neatly to lay social and political conservatives. The science of evolutionary biology has responded to and improved in response to their critique. But many non-specialists

---

[565] Gould & Lewontin (1979) at pgs. 581-598; Pigliucci & Kaplan (2000) at pgs. 66-70; Wilson (2012) at pgs. 30-31.

[566] Gould & Lewontin (1979) at pg. 585.

[567] E.g. Buss et a.. (1998) at pg. 536-537.

continue to treat existing social behaviours and strategies as adaptive by default and novel social behaviours and strategies as maladaptive. Conservatives, for example, will argue that economic inequality enhances fitness because it provides incentives for individual striving and punishments for poor performance. To the extent that this is untrue, in the sense that wealth and high incomes are rarely a true reward for effort, and living in the lower part of the social hierarchy tends to stress and demoralise people, cleverer conservatives and liberals invoke the second part of the adaptionist formula. Inequality may not be a perfect social structure but the population-level advances provided by the concentration of wealth and income (i.e. capital-intensive 'innovation') makes society as a whole better off even if there are relative fitness costs borne unfairly by some segments of society.

Gould & Lewontin argued that adaptionist thinking is unscientific and unfalsifiable. It permits the conservative to come up with an unending series of 'just so' stories to justify the adaptive function of the existing order by establishing a frame of reference in which the virtue of the status quo is assumed. If one justification is disproved, others can be invented without having to fundamentally change one's worldview. So in this way, conservative opposition to homosexuality shifts seamlessly from opposition on the basis of divine command, to the basis of its supposed unnaturalness, to the basis of effect on social order and family relations, to its effect on social health, to 'confusing children'. And resistance to changing our energy strategies to deal with climate change can move from 'climate change isn't real', to 'climate change isn't cause by humans', to 'climate change is a communist plot', to 'climate change isn't that bad, actually', to believing that capitalism will permit out existing social and political arrangements to survive the transition to a warmer world. Conservatives have no need to be consistent – their commitment to the existing social order precedes their ostensible justifications for it and they're free to adapt the narrative which produces the best results in a given dialectical context.

Further, even if adaptionists cannot arrive at a socially-acceptable justification of social norms, they assume that one must exist[568]. The conservative is free to argue that even if a social behaviour appears to be harmful or maladaptive, it must exist for reasons we cannot understand. Either because the existing social order was put in place by a divine being whose will and intent we cannot possibly know, or because inherited norms represents the accumulated wisdom of nature or 'the ancients', or because the 'invisible hand' of the market provides the perfect allocation of goods and services in the economy. Even though there are people in society whom a given rule harms and who are agitating for change, we might not understand the full reasons why a particular behaviour evolved. In a limited sense, this is not incorrect. We may not know or appreciate the full evolutionary history of a particular behaviour, and changing it may have consequences that are poorly understood. But the default presumption that an extant norm is more fit than the alternatives, even in the face of evidence of specific and demonstratable costs, distinguishes the merely cautious from the innately conservative.

* * *

The *Spandrels of St Marco* paper challenges us to ask what kind of evidence might we need to show that a trait, behaviour, organ or institution is adaptive or maladaptive.[569] The paper, and the body of research subsequently inspired by it, establishes a series of alternative hypotheses about the evolutionary origins of social behaviour that are no more or less credible than the adaptiveness hypothesis. Only by the careful elimination of alternative hypotheses is it possible to settle on a falsifiable theory of the evolutionary origins of a particular organ or cultural behaviour.

The most well-known alternative hypothesis, and the one for which the *Spandrels of St Marco* paper is named, is that an evolved trait or behaviour may be a so-called 'spandrel'. Gould & Lewontin noted that the triangular

---

[568] Gould & Lewontin (1979) at pg. 586.

[569] Pigliucci & Kaplan (2000) at pgs. 66-70.

spaces featuring Biblical imagery in many medieval churches – notably in St Mark's Cathedral in Venice – appear so 'elaborate, harmonious and purposeful' that we can't help but to presume that their artistic function was central to the entire design of the edifice. Yet in fact these spaces, which Gould [perhaps mistakenly[570]] called 'spandrels', arise as an architectural consequence of mounting domed structures on top of arches. The trait of the building started out as a by-product of physical constraints on the building's form. Spandrels themselves are non-adaptive and not directly subject to selection, and are maintained because of their neutral fitness effect. But the presence of non-adaptive traits in the population creates the possibility that they could become co-opted by natural selection later. Gould later divided spandrels into two types: pre-adaptions (non-adaptive structures) and exaptions (structures that were once non-adaptive but subsequently became fitness-enhancing)[571].

Most examples of spandrels in biological organisms involve physical by-products of the growth and development process. The shape and design of many arthropod shells, for example, arises largely from the chemical limitations of growing a hardened mineral carapace throughout the lifetime of the animal. And in many species of mammal, hormones of sex and development produce a long list of physical changes – and its challenging to identify which changes are fitness-enhancing benefit and which are merely by-products which have been retained by natural selection because of the overwhelming reproductive advantage sex hormones provide[572]. The stress hormone cortisol, for example, activates the fight-or-flight response, supports the short-term survival of animals and is therefore adaptively maintained by natural selection. But it's long-term negative effects on health and cognition are a by-product of this action and may in fact decrease the long-term fitness of chronically stressed populations.

Indeed, domestication of many animal (and plant) species followed

---

[570] Houston (1997); Gould (1997) at pgs. 10750–10755.

[571] Gould & Vrba (1982) at pgs. 4-15; Buss et al. (1998) at pg. 539–540.

[572] Gould (1997) at pgs. 10750–10755; Buss et al. (1998) at pg. 536.

precisely this pattern. It can certainly be shown that many features of the domestic dog, including its facial morphology, tail wagging and general playfulness are traits that have been artificially selected in order to promote their integration into human social groups. And indeed, there's emerging evidence that dog facial muscles and dietary preferences have been under positive genetic selection over recent evolutionary history[573]. But many of the physical and behavioural differences between domestic species and their wild ancestors are likely to be by-products of humans selecting for a single trait – sociability or lowered aggression. By preferentially breeding animals with lower levels of stress and aggression hormones, humans have triggered a host of secondary changes including in size, shape, colouration, behaviour and cognition[574]. These changes are not necessarily adaptive, but may become desirable later (i.e. become exaptions) as a result of cultural selection on breeds.

We can apply the same analysis to cultural traits, norms and institutions. Are traditionalist notions of gender roles, in which women are presumed to perform the majority of reproductive labour, a necessary social structure that maximises fitness, or merely a cultural by-product of economic arrangements which privileged the wages and social status of fighting-age males? Certainly, there's ample evidence from capitalist history of periods in which women performing the bulk of agricultural or manufacturing labour that one could argue persuasively that gender roles are a spandrel: a by-product of the mode of economic production.

One of the primary 'architectural' limitations on evolutionary adaption is the correlation between size and form ('allometry'). As animal size increases, the physical limitations on bodies become more important. Crustaceans cannot grow above a certain size without losing their capacity to respirate; larger land animals need thicker bones, higher blood pressure, bigger lungs and more energy-rich diets. Growth periods are prolonged,

---

[573] Kaminski et al. (2019) at pgs. 14677-14681; Axelsson et al.(2013) at pgs. 360-364.

[574] Trut (1999); Trut et al. (2009) at pgs. 349-360; Wilkins et al. (2014) at pgs. 795-808; Wright (2015) at pgs. 11-20.

and this in turn creates spandrels as parents have to spend more time and energy investing in the survival of their young. Necessary architectural and behavioural responses to larger or smaller physical size (driven, for example, by increased predation or changing environmental conditions) can lead to a cascade of by-products in terms of cognition and behaviour. It's highly likely that at least two species of humans (*homo naledi* and *homo floriensis*) experienced a host of physical and cognitive changes in response to decreasing body size even at a very late date in human evolution – at the same time that the environment of other early humans was favouring larger brains and more complex social organisation.

We can apply the same analysis to culture and institutions. As governments cover more extensive populations and territories, the norms governing social interaction tend to become more anonymous and impartial. As we exceed the capacity of humans to memorise the kin relationships and reputational status of the majority of individuals they interact with, we by necessity come to rely on more symbolic and abstracted markers of group identity. These markers are not necessarily more efficient at sustaining group cohesiveness on small scales (in fact, they may be strictly inferior) but they are necessary adaptions as society scales up. With this increasing anonymity comes a whole host of other changes, including the need for stronger impartial enforcement of law and contracts, growing social isolation and an increase emphasis on formal manners and rules of exchange. In the same vein, as bureaucratic institutions scale up in order to govern ever-larger populations, their forms and rules change and adapt – and not all of these changes are positive. Bureaucracies become more impersonal, hierarchical, labyrinthine, rule-bound and resistant to change. These changes may not be adaptive but instead a necessary by-products of allometric changes which secure the cultural reproduction of the social whole.

* * *

Other alternative hypotheses tend cluster around three major types of cognitive error or bias: first, assuming the equal strength of the selective pressure on strategies; secondly, underestimating the role of contingency and change; and thirdly, simplifying how traits interact to make up the whole.

We must begin by recognising that natural selection does not exert the same pressure equally on all organisms and groups in the environment at the same time, or even the same pressure on all traits in the same organism. Species and groups which experience material abundance, and which face minimal competition from other species and groups, may face weak selective pressures. Under these conditions, mutations can start to accumulate in the genetic and cultural structure of a population, and its traits and behaviours can diverge from the local fitness maximum.

In the same way that a species may gradually change over time as a result of such *genetic noise* or *drift*, societies may find their norms and behaviours changing over time because of *cultural drift*[575]. Consider for example the emergence of new religious beliefs and practices. In any society with symbolic culture, individual agents may randomly innovate new beliefs and practices and spread them to their followers. When a population is subject to strong selective pressures, only those beliefs and practices which generate a fitness advantage for the group are likely to survive and thrive. But when inter-group competition is weak, new beliefs and practices may spread essentially at random: some will die off, and others become incredibly popular. So over time, the norms of a society may change in ways that are nonadaptive – and indeed two groups which started out with the same culture operating in the same environment may come to see themselves as entirely different peoples simply through random drift.

Cultural drift is especially important for understanding elements of symbolic culture that are not under strong elective pressure. This includes the evolution of names, language, the visual arts and music. In these fields,

---

[575] Gould & Lewontin (1979) at pgs. 590-591; Koerper & Stickel (1980) at pgs. 463-469; Buss et al. (1998) at pg. 536; Bentley et al. (2004) at pgs. 1443-1550; Boyd & Richerson (2005) at pg. 69.

taste and fashion can change quickly and seemingly at random, with little or no meaningful adaptive reason for doing so. Wearing the right style of clothing, or listening to the right genre of music, or being a fan of a particular esoteric subculture, can have important consequences for social status and reproductive success. But there are no evolutionary criteria on which we might judge that a particular style of clothing, or arrangement of harmonies, or abstract arrangement of colours, is any more or less fit than any other. Language, and in particular vocabulary, is best understood in this way. While there may be more-or-less fit ways of conveying information quickly and accurately, leading to a broad but not indefinite range of common grammatical structures, the actual sounds used to represent particular ideas and concepts are essentially arbitrary, so language usage tends to drift over time, leading to the vulgarisation of forms and the emergence of new regional dialects and languages.

Another important aspect of the strength of selective pressure to consider is the rate of evolutionary change compared to the rate of change in the material and cultural environment[576]. Much earlier in this text, we noted that rate at which adaption takes place depends on the predictability of the natural environment. When conditions are stable over geological time periods, genetic evolution can provide a species all the adaptive potential it requires. When conditions are more unstable, a social species may develop cumulative culture, which permits it to adapt to changes in the environment faster than it can accumulate genetic mutations. But when conditions change from generation-to-generation, and even inherited culture is unlikely to reproduce reliably fitness-enhancing behaviours, the only option is for organisms to be highly individually adaptable, capable of adopting a variety of possible traits and behaviours depending on the present conditions during early development.

Owing to mismatch between the rate of natural selection and the rate of change in its environment, a species may possess a number of genetically-

---

[576] Pigliucci & Kaplan (2000) at pg. 67; Buss et al. (1998) at pg. 536

controlled traits which have become maladaptive or vestigial[577]. Many species which adapt to life on isolated continents and islands act in ways which make them highly vulnerable to newly-introduced predators. And indeed, modern-day genetic essentialists who apply this model to human behaviour make many of the same analogies[578]. For example, obesity and increasing rates of Type 2 diabetes in humans (and domesticated dogs and cats) are hypothesised to be a maladaptive consequence of digestive systems operating in a far more calorie-rich nutritional environment than they evolved in.

"All evolutionary explanations of the existence of species-wide mechanisms are to this extent explanations in terms of the past fitness effects of that kind of mechanism that led to the current existence of the mechanism in the species. The fact that a mechanism currently enhances fitness, by itself, cannot explain why the mechanism exists or how it is structured" [Buss][579]

Evolutionary mismatch is an important concept, but it's easily misapplied in social species which are not only subject to variable rates of selection and variable rates of environmental change, but also *variable mechanisms of selection*. Remember, gene-culture evolution argues that behaviour in social species is the result of both biological and cultural selection. So we often find "Capital-E, Capital-P" Evolutionary Psychologists and conservatives arguing that an evolutionary mismatch between the environment of evolutionary adaptiveness ('EEA') and modern life is the only valid hypothesis for irrational behaviours with negative fitness consequences[580]. But they ignore the 50,000 years or more of cultural evolution which play a role in how biological traits are regulated and reproduced in modern humans. Diet-induced increases in human obesity are caused just as

---

[577] Giphart & van Vugt (2018)

[578] Alvergne et al. (2016)

[579] Buss et al. (1998) at pg. 540.

[580] Addressed in Chapter 5 of Boyd & Richerson (2005)

much by the exploitation of human pleasure drives by profit-seeking institutions, the way in which food is manufactured at the cheapest cost and the inability or unwillingness of governments to regulate. This cultural and economic context cannot simply be assumed to be a fixed and unchanging environment – it is an adaptive system in its own right.

The second major cognitive error is to underestimate the role of contingency in human affairs – and to assume pattern and causation where there is none. Thanks to Niko Tinbergen we know that the 'reasons' for a given behaviour include everything from its deep evolutionary history, its current fitness effects, its role in the development of the social agent and its physical mechanisms of action. Evolutionary game theory shows us that for any given social dilemma, there may be many evolutionarily stable strategic equilibria[581]. Some of these equilibria may be attractors towards which a wide variety of different populations will converge regardless of their initial position. Others may be unstable states that are difficult to access, or local attractors which are only reachable from a small subset of positions not including a populations' current composition. Even if a particular behaviour is adaptive, it may only be *locally adaptive* and may not represent the optimal solution to an evolutionary dilemma[582].

Put another way, the particular traits and behaviours that an organism inherits critically depend on the evolutionary trajectory and history of the population as a whole. Some biological organs are 'inefficiently' designed in a way that create significant health risks for the organism, but could not be otherwise because of the route that organ took to perform its current function. Cultural institutions are the same way – they may be highly ritualised or inefficient, but they are difficult to reform because cultural evolution made do with the tools available at the time[583]. This has two consequences. First of all, adaptionists cannot argue that that we live in the best of all possible worlds, because evolution strongly suggests alternative

---

[581] Gould & Lewontin (1979) at pgs. 593.

[582] Buss et al. (1998) at pg. 537.

[583] Boyd & Richerson (2005) at pgs. 151-152.

worlds could have and might still exist (see the next Chapter).

But secondly the identification of a hypothetical alternative social structure with a higher fitness is no *guarantee that it such a structure would be accessible by the current population*. This is where both conservative reactionaries and utopian or revolutionary socialists often go wrong. They employ "Capital-R" Reason or some form of Intuition to identify a superior form of social organisation. But their attempt to force a social transition involves crossing unstable strategic territory. Attempting to move towards a different social structure may unleash evolutionary forces and currents than send a population back to its original position, or careening off on an entirely unforeseen path. No matter how well-intentioned, the French and Russian Revolutions demonstrated that the attempt to force a social phase transition while leaving the cultural evolutionary forces which supported the previous equilibrium in place was more likely than not doomed to produce results that the revolutionaries did not intend and could not anticipate. More on this in the next Chapter.

The final set of hypotheses about the evolutionary origins of particular traits and behaviours are grouped together as constraints, trade-offs and costs. This has traditionally formed part of the adaptionist methodology critiqued by Gould & Lewontin[584], but is better explained by multi-level selection than any alternative theory. In order for an organism to develop a biological or cultural function, it may require other parts of itself to pay a cost or develop inefficiently – to behave altruistically. Stable equilibria are complex, delicately balanced and may require maintenance of organs or institutions that are imperfect or destructive[585]. Growing advances in genetic knowledge have demonstrated that many genes – and the proteins they encode – are *pleiotropic*[586]. Rather than a single gene controlling a

---

[584] Gould & Lewontin (1979) at pgs. 591; Gould (1980) at pgs. 39-52; Cheverud (1984) at pgs. 155–171; Maynard Smith et al. (1985) at pgs. 265-287; Boyd & Richerson (2005) at pgs. 155-156.

[585] Buss et al. (1998) at pgs. 538-539.

[586] Baatz & Wagner (1997) at pgs.49–66.

single trait, each gene governs a small percentage of the function of multiple traits, and any individual trait is governed by the overlapping effects of very many different genes.

Genes and traits cannot be considered in isolated adaptive contexts because their replication critically depends on the survival of the whole[587]. Organs and institutions may work less efficiently than they otherwise might because of the need to cooperate with other organs and institutions with their own separate evolutionary history and adaptive function. Law enforcement, for example, could be made more 'efficient' if it were freed from constraints imposed on it by other social institutions, such as norms favour individual rights, freedom from arbitrary torture, detention and punishment, and general protections of privacy and access to justice. But we generally accept these trade-offs because the social value of those rights exceeds the fitness advantages law enforcement organs might potentially gain if these norms were loosened. In fact, having a social institution break free of its evolutionary constraints is one of the major warning signs that your population has developed a social cancer.

Boyd & Richerson have argued that we should in fact expect cultural strategies to be maladaptive more often than biological ones[588], because the speed at which cultural variants can be transmitted through a population involves a *necessary* trade off against the ability of social agents to assess whether or not novel strategies are fitness enhancing. Humans may be so terrible at judging whether or a not a socially transmitted behaviour is adaptive or maladaptive precisely because the 'collective brain' of the community prefers strategies to be transmitted widely and rapidly in order for their fitness to be assessed by the population as a whole - even if the consequences are dire for individuals that adopt that strategy. In other words, it's possible that the survival of early humans depended to such an extent on relentless imitation of new behaviours on the off chance that one increased group survival that even today we are poorly equipped to make

---

[587] Buss et al. (1998) at pg. 538-539.

[588] Boyd & Richerson (2005) from pg. 155-.

individual decisions about the suitability of behaviours. This trade-off, or dilemma, between the interests of the individual and the interests of the group results in a pattern of human behaviour that may not appear strictly rational at either level.

For many reasons, multilevel selection is the best theoretical framework for explaining these trade-offs and constraints because it best explains – in both a biological and cultural context – how and why sub-components of a social organism can evolve to cooperate with one another and self-limit their behaviour in order to promote the survival of the whole. Much of this book has been devoted to showing that cooperative and altruistic strategies are evolutionary stable in a context in which they are part of a population of similar strategies competing against other populations at a higher level of organisation.

* * *

Science is an act of imagination. The quality of our theories about the world depends on the conception and disproving of alternative hypotheses. The scientific method cannot tell us what is true, only what is falsifiable. Political science and sociology are much the same. The adaptionist paradigm can conceive of only a limited range of possibilities: social behaviours are either the best solution available, or an maladaptive deviation that must be confronted and rooted out. But with a little more imagination, we can conceive of numerous credible hypothesis about why people behave the way they do – we make presumptions about the adaptiveness of their choices at our peril.

When political actors examine social practices and hierarchies which appear to be inefficient or harmful, there are a number of alternative hypotheses we can draw upon. The conservative or adaptionist will default to the null hypothesis that every social behaviour in their own in-group is adaptive. The genetic essentialist may agree that a behaviour is maladaptive, but naturalise it as the product of a genetic legacy that cannot be easily changed. Whereas the evolutionary socialist will note that political and economic structures are cultural products that are not only modifiable, but the result of economic and material conditions that are themselves open to manipulation by social agents.

Anyone whose default hypothesis is that current social norms and structures are adaptive lacks the imagination to see that other worlds are possible (see Chapter 18: "Freedom is Scary"). On almost too many social issues to count – from racial integration, to homosexuality, divorce, non-monogamy and gender roles – the presumption that the pre-existing social order was the only possible equilibrium for society has been exposed as a *post hoc* justification of arbitrary and historically contingent arrangements. Human beings are natural story tellers, and we're very talented at fabricating justifications for our behaviour that are superficially plausible. Science is often co-opted for this purpose, but hopefully this Chapter has helped show that evolutionary science doesn't take have a conservative bias.

As technology brings us into daily contact with a wider variety of cultures and sub-cultures, it's increasingly important that we recognise that the beliefs and practices of others are the product of their particular cultural and evolutionary history, or that material conditions have changed faster than that group or sub-group has been able to adapt, or that even if our local adaptive equilibria were available to them that the costs and risks of transition would be non-trivial. Liberal societies have done tremendous harm to indigenous and colonised societies by attempt to forcibly shift their culture onto our own evolutionary path; if we truly had confidence in the fitness of our beliefs and practices then the better approach would have been to provide other cultures with the time and space to adapt to changing material circumstances while preserving the continuity of their culture and unique learning and wisdom.

17

THE NATURALIST FALLACY

Key Points

- It's impossible to judge whether any complex social equilibria are optimal. Social structure is contingent – the world could have been other than it is and therefore could be different in future.
- Conservatives insure a population against destabilising social or environmental changes by pulling it in the direction of prior equilibria points. Conservatives believe [wrongly] that social learning can only occur when elites transmit new knowledge to non-elites.
- Both progressives and conservatives have a responsibility to seek social and political change through means that preserve the viability of the social organism. Revolutionary or counter-revolutionary breaks are highly unlike to move society to the desired end-point.

In the twentieth century – unlike in the nineteenth – progressive-minded people tended to keep their distance from evolutionary accounts of human behaviour. They made two core critiques of sociobiology, the effort to study human behaviour in the context of the material world in which it evolved. Firstly, although it makes no pretence to offering normative guidance, cultural evolution can be used to argue that existing social rules, norms and institutions are already effective mechanisms to govern a society – and thus weaken demand for necessary social reform. As we saw in the previous Chapter, it often requires creative thinking to falsify a default assumption of the fitness of observed behaviour. Sociobiology is often interpreted as supporting political conservatism because it's simply easier to assume that existing social rules, norms and institutions are fit for purpose than to argue or demonstrate the contrary.

Secondly, an evolutionary approach can be seen as a rejection of enlightenment humanism, since it's sceptical on its face that we can use "capital-R" Reason alone to improve society. In the place of modernist optimism about the future, it locates the drivers of social, political and economic progress in historical, cultural and biological processes that are beyond individual control. Instead of reifying human cognitive capacities, cultural evolution instead sees the cumulative wisdom of society as a whole – its inherited practices and technologies, its capacity for widespread trial-and-error learning, and its complex modes of production – as the locus of human development. This is a leap that socialists and dialectical materialists made long ago, but which remains anathema to liberal individualists. Socialists are humanists, yes, but pessimistic about the capacity of individuals alone to fundamental change anything about their social circumstances. They identify the greatest potential for progress in the collective.

But the progressive critics of sociobiology tend to fallaciously confuse analysis about how social organisation ought to be with descriptive accounts of how it is and how it came to be. Sociobiology is often embraced by cultural and political conservatives who are prone to precisely the same naturalistic and adaptionist thinking. This includes some contemporary moral and evolutionary psychologists, such as Jon Haidt and Sam Harris, biologists like Robert Trivers [the discoverer of reciprocal altruism] and Brett Weinstein, and writers for the mass market such as Stephen Pinker and Jordan Peterson. What these writers and thinkers have in common is what I will term a naturalistic conservatism. They find moral and normative justification for existing social hierarchies not in divine command or positive law but in a scientifically-grounded belief that the world cannot be other than it is. They are the heirs of Herbert Spencer and Francis Galton – men [and it is usually men˷ who seek and find in nature the *telos* of their own [mostly unearned] social and economic privileges.

Naturalist conservatives tend to see political, social and economic inquiry as a scientific problem involving the identification of and solution of social dilemmas. This can only be done with any degree of rigor for relatively simple problems subject to static and deterministic processes. But in lieu of evidence, they hypothesise that contemporary (chauvinistically culturally Western) social norms are not historically contingent structures that emerged under a particular set of historical and environmental conditions, but Platonic ideal forms which embody social truths across time and culture. Faced with the terrifying possibility that other, better worlds are possible, they retreat into reification of the social relations with which they are most familiar and comfortable.

Although Gould & Lewontin's *Spandrels* paper is best-known for its critique of the adaptionist programme in science, it also makes a broader point about this 'Panglossian paradigm' – the conservative belief that we live in the 'best of all possible worlds'. Dr Pangloss is a literary invention of Voltaire, a parody of the Enlightenment philosopher and polymath Gottfried Leibnitz. Early in the novel *Candide*, the irrepressible Dr Pangloss outlines his philosophy to the protagonist, combining both a misplaced faith in his own reasoning and the inherently conservative social conclusions that follow from it.

"It is demonstrable that things cannot be otherwise than as they are; for all being created for an end, all is necessarily for the best end. Observe, that the nose has been formed to bear spectacles – thus we have spectacles. Stones were made to be hewn, and to construct castles – – therefore my lord has a magnificent castle." [Voltaire, Candice][589]

Dr Pangloss uses his Reason in a way it was likely adaptive to do so for clever individuals over long evolutionary periods: as a rhetorical tool to justify

---

[589] Voltaire, "Candide" (1759) at pg. 3.

one's own position in the social hierarchy and to persuade others to support that privilege. Today's naturalist conservatives are little better than modern echoes of Voltaire's parody.

But in evolution properly understood, the world is shaped by stochastic [random] events and multiple equilibrium states are possible. It's impractical to calculate in advance the end-state of a given population in a complex system other than in terms of broad trends, similarities and patterns. Thinking this way reveals that any given social structure is the product of random and imperceptible influences, which taken together generate its emergent properties.

"[T]he exploration of this inefficient world that we do inhabit implies, since it is contingent on the path taken at an earlier juncture, the existence of other counterfactual worlds. These worlds are accessible, and given the right dose of insight, leadership sacrifice and courage we might still find them accessible and substantially more habitable than the world of our frozen accidents" [Lustick, Taking Evolution Seriously][590].

If the world could have been otherwise, then there are not only alternative futures but also alternative presents. There is no Platonic social ideal, but instead a series of historical – and indeed, cosmic – accidents. The particular combination of genetic and cultural strategies in a given population is not the best of all possible worlds but records a population's past and sets the current horizon of its possible futures. The task of evolutionary socialists is to understand the processes that got us to where we are, as well as the dynamic tensions and institutions which maintain the status quo, so that we might reform society more efficiently and without precipitating a total rupture in cultural continuity.

* * *

---

[590] Lustick (2011) at pg. 201.

Not all conservatives necessarily idealise some kind of permanent social stasis. While there have certainly been no shortage of social ideologies and movements chasing utopian idylls, very few conservative regimes resemble Tsarist Russia, Nazi Germany or North Korea. Tellingly, the most reactionary societies tend fare extremely poorly in competition with other groups – they are unfit for their environment, relics of an earlier evolutionary age. Most societies recognise, even if forced to do so by material circumstances, that their survival depends on adapting to the social and physical environment – which is constantly changing. Population growth, migration and technological change will force any interacting population to adapt at least some of its behaviours over time.

Following Edmund Burke, modern conservatives tend not to reject change out of hand. They accept that any society is very far from knowing 'ultimate' moral truths[591]. Instead their focus is on pragmatic control of the rate and direction of social change. Social transformations are only permissible if driven and led by legitimate authorities for legitimate reasons. This mindset unites traditionalists who pine after church and aristocracy, libertarians who privilege the property rights of the [successful] capitalist, neoliberal technocrats who prize managerial skill, and 'classical liberals' who think of themselves as the natural social and economic elite of society. What these worldviews share is a belief that social learning is a top-down process – disseminating useful information from elites to the people – and not the other way around. Whether legitimate reasons are given by God, Emperor, Jeff Bezos, the invisible hand of the market or the sensibilities of media elites, it's elites and not the people who determine whether or not a social strategy is adaptive or maladaptive. By pure coincidence, this means that no one who holds power or influence under the status quo is under threat of losing that power as social relations change.

Burkean conservatives are not necessarily wrong on their face. High status individuals do in fact have significant advantages in disseminating

---

591 Taylor, "Multiculturalism: Examining the Politics of Recognition" in Gutmann (ed.) (1994) at pg. 73.

social norms and sustaining social equilibria, and hegemonic coalitions of powerful actors, as we know, are often historically important for initiating large-scale social re-organisation. As the winners of previous rounds of the social game, elites may indeed possess the fittest strategies – at least of their time. Community elders may preserve knowledge and traditions which, because of gradual changes in a group's way of life, have not been passed on to the current generation. Cultural transmission of knowledge, as we know, is important when conditions change more slowly than the life of single individuals, but faster than biology can generate mutations and adaptions. If a social species faces an environmental threat – or increased competition from a another group – which it has not faced during the developmental period of the current generation, then they can, and will, look to successful elders to point the way forward by recalling how things were in the past.

Conservatives preserve, maintain and defend a lived or imagined version of a previous social equilibrium – either because they were personally socialised into it, or because they have come favour an earlier social form for normative, ideological or aesthetic reasons. In essence, conservatives 'backup' a culture in case new or emerging social norms are off-equilibrium, exploitative or unstable – they exert a cultural pull in the direction of prior equilibria. In an era of liberal bourgeois revolutions, for example, the ultimate outcome of which was uncertain, the stability and predictability of monarchical government must have seemed worth defending. If the social costs of a new form of social organisation prove to be too high, conservatives can return to political and social power promising to restore the *status quo ante*. They are an insurance system against the unpredictability of social evolution – a save file or restore point – that ensures that not everything will be lost if things go wrong.

Reaction, therefore, intensifies when a social or cultural group has experienced a significant decline in its average fitness – defeat in war, economic collapse, or social revolution gone awry. Conservatives are particularly useful for dealing with recurrent threats that emerge periodically beyond the lifetime of individuals, such as major interstate warfare or pandemics. Hierarchical traditions that venerate self-sacrifice and obedience to authority are preserved during periods of relative peace in specialised social institutions, preserving the knowledge of how to fight and win wars or defeat plagues until needed. Conservatives are less successful in dealing with regular or endemic crises, such as cyclical economic downturns, which occur often enough that the population as a whole recognises the futility of returning to previous modes of social organisation.

For this reason, we should expect that natural selection will retain conservatism [as a social and political strategy] at a not insignificant frequency as part of a complex social equilibrium. Conservatism provides a mechanism by which a cultural group can recover from infrequent catastrophes. Because the past is a known, or at least knowable, quantity, conservatives tend to share more in common with one another than progressives, whose ideological and aesthetic ideals can diverge as widely from one another as the human imagination allows. Because the future is unknowable, progressives are prone to strong internal disagreements about where they're going and how to get there.

But the past is also an imperfect guide. The conservative imagination is limited to those previous cultures which can be transmitted orally by people still living, or preserved in cultural artefacts (replicators) such as novels, histories or architecture. Which of these prior social forms is best adapted to our current problems? The answer may very well be none of them, and the act of trying to restore some earlier age may be more harmful than whatever crisis has provoked a reactionary turn in the first place.

In complex systems, social orders are historically contingent and are the product of a web of interrelationships that can't be easily mapped and never artificially replicated. Trying to cross a fast-moving stream may appear as simple as moving from one bank to another, but that stream may have unpredictable and dangerous currents. Similarly, trying to move a society towards a different [earlier] equilibrium point may push conservatives even further away from the outcomes they want. As Heraclitus observed, you can't ever step in the same stream twice. Nothing stands still.

As society evolves, its internal composition changes *and* the external environment in which it lives changes. When a population moves between social equilibria, multilevel selection suggests you also necessarily change the internal equilibrium of all the agents in that system *and* you change the equilibrium of the external network of societies which it inhabits. The fitness consequences for a society of changing its internal structure is always *relative* to the level of competition between societies in the international system. The growth of socialist and social democratic parties in the first half of the twentieth century had become a stabilising presence for addressing the demands of workers under capitalism, but removing them destabilised the liberal order. In trying to undermine social democracy and preserve the capitalist system between the World Wars, Western liberals ended up driving their societies into the arms of fascists.

Social and political conservatives are actors in a complex and interdependent system who cannot predict the outcome of their desired policies with any certainty. Like any revolutionary movement, they are likely to be disappointed – possibly catastrophically so – by making the attempt to put their beliefs into action. And in this way the social equilibrium is broadly stabilised, because no social movement seeking to go *too far back* can escape failure and collapse in the face of cultural selection. The challenge is equally salient for progressives: can the march of social evolution be forced, and if so, how far?

* * *

What is the evolutionary socialist theory of change? Is social reform a process of gradual adaptions accumulating at different speeds in different parts of the body politic, as Eduard Bernstein, the Fabians and the social reformists who followed them believed? Are we resigned to an essentially unchanging social order which accumulates cultural and economic mutations slowly until a rapid phase change – a revolution – occurs in which a new social order is established all at once, as many Marxists [and Stephen Jay Gould[592]] would have hoped? Or can socialists force social improvements

---

[592] Gould & Eldredge (1977) at pgs. 115-151.

against the wishes of a cruel and uncaring nature, using our powers of Reason and empirical science to take short-cuts on our evolutionary journey – a view shared by Pinker, Robespierre and Lenin alike. We can think of these as the reformist, revolutionary and Leninist currents in socialist thought.

Societies are learning systems. By maintaining a diversity of opinions and behaviours, which almost every non-totalitarian society must, they endogenously generate new information and new social strategies at all levels. Trial-and-error experimentation offers both adaptability to changes in environmental or strategic conditions, and a capacity for a long-term improvement in a population's material and social condition. Conservatives seek to control the operation of this process in two crucially undemocratic ways. Firstly, limiting social learning to a top-down, elite-driven process means that social norms, values and institutions reflect elite knowledge and interests – which may come at a fitness cost to the community since elites have an incentive to defect from mechanisms of social cooperation and control (recall Chapter 13: "Social Cancers"). And secondly, by privileging the hegemons of the past who established the outlines of the current status quo, they risk a mismatch between the information or learning on which social norms are based and the social and material environment of the present.

The best critique of this latter position was set out by Thomas Paine, writing in direct opposition to Burke more than two hundred years ago.

"[T]here never can exist . . . any generation of men, in any country, who possess of the right or the power of binding and controlling posterity to the end of time, or of commanding forever how the world shall be governed . . . Every age and generation must be free to act for itself, in all cases, as the ages and generations which preceded it. The vanity and presumption of governing beyond the grave, is the most ridiculous and insolent of all tyrannies. . . It is the living, and not the dead, who are to be accommodated." [Paine, the Rights of Man][593]

---

[593] Paine, "Rights of Man, Part One" (1791).

The fundamentally democratic nature of socialist ideology also produces a different interpretation of social learning. Socialists believe that social and cultural learning is optimised when it is pluralistic and egalitarian – when every social agent has the opportunity to contribute new knowledge to the whole, and when every social agent affected by the operation of a social norm, rule of institution can freely decide whether or not to comply with it. That's not to say that societies can't evolve specialist institutions for the production and dissemination of knowledge, or that every social agent has an equal chance of having their idiosyncratic strategy imitated. Only that such institutions should be set up in such a way as to guard against the entrenchment of elite privilege.

Following from their reluctance to accept the feasibility of spontaneous, self-generating social order, social conservatives are reluctant to recognise the possibility of spontaneous, endogenous social learning. Just as social order is constructed by a hierarchy of power, social progress occurs in a hierarchy of knowledge in which philosopher-kings deliver "capital-T" Truth to the masses. Socialists and other progressives recognise that everyone, no matter their formal education or social class, is an adaptive agent capable of generating ways of knowing, ways of doing and ways of being that are best adapted for their lived material conditions. Society may find through this bottom-up process modes of social, economic and political organisation that would be fitness-enhancing if widely adopted. This is the libertarian socialist 'dual power' theory of change - to build influence both within and without existing institutions of power.

Critically, the evolutionary perspective is activist, not quietest. It does not resign us to accept the passive operation of the natural selection algorithm. Cultural rules, norms and institutions can and should be routinely challenged. Doing so creates the very behavioural variation and mutation that cultural selection needs to operate – *not* challenging the status quo may allow poorly adapted norms to survive longer than they otherwise would have. Everyone is free to try different strategies, and their success or failure determines whether the proposed change is replicated into the next generation. What motivates individuals to political action is largely secondary. Whether we challenge traditional norms on the basis of Reason (i.e. *this* mode of economic organisation is more efficient) or Intuition (i.e. *this* social norm in inegalitarian and unjust), the net result may be an increase in group fitness.

"The materialist doctrine that men are products of circumstances and upbringing, and that, therefore, changed men are products of changed circumstances and changed upbringing, forgets that it is men who change circumstances and that the educator must himself be educated." [Marx, Third Thesis on Feuerbach][594]

For social agents seeking reform, the most effective thing to do to is to advocate for one's beliefs as strongly possible and let forces of cultural evolution go to work. Everyone finds their own ethical *should* from within themselves, and by employing their power and agency may be able to influence social outcomes to increase the likelihood of their preferred outcome. Importantly, by working together with like-minded others, they might be able to *substantially change the probability of their preferred strategy becoming fixed in the population.* If cultural selection ultimately disappoints, it is because neither moral Intuitions nor abstract Reason provides a reliable means of discovering optimal social equilibria in all circumstances.

Progressives, therefore, should see their activism as running a series of natural experiments. Whether in the form of social organising, movement activism or electoral politics, our attitude should always be that of the tinkerer or scientist. They should move quickly and resolutely to establish the kinds of social arrangements they would like to see in the world, give them the best opportunity to flourish, and then re-assess if the results do not live up to our expectations. This does not mean that change is or should be slow, or that social experiments can only take the form of adjustments to existing arrangements. The behaviours, strategies and signals which foreshadow another form of social organisation grow under the dynamic processes of the current system and phase transitions between

---

[594] Marx, "Theses on Feuerbach" (1845).

vastly different modes of social organisation can occur extremely rapidly. Over a very short period of time, changes in the social, political and economic life of a community can appear abrupt, even revolutionary. Not every social state is stable, and rapid transition through periods of uncertainty is more likely to be successful than a gradual walk.

Where evolutionary or Darwinian socialism diverges from orthodox Marxism is in recognising that the outcome of this process is not pre-ordained. We should be sceptical that we can know with any certainty that alternative social arrangements we prefer would prove politically, culturally and economically stable. Capitalism is not a rigidly determined machine, whose internal processes of accumulation and exploitation have only one result. Rather, as Bernstein, Gramsci and other theorists recognised, it is embedded in a social order which is able to learn, adapt and compensate. Ironically, the economism of the early Marxists was anything but scientific: like Social Darwinism and other nineteenth-century pseudo sciences, it assumed a rigid social procession through a series of stages towards an end-state amenable to the aesthetic and ideological preferences of its progenitors.

"In reality, one can 'scientifically' foresee only the struggle, but not the concrete moments of the struggle, which cannot but be the results of opposing forces in continuous movement . . . In reality, one can 'foresee' to the extent that one acts, to the extent that one applies a voluntary effort and therefore contributes concretely to creating the result." [Gramsci, Prison Notebooks]

Socialists can be bold, they can be radical. But they must also be humble. They are seeking to direct social forces subject by natural and cultural pro-cesses many times more powerful than the mediocre abilities of individual humans. The absolute best they can hope for is to fight hard for what they believe in within the context of the ongoing social system and have confidence that, in the end, the mathematics of altruism and cooperation are on their side – and not that of the reactionaries.

The greatest challenge for the political activist is to pursue social change without crashing the ecosystem which the population relies upon for its survival. This has both an environmental sense and a cultural one. They must ensure that the social and economic structures they advocate for don't damage the long-term habitability of our environment. The Soviets made this mistake over and over again, rendering vast swathes of Central Eurasia virtually uninhabitable and hastening their own cultural and political collapse. We cannot provide cheap energy to the masses if we do so by burning fossil fuels and driving the planet's climate and ecology through an irreversible transition to a warmer world. We cannot feed ourselves if by doing so we leech the land of its ability to regenerate, crash biodiversity and institute mono-cultures that expose us to ever-increasing risks from pests, disease and climate change.

And just as we are custodians of the physical environment in which our species lives, we are also custodians of the social environment. We may wish to, as Paine said, free ourselves from the tyranny of the dead but we cannot set ourselves up as tyrants over those generations yet to be born. This way of seeing society as a complex adaptive system therefore suggest three overriding ethical imperatives for the political actor, which cannot be derived *a priori* from other universal belief systems.

- Firstly, political and economic change can occur only in ways which guarantee the survival of the social organism. Unless one is prepared to engage in utopian separatism, any political activism should aim to preserve the cohesion of a democratic society.
- Secondly, social agents must be prepared to defend liberal society against those that would seek to undermine or exploit it – including against exploitative strategies that we are ideologically or aesthetically sympathetic to.
- Lastly, in the event that a cohesive society is destroyed, split or ceases to exist – through war or revolution – social species should aim to restore an open, democratic society as their first priority. The dominance of a single hegemonic coalition is a recipe for long-term evolutionary failure.

If our social and economic experiments rip apart the social fabric in order to replace it with something entirely new, then we have acted no differently from a social cancer. The wrong way to pursue change – the revolutionary way – would be to try to break the ongoing social system so as to achieve permanent decision dominance over others by excluding alternative world views. If political actors are to be Darwinians and scientists, they must consider the ethical consequences of their social experiments no more or less rigorously than the nuclear physicist, the germ researcher or psychologist. To experiment on human culture an awesome responsibility - and many who would do so on both right and left are little better than mad scientists.

18

FREEDOM IS SCARY

Key Points

- Since social agents have evolved to live in groups and inherit information and strategies through social learning, they experience existential anxiety in a cultural environmental that fails to convey strong expectations about behaviour.
- The authoritarian desire for order reflects one solution to the problem of existential anxiety: to increase levels of certainty about the required behaviour of both oneself and others.
- Because it fundamentally misunderstands human nature, choice liberalism leads inevitably to increasing social support for authoritarian politics. Socialists understand that only by providing citizens with existentia security can they be truly free.

Social species come into the world equipped with learning rules to acquire cultural information from both parents and non-parents alike in order to efficiently adapt their behaviour for their social and material circumstances. Human beings need to learn about social rules, norms and institutions in order to behave appropriately in complex social, economic and political interaction – they are not born with this knowledge; it's not carried in their genes. Appropriate strategies for every scenario could also not possibly be discovered anew by each individual. Being human without inheriting an information-dense body of cultural know-how would be extremely inefficient and stressful.

Both classical game theory and liberal philosophy are predicated on the same ontological foundation – that of the individual actor free to choose their social strategy at will. John Rawls, perhaps the greatest liberal philosopher of the twentieth century, accepted relatively uncritically that the first principle of any system of 'justice' would be that everyone should enjoy *"the most extensive basic liberty compatible with a similar liberty for others"*[595]. Rawls was writing explicitly within the tradition of choice liberalism – his social agents are instrumentally, not adaptively, rational and care only about absolute, not relative gains[596]. Rawlsian liberalism is noble social structure – one that most liberals and socialists would agree is a desirable first step. And societies organised on liberal principles have proven remarkably stable over recent human history, thanks largely to their capacity for adaptive social learning.

Yet we have an empirical puzzle. Significant numbers of people – including highly educated, liberal elites – are discomforted by Rawls' first principle of justice. They reflect on the social freedoms which they inherit by right of citizenship and reject them as an appropriate basis for morality. Many have come to believe there to be an evolutionary mismatch between the liberal notion of freedom and the reality of human existence. Human beings are social creatures, yes, but we may not be well adapted for social structures which lack shared meaning, stable beliefs and categories, and which leave the choice of moral action up to the individual. Freedom, put simply, can make people unhappy and lead them to prefer social and political structures that are more rigid, collectivist and hierarchical. Rather than wanting liberty for themselves and others, a significant minority of people prefer security to freedom. So perhaps, they reason, liberty should be reserved only for those prepared to wield it.

---

[595] Rawls (1971), at pgs. 60, 250.

[596] Rawls (1971), at pgs. 143-144.

This final Chapter is all about authoritarianism. Authoritarianism is a trait, or set of traits, which aspires to order and patterned regularity in behaviour, and generates biases in favour of rule-following and systemic defence. Authoritarians do not value *particular* social arrangements, they value the order and regularity that rigid social structures – any structures – provide. Authoritarianism may have both genetic and cultural replicators, and is likely maintained in an evolving population of social agents – even liberal populations – at some not insignificant frequency because it offers some benefit to the group. This chapter will make the argument that the function of the authoritarian impulse is to reduce the existential anxiety of behaviourally flexible social agents inhabiting a world in which alternative social arrangements are not only accessible but actively present in the population.

The perfectly understandable desire to reduce uncertainty about social behaviour – to know for certain which strategies are right, and true, and good – lies at the root of the authoritarian impulse. Authoritarians do not merely crave order as a route to social and political power; instead, they crave it because having a defined social role provides existential relief. Traditionalist women, for example, do not support the patriarchy because they want to be men, but because they are reassured by a social role that is subservient but secure. The impulse to follow the rules and not stand out from the crowd is a product of cultural selection favouring strategy sets whose social fitness is no worse than average, while potentially punishing severely those that deviate even a little from the mean. And it often turns out that the best way to avoid social dilemmas is to be part of a tight-knit community which rigid social norms and little scope for individual variation in behaviour.

It's important to note at the outset that while there are significant overlaps between conservatism and authoritarianism, liberals and progressives are in no way immune from the authoritarian impulse. Liberal (and progressive) elites often respond unhelpfully to the popular desire for order and community – they often behave in deeply undemocratic ways[597]. Perhaps, they tell themselves in private, freedom is something that is best reserved only for elites. The mob can cling to outmoded ways of being, if only they can be controlled. A certain paternalism is therefore inherent to the way liberalism has been and continues to be practiced. So we'll begin our discussion at the beginning – with the enlightenment project, the cult of Reason, and what the early modern philosophers had to say about anxiety.

* * *

In the eyes of Immanuel Kant, writing near its end, the defining characteristic of the liberal Enlightenment era had been courage rather than wisdom. It was the brave individual who was willing to challenge the dogmas of the past, even after the tools to do so had been widely developed and disseminated. For the majority of people, however:

"[I]t is very difficult for the individual to work himself out of the [dependency] which has become almost second nature to him. He has even grown to like it, and is at first really incapable of using his own understanding because he has never been permitted to try. Dogmas and formulas . . . are the fetters of an everlasting [dependency]. The man who casts them off would make an uncertain leap over the narrowest ditch, because he is not used to such free movement." [Kant, What Is Enlightenment?][598]

Kant saw, accurately, that adherence to the status quo provides psychological reassurance and that the liberal promise of behavioural freedom and epistemic uncertainty could be anxiety-inducing. An elitist, in addition to being one of history's greatest philosophers, Kant shared the view of Burke – and Hobbes – that change through revolutionary means was neither

---

[597] Adler (2018).

[598] Kant, "Answering the Question: What Is Enlightenment?" (1784).

possible nor desirable[599]. No one had the right to rebel against a legitimate authority which used public Reason to exercise just guardianship over those unprepared for self-rule – Kant's ideal prince was Frederick II of Prussia, not Robespierre. Reason was a tool used by elites to write the social contract; it was not an instrument the mob could use to challenge or reform that social order from below[600].

But in the aftermath of the French Revolution and the Napoleonic Wars, European intellectuals were far less likely than they had been to see the enlightenment as ushering in a new era of social and economic justice. Nietzsche was a fierce critic of Kant and the project he represented. He saw the enlightenment as a lost opportunity[601]. Rather than learning to be comfortable with existential anxiety and a diversity of perspectives, the enlightenment *philosophes* elevated Reason as the new source of all Truth and authority. The new liberal elite were cultural super predators, able to exploit new social strategies and cast aside the restraints of unnecessary institutions and beliefs. But they were no less brutal and authoritarian than the hegemons they replaced. The freedom to explore new strategic space and innovate was a privilege reserved to only a few – the masses and colonised peoples continued to take their social cues from their political masters at the top of the social hierarchy.

During this period, the pre-existentialist philosopher Soren Kierkegaard also wrote about anxiety – describing it as an emotion akin to that dizzy feeling one gets standing on a precipice and looking down into an abyss. It's more than fear – an emotional reaction to a known threat. Anxiety is fear of the unknown. *"Anxiety is the dizziness of freedom, which emerges when the spirit wants [the] freedom to look down into its own possibility, . . Freedom*

---

[599] Kant, "Answering the Question: What Is Enlightenment?" (1784). "[The] public can achieve enlightenment only slowly. A revolution may bring about the end of a personal despotism or of avaricious tyrannical oppression, but never a true reform of modes of thought. New prejudices will serve, in place of the old, as guide lines for the unthinking multitude."

[600] Kant, "Groundwork of the Metaphysics of Morals" (1785) Vol 6, pg. 320 & Vol. 8 pgs. 297-302.

[601] Nietzsche (1886), esp. Chapter V.

succumbs to dizziness. . . . In [such dread], there is the egoistic infinity of possibility, which does not tempt like a definite choice, but alarms and fascinates with sweet anxiety."[602] Kierkegaard was a devout Christian, and saw in the Genesis myth the archetype of all social anxiety: the first humans had a choice to eat the fruit of the tree that gave knowledge of good and evil. In that moment, humanity experienced existential dread, metaphorically, for the first time. *"If man were a beast"*, Kierkegaard concluded, *"he would not be able to [feel] dread. . . . Anxiety is the possibility of freedom."*[603]

The liberal project, and the corresponding growth in the diversity of tolerated social strategies, led to profound changes in the social and emotional life of those populations subject to it. The dissolution of communal bonds brought about by liberal capitalism lies at the historic root of its rejection by both utopian socialists and conservatives. For people living through the industrial revolution in England – and later in other parts of the world – the proletarian city was a site of moral decay. The sons and daughters of farmers cast off the social bonds of agrarian society to operate in a world that both gave them personal freedom and subjected them to a degree of exploitation and abuse that would have been inconceivable to their parents. Some found in the new world the opportunity to express themselves differently, to love in new ways and use their talents to achieve careers that were never before accessible. Many more suffered from the absence of social safety nets, the denial of basic dignity, and by being forced to adopt coping strategies to deal with the stresses of capitalist production.

"[E]verlasting uncertainty and agitation distinguish the bourgeois epoch from all earlier ones. All fixed, fast-frozen relations, with their train of ancient and venerable prejudices and opinions, are swept away, all new-formed ones become antiquated before they can ossify. All that is solid melts into air, all that is holy is profaned, and man is at last compelled to face with sober senses his real conditions of life, and his relations with his kind." [Marx & Engels, The

---

[602] Kierkegaard, "The Concept of Anxiety" (1844), Chapter I, pgs. 54–55.

[603] Kierkegaard (1844), Chapter V, pg. 140.

Communist Manifesto].

Socialists have historically vacillated between horror and fascination at the way capitalism tears apart and atomises the social order. Those in the Marxist tradition, unlike the utopians, see proletarianization as necessary process that paves the way for new forms of social organisation. Put simply, liberalism clears strategic space for new forms of social and economic organisation among the working class. For the first time, it brings them together as workers with the common experience of commodity production, instead of dividing them by superficial barriers of race, tribe, religion, sex, or language. The existential anxiety caused by the dissolution of all prior communities motivates atomised liberal social agents to agitate for their rights and come together in new, solidaristic movements.

Most progressives recognise that the enlightenment model of individual courage and opportunity is in some way incomplete – that structures of oppression persisted long after the feudal and colonial architecture that legitimised them had been swept away. Socialists go furthest in acknowledging that as social beings a significant percentage of the population will have psychological needs for community and structure that cannot be met under capitalism. Because they understand human nature better, evolutionary socialists may be best placed to harness the emotional needs of individuals for community in order to build something radical and new.

Liberals, on the other hand, assumed on the basis of a flawed model of human nature that wealth (higher payoffs) would make societies stable and happy. They were wrong. As (neo-)liberalism resumed its long march through social institutions in the waning decades of the twentieth century, replacing cooperative strategies with ones based on competition and self-help levels of social anxiety and individual isolation rose in step – even among social strata that saw their wealth and incomes increase exponentially.

By ever-increasing the number of brands, variations and specialisations of basic products – even as those goods are produced by an ever-shrinking number of monopolies – late stage capitalism has paradoxically made choice more difficult for consumers and generated an endemic level of stress that psychologists have labelled 'choice overload'[604].

"There comes a time when choice, rather than freeing the individual, becomes so complex, difficult and costly, that it turns into the opposite. There comes a time, in short, when choice turns into overchoice and freedom into un-freedom." [Toffler, Future Shock]

Human beings are not relentlessly calculating utility optimisers, who derive pleasure and satisfaction from making efficient market decisions. Instead, as this book as shown repeatedly, we are error-prone and irrational status-seekers, who are concerned above all to do no worse than our social peers. We cannot know in advance if the good or service we are purchasing will be fitness-enhancing, and as a result experience existential dread about even mundane everyday decisions. Limitations on the information available to us are not merely a market failure, but an innate feature of a universe in which time flows in only one direction. In order to manage this paradox of choice, we turn to heuristics that simplify our decision-making: what did our parents purchase for us as children? What brands advertise most heavily? What products are favoured by celebrities whose lifestyles we aim to emulate?

As neoliberals privatise more and more formerly cooperative social services, putting public capital in private hands in a desperate effort to indefinitely sustain a world of endless profit, they introduced the illusion of choice into social services which are necessary to meet existential needs. In the twenty-first century, the vast majority of parents in advanced western democracies are faced with recurrent 'choices' about their children's schooling – starting in child-care and running all the way through their tertiary education. These decisions can have vast fitness consequences which cannot be known with any certainty. As healthcare systems are privatised, the number of providers and healthcare plans proliferates

---

[604]Toffler (1970); Schwartz (2000) at pgs. 79-88; Schwartz (2004).

seemingly endlessly, offering a wide range of coverage at an equally absurd variety of prices. The healthcare 'consumer' is faced with a paradox of choice – how much is dental care worth to me; what are my odds of experiencing a medical emergency; am I likely to get pregnant in coming years?

Social security systems have also been privatised, so that an large proportion of the working class' retirement income depends on the vagaries of the market. We are presented the choice of ethical investing, aggressive growth, or blue chip stocks. But we have little control over the outcomes of these decisions. Our education outcomes, our standard of living in retirement, and indeed our very health is rendered essentially a roll of dice. But because these are fundamental human needs, our anxiety about these potentially life-altering decisions has grown to crisis proportions.

The neoliberal would argue that increasing the variety of choice is not necessarily an end in its own right. Unlike libertarians, neoliberals value the efficient functioning of the market more than they value the freedom and well-being of the individual. Yet the goals of the two groups are aligned. Increasing the variety of producers, or brands, in a competitive market permits producers who deliver a higher quality good at a lower cost to grow while punishing less efficient, less productive suppliers. Remember the third axiom of capitalist ideology, introduced at the start of this book: competitive, self-help strategies are empirically and normatively superior to cooperative ones.

Socialists can argue the merits of their case: that capitalist competition more often than not produces inefficient monopolies that are hostile to the consumer, particularly when essential public services are placed under private control. But they have a second line of attack, against the first axiom of capitalist ideology: humans are simply not purely egotistic utility-maximising individualists. *Even if it were true that competition in education, healthcare and other essential services improved outcomes [and it's not]*, neoliberals advocate a social model that immiserates and alienates populations who adopt their strategies. The first decades of the twenty first century have demonstrated that neoliberalism, left unchecked, is politically unstable and ungovernable *even as it increases economic output.*

Conservatives, witnessing the same social trends that fascinated and appalled the early Marxists, offered a similar diagnosis but a different cure. For Dostoyevsky, man would always be afraid of freedom. It was up to the authoritarian patrician – represented in Russia by God, Tsar, and State – to provide social order. In this, the orthodox conservatives were no less elitist than the enlightenment liberals – but for conservatives, leaders are tragic figures who intercede between a world of unfathomable mysteries and the world of men, not heroic scientists seeking to expose and simplify those mysteries.

"[They] shall have an answer for all. And [the people] will be glad to believe [the] answer, for it will save them from the great anxiety and terrible agony they endure at present in making a free decision for themselves. And all will be happy, all the millions of creatures except the hundred thousand who rule over them. For only [they] who guard the mystery, shall be unhappy." [Dostoevsky, The Brothers Karamazov]

The rejection of individual freedom remains the central underpinning of all stripes of authoritarian to this day. Individuals are not free to mix and match from among the forms of personal expression that are now available, but rather constrained by God or society or nature to perform fixed social roles and behaviours. Groups are bearers of innate traits that to a large degree shape their social outcomes – whether understood in terms of sin, genes or culture, individuals cannot escape their place in the social hierarchy and any attempt to do so would result in unhappiness, inefficiency and disorder. Liberals at least permit individuals the theoretical freedom to improve their social status.

The Canadian communitarian philosopher Charles Taylor locates the origins of neoliberal anxiety in the dialogue between culture and the individual i.e. the awareness of one's freedom of action. While the individual seeks social recognition of the validity of their choices, culture sets the conditions upon which that recognition is granted.

"One could argue that it is reasonable to suppose that cultures that have provided the horizon of meaning for large numbers of human beings, of diverse characters and temperaments, over a long period of time – that have, in other words, articulated their sense of the good, the holy, the admirable – are almost certain to have something that deserves our admiration and respect, even if it is accompanied by much that we have to abhor and reject. . . . it would take a supreme arrogance to discount this possibility a priori." [Taylor, The Politics of Recognition][605]

Taylor does recognise that cultural norms are specific to certain populations at particular moments in their history. But he sees the absence of authoritative social scripts under liberalism as having increased the likelihood that many people will go through life not only lonely but incapable of knowing what to do to be validated as a member of a community – any community[606]. This existential malaise is not only a source of stress and anxiety, but the driving force behind why so many subaltern groups living under late stage capitalism cling desperately to exclusionary forms of identity.

Taylor was one of the first conservative theorists to critique what is now often termed 'identity politics' – the rejection of both liberalism and class politics in favour of narrower group interests based on race, gender or sexuality. He saw this as the inevitable result of liberalism's social values being too 'thin' to provide sufficient social certainty for social agents to properly govern their own lives. But the communitarian critique is not the only route out of this paradox. Instead, it is reflective of the historical failure of socialists to build viable alternative institutions of community and belonging based on people's shared experience of their material condition, and that are inclusive rather than exclusionary.

* * *

---

[605] Taylor (1994) at pg. 72.

[606] Taylor (1991)

Authoritarianism, or at least for the potential for it, is inherent in every social structure. The biological and cultural processes by which a child is socialised into the norms and practices of their community start operating well before they are capable of systematic thought, and many years before our societies consider them to be responsible, legal adults. We do not get to freely pick and choose the strategies which govern our behaviour – we inherit them through our genes, from observing our parents and by absorbing the cultural norms and expectations of the population in which we grow up. Before we even have an individual sense of self, we are already absorbing a body of collective knowledge that closes off some developmental paths and privileges others. There's a reason why the authority of parents is the political model of all despotic government: because the raising of children is the primal dictatorship. There is not a single moment in the life of a social agent when their behaviour is genuinely free and unbounded.

When much of what individuals believe and how they act is a product of evolutionary processes, how can we decide whether a social rule, norm or institution 'legitimate' and therefore worth preserving? How can we judge when someone else's social norm or behaviour is illegitimate and therefore open to challenge? How courageous do we need in order to criticise an unjust law – must we be, as Kant might insist, exceptional minds with impeccably marshalled evidence and argument? How much can we trust in the intentions of our fellow citizens when they perform behaviours that are outside our own social context? Do we given in to our authoritarian instincts and call them out, engaging in punishment and ostracism of someone who, for all we know, is performing their own culturally-sanctioned actions? Or can we be brave, letting others be and trusting that the social equilibrium of the community of the whole can tolerate strategic variants we've never seen before and don't understand?

In classical liberalism, a social structure is legitimate when its laws, norms and institutions reflect a hypothetical contract or agreement between all its members decided upon through public Reason. Since social agents are conceived of as rational utility-maximisers, they consent to those arrangements and behaviours which are best adapted to their interests, as determined by the elite arbiters of social order.

As a thought experiment, the social contract is mere fiction[607] – no less an act of fantasy than any other origin myth legitimising the rule of some tyrants over others. There's the obvious critique of Paine: that social contracts cannot bind future generations without becoming tyrannies – they must therefore include mechanism through which social norms are routinely updated and re-written. Then there's the issue of group membership – that by virtue of being born in a particular territory or to particular parents, one assumes all the rights, duties and obligations of a society without ever explicitly ratifying one's agreement to the existing social contract. And finally, how much power does any individual possesses to dissent from social arrangements – is the individual sovereign, in that they can veto the application of any norm on themselves, or are the people as a whole sovereign, in the sense that social arrangements reflect a compromise or negotiation that is stable and consensual for the vast majority?

The evolutionary account of social order is parsimonious with Locke's conception of the social contract as legitimized in each generation by implied, or 'tacit', consent.[608] Social norms are not established via explicit contract, but replicated through shared understandings or expectations about individual behaviour (i.e. an equilibrium in beliefs and practices). What renders an social order legitimate is not that it is positively chosen, but that is it is not actively resisted. We are not *obligated* to follow social convention, but preserve at all times the option to rebel against it. Upon encountering injustice, we can consciously challenge a norm, work actively to change it and pass on new behaviours to the next generation. But we can otherwise live our lives secure in the knowledge that the strategies we inherited as children remain fit for purpose.

Where does that leave the individual? The instinctive heuristic systems

---

[607] Hume, "Of Civil Liberty" (1742).

[608] Locke, 'Second Treatise on Government', Yale University Press (2003) at pgs. 74-6, pgs. 116-7.

that we are equipped with by our genes and by our upbringing work perfectly well most of the time – up until the point that they don't. We acquiesce to our in-built moral prejudices by acting in accordance with them, and if we ever stopped to think about our actions using our 'System 2' capabilities, we could and would probably construct elaborate arguments and justifications for them in abstract or universal terms. But we also have the capacity to override our instincts and adjust our behaviour upon encountering contrary motivating signals of sufficient salience.

So social rules, norms and institution are legitimate to the extent that they generate tacit acquiescence to the status quo. We always have choice but don't need to exercise it most of the time. That tacit acceptance of the status quo provides a baseline of existential security and psychological well-being. But individuals are free to decide for themselves to implement or adopt variant social behaviours, so long they do not put the survival of the community of the whole at risk (as we discussed at the end of the previous Chapter). Often, the trigger for individual activism will be that a given social norm causes material or psychological harms which outweigh the safety of compliance. So those most adversely affected by the behaviour of others – the oppressed, downtrodden, marginalised and disadvantaged – are most likely to demand reform. Those atop the social hierarchy have the most existential security, and so while they're least likely to dissent from the status quo, they paradoxically have the greatest freedom of social experimentation. The homeland of authoritarianism is the middle class – those who are somewhat existentially insecure but not sufficiently oppressed by the status quo to endorse rebellion against it.

Criticising the behaviour of others is legitimate when it is conscious and considered – when we have weighed the social costs and benefits of punishing or ostracising a stranger, and judged the social price worth paying. In a liberal society, making judgements about the behaviour of others must be careful, costly and deliberative - which perhaps is why modern legal systems have thoroughly ritualised ways of doing so. Judgment of others is illegitimate when we are merely acting instinctively, or performing a social script we have inherited from others.

"[I]t might be part of the 'ethos' of a good citizen that we do not pry into the (ir)responsibility of others, but rather trust that they are trying to be as responsible for their own choices and demands as we are in ours. Of course, this means we may be taken advantage of by some of our less scrupulous citizens. . . .[but a social order] that encourages everyone to view their co-citizens as putative cheats is not a promising basis for developing trust and solidarity." [Kymlicka][609]

The negative emotional valence we feel towards social deviance, and the motivation it provides to inflict punishment (either direct or third-party) is not brave – it is cowardly, privileging our own sense of existential security against the dignity and respect owed to our fellow citizens. To employ vigilante violence against interracial or same-sex couples, to curse and humiliated the gender-deviant or cultural rebel, was until relatively recently to feel safe, comfortable and protected by the social status quo. On the other hand, to critique the powerful, to fight against social cancers, to serve the community by defending its solidarity and survival, required courage and self-confidence.

So Kant was partially right – but it's not courage that is necessary to advance social and political progress. Courage is a virtue: innate to the individual and disconnected for their social and economic position. What is required in truth is *existential security*, which is a product of material circumstances. To crave social order, to lack trust in the competence of fellow citizens to make decisions for themselves, is the product of a lack of self-security. Authoritarians represent that population fraction whose desire for existential security cannot be satisfied – they crave certainty even if it means the ruin of the community of the whole. By reducing the existential security of the average citizen, by putting a choice architecture around everyday decisions, neoliberals increase social anxiety and thus, inevitably, support for authoritarianism. The rise of fascism, populism and identity politics catches liberals by surprise because their account of human nature is fundamentally at odds with the adaptive nature of social species.

---

[609] Kymlicka (2002), Chapter 3, at pg. 95.

Socialists are not interested in maximising choice for its own sake – at least when it comes to the provision of basic human rights and needs which are necessary to ensure the equal dignity of all. Unlike liberals, socialists don't mind putting limits on individual freedom, if doing so results in universal social programs that guarantee everyone fair fitness outcomes over the course of their life. We can have fifty flavours of ice cream – that choice is not going to fundamentally change someone's life outcomes. But there must not be fifty different possible rolls of the dice for children born into the same society, or for people who develop a serious illness, or who work hard their entire lives and want to retire without falling into poverty. Because their vision of social behaviour is evolutionary, socialists can recognise that being part of a community may mean implicitly reducing freedom in some domains in order to give social agents the existential security they need to exercise their freedom to thrive in others.

Strategic variation is a wonderful and necessary thing. But if social agents are anxious about how they'll meet their daily needs, they'll never have the physical or psychological security necessary to take Kierkegaard's leap of faith and genuinely experiment with their social, political or economic organisation. Socialists should focus their efforts on meeting those fundamental social needs that provide real social agents the most existential security – their health, housing, education, social security and even employment. Only once these basic needs are met can we expect levels for support for political and cultural authoritarianism to fall in any kind of enduring manner. In the final analysis, and if they do their job correctly, socialists may be better at defending freedom than liberals themselves.

Belief in Progress

We have now come to the end, or at least the end of the beginning. In perhaps too grand a sweep, this book has endeavoured to sketch the outline of a comprehensive evolutionary theory of human politics and society. We began with very small and simple social dilemmas, and have worked our way to the edge of big picture questions of social ontology, epistemology, meta-ethics and existentialism. I have sought to demonstrate that the use of naturalistic narratives to justify the status quo distribution of power and resources under capitalism is, and always has been, a fraud. Whether or not the alternative model outlined here comes to be accepted as lending support for an evolutionary, or Darwinian, socialism, readers of this book should be better equipped to challenge the central myths of the capitalist paradigm.

Humans are social beings, evolved and adapted to live in groups. Our cognitive specialisations, reliance on social learning and emotional biases mean that individuals can only fulfill their development potential in the context of society. We are not selfish, utility-maximising computers – quite the contrary. We are extremely poor rationalists by even the most rudimentary standard, and cannot achieve anything of note – least of own secure our physical and emotional security – alone. Contrary to the simplified models of economists, there are cooperative, trusting strategic solutions to many social games. Much of human behaviour and decision-making which appears irrational or inexplicable may, in fact, reflect the operation of adaptive heuristics that have been handed down to us as a result of the collective unconscious learning of previous generation. In short, we are not compelled to be selfish because our genes are selfish. Our nature includes considerable capacity for cooperation under the right conditions, and it is this aspect of human nature which has led our species to dominate the little blue planet we call home.

In the late nineteenth century, Darwinian socialists like Kropotkin lost their battle for the soul of science, which was colonised by the social prejudices of the existing elite. In the early part of the twenty-first, fuelled by new discoveries and ongoing public interest, popular writers like Steven Pinker, Sam Harris and Jordan Peterson are performing the same trick as Spencer, Galton and Wallace: defending existing social hierarchies on the basis of their supposedly natural origin. The longer that liberalism faces a crisis of popular legitimacy – brought on by its own failure to understand the human subject as a material being and not an ideal abstraction – the more the defenders of the status quo will lean on behavioural economics, genetic essentialism and Evolutionary Psychology to manage, ideologically disarm and continue to exploit society.

"The left's understandable but unfortunate mistake in regard to Darwinian thinking has been to accept the assumptions of the right, starting with the idea that the Darwinian struggle for existence corresponds to the vision of nature suggested by Tennyson's memorable phrase 'nature red in tooth and claw'. From this position it seemed only too clear that, if Darwinism applies to social behaviour, then a competitive marketplace is somehow justified, or shown to be 'natural', or inevitable". [Singer, A Darwinian Left] [610]

I don't agree with the utilitarian philosopher Peter Singer on much, but his critique here is accurate. For almost a century, the Western left has struggled in vain to achieve its social and political objectives because it entered the field already having conceded to the philosophical framework of our opponents. There's an elitist flaw at the heart of even the most well-meaning progressive liberalism: by implicitly accepting a model in which individuals are prefigured as self-interested egoists, and Reason is the only route to justice, it accepts that possession of a highly abstracted form of intelligence grants individuals virtue and dignity – and that authoritarian

---

[610] Singer (1999)

paternalism is the only remedy for those unfortunates whose genes, culture or development put them at odds with the ideal social order. Socialists must take back the narrative by returning to the dialectical understanding of Marx and Kropotkin. They must fight for their goals equipped with a model of society that is both empirically grounded and unequivocally owned by the left. Evolutionary socialists want to live in a world whose foundational tenet is recognition of humanity's social and cooperative nature.

But they must enter that battle as empiricists, not idealists. As we have seen throughout this book, social species are not universal co-operators – strategies of unconditional cooperation are not evolutionarily stable because, in the absence of strong punishments, exploitative strategies will over time erode and disrupt them. Human beings are *conditional* co-operators. We have introduced the notion that there are essentially four, mathematically equivalent, social structures which can render altruistic cooperation stable. These are kinship (i.e. genetic and strategic relatedness), network or physical proximity, reciprocity and reputation (i.e. do unto others as they do unto you) and culturally- or symbolically-denoted group identities. All mechanisms of social trust and social order must be predicated on some combination of these structures. For altruism to be evolutionarily stable it must be parochial – the selective pressure between groups must be greater than the selective pressure within them.

For the right-wing of the socio-biology movement, who are either genetic essentialists or sceptical of mutual recognition being validly grounded upon symbolic identities, this view of human nature leads to pessimistic conclusions. They believe social species are doomed to exist in a world in which it's not only expected but normalised that individuals would privilege members of their own family, ethnic group or immediate social circle. And that these relatively narrow and self-interested social groups are forced to conduct a war of all against all, for ever, trading places in the political hierarchy but never fundamentally changing its structure. However, for sociobiologists who recognise that culture provides an essentially infinite variety of symbolic behaviours capable of generating mutual recognition between social agents – a mental ability that as far as we know no other species on our planet has developed – we can be far more optimistic about altruism and our capacity to make major evolutionary transitions that render group differences meaningless.

Symbolic culture permits a social species to expand membership of their communities beyond kin, their direct social network and neighbours. It means that strangers who have never previously met, and who carry radically different external identity markers or tags, can recognise one another as having the same altruistic social strategy simply through the mutual recognition of shared expectations and behaviours. It does not matter whether this mutual recognition is motivated by rational self-interest (i.e. you have something to sell that I want to buy) or by some irrational and costly ritual. What matters is that unlike every other social species we know of, human social groups are flexible, expandable and adaptable. We routinely cooperate with tens of millions of genetically unrelated individuals – an achievement that is unprecedented in the history of life. Because human parochialism is almost infinitely flexible, we've already made several major phase transitions in our journey to the present, scaling up and specialising our social norms, rules and institutions to bring political order to ever-larger populations.

These observations explain a considerable amount of everyday political behaviour. Humans are remarkably good pattern matchers – we are biologically and cognitively primed to make associations about group membership, moral status and conditional behaviour. So when we're stressed or otherwise under a heavy emotional and cognitive burden, we tend to the see the worst aspects of our nature come to the forefront: bigotry, discrimination, exclusion, hostility and even violence. But as we've learned, in a social species like ours behaviour is the product of both biological and cultural influences. Our capacity to categorise and classify can be honed as delicate surgical instrument that identifies true threats to the community – fascists and self-interested elites – while learning to stay our hand when our biology is otherwise screaming at us that strangers pose a threat. But conservatives and reactionaries can also manipulate our culture to wield that capacity to discriminate like a sledgehammer, priming citizens to fear and hate those different from themselves, to exclude others from the community and use violence against them.

Political liberalism has made tremendous strides expanding the circle of cooperation on the basis of the equal dignity of every human being. As a species, we have shown that societies built on breaking down hegemonies and replacing them with mutual recognition and respect are wiser and more robust than more closed societies – although they're not immune from social cancers undermining them from within. But Rousseau wrote that we *"do not know what our nature permits us to be"*[611] and it takes a supreme act of intellectual arrogance to presume that the social order that currently exists is the best of all possible worlds. We do not know for certain how wide the circle of cooperation can be expanded using our existing cultural tools and institutional arrangements. We do not know if there are alternative social equilibrium that are accessible to us, and which sub-groups in our own community might develop or have developed organisational tools to build the basis of an alternative, more just order.

As we proceed from here, we must always be aware that materialist theories of political and cultural evolution can all too easily slip into justificatory narratives of supposedly ideal forms. Comte and Spencer were wrong in seeing laissez-faire capitalism as the highest stage of cultural development but Marx and his interpreters sometimes made similar errors. Evolutionary politics guarantees continuous change, but makes few promises about its direction – or of the moral desirability of the order that eventually emerges. To the extent we perceive a direction to history, it bends only ever-so-slightly towards justice. Though perhaps we couldn't exist otherwise, our capacity for altruism is a fragile miracle born of millions of years of highly contingent evolutionary history.

Evolutionary socialism categorically rejects the idea of an End of History. In this, we must break in spirit with old ideas of both scientific and idealistic socialists who presume in their enthusiasm for a better world to know the shape that world should take. Socialism is a process, a movement, an

---

[611] Rousseau, "Emile, or On Education" (1762).

action. The end result of activism is unknown and unknowable. In this, the evolutionary socialist Eduard Bernstein was much closer to Marx than his orthodox critics would ever admit. We reject category, description, ideal forms and determinism – in their place, we have process, relationships, dialectics and conflict. To seek social change as a progressive is to make a leap of faith – to know that as individual actors we cannot possibly change the course of human history. But to hope that by throwing our individual and collective political weight against the social tide we might influence the path that history takes ever so slightly. Sometimes that tide might shift suddenly underneath us, all at once, as we discover that we were much closer to an alternative social and economic order than we every through possible. The Revolution is probably not going to break out tomorrow, but it might.

"We have no means of measuring this vast machine, we are unable to calculate its workings . . . we do not know ourselves, . . we scarcely know whether man is one or many; we are surrounded by impenetrable mysteries. [W]e think we can penetrate them by the light of reason, but we fall back on our imagination. Through this imagined world each forces a way for himself which he holds to be right; none can tell whether his path will lead him to the goal." [Rousseau, Emile][612]

The evolutionary socialist is acutely aware of the fragility of the existing social order. We can recognise both the immense improbability of the series of events that brought the status quo into being, and the remarkable ease with which selfish strategies – if left unchecked – could erode even the most fundamental social values of community and solidarity. Progress is not irreversible. In the early decades of the twenty first century, the dominant pro-market forms of liberalism are experiencing an acute social, political, economic and ecological crisis. Our political leaders have wandered into a strategic *cul de sac* because an entire generation of Western elites have been socialised with a model of human nature that is fundamentally false.

---

[612] Rousseau, "Emile, or On Education" (1762).

Neoliberal regimes have atomised our social and economic lives, made market competition the sole way of accessing fundamental human rights, and failed to manage existential threats to our survival, including climate change, overfishing and biodiversity collapse.

Evolutionary socialists recognise that we are all custodians of a social order that depends upon stewardship of both the natural and social environment. That a healthy and self-assured people make for a healthy and self-assured society. We are not slaves to algorithmic optimisation – to artificial metrics of economic output, job creation and infrastructure built. Whether the authoritarian Soviet Union or the authoritarian capitalist firm, institutions that are structured so as to consciously maximise of their own fitness at the expense of the organic whole have led to environmental degradation, social cancers and totalitarian social forms that undermine the bases of long-term social and psychological well-being. For that reason, this book has warned both revolutionary socialists and conservatives that any effort to overthrow liberal democratic orders by force is like to falter on the hidden rocks and shoals of cultural selection.

So long as human beings live in relatively tolerant liberal democracies, or their structural equivalent at other times and places, which take a relaxed and confident approach to individual behavioural variation and maintain a thin, yet universal, set of markers of citizenship, cultural evolution will generate endogenous knowledge *even if the broader natural and social environment remains unchanged.* Through trial-and-error experimentation, we make incremental innovations that increase the productivity of labour and capital over time. But we are also constantly improving *all* of our social arrangements: we reform our laws and institutions so that they operate more effectively, we develop new ways of managing people and institutions, and we discover new ways of being which – usually after some struggle for acceptance – form part of a new social fabric. With every marginal increase in human knowledge, we move a step closer to a social structure in which no one is anxious about their material and psychological needs.

Socialism may be nearly two centuries old, and liberalism much older, but as a species we have never really experienced a society in which everyone was truly free. Citizens of more equal societies with stronger institutions of social cooperation are happier and healthier than those dominated by capitalist norms of competition and self-help[613]. Socialists should focus above all on building a society in which citizens enjoy the existential security to experiment with alternate behaviours and social forms – to be truly free. Such a social structure would not only reduce the appeal of conservative and authoritarian rhetoric from the right in the immediate future, but lay the foundations for a culture truly prepared to leap together into the unknown.

---

[613] Pacek & Radcliff (2008) at pgs. 267-277; Wilkinson & Pickett (2009).

Bibliography

Adami & Hintze, "Winning isn't everything: Evolutionary stability of zero determinant strategies" Nature Communications Vol. 4 No. 10,1038 (2012)

Adami et al. "Evolutionary game theory using agent-based methods" Physics of Life Reviews Vol. 19 (2016) at pgs. 1-26.

Adams, "Formulating an Anarchist Sociology: Peter Kropotkin's Reading of Herbert Spencer" Journal of the History of Ideas Vol. 77 No. 1 (2016) at pgs. 49-73

Adler, "The Centrist Paradox: Political Correlates of Democratic Discontent" SSRN (2018)

Ainslie & Herrnstein, "Preference Reversal and delayed reinforcement" Animal Learning and Behaviour Vol. 9 No. 4 (1981) at pgs. 476-482

Ainslie, "The Cardinal Anomalies that Led to Behavioural Economics: Cognitive or Motivational?" Managerial and Decision Economics Vol. 37 (2015) at pgs. 261-275

Akin, "The Iterated Prisoners Dilemma: Good Strategies and Their Dynamics" Ergodic Theory, Advances in Dynamical Systems (2016) at pgs. 77-107

Alexander, ' The Biology of Moral Systems" Aldine de Gruyter (1987)

Alexander, "The Micro-Macro Link" University of California Press (1987)

Alford & Hibbing, "The Origin of Politics: An Evolutionary Theory of Political Behaviour" Vol. 2 No. 4 (2004) at pgs. 707-723.

Allen et al., "Against Sociobiology" The New York Review of Books Vol. 22 (1975) at pg. 18.

Alvergne et al., "Evolutionary Thinking in Medicine" Springer (2016)

Anderson, ' Beyond Homo Economicus: New Developments in Theories of Social Norms" Philosophy and Public Affairs Vol. 29 No. 2 (2000) at pgs.

170-200

Anderson, "Imagined Communities: Reflections on the origin and spread of nationalism" Verso (1983)

Anderson, "What's the Point of Equality?" Ethics Vol. 109. No. 2 (1999) at pgs. 287-337.

Angus, "Marx and Engels . . . and Darwin?" International Socialist Review Vol. 65 (2009) at pgs. 17-29.

Aoki, "A Condition for Group Selection to Prevail over Counteracting Individual Selection" Evolution Vol. 36 (1982) at pgs. 832-842.

Ariely et al. "Doing Good or Doing Well? Image Motivation and Monetary Incentives in Behaving Prosocially" The American Economic Review Vol. 99 No.1 (2009) at pgs. 544-555

Asch, "Opinions and social pressure" Scientific American Vol. 193 (1955) at pgs. 31-35

Askew et al., "The Effect of Disgust and Fear Modelling on Children's Disgust and Fear for Animals" Journal of Abnormal Psychology Vol. 123 No.3 (2014) at pgs. 566-577

Aumann, "Correlated Equilibrium and an Expression of Bayesian Rationality" Econometrica Vol. 55 (1987) at pgs. 1-18

Aumann, "Subjectivity and Correlation in Randomising Strategies" Journal of Mathematical Economics Vol. 1 (1974) at pgs. 67-96

Axelrod & Dion, "The Further Evolution of Cooperation" Science Vol. 242 No. 4884 (1988) at pgs. 1385-1390

Axelrod & Hamilton, "The Evolution of Cooperation" Science Vol. 211 (1981) at pgs. 1390-1396.

Axelrod & Hammond, "The Evolution of Ethnocentrism" Journal of Conflict Resolution Vol. 50 No. 6 (2006) at pgs. 926-936.

Axelrod (ed.), "The Complexity of Cooperation" Princeton University Press (1997)

Axelrod, "An Evolutionary Approach to Norms," The American Political Science Review Vol. 80 No. 4 (1986) at pgs. 1095-1111.

Axelrod, "On Six Advanced in Cooperation Theory" Analyse & Kritik Vol. 22 (2000) at pgs. 130-151

Axelrod, "The Complexity of Cooperation: Agent-Based Models of Competition and Collaboration" Princeton University Press (1997).

Axelrod, "The Evolution of Cooperation", Penguin Press (1984)

Axelsson et al., "The genomic signature of dog domestication reveals adaptation to a starch-rich diet" Nature Vol. 495 (2013) at pgs. 360-364

Ayer, "Language, Truth and Logic" Gollancz (1936)

Baatz & Wagner, "Adaptive inertia caused by hidden pleiotropic effects" Theoretical Population Biology Vol. 51 (1997) at pgs. 49-66

Bakunin, "Man, Society and Freedom" (1871)

Baldwin, "A New Factor in Evolution" The American Naturalist Vol. 30 No. 354 (1896) at pgs. 441-451

Ball, "Marx and Darwin: A Reconsideration" Political Theory Vol. 7 No. 4 (1979) at pgs. 469-483

Banton, "Racial and Ethnic Competition" Cambridge University Press (1983)

Baranowski et al. (eds.), "A Companion to Nazi Germany" Wiley & Sons (2018)

Barth (ed.), "Ethnic Groups and Boundaries" Little Brown (1969)

Beall et al., "Higher offspring survival among Tibetan women with high oxygen saturation genotypes residing at 4,000m" Proceedings of the Natural Academy of Sciences Vol. 101 No. 39. (2004) at pgs. 14300-14304

Bentham, "Anarchical Fallacies" (1816)

Bentley et al., "Random Drift and Culture Change" Proceedings of the Royal Society B Vol. 271 No. 1547 (2004) at pgs. 1443-1550

Bergstrom, "Evolution of Social Behaviour: Individual and Group Selection" Journal of Economic Perspectives Vol. 16 (2002) at pgs. 67-88

Bergstrom, "The Algebra of Assortative Encounters and the Evolution of Cooperation" International Game Theory Review Vol. 5 No. 3 (2003) at pgs. 211-228

Bernstein, "Evolutionary Socialism: A Criticism and Affirmation" (1899)

Bessant, "Why I am a Socialist" (1886)

Bhavnani & Backer, "Localised Ethnic Conflict and Genocide: Accounting for Differences in Rwanda and Burundi" Journal of Conflict Resolution Vol.

44 No. 3 (2000) at pgs. 283-306

Bhavnani et al., "Three Two Tango: Territorial Control and Selective Violence in Israel, the West Bank, and Gaza," Journal of Conflict Resolution Vol. 55, No. 1 (2012) at pgs. 133-158

Bhavnani et al., "Violence and Control in Civil Conflict: Israel, the West Bank, and Gaza," Comparative Politics Vol. 44, No. 1 (2011) at pgs. 61-80

Bhavnani, "Ethnic Norms and Interethnic Violence: Accounting for Mass Participation in the Rwandan Genocide" Journal of Peace Research Vol. 43 No. 6 (2006) at pgs. 651-669

Bialas, "Nazi Ethics: Perpetrators with a Clear Conscience" Studies on the Holocaust Vol. 27 No. 1 (2013) at pgs. 3-25

Bicchieri, "Rationality and Coordination" Cambridge University Press (1993)

Bicchieri, "The Grammar of Society: The Nature and Dynamics of Social Norms" Cambridge University Press (2006)

Binmore, "Natural Justice" Oxford University Press (2005)

Birch & Okasha, "Kin Selection and Its Critics" Bioscience Vol. 65 No. 1 (2014) at pgs. 22-32.

Blute, "Darwinian Sociocultural Evolution: Solutions to Dilemmas in Cultural and Social Theory" Cambridge University Press (2010)

Boehm, "Hierarchy in the Forest: The Evolution of Egalitarian Behaviour" Harvard University Press (2001)

Bomze & Burger, "Stability by Mutation in Evolutionary Games" Games and Economic Behaviour Vol. 11. No. 2 (1995) at pgs. 146-172

Boone, "The Evolution of Magnanimity: When Is It Better To Give Than Receive?" Human Nature Vol. 9 (1998) at pgs. 1-21

Borello, "Evolutionary Restraints: The Contentious History of Group Selection" University of Chicago Press (2010)

Bowlby, "Attachment and Loss, Volumes I & II" Basic Books (1969, 1973)

Bowles & Gintis, "A Cooperative Species: Human Reciprocity and its Evolution" Princeton University Press (2011)

Bowles et al., "The punishment that sustains cooperation is often coordinated and costly" Behavioural and Brian Sciences Vol. 35 No. 1 (2012) at pgs.

20-21

Boyd & Richerson, "Built for Speed, Not For Comfort: Darwinian Theory and Human Culture" History and Philosophy of Life Sciences 23 (2001) at pgs. 425-465

Boyd & Richerson, "Culture and the Evolutionary Process", Chicago University Press (1985)

Boyd & Richerson, "Not by Genes Alone: How Culture Transformed Human Evolution" Chicago University Press (2005)

Boyd et al., "The evolution of altruistic punishment" Proceedings of the National Academy of Sciences Vol. 100 No. 6 (2003) at pgs. 3531-3135.

Boyd, "Mistakes Allow Evolutionary Stability in the Repeated Prisoner's Dilemma Game" Journal of Theoretical Biology Vol. 136 (1989) at pgs. 47-56

Buckholtz et al., "The Neural Correlates of Third Party Punishment" Neuron Vol. 60 No. 5 (2008) at pgs. 930-940

Burnham, "Toward a neo-Darwinian synthesis of neoclassical and behavioural economics" Journal of Economic Behaviour & Organization Vol. 90S (2003) at pgs. S113-157

Buss et al., "Adaptions, Exaptions and Spandrels" American Psychologist Vol. 53. No. 5 (1998) at pg. 533.

Buss, "Evolutionary Psychology: A New Paradigm for Psychological Science" Psychological Inquiry Vol. 6 No. 1 (1995) at pgs. 1-30.

Caldwell (ed.), "The Collected Works of F.A. Hayek Vol. 13" (2010)

Cavalli-Sforza & Feldman, "Cultural Transmission and Evolution: A Quantitative Approach" Princeton University Press (1981)

Cavalli-Sforza & Feldman, "Cultural versus Biological Inheritance: Phenotypic Transmission from Parents to Children (A Theory of the Effect of Parental Phenotypes on Children's Phenotypes)" American Journal of Human Genetics Vol. 25 (1973) at pgs. 618-635

Cavalli-Sforza & Feldman, "Models for Cultural Inheritance: Within Group Variation" Theoretical Population Biology Vol. 42. No. 4 (1973) at pgs. 42-55

Cederman, "Endogenizing geopolitical boundaries with agent-based modelling" Proceedings of the National Academy of Sciences Vol. 99.

Supplement 3 (2002) at pgs. 7296-7303.

Cheng et al. (eds.), "The Psychology of Social Status" Springer (2014)

Cheng et al., "Two ways to the top: Evidence that dominance and prestige are distinct yet viable avenues to social rank and influence" Journal of Personality and Social Psychology Vol. 104 No. 1 (2013) at pgs. 103-125

Cheverud, "Quantitative genetics and developmental constraints on evolution by selection." Journal of Theoretical Biology Vol. 110 (1984) at pgs. 155-171

Choi & Bowles, "The Coevolution of Parochial Altruism and War" Science Vol. 318 No. 26 (2007) at pgs. 636-640

Christian, "Maps of Time: An Introduction to Big History" University of California Press (2004)

Chung & Herrnstein, "Choice and Delay of Reinforcement" Journal of the Experimental Analysis of Behaviour Vol 10 No. 1 (1967) at pgs. 67-74

Cialdini & Goldstein, "Social Influence: Compliance and Conformity," Annual Review of Psychology Vol. 55 (2004) at pgs. 591-621

Clark, "Agents and Structures: Two Views of Preferences, Two Views of Institutions" International Studies Quarterly 42 (1998) at pgs. 245-270

Collins, "Please, Not Another Bias! The Problem with Behavioural Economics" Evonomics (September 2016)

Comte, "System of Positive Polity" (1851)

Corning, "Holistic Darwinism: Synergy, Cybernetics and the bioeconomics of evolution" University of Chicago Press (2005)

Cosmides & Tooby, "Evolutionary Psychology: A Primer". Available at https://www.cep.ucsb.edu/primer.html

Cosmides & Tooby, "Evolutionary Psychology: New Perspectives on Cognition and Motivation" Annual Review of Psychology Vol. 64 (2013) at pgs. 201-229

Cosmides, Tooby & Barkow (eds.), "The Adapted Mind: Evolutionary Psychology and the generation of culture" Oxford University Press (1992)

Crenshaw, "Demarginalizing the Intersection of Race and Sex: A Black Feminist Critique of Antidiscrimination Doctrine, Feminist Theory and Antiracist Politics" University of Chicago Legal Forum Vol. 139 (1989) at pgs. 139-167

Crenshaw, "Mapping the Margins: Intersectionality, Identity Politics, and Violence against Women of Color" Stanford Law Review Vol. 43. No. 6 (1991) at pgs. 1241-1299

Curtis et al., "Evidence that Disgust Evolved to Protect From Risk of Disease" Proceedings of the Royal Society B Vol, 271 (2004) at pgs. S131-S133.

Cutler, "The Basic Bakunin: Writings 1869-1871" Prometheus Books (1992)

Daly & Wilson, "The Truth about Cinderella: A Darwinian View of Parental Love" Yale University Press (1999)

Damasio, "Descartes Error: Emotion, Reason and the Human Brain" Avon Books (1995)

Danziger, Levav & Avnaim-Pesso, "Extraneous factors in judicial decisions" Proceedings of the National Academy of Sciences Vol. 108 No. 17 (2011) at pgs. 6889-6892

Darwin, "On the Origin of Species by Natural Selection" (1859)

Darwin, "The Descent of Man, and Selection in Relation to Sex" (1871)

Darwin, "The Expression of Emotions in Man and Animals" (1872)

Dawkins, "The Extended Phenotype: The Gene as the Unit of Selection" Oxford University Press (1982)

Dawkins, "The Selfish Gene" Oxford University Press (1979)

Dear et al., "Do 'watching eyes' influence antisocial behaviour? A systematic review & meta-analysis" Evolution and Human Behaviour Vol. 40 (2019) at pgs. 269-280

Delisle (ed.), "The Darwinian Tradition in Context" Springer International Publishing (2017)

Dennett, "Darwin's Dangerous Idea: Evolution and the Meaning of Life" Simon & Schuster (1995)

Dennett, "Elbow Room: The Varieties of Free Will Worth Wanting" MIT Press (1984)

Deutsch & Gerard, "A Study of normative and informational social influences upon individual judgment" Journal of Abnormal Social Psychology Vol. 51 No. 3 (1955) at pgs. 629-636

Dingli & Nowak, "Infectious tumour cells" Nature Vol. 443 (2006) at pgs. 35-36

Dobzhansky, "Nothing in Biology Makes Sense except in the Light of Evolution" The American Biology Teacher Vol. 35 No. 3 (1973) at pgs. 125-129

Donnelly, "Universal Human Rights in Theory and Practice" Cornell University Press (2013)

Drexler, "Engines of Creation: The Coming Era of Nanotechnology" Doubleday (1986)

Dugatkin, "The Prince of Evolution: Peter Kropotkin's Adventures in Science and Politics" Createspace (2011)

Dunbar, "Grooming, gossip, and the evolution of language" Harvard University Press (1998)

Dunbar, "Human Evolution" Pelican Books (2014)

Dunbar, "Neocortex size as a constraint on group size in primates" Journal of Human Evolution Vol. 22 No. 6 (1992) at pgs. 469–493

Durham, "Co-evolution: Genes, Culture and Human Diversity" Stanford University Press (1991);

Durkheim, "The Division of Labour in Society" (1893)

Durkheim, "The Rules of Sociological Method" (1895)

Edgeworth, "Mathematical Psychics: An Essay on the Application of Mathematics to the Moral Sciences" (1881)

Efferson, Rafael & Fehr, "The Coevolution of Cultural Groups and Ingroup Favoritism" Science Vol. 321 No. 5897. (2008) at pgs. 1844-1849.

Einstein, "Why Socialism?" The Monthly Review, May 1949

Engels, "Socialism: Utopian and Scientific" (1880)

Engels, "The Part played by Labour in the Transition from Ape to Man" Progress Publishers (1934)

Engen, "Killing for the Country: A New Look at 'Killology'" Canadian Military Journal Vol. 9. No. 2 (2011)

Ernest-Jones et al., "Effects of eye images on everyday cooperative behaviour: a field experiment" Evolution and Human Behaviour Vol. 32 No. 3 (2011) at pgs. 172-178

Eshel & Cavalli-Sforza, "Assortment of Encounters and evolution of cooperativeness" Proceedings of the National Academy of Sciences of the United States cf America Vol. 79. No. 4 (1982) at pgs. 1331-1335

Esko et al., "Genetic Structure of Europeans: A View from the North-East" PLOS ONE Vol. 5 No. 3 (2010)

Faludi, "Backlash: The Undeclared War Against American Women" Crown Publishing Group (1991).

Fan et al., "Going global by adapting local: A review of recent human adaptation" Science Vol. 354. No. 6308 (2016) at pgs. 54-59

Fearon & Laitin, "Explaining Interethnic Cooperation" The American Political Science Review Vol. 90 No. 4 (1996) at pgs. 715-735

Fehr & Fischbacher, "Third Party Punishment and Social Norms" Evolution and Human Behaviour Vol. 25 (2004) at pgs. 63-87

Fehr & Gachter, "Altruistic Punishment in Humans" Nature Vol. 415 No. 6868 (2002) at pgs. 137-140

Fehr & Gachter, "Cooperation and Punishment in Public Goods Games" The American Economic Review Vol. 90. No. 4 (2000) at pgs. 980-994

Fehr & Schneider, "Eyes are on us, but nobody cares: are eye cues relevant for strong reciprocity?" Proceedings of the Royal Society B Vol. 277 No. 1686 (2009) at pgs. 1315-1323.

Ferguson & Whitehead (eds.), "War in the Tribal Zone" School of American Research Press (1992)

Fiorini, "The Evolution of International Norms" International Studies Quarterly 40 (1996) at pgs. 363-389

Fisher & Ury, "Getting to Yes: Negotiating Agreement Without Giving In" Penguin (1981)

Fisher, "Capitalist Realism: Is There No Alternative?" Zero Books (2009)

Fletcher & Michener (eds.), "Kin recognition in animals" Wiley (1987)

Fodor, "Modularity of Mind" MIT Press (1980)

Foulsham et al., "Gaze allocation in a dynamic situation: Effects of Social Status and Speaking" Cognition Vol. 117 (2010) at pgs. 319-331

Fox (ed.), "Biosocial anthropology" Malaby Press (1975)

Fraser & Jaeggi, "Capitalism: A Conversation in Critical Theory" John

Wiley & Sons (2018)

Friedman, "A Non-cooperative Equilibrium for Supergames" Review of Economic Studies Vol. 38 No. 113 (1971) at pgs. 1-12

Fry & Soderberg, "Lethal Aggression in Mobile Forager Bands and Implications for the Origin of War" Science Vol. 341, No. 6143 (2013) at pgs. 270-273

Fry (ed.), "War, Peace and Human Nature: The Convergence of Evolutionary and Cultural Views" Oxford University Press (2013)

Gale et al., "Learning to be Imperfect: The Ultimatum Game" Games and Economic Behaviour Vol. 8 No. 1 (1995) at pgs. 56-90

Galor & Ozak, "The Agricultural Origin of Time Preference" American Economic Review Vol. 106. No. 10 (2016) at pgs. 3064-3103

Gangestad, Haselton & Buss, "Evolutionary Foundations of Cultural Variation: Evoked Culture and Mate Preferences" Psychological Inquiry Vol. 17 No. 2 (2006) at pgs. 75-95

Gardner & West, "Greenbeards" Evolution Vol. 64 No. 1 (2010) at pgs. 25-38

Gelfand, "Rule Makers, Rule Breakers: How Culture Wires our Minds, Shapes our Nations, and Drives our Differences" Scribner (2018)

Gerratana, "Marx and Darwin" New Left Review Vol. 35 (1974) at pgs. 60-82

Gigerenzer & Gaissmaier, "Heuristic Decision Making" Annual Review of Psychology Vol. 62 (2011) at pgs. 451-482

Gigerenzer & Selten (eds.), "Bounded Rationality: The Adaptive Toolbox" MIT Press (2002)

Gigerenzer, "How to Explain Behaviour" Topics in Cognitive Science (2019) at pgs. 1-19

Gigerenzer, "Why Heuristics Work" Perspectives on Psychological Science Vol. 3 No. 1 (2008) at pgs. 20-29.

Gilpin, "War and Change in World Politics" Cambridge University Press (1981)

Gintis, "A Framework for the Unification of the Behavioural Sciences" Behavioural and Brain Sciences Vol. 30 No 1. (2007) at pgs. 1-16

Gintis, "Game Theory Evolving, Second Edition: A Problem-Centered Introduction to Modelling Strategic Interaction" Princeton University Press (2009)

Gintis, "Individuality and Entanglement: The Moral and Material Basis of Social Life" Princeton University Press (2017)

Gintis, "Social Norms as Choreography" Politics, Philosophy and Economics Vol.9 No. 3. (2010) at pgs. 251-263

Gintis, "The Bounds of Reason: Game Theory and the Unification of the Behavioural Sciences" Princeton University Press (2009)

Gintis, "The Hitchhiker's Guide to Altruism: Gene-Culture Co-evolution, and the Internalization of Norms" Journal of Theoretical Biology Vol. 220 No. 4 (2003) at pgs. 407-418

Giphart & van Vugt, "Mismatch: How Our Stone Age Brain Deceives Us Every day (And What We Can Do About It)" Robinson (2018)

Goodnight & Stevens, "Experimental Studies of Group Selection: What do they tell us about Group Selection in nature?" The American Naturalist Vol. 150 (1997) at pgs. s59-s79

Gorman, "Michael Harrington: Speaking American" Routledge (1995)

Gould & Eldredge, "Punctuated equilibria: the tempo and mode of evolution reconsidered" Paleobiology Vol. 3 No. 2 (1977) at pgs. 115-151

Gould & Lewontin, "The Spandrels of St Marco and the Panglossian Paradigm: A Critique of the Adaptionist Programme" Proceedings of the Royal Society of London B Vol. 205 (1979) at pgs. 581-598

Gould & Vrba, "Exaption – a missing term in the science of form" Paleobiology Vol.8 No. 1 (1982) at pgs. 4-15

Gould, "The exaptive excellence of spandrels as a term and prototype", Proceedings of the National Academy of Sciences of the United States of America Vol. 94 No. 20 (1997) at pgs. 10750–10755

Gould, "Caring Groups and Selfish Genes" Natural History Vol. 86. No. 10 (1977) at pg. 20-.

Gould, "Darwinian Fundamentalism" New York Review of Books, 12 June 1997

Gould, "Kropotkin Was No Crackpot" Natural History Vol. 97 No. 7 (1997) at pgs. 12-21.

Gould, "The evolutionary biology of constraint" Daedalus Vol. 109 (1980) at pgs. 39-52

Gould, "The Panda's Thumb: More Reflections in Natural History" W.W. Norton & Company (1980)

Gould, "The Structure of Evolutionary Theory" Harvard University Press (2002)

Govindan et al., "A Short Proof of Harsanyi's Purification Theorem" Games and Economic Behaviour Vol. 45 No. 2 (2003) at pgs. 369-374

Gowdy et al., "The evolution of hyperbolic discounting: Implications for truly social valuation of the future" Journal of Economic Behaviour & Organization Vol. 90S (2013) at pgs. S92-104

Gracia-Lazaro et al., "Human behaviour in Prisoners Dilemma experiments suppresses network reciprocity" Scientific Reports Vol. 2 (2012) at pgs. 1-4

Graeber, "Debt: The First 5,000 Years" Melville House (2011)

Grafen, "An Inclusive Fitness Analysis of Altruism on a Cyclical Network" Journal of Evolutionary Biology Vol. 20 (2007) at pgs. 2278-2283

Grafen, "Biological Signals as handicaps" Journal of Theoretical Biology Vol. 144 No. 4 (1990) at pgs. S187-546

Gramsci, "Selections from the Prison Notebooks" ElecBooks (1999)

Grant et al., "The cognitive and cultural foundations of moral behaviour" Evolution and Human Behaviour Vol. 39 No. 5 (2018) at pgs. 490-501

Greene, "Moral Tribes: Emotion, Reason and the Gap Between Them and Us" Atlantic Books (2013)

Grief, "Contract Enforceability and Economic Institutions in Early Trade: The Magribi Traders' Coalition" The American Economic Review Vol. 82 No. 3 (1993) at pgs.525-548

Grief, "The Birth of Impersonal Exchange: The Community Responsibility System and Impartial Justice" Journal of Economic Perspectives Vol. 20 No. 2 (2006) at pgs. 221-236

Grossman, "On Killing: The Psychological Cost of Learning to Kill in War and Society" Back Bay Books (1996)

Grune-Yanoff, "Models of Temporal Discounting 1937-2000: An Interdisciplinary Exchange between Economics and Psychology" Science in Context Vol. 28 No. 4 (2015) at pgs. 675-713

Guth & Tietz, "Ultimatum Bargaining Behaviour: A Survey and Comparison of Experimental Results" Journal of Economic Psychology Vol. 11 (1990) at pgs. 417-449;

Guth et al., "An Experimental Analysis of Ultimatum Bargaining" Journal of Economic Behaviour and Organisation Vol. 3 (1982) at pgs. 367-388

Güth, Schmittberger, & Schwarze, "An Experimental Analysis of Ultimatum Bargaining" Journal of Economic Behaviour & Organization Vol. 3 (1982) at pgs. 367-388

Gutmann (ed.), "Multiculturalism. Examining the Politics of Recognition" Princeton University Press (1994) at pgs. 25-73

Haidt, "The emotional dog and its rationalist tail: a social intuitionist approach to moral judgment" Psychological Review Vol. 108. No. 4 (2001) at pgs. 814-;

Haidt, "The Righteous Mind: Why Good People are Divided by Politics and Religion" Penguin Books (2012)

Haldane, "Marxist Philosophy and the Sciences" Books for Libraries Press (1939)

Haldane, "The Causes of Evolution" Longman, Greens & Co. (1932)

Haley & Fessler, "Nobody's Watching? Subtle cues affect generosity in an anonymous economic game" Evolution and Human Behaviour Vol. 26. No. 3 (2005) at pgs. 245-256

Hamilton, "The Genetical Evolution of Social Behaviour, I & II" Journal of Theoretical Biology Vol. 7 (1965) at pgs. 1-16, and 17-52

Hamlin & Wynn, "Young infants prefer prosocial to antisocial others" Cognitive Development Vol. 26 No. 1 (2011) at pgs. 30-39

Hamlin et al., "How infants and toddlers react to antisocial others" Proceedings of the National Academy of Sciences Vol. 108 No. 50 (2011) at pgs. 19931-19936

Hardin, "The Tragedy of the Commons" Science Vol. 162 No. 259 (1968) at pgs. 1243-1248

Harrington & Gelfand, "Tightness-Looseness across the 50 united states" Proceedings of the National Academy of Sciences of the United States of America Vol. 111. No. 22. (2014) at pgs. 7990-7995

Harrison (ed.), "Complexity in World Politics" State University of New York Press (2006)

Harsanyi, "Games with Randomly Distributed Payoffs: A New Rationale for Mixed-Strategy Equilibrium Points" International Journal of Game Theory Vol. 2 No. 1 (1973) at pgs. 1-23

Harsanyi, "Rational-Choice Models of Political Behaviour vs. Functionalist and Conformist Theories" World Politics Vol. 21 No. 4 (1969) at pgs. 512-538

Hawkins, "Social Darwinism in European and American Thought, 1860-1945" Cambridge University Press (1997)

Henrich & Boyd, "Why People Punish Defectors: Weak Conformist Transmission can Stabilize Costly Enforcement of Norms in Cooperative Dilemmas" Journal of Theoretical Biology Vol. 208. No.1 (2001) at pgs. 79-89

Henrich & Ensminger (eds.), "Experimenting with Social Norms: Fairness and Punishment in Cross-Cultural Perspective" Russel Sage Press (2014)

Henrich et al., "'Economic Man' in cross-cultural perspective: behavioural experiments in 15 small-scale societies" Behavioural and Brain Sciences Vol. 28 (2005) at pgs. 795-855

Henrich et al., "In Search of Homo Economicus: Behavioural Experiments in 15 Small-Scale Societies" American Economic Review Vol. 91. No. 2 (2001) at pgs. 73-78

Henrich, "The Secret of Our Success: How Culture is Driving Human Evolution, Domesticating Our Species and Making us Smarter" Princeton University Press (2016)

Herdt & Keesing (eds.), "Rituals of Manhood: Male Initiation in Papua New Guinea" University of California Press (1992)

Hermann et al., "Humans have evolved specialised skills of social cognition: the cultural intelligence hypothesis" Science Vol 317. No. 5843 (2007) at pgs. 1360-1366;

Hermann et al., "The structure of individual differences in the cognitive abilities of children and chimpanzees" Psychological Science Vol. 21. No. 1 (2010) at pgs. 102-111

Herrnstein, 'Relative and Absolute Strength of Response as a Function of Frequency of Reinforcement" Journal of the Experimental Analysis of Behaviour Vol. 4 No. 3. (1961) at pgs. 267-272

Hilbe, Nowak & Sigmund "Evolution of extortion in iterated Prisoner's Dilemma games" Proceedings of the National Academy of Sciences of the United States of America Vol. 110 No. 17 (2013) at pgs. 6913–6918

Hintze & Adami, "Punishment in public goods games leads to meta-stable phase transitions and hysteresis" Physical Biology 12 (2015)

Hintze & Adami, "Thermodynamics of evolutionary games" Physical Review E Vol. 97 No. 6 (2018)

Hobbes, "Leviathan" (1651)

Hodgson, "Understanding organizational evolution: Toward a research agenda using generalized Darwinism", Organization Studies 34 (2013) at pgs. 973-992.

Hofbauer & Sigmund, "Evolutionary Games and Population Dynamics" Cambridge University Press (1998)

Hofstadter, "Social Darwinism in American Thought" Beacon Press (1955)

Holland, "Adaptive Algorithms for Discovering and Using General Patterns in Growing Knowledge Bases" International Journal of Policy Analysis and Information Systems Vol. 4 (1980) at pgs. 245-268

Holland, "Hidden Order: How Adaption Builds Complexity" Addison Wesley (1995)

Horner & Whiten, "Causal knowledge and imitation/emulation switching in chimpanzees (pan troglodytes) and children (homo sapiens)" Animal Cognition Vol. 8 No. 3 (2005) at pgs. 164-181

Houston, "Are the spandrels of St Marco really Panglossian pendentives?" Trends in Ecology and Evolution Vol. 12 No. 3 (1997)

Hume, "A Treatise on Human Nature" Oxford University (1739)

Hume, "Of Civil Liberty" (1742)

Huxley, "Address to the Anthropological Department of the British

Association, Dublin, 1878" Nature Vol. 18 (1878) at pgs. 445-448

Huxley, "Evolution and Ethics" MacMillan & Co. (1895)

Ibn Khaldun, "The Muqaddimah: An introduction to history" (1378)

Ilardo et al., "Physiological and Genetic Adaptations to Diving in Sea Nomads" Cell Vol. 173. No. 3 (2018) at pgs. 569-580

Inoue & Matsuzawa, "Working memory of numerals in chimpanzees" Current Biology Vol. 17 No. 23 (2007) at pgs. 1004-1005

Ivanova & Markin, "Piotr Alekseevich Kropotkin and his Monograph Researches on the Glacial Period (1876)" Geological Society of London Special Publications Vol. 301 (2008) at pgs. 117-128

Jablonka & Lamb, "Evolution in Four Dimensions: Genetic, Epigenetic, Behavioural and Symbolic Variation in the History of Life" MIT Press (2005)

Jamieson (ed.), "The Criminology of War" Routledge (2017)

Jaspers, "The Origin and Goals of History" Routledge (1949)

Jenkins, "Categorization: Identity, Social Process and Epistemology" Current Sociology Vol. 48 No. 3 (2000) at pgs. 7-25

Jing, "The Temple of Memories: History, Power and Morality in a Chinese Village" Stanford University Press (1996)

John, "Ideas and interests; agendas and implementation: an evolutionary explanation of policy change in British local government finance", British Journal of Politics and International Relations 1(1) (1999) at pgs. 39-62

Johnson, "The Struggle for Coexistence: Peter Kropotkin and the Social Ecology of Science in Russia, Europe and England, 1859-1922" PhD Thesis, University of British Colombia (Vancouver) (2019) at pg. 18.

Jost & Amodio, "Political ideology as motivated social cognition" Motivation and Emotion Vol. 36 (2012) at pgs. 55-64

Jost et al., "Political Conservatism as Motivated Social Cognition" Psychological Bulletin Vol. 129. No. 3. (2003) at pgs. 339-375

Jost et al., "Political Ideology: Its Structure, Functions and Elective Affinities" The Annual Review of Psychology Vol. 60 (2009) at pgs. 302-337

Jost, 'The end of the end of ideology', American Psychologist Vol. 61, No. 7 (2006) at pgs. 651-

Kahneman & Tversky "Prospect Theory: An Analysis of Decision under

Risk" Econometrica Vol. 47 No. 2 (1979) at pgs. 99-127

Kahneman & Tversky, "Rational Choice and the Framing of Decisions" The Journal of Business Vol. 59 No. 4 (1986) at pgs. 251-278

Kahneman, Knetsch & Thaler, "Fairness and the Assumptions of Economics" Journal of Business Vol. 59 (1991) at pgs. 285-100

Kalyvas & Kocher, "Ethnic Cleavages and Irregular War: Iraq and Vietnam" Politics and Society Vol. 35 No. 2 (2007) at pgs. 183-223

Kalyvas, "Micro-level Studies of Violence in Civil War: Refining and Extending the Control-Collaboration Model" Terrorism and Political Violence Vol. 24 No. 4 (2012) at pgs. 658-668

Kalyvas, "The Logic of Violence in Civil Wars" Cambridge University Press (2006)

Kalyvas, "The Ontology of Political Violence: Action and Identity in Civil Wars" Perspectives on Politics Vol. 1 No. 3 (2003) at pgs. 475-494

Kaminski et al., "Evolution of facial muscle anatomy in dogs" Proceedings of the National Academy of Sciences Vol. 11 No. 29 (2019) at pgs. 14677-14681

Kant, "Answering the Question: What Is Enlightenment?" (1784)

Kant, "Groundwork of the Metaphysics of Morals" (1785)

Kant, "Perpetual Peace: A Philosophical Essay" (1795)

Keohane, "After Hegemony: Cooperation and Discord in the World Political Economy" Princeton University Press (1984)

Keynes, "The General Theory of Employment, Interest and Money" Harcourt Brace & Co. (1935)

Kierkegaard, "The Concept of Anxiety" (1844)

Killingback & Doebeli, "Spatial Evolutionary Game Theory: Hawks and Doves Revisited" Proceedings of the Royal Society B Vol. 263 No. 1374 (1996) at pgs. 1135-1144

Kindelberger, "The World in Depression: 1929-1939" University of California Press (1973)

Kinna, "Fields of Vision: Kropotkin and Revolutionary Change" SubStance Vol. 36. No. 2 (2007) at pgs. 67-86

Kinzler et al., "Accent Trumps Race in Guiding Children's Social Preferences" Social Cognition Vol. 27 No. 4 (2009) at pgs. 623-634

Knetsch, "The endowment effect and evidence of nonreversible indifference curves" American Economic Review Vol. 79 (1989) at pgs. 1277-1284

Knight & Sened (eds.), "Explaining social institutions" University of Michigan Press (1995) at pgs. 22-23

Koerper & Stickel, "Cultural Drift: A primary process of cultural change" Journal of Anthropological Research Vol. 36 No. 4 (1980) at pgs. 463-469

Kropotkin, "Mutual Aid Among Savages", The Nineteenth Century, April 1891

Kropotkin, "Mutual Aid: A Factor in Evolution" (1902)

Kropotkin, "Revolutionary Studies" The Commonweal, January 1892

Kuhn et al., "The Work of John Nash in Game Theory," Journal of Economic Theory Vol. 69 (1996) at pgs. 153-185

Kydd, "International Relations Theory: The Game Theoretic Approach" Cambridge University Press (2015)

Kymlicka, "Contemporary Political Philosophy: An Introduction" Oxford University Press (2002)

Kymlicka, "Multicultural Citizenship," Oxford University Press (1995)

LaFollette (ed.), "The Blackwell Guide to Ethical Theory" Wiley-Blackwell (2000) at pgs. 400–419

Laibson, "Golden Eggs and Hyperbolic Discounting" Quarterly Journal of Economics (1997) at pgs. 443-491

Laitin, "Marginality: A Microperspective" Rationality and Society Vol. 7 (1995) at pgs. 31-57

Laland & Brown, "Sense & Nonsense: Evolutionary Perspectives on Human Behaviour" Oxford University Press (2011)

Laland, "Darwin's Unfinished Symphony: How Culture Made the Human Mind" Princeton University Press (2017)

Lehmann & Feldman, "War and the Evolution of Belligerence and Bravery" Proceedings of the Royal Society of London B Vol. 275 No. 1653 (2008) at pgs. 2877-2885

Lehmann et al., "The Evolution of Helping and Harming on Graphs: the Return of the Inclusive Fitness effect" Journal of Evolutionary Biology Vol.

20 (2007) at pgs. 2284-2295

Leigh, "Adaption and Diversity" Cooper Press (1971)

Lenin, "Imperialism: The Highest Stage of Capitalism" (1914)

Levine et al., "Self-Categorization and Bystander Non-Intervention: Two Experimental Studies" Journal of Applied Social Psychology (2002) at pgs. 1452-1463

Lewis, "Convention: A Philosophical Study" Harvard University Press (1969)

Lewontin et al., "Not in Our Genes: Biology, Ideology and Human Nature" Pantheon Books (1984)

Lewontin, "Biological Determinism" The Tanner Lectures in Human Values (1982)

Lewontin, "Biology As Ideology: The Doctrine of DNA" House of Anansi Press (1991)

Lewontin, "The Fallacy of Biological Determinism" The Sciences, Vol. 16 No. 2 (1976) at pgs. 6-10

Lewontin, "The Units of Selection" Annual Review of Ecology and Systematics Vol. 1 (1970) at pgs. 1-18

Lieberman et al., "Evolutionary Dynamics on Graphs" Nature Vol. 433 No. 7023 (2005) at pgs. 312-316

Locke, 'Second Treatise on Government', Yale University Press (2003)

Lumdsen & Wilson, "Genes, Mind and Culture: The Coevolutionary Process" Harvard University Press (1981)

Lustick, "Taking Evolution Seriously: Historical Institutionalism and Evolutionary Theory" Polity Vol. 43 No 2 (2011) at pgs. 179-209

Machiavelli, "Discourses on Livy" (1531)

Mahajan et al., "The Evolution of Intergroup Bias: Perceptions and Attitudes in Rhesus Monkeys" Journal of Personality and Social Psychology Vol. 100 (2001) at pg. 387-

March & Olsen, "The Logic of Appropriateness" The Oxford Handbook of Political Science (2011)

March, "Bounded Rationality, Ambiguity and Engineering of Choice" The Bell Journal of Economics Vol. 9 No. 4 (1970) at pgs. 570-592

Margolis, "Patterns, Thinking and Cognition: A Theory of Judgment" University of Chicago Press (1987)

Margulis, "Origin of Eukaryotic Cells" Yale University Press (1970)

Marx, "A Contribution to the Critique of Political Economy" (1859)

Marx, "A Critique of The German Ideology" Progress Publishers (1968)

Marx, "The Poverty of Philosophy" (1847)

Marx, "Theses on Feuerbach" (1845)

Maynard Smith & Price, "The Logic of Animal Conflict" Nature Vol. 246 No. 5427 (1972) at pgs. 15-18

Maynard Smith & Szathmary, "Major Transitions in Evolution" Oxford University Press (1995)

Maynard Smith & Szathmary, "The Major Evolutionary Transitions" Nature Vol. 374. No. 6519. (1995) at pgs. 227-232

Maynard Smith & Szathmary, "The Origins of Life: From the Birth of Life to the Origin of Language" Oxford University Press (1999)

Maynard Smith et al. "Developmental constraints and evolution" Quantitative Review of Biology Vol. 60 (1985) at pgs. 265-287

Maynard Smith, "Models of a Dual Inheritance System" Journal of Theoretical Biology Vol. 143 No. 1 (1990) at pgs. 41-53

Maynard Smith, "Evolution and the Theory of Games" Cambridge University Press (1982)

Maynard Smith, "Group Selection and Kin Selection" Nature No. 4925 (1964) at pgs. 1145-1147.

Maynard Smith, "The Theory of Games and the Evolution of Animal Conflicts" Journal of Theoretical Biology Vol. 47. No. 1 (1974) at pgs. 209-221

Mayr, "Cause and effect in biology" Science Vol. 134 (1961) at pgs. 1501–1506

Mayr, "What Makes Biology Unique?" Cambridge University Press (2004)

McAuliffe et al., "Costly third-party punishment in young children" Cognition Vol. 134 (2015) at pgs. 1-10

McCarty & Meirowitz, "Political Game Theory: An Introduction" Cambridge University Press (2007)

McElreath & Boyd, "Mathematical Models of Social Evolution: A Guide for the Perplexed" University of Chicago Press (2007)

McElreath, Boyd & Richerson, "Shared Norms and the Evolution of Ethnic Markers" Current Anthropology Vol. 44. No. 1 (2003) at pgs. 122-130

McKelvey & Palfrey, "An Experimental Study of the Centipede Game" Econometrica Vol. 60 No. 4 (1992) at pgs. 803-836

McRae, 'Social consequences of experiential openness', Psychological Bulletin Vol. 120 (1996) at pgs. 323-

Mercier & Sperber, "Why Do Humans Reason? Arguments for an Argumentative Theory" Behavioural and Brain Sciences Vol. 34 (2011) at pgs. 57-111

Mesoudi et al., "Towards a unified science of cultural evolution" Behavioural and Brain Sciences Vol. 29 No. 4 (2006) at pgs. 329-347

Mesoudi, "Pursuing Darwin's curious parallel: Prospects for a science of cultural evolution" PNAS Vol. 114 No. 30 (2017) at pgs. 7853-7860

Michels, "Political Parties: A Sociological Study of the Oligarchical Tendencies of Modern Democracy" The Free Press (1911)

Minkel, "Psyching Out Evolutionary Psychology: Interview with David J. Buller" Scientific American, 4 July 2005

Modelski, "Evolutionary Paradigm for World Politics" International Studies Quarterly Vol. 40 (1996) at pgs. 321-342

Morgan & Laland, "The biological basis of conformity" Frontiers in Neuroscience Vol. 6 (2012)

Morrow, "Game Theory for Political Scientists" Princeton University Press (1994)

Muir et al., "Multilevel selection with kin and nonkin groups, experimental results with Japanese quail (Coturnix japonica)" Evolution Vol. 6 (2013) at pgs. 1598-1606

Muir, "Group selection for adaption to multiple-hen cages: selection program & direct responses" Poultry Science Vol. 75 (1996) at pgs. 447-458

Muller et al., "Prosocial Consequences of Imitation" Psychological Reports Vol. 110 (2012) at pg. 891

Muthukrishna et al., "The Cultural Brain Hypothesis: How culture drives brain expansion, sociality, and life history" PLoS Computational Biology Vol. 14 No. 11 (2018)

Nagel & Tang, "Experimental Results on the Centipede Game in Normal Form: An Investigation on Learning" Journal of Mathematical Psychology Vol. 42 (1998) at pgs. 356-384

Nietzsche, "Beyond Good and Evil: Prelude to a Philosophy of the Future" (1886)

Nietzsche, "On Truth and Lies in a Nonmoral Sense" (1873)

Nitecki & Robinson (eds.), "Global Theory of dynamical systems" Springer (1980)

Novoa, "Social Darwinism: A Case of Designed Ventriloquism" in "Truth and Reconciliation for Social Darwinism", This View of Life Magazine (2016); Available at: https://evolution-institute.org/wp-content/uploads/2016/11/2Social-Darwinism_Publication.pdf

Nowak & May, "Evolutionary Games and spatial chaos" Nature Vol. 359 No. 6398 (1992) at pgs. 826-829

Nowak & Sigmund, "Cooperation versus Competition" Financial Analysts Journal Vol. 56 No. 4 (2000) at pgs. 13-22

Nowak & Sigmund, "Evolution of Indirect Reciprocity" Nature Vol. 437 (2005) at pgs. 1291-1298

Nowak et al., "Evolutionary Dynamics in Structured Populations" Philosophical Transactions of the Royal Society B Vol. 365. No. 1537 (2010) at pgs. 19-30

Nowak et al., "Spatial Games and the Maintenance of Cooperation" Proceedings of the National Academy of Science of the United States of America Vol. 91. No. 11 (1994) at pgs. 4877-4881

Nowak, "Five rules for the evolution of cooperation" Science Vol. 314 No. 5805 (2006) at pgs. 1560-1563

Nowak, Page, & Sigmund, "Fairness Versus Reason in the Ultimatum Game" Science Vol. 289 No. 5485 (2000) at pgs. 1773–1775

Nowak, Tarnita & Wilson, "The Evolution of Eusociality" Nature Vol. 466 (2010) at pgs. 1057-1062

Nozick, "The Nature of Rationality" Princeton University Press (1993) at pgs. 139-151

Odling-Smee et al., "Niche Construction: The Neglected Process in Evolution" Princeton University Press (2003)

Ohtsuki et al., "A simple rule for the evolution of cooperation on graphs" Nature Vol. 441 No. 7092 (2008) at pgs. 502-505

Olson & Zeckhauser, "An Economic Theory of Alliances" The Review of Economics and Statistics 48(3) (1966) at pgs. 266-279

Olson, "The Logic of Collective Action" Harvard University Press (1965)

Osbourne, "An Introduction to Game Theory" Oxford University Press (2004)

Ostrom & Janssen, "Working Together: Collective Action the Commons and Multiple Methods in Practice" Princeton University Press (2010)

Ostrom, "A Behavioural Approach to the Rational Choice Theory of Collective Action" Vol. 92 No. 1 (1998) at pgs. 1-22

Ostrom, "Beyond Markets: Polycentric Governance of Complex Economic Systems" American Economic Review Vol. 100 (2010) at pgs. 1-33

Ostrom, "Collective Action and the Evolution of Social Norms" The Journal of Economic Perspectives" Vol. 14 No. 3 (2000) at pgs. 137-158

Ostrom, "Governing the Commons: The Evolution of Institutions for Collective Action" Cambridge University Press (1990)

Pacek & Radcliff, "Assessing the Welfare State: The Politics of Happiness" Perspectives on Politics Vol. 6 No. 1 (2008) at pgs. 267-277

Page & Nowak, "Unifying Evolutionary Dynamics" Journal of Theoretical Biology Vol.219 No. 1 (2002) at pgs. 93-98

Paine, "Rights of Man" (1791)

Parfit, "Reasons and Persons" Oxford University Press (1984)

Pigliucci & Kaplan, "The fall and rise of Dr Pangloss: adaptionism and the Spandrels paper 20 years later" Trends in Ecology and Evolution Vol. 15 No. 2 (2000) at pgs. 66-70;

Piketty, "Capital in the Twenty-First Century" Harvard University Press (2013)

Pinker, "Enlightenment Now: the Case for Reason, Science, Humanism, and Progress" Viking Books (2018)

Pinker, "The Better Angels of Our Nature: Why Violence Has Declined" Viking Books (2011)

Pinker, "The Blank Slate: The Modern Denial of Human Nature" Harvard University Press (2002)

Pinker, "The False Allure of Group Selection" Edge, 18 June 2012

Pittenger, "American Socialists and Evolutionary Thought, 1870-1920" University of Wisconsin Press (1993)

Plotkin (ed.), "The role of behaviour in evolution" MIT Press (1988)

Pohley & Thomas, "Non-linear ESS models and frequency-dependent selection" Biosystems Vol. 16 No. 2 (1983) at pgs. 87-100

Pollan, "The Omnivore's Dilemma: A Natural History of Four Meals" The Penguin Press (2006)

Popper, "The Logic of Scientific Discovery" Routledge (1959)

Popper, "The Open Society and Its Enemies" Routledge (1947)

Press & Dyson, "Iterated Prisoner's Dilemma contains strategies that dominate any evolutionary opponent" Proceedings of the National Academy of Sciences of the United States of America Vol. 109. No. 26 (2012) at pgs. 10409-10413

Price, "A Review of the Principle Questions in Morals" (1758)

Price, "Extension of Covariance Selection Mathematics" Annals of Human Genetics Vol. 35 (1972) at pgs. 485-490

Proudhon, "What is Property? An Inquiry into the Principle of Right and Government" (1831)

Prunier, "The Rwanda Crisis: History of the Genocide" Columbia University Press (1995)

Raihani et al., "Punishment and cooperation in nature" Ecology & Evolution Vol. 27 No. 5 (2012) at pgs. 288-295

Rawls, "A Theory of Justice", Harvard University Press (1971)

Rawls, "Justice as Fairness: A Restatement" Belknap Press (2001)

Rawls, "Justice as Fairness: Political not Metaphysical" Philosophy and Public Affairs Vol. 14 (1985) at pgs. 223-251

Rawls, "Political Liberalism" Columbia University Press (1993)

Reismann, "Capitalism: A Treatise on Economics" TJS Books (1998)

Richerson & Henrich, "Tribal Social Instincts and the Cultural Evolution of Institutions to Solve Collective Action Problems" Cliodynamics Vol. 3 No. 1 (2012)

Riedl et al., "No third-party punishment in chimpanzees" Proceedings of the National Academy of Sciences Vol. 109 No. 27 (2012) at pgs. 14824-14829

Riolo, Cohen & Axelrod, "Evolution of Cooperation without Reciprocity" Nature Vol. 414 (2001) at pgs. 441-443

Roach et al., "Analysis of Genetic Inheritance in a Family Quartet by Whole-Genome Sequencing" Science Vol. 328 No. 5978 (2010) at pgs. 636-639

Robson & Samuelson, "The Evolutionary Foundations of Preferences" in the "Handbook of Social Economics, Volume 1" North-Holland (2011) at pgs. 221-310.

Robson, "A Biological Basis for Expected and Non-expected Utility" Journal of Economic Theory Vol. 58. (1996) at pgs. 397-424

Robson, "Why would nature give individuals utility functions?" Journal of Political Economy Vol. 109 No. 4 (2001) at pgs. 900–914

Rosas, "Evolutionary game theory meets social science: Is there a unifying rule for human cooperation?" Journal of Theoretical Biology 264 (2010) at pgs. 450-456

Rosenthal, "Games of Perfect Information, Predatory Pricing and the Chain Store" Journal of Economic Theory Vol. 25. No. 1 (1981) at pgs. 92-100

Roth et al., "Bargaining and Market Behaviour in Jerulsalem, Ljubljann, Pittsburgh and Tokyo: An Experimental Study" American Economic Review Vol. 81 No. 1 (1991) at pgs. 162-202

Rousseau, "A Discourse on the Origin and Basis of Inequality Among Men" (1754)

Rousseau, "Democracy & War: Institutions, Norms and the Evolution of International Conflict" Stanford University Press (2005)

Rousseau, "Emile, or On Education" (1762)

Rowe, "It's Time to Base Economics on Human Nature, Not Homo Economicus" Evonomics (2016)

Sagarin & Taylor (eds.), "Natural Security: A Darwinian Approach to a Dangerous World" University of California Press (2008)

Sapolsky, "Behave: The Biology of Humans at Our Best and Worst" Bodley Head (2017)

Schank & Abelson, "Scripts, Plans, Goals and Understanding" Erlbaum Associates (1977)

Schmidt, Call & Tomasello, "Young children enforce social norms" Current Directions in Psychological Science Vol. 21 No. 4 (2012) at pgs. 232-236

Schofield & Caballero (eds.), "Political Economy of Institutions, Democracy and Voting" Springer (2011)

Schrodt, "Patterns, Rules and Learning: Computational Models of International Behaviour" Parus Analytical Systems (2004)

Schuster & Sigmund, "Replicator Dynamics" Journal of Theoretical Biology Vol. 100 No. 3 (1983) at pgs. 533-538

Schuster (ed.) "Reviews of nonlinear dynamics and complexity, Vol. 2" Wiley-VCH (2009)

Schwartz, "Self-determination: The Tyranny of Freedom" The American Psychologist Vol. 55 No. 1 (2000) at pgs. 79-88

Schwartz, "The Paradox of Choice: Why More is Less" Harper Perennial (2004)

Selten, "Re-examination of the Perfectness Concept of Equilibrium in Extensive Games" International Journal of Game Theory Vol. 4 (1975) at pgs. 25-55

Sen, "Identity and Violence: The Illusion of Destiny" W.W. Norton & Co (2006)

Sethi & Somanathan, "The Evolution of Social Norms in Common Property Resource Use" The American Economic Review Vol. 86. No. 4 (1996) at pgs. 766-788

Sherif et al., "Intergroup Conflict and Cooperation: The Robbers Cave Experiment" The University Book Exchange (1961)

Simon, "A behavioural model of rational choice" Quarterly Journal of Economics Vol. 69 (1955) at pgs. 99-118

Simon, "Rational Choice and the Structure of the Environment" Psychological Review Vol. 63. No. 2 (1956) at pgs. 129-138

Sinervo & Lively, "The rock-papers-scissors game and the evolution of alternative male strategies" Nature Vol. 380 (1996) at pgs. 240-243

Singer, "A Darwinian Left: Politics, Evolution and Cooperation" Weidenfeld & Nicholson (1999)

Skews, "Politics for the New Dark Age: Staying Positive Amidst Disorder" Hybrid Publishers (2017)

Skinner, "Selection by Consequences" Science Vol. 213. No. 4507 (1981) at pgs. 501-504

Skyrms, "Evolution of the Social Contract, Second Edition" Cambridge University Press (2014)

Skyrms, "Signals: Evolution, Learning and Information" Oxford University Press (2010)

Slobodian, "Globalists: The End of Empire and the Birth of Neoliberalism" Harvard University Press (2018)

Smaldino, Schank & McElreath, "Increased costs of cooperation help cooperators in the long run" American Naturalist Vol. 181 No. 4 (2013) at pgs. 451-463

Smith, "The Theory of Moral Sentiments" (1759)

Snidal, "Relative gains and the pattern of international cooperation" American Political Science Review 85 (1991) at pgs. 701-26

Snidal, "The Limits of Hegemonic Stability Theory" International Organisation Vol. 39 No. 4 (1985) at pgs. 579-614

Sober & Wilson, "Unto Others: The Evolution and Psychology of Unselfish Behaviour" Harvard University Press (1998)

Sober (ed.) "Did Darwin Write the Origin Backwards: Philosophical Essays on Darwin's Theory" Prometheus (2010)

Sosis, "Costly Signalling and Torch Fishing on Ifaluk Atoll" Evolution and Human Behaviour Vol 21, No. 4 (2000) at pgs. 223-244

Spencer, "A Theory of Population, Deduced from the General Law of Human Fertility" Westminster Review Vol. 57 (1852) at pgs. 468-501

Spencer, "Principles of Biology" (1864)

Spencer, "Principles of Ethics Part I: the Data of Ethics" (1879)

Spencer, "Social Statics" (1851)

Spencer, "The Social Organism" (1860)

Sperber, "Explaining Culture: A naturalistic approach" Blackwell (1996)

Spitzer et al., "The Neural Signature of Social Norm Compliance" Neuron Vol. 56 No.1 (2007) at pgs. 185-196

Stack, "The First Darwinian Left: Socialism and Darwinism, 1859-1914" New Clarion Press (2003)

Stephen & Sulikowski, "Tinbergen's Four Questions" in "The Encyclopedia of Evolutionary Psychological Science" Springer Nature (2019)

Sterenly, "Dawkins vs. Gould: Survival of the Fittest" Icon Books (2007)

Stern (ed.), "Institutions for Managing the Commons" National Research Council (2001)

Stewart & Plotkin, "From extortion to generosity, evolution in the iterated Prisoners Dilemma" Proceedings of the National Academy of Sciences of the United States of America Vol. 110. No. 38 (2013) at pgs. 15348-15353

Stiglitz, 'The Price of Inequality' Penguin (2012)

Stoelhorst & Richerson, "A naturalistic theory of economic organization" Journal of Economic Behaviour & Organization Vol. 90S (2013) at pgs. S45-S56

Stone et al., "Choosing How to Cooperate: A Repeated Public-Goods Model of International Relations" International Studies Quarterly 52 (2008) at pg. 335-

Sugden, "The Economics of Rights, Co-operation, and Welfare (2nd edition)" Palgrave McMillan (2004)

Szejnmann, "Nazism in Central Germany: The Brownshirts in 'Red' Saxony" Berghahn Books (1999)

Taleb, 'Antifragile: Things That Gain from Disorder' Random House (2012)

Taylor & Jonker, "Evolutionarily Stable Sets and Game Dynamics" Mathematical Biosciences Vol. 1 No. 1-2 (1978) at pgs. 145-156

Taylor, "The Malaise of Modernity" House of Anansi Press (1991)

Thaler & Sunstein "Nudge: Improving Decisions About Health, Wealth, and Happiness" Penguin Books (2009)

Thaler, "Some empirical evidence on dynamic inconsistency" Economics

Letters Vol. 8 No. 3. (1981) at pgs. 201-207;

Thomas, "Evolutionary Stability: States and Strategies" Theoretical Population Biology Vol. 26 No. 1 (1984) at pgs. 49-67

Thomas, "On Evolutionarily Stable Sets" Journal of Mathematical Biology Vol. 22 (1985) at pgs. 105-115

Thorisdottir & Jost, "Motivated Closed-Mindedness Mediates the Effect of Threat on Political Conservatism" Political Psychology Vol. 32. No. 5 (2011) at pgs. 785-811

Tilly, "The Formation of Nation States in Western Europe" Princeton University Press (1975)

Tinbergen, "Derived activities: Their causation, biological significance, origin and emancipation during evolution" Quarterly Review of Biology 27 (1952)

Tinbergen, ' On Aims and Methods in Ethology" Zeitschrift für Tierpsychologie Vol. 20 (1963) at pgs. 410–433

Toffler, "Future Shock" Random House (1970)

Trivers, "The Evolution of Reciprocal Altruism" The Quarterly Review of Biology Vol. 46 No. 1 (1971) at pgs. 35-57

Trut et al., "Animal evolution during domestication: the domesticated fox as a model" BioEssays Vol. 31 No. 3 (2009) at pgs. 349-360

Trut, "Early Canid Domestication: The Farm-Fox Experiment" American Scientist Vol. 87 (1999) at pgs. 160-169.

Turchin, "Ultra Society: How 10,000 years of War Made Humans the Greatest Co-operators on Earth" Beresta Books (2016)

Tversky & Kahneman, "The Framing of decisions and the psychology of choice" Science Vol. 211 No. 4481 (1981) at pgs. 453–58

Van der Linden, "How the Illusion of Being Observed can Make You a Better Person" Scientific American (2011)

Vargas, "Urban Irregular Warfare and Violence Against Civilians: Evidence From a Colombian City," Terrorism and Political Violence Vol. 21, No. 1 (2009) at pgs. 110–132

Voltaire, "Candide" (1759)

Von Neumann & Morgenstern, "The Theory of Games and Economic

Behaviour" Princeton University Press (1944)

Wade et al., "Group Selection and social evolution in domesticated animals" Evolutionary Applications Vol.3 No. 5-6 (2013) at pgs. 453-465

Waltz, "Theory of International Politics", Addison-Wesley (1979)

Wang et al., "How time preferences differ: Evidence from 53 countries" Journal of Economic Psychology Vol. 52 (2016) at pgs. 115-135

Waring & Smaldino, "The coevolution of economic institutions and sustainable consumption via cultural group selection" Ecological Economics Vol. 131 (2017) at pgs. 524-532

Weikart, "Socialist Darwinism: Evolution in German Socialist Thought from Marx to Bernstein" International Scholars Publications (1998)

West et al., "Sixteen common misconceptions about the evolution of cooperation in humans" Evolution and Human Behaviour Vol. 32. (2011) at pgs. 231-265

Whitley & Kite, "The Psychology of Prejudice and Discrimination" Wadsworth (2019)

Wilkins et al., "The "Domestication Syndrome" in Mammals: A Unified Explanation Based on Neural Crest Cell Behaviour and Genetics" Genetics Vol. 197 No. 3 (2014) at pgs. 795-808

Wilkinson & Pickett, "The Spirit Level: Why More Equal Societies Almost Always Do Better" Allen Lane (2009)

Williams, "Adaption and Nature Selection" Princeton University Press (1966)

Wilson & Gowdy, "Evolution as a General Theoretical Framework for Economics and Public Policy" Journal of Economic Behaviour and Organisation Vol. 90S (2013) at pgs. S3-S10

Wilson & Henrich, "Scientists Discover What Economists Haven't Found: Humans" Evonomics, July 2012

Wilson & Holldobler, "The Ants" Belknap Press (1990)

Wilson & Sober, "Reintroducing group selection to the human behavioural sciences" Behavioural and Brain Sciences Vol. 17 No. 4 (1994) at pgs. 685-608

Wilson & Wilson, "Rethinking the Theoretical Foundation of Sociobiology" Quarterly Review of Biology Vol. 82 No. 4 (2007) at pgs. 327-348

Wilson, "A Tale of Two Classics" New Scientist Vol. 213 No. 2857 (2012) at pgs. 30-31

Wilson, "A Theory of Group Selection" Proceedings of the Natural Academy of Sciences" Vol. 72 No. 1. (1975) at pgs. 143-146

Wilson, "Consilience: The Unity of Knowledge" Vintage (1998)

Wilson, "Darwin's Cathedral: Evolution, Religion and the Nature of Society" University of Chicago Press (2003)

Wilson, "Does Altruism Exist? Culture Genes and the Welfare of Others" Yale University Press (2015)

Wilson, "Genesis: The Deep Origin of Societies" Liveright (2019)

Wilson, "On Human Nature" Harvard University Press (1979)

Wilson, "Reaching a New Plateau for the Acceptance of Multilevel Selection" The Evolution Institute, 22 September 2017

Wilson, "Sociobiology: The New Synthesis" Harvard University Press (1975)

Wilson, "Structured Demes and the Evolution of Group Advantageous Traits" The American Naturalist Vol. 111 No. 977 (1977) at pgs. 157-185

Wilson, "The Neighbourhood Project: Using Evolution to Improve My City, One Block at a Time" Little, Brown & Company (2011)

Wilson, "The Social Conquest of Earth" Norton (2012)

Wilson, "This View of Life: Completing the Darwinian Revolution" Knopf Doubleday (2019)

Wilson, "Weak Altruism, Strong Group Selection" Oikos Vol. 59 (1990) at pgs. 135-148

Wilson, "What Milton Friedman Got Wrong: Biologists Destroy Homo Economicus" Evonomics, February 2013

Wilson, Ostrom & Cox, "Generalizing the Core Design Principles for the Efficacy of Groups" Journal of Economic Behaviour and Organisation Vol. 90S (2013) at pg. S24-S25

Witkower et al., "Two Signals of Social Rank: Prestige and dominance are associated with distinct nonverbal displays" Journal of Personality and Social Psychology Vol. 18 No. 1 (2020) at pgs. 89-

Witt & Schwesinger, "Phylogenetic footprints in organizational behaviour" Journal of Economic Behaviour & Organization Vol. 90S (2013) at pgs. S33-S44

Wright, "A Short History of Progress" House of Anansi Press (2004)

Wright, "The Genetic Architecture of Domestication in Animals" Bioinformatics and Biology Insights Vol. 9 Supp. 4 (2015) at pgs. 11-20.

Wynne-Edwards, "Animal Dispersion in Relation to Social Behaviour" Oliver & Boyd (1962)

Yamagishi et al., "Bounded Generalised Reciprocity: Ingroup boasting and Ingroup favouritism" Advances in Group Processes Vol. 16 No. 1 (1999) at pgs. 161-197

Ye et al., "Sympathy and Punishment: Evolution of Cooperation in Public Goods Game" Journal of Artificial Societies and Social Simulation Vol. 14 No. 4 (2011) at pgs. 20-

Yeates et al. "Dynamics of prebiotic RNA reproduction illuminated by chemical game theory" Proceedings of the National Academy of Sciences of the United States of America, Vol. 113 No. 18 (2016) at pgs. 5030-5035

Zahavi, "Mate selection – a selection for handicap" Journal of Theoretical Biology Vol. 53 No. 1 (1975) at pgs. 205-214

About the Author

Anthony Skews is a former diplomat with over a decade's experience working as a political analyst for the Australian government. A graduate of the University of Melbourne and Australian National University, he completed his dissertation in cultural evolution and political science at the Graduate Institute of International and Development Studies in Geneva. With a background in science, international law and political theory, he brings together a unique perspective on modern social and political life informed by his personal commitment to social and economic justice.

You can connect with me on:

🌐 http://www.anthonyskewspolitics.com

🐦 https://twitter.com/ASkews2000

Also by Anthony Skews

Politics for the New Dark Age: Staying Positive Amidst Disorder

Politics for the New Dark Age provides a comprehensive introduction to left-wing thought for the 'post-fact', politically polarised era. Voters appalled by the recourse to petty nationalisms and xenophobia will respond to leaders that articulate a cohesive and genuine progressivism. This book provides the framework for politicians and activists to deliver that vision, organised around the themes of cooperative solutions to social problem-solving and a social contract centred on rights and equal dignity of all people. It advocates for a millennial political identity that is both libertarian and socialist, rooted in the struggle for democratic control over the decisions that affect our lives.

Synthesising contemporary psychological and economic research with classical political theory, the book begins with the premise that dynamic conflict between left and right is a fixed aspect of human political and social life. Drawing on contemporary Australian examples, it shows how the partisan divide recurs in policy debates from civil rights, to inequality, to economic growth, to the environment and foreign policy. Rather than lament the impossibility of technocratic consensus, *Politics for the New Dark Age* argues that we should re-commit to fighting for our democracy in order to manage social differences and channel them into opportunities for social progress.

www.ingramcontent.com/pod-product-compliance
Lightning Source LLC
Chambersburg PA
CBHW021845020426
42334CB00013B/199